BREAKDOWN
A PERSONAL CRISIS AND A MEDICAL DILEMMA

BREAKDOWN

A PERSONAL CRISIS AND A MEDICAL DILEMMA

STUART SUTHERLAND

pinter & martin

PINTER & MARTIN

Breakdown
First edition published by Weidenfeld & Nicholson 1976
Second edition published by Oxford University Press 1998
This reprint edition with a new foreword published by Pinter & Martin Ltd 2010

ISBN 978-1-905177-20-2 (paperback)
ISBN 978-1-905177-78-3 (ebook)

British Library Cataloguing-in-Publication Data
A catalogue record for this book is available from the British Library.

Set in Garamond

Printed and bound in Great Britain by TJ International Ltd, Padstow, Cornwall

Pinter & Martin Ltd
6 Effra Parade
London SW2 1PS

www.pinterandmartin.com

Foreword

As a psychology undergraduate at the time, I recall the stir created by Stuart Sutherland's frank and painfully honest account of his developing bipolar disorder, and subsequent treatment at the hands of the NHS mental health services in the 1970s. *Breakdown* was first serialised in a Sunday paper and later inspired a successful stage play, *Melon*, starring Alan Bates. It was a sensation.

Breakdown was the first of a genre in which prominent people 'came out' and shared their experiences with their peers and the wider public. Today, many household names have followed in Stuart Sutherland's footsteps and used their celebrity to facilitate wider understanding and acceptance of this highly stigmatising diagnosis: Stephen Fry, Spike Milligan, Frank Bruno, Carrie Fisher, Richard Dreyfuss and Tony Slattery. But what was, and remains, remarkable about *Breakdown* is that Stuart Sutherland was Professor of Experimental Psychology at the University of Sussex and an internationally renowned figure in the psychology of learning; indeed I recall reading *Breakdown* out of curiosity, having read many of his scientific papers and books as an undergraduate. His scientific curiosity and considerable analytical skill are brought gloriously to bear upon on the nature of his thinking and mood change, the scientific foundations of the treatments he was offered and, as we would say today, the 'user experience' of care. He would have been terrific as an expert member of the UK NICE committee developing the guidelines for the treatment of bipolar disorder. But the fact that he chose to write this book, given the prejudices of the time and the position he was in, was a massive personal risk; but it was this fact that lent it such pathos and added to its impact. There is, for example, his extraordinary account of a University Dean asking him to resign in the light of his behaviour and shame brought upon the University. You can imagine how that would go down in an industrial tribunal today

I have re-read this book after 30 years. It is a riveting read. The success of this book remains in its ability to weave a vivid account of the unfolding story of his mood swings and journey of discovery around a prosaic life narrative that would not be out of place in a soap opera. The ups and downs of his marriage, the infidelities, the arguments about his behaviour and the reaction of his colleagues is brilliantly described and a page turner. The account of his treatment in hospital, and the professionals and fellow patients he meets there, is well observed. There are many hilarious moments where the man of science meets the man of intuition:

"Some of the psychiatrist's sayings and advice were not a little bizarre. At one point, and for no clear reason, he wrote on the board the details of our family trees. Since Josie's mother was a bastard, the identity of her grandfather was a mystery. On learning this he remarked: 'Ah, so your grandfather is just a faceless penis to you'. We were both sane enough at the time to disregard this remark, but had we been more distressed we might have been deeply puzzled by it and spent agonizing hours to fathom its significance. As it was, I assumed we had reduced the psychiatrist to a state of incoherence, in which he was desperately trying to say something clever, no matter how meaningless." (p67)

Of course many things have changed in NHS mental health services, but one still recognises much of what is described here. I think mental health professionals will find it fascinating (and a touch embarrassing) to see how some things haven't changed. The science of bipolar disorder has also moved on and it is interesting to read his balanced account of the 'state of the art' in the 1970s and 80s. Nowadays, there is very little analytical psychotherapy that is used or researched in bipolar disorder; cognitive behavioural therapy has a firmer empirical basis and promotes understanding and self-management of the triggers and moderators of mood (it is interesting that much of Stuart Sutherland's professional work paved the way for the move from behaviourism to cognition and mental representation). There have been advances in the molecular genetics of bipolar disorder including the finding that bipolar disorder shares genetic linkage, and lies on a continuum with schizophrenia.

In my opinion *Breakdown* remains the best first person account of bipolar disorder. It is written with enormous clarity, understanding, candour and humour. Whether sufferer, mental health professional, concerned relative or friend, this book will be of benefit to you. As the Hollywood strap lines might say, 'this will make you laugh and cry . . . unmissable'.

Professor Max Birchwood
University of Birmingham and Birmingham
and Solihull Mental Health Foundation Trust
June 2010

Preface

When, 20 years after it was written, I reread my account of my manic-depressive illness, I was surprised and even startled by its frankness: it makes Jean-Jacques Rousseau seem a model of reticence. Perhaps I wrote the more revealing parts when in a near manic mood.

The first edition appears to have set a fashion, for since it was published not only other psychologists, but novelists, scientists, musicians, actors, and others have come out of the closet and described their own manic-depressive illnesses both in writing and on television. Indeed, so fashionable has this disorder become that many psychologists, perhaps particularly those who are manic-depressives themselves, declare that it is closely allied to genius. For myself, I make no such claim.

Manic-depression may be à la mode, but for better or worse—and many may think for worse—I suspect that *Breakdown* remains the frankest and most detailed account. I have tried to give an exact description of what took place in the years of my illness, sparing neither myself nor those who treated me. This part of the book is not greatly changed: I have brought it up to date and added some telling incidents that for various reasons did not appear in previous editions.

The autobiographical part of the book was written partly to comfort fellow sufferers, many of whom wrongly believe their condition is unique. In retrospect, however, many of the events of my illness were so bizarre that, however agonizing at the time, they deserve to be recorded.

The second half of the book, which has been almost completely rewritten, is intended to inform the general public about mental illness—its nature, origins and treatment. Apart from its objective interest, it may help those who are mentally disordered or their friends and relatives to choose the best treatment. I hope this part will also be found useful by students needing an elementary introduction to the subject, but, for three reasons, it does not resemble a textbook.

First, while outlining the difficulties of those who treat mental illness, it is in places extremely critical of their activities. Because teachers are unlikely to recommend books that attack their favourite views, textbooks tend to distribute prizes to all schools of thought and to all methods of treatment, a bland outlook that I have sedulously avoided. Second, it is at least as important to know what is wrong with a profession as what is right: the latter does not need changing, the former does. At the cost of offending some readers, my criticisms are forthright, particularly those of certain forms of psychotherapy. The reliance on intuition to determine the efficacy of a procedure has led many psychotherapists wildly astray. As someone remarked, 'Intuition is the faculty that tells you you are right when you are wrong.' There is no substitute for large carefully controlled trials. It is, moreover, important for anyone thinking of making a career in any aspect of mental health to know its pitfalls. Third, I have tried to enliven this part by illustrating it with some of the weird events that occur in the treatment of the mentally ill, including those in which I participated. The fact that I occasionally use a light touch should not detract from the seriousness of the topic. The only chapter that may present the lay reader with difficulties is that on how drugs for mental disorder may affect the brain, a complex but burgeoning topic.

It may be thought that I have allocated too much space to psychotherapy, some of which is of doubtful value. The different therapies are, however, of general interest: they have both shaped society's attitudes and have in turn often reflected them. Moreover, both the demand for, and the supply of, psychotherapy is growing at an alarming rate and the confident but misplaced belief of both governments and individuals that it is the answer to most of the problems of the age—from teenage crime to middle-aged anxiety —remains unshakeable.

On more practical matters, the chapters forming Part I were written at different times. To preserve their freshness I have left the time perspective unchanged, later adding some telling episodes that were originally omitted. Where an addition refers to later events and could not have been written at the time, it is placed in square brackets.

The times at which the chapters were written are: Chapters 1-7, 1972; 8, 1987; 9, 1997. Finally, although I cannot lay claim to political correctness, in deference to the majority of potential readers, I have deliberately used 'they', 'them', and 'their' as singular pronouns meaning 'he or she' and so on.

Acknowledgements

I thank Peter Clifton and Dai Stephens for advice on some of the physiological aspects of the book, Julia Purcell for helping me to clarify some of the chapters in Part II, and my secretary Ann Doidge for her tireless typing and retyping of the MS, as well as those acknowledged in the first edition.

N. S. S.
July 1997

Contents

PART I

Manic-depression: a personal account

'Post-therapeutic confessionals, written under intense abreactive pressure and unneutralized exhibitionism, often betray their underlying motives of subtle revenge towards the disappointing treatment.'

J. Kavka (Member of the Chicago Institute for Psychoanalysis),
from *Contemporary Psychology, 1975*

1

Onset

About three years ago, in my mid-forties, I had a sudden and severe mental breakdown. There was nothing unusual about the breakdown itself, nor about the events in my own life that led up to it. The only exceptional feature was that I am a psychologist and should therefore be able to view my illness from two standpoints—subjectively as the patient and more objectively as the detached professional observer. [Before continuing, I should explain that in order to retain its freshness I have not changed the time perspective of the account of my original breakdown. Chapters 1–7 were written in 1974, about three years after the first breakdown. I have added a few later comments which appear in square brackets.]

Until I broke down I had always regarded myself as reasonably well-balanced: although I had sometimes worried about physical illness, the idea that I might be subjected to the torture and humiliation of a severe mental illness had never crossed my mind. For many years I had been outgoing, efficient, continually active and reasonably cheerful: I thought of myself as well-meaning, though possibly somewhat insensitive both to my own and others' feelings. It never occurred to me that one day my existence would disintegrate within the space of a few hours. For half a year I lived in mental anguish, a prey to obsessive and agonizing thoughts. I had neither interest in nor ability to cope with the outside world which formerly I had found so fascinating. I hated myself and I hated others, and so unremitting and painful were my thoughts that I was virtually unable to read: I could not even concentrate sufficiently to peruse the daily paper. In five months all I read were a few brief case histories of neurotic breakdowns which were sufficiently similar to my own to seize my interest. For someone accustomed to spending most of the day reading and writing, the complete inability to do either was a singularly refined torture.

There were two aspects of the breakdown that were particularly painful, and took me by surprise since I had never experienced anything similar. The onset was marked by levels of physical anxiety that I would not have believed possible. If one is almost involved in a road accident, there is a delay of a second or two and then the pit of the stomach seems to fall out and one's legs go like jelly. It was this feeling multiplied a hundredfold that seized me at all hours of the day and night. My dreams were often pleasant, but as soon as I woke panic set in and it would take a few moments to work out what it was about. The realization brought anguish: an irrevocable and cataclysmic event had occurred from which I could imagine no recovery. Sleep was difficult to come by even with the help of sleeping pills, to which I soon resorted. I would awake in terror twenty or thirty times a night. I would sometimes doze off in the daytime, and dream pleasant dreams for what seemed an eternity only to wake panic-stricken to discover that I had been asleep for no more than a few minutes.

The second unexpected consequence of the breakdown was the most extreme boredom. I could concentrate on nothing except my own pain. At first I would try to go to the theatre, or the cinema, but invariably I became so agitated that I had to leave after a few minutes. In my previous existence, there had always been something to look forward to: now there was nothing, except the fitful mercy of sleep. I spent the day longing for the night to come.

I am conscious that, without being a poet, it is difficult to capture in words the quality of the pain and boredom that I suffered. Indeed it is difficult even to recall in my present mood the bitterness of my experience. Perhaps nature is merciful in making it so difficult to remember pain: it is said that no woman would ever bear a second child if she could remember the agony of her first birth. A friend recently pointed out that I have a tendency to dramatize. He said: 'If you have a breakdown, it has to be the biggest and best of all time, just as if you have seen a donkey and a girl in Port Said, you come back saying it was the only show of its kind to be done on roller skates'. My breakdown was not the biggest and the best, but it was severe enough, and I believe my experiences were characteristic of those of other sufferers.

The reader may wonder what dire misfortune could have occurred to reduce to such misery someone who had counted himself as having a happy marriage and many friends, who was pursuing an interesting and not un-successful career, and who enjoyed many other diversions. The breakdown was in fact triggered by a banal, if somewhat old-fashioned, emotion—sexual jealousy. For some years I had known that my wife—Josie—had been having a sporadic affair. I had been upset when I first heard about it from her, but had tolerated it since I had always regarded sexual jealousy as a particularly despicable and selfish emotion. Furthermore, she had told me her lover was an accountant, and after all who can feel jealous of an accountant? Finally, I had myself had a number of affairs, although

I had always tried to avoid too much involvement: I therefore had no right to recriminate. She had confided many of the details of her affair to me, and I had even admired some of the extravagant gifts with which it was punctuated. She had, however, told me that the man was someone I did not know. When eventually I discovered the truth, my reactions were very different.

About three years after Josie's affair began, I returned from a trip abroad to find her unusually cold. In the deepest part of the night, she revealed the name of the man: despite the lapse of a further three years I still cannot bring myself to write the word 'lover'. It turned out to be a fairly close friend of mine whom I had known for many years. I found this news desperately upsetting, possibly because my attitude towards him had always been ambivalent. In retrospect it seems as though he had always behaved towards me in a spirit of petty rivalry and I had tolerated this behaviour, ascribing it to gaucheness rather than to animosity. He was in many ways the opposite of how I pictured myself: he appeared to be emotionally closed up, mean and humourless, but along with such less desirable traits he possessed one that I admired—he was completely self-reliant and needed sympathy from nobody. The self-reliance was accompanied by a boastful smugness that I and some of our mutual acquaintances found hard to bear: some referred to him as 'the lout', and I had from time to time found myself defending his behaviour as arising from awkwardness rather than from malice. In the light of what took place, I cannot of course pretend to be presenting a fair or sympathetic portrait of him: the description is intended primarily to reveal my own feelings. It is given to few to be completely objective about such matters.

While the affair had been going on, Josie and I had together been seeing this friend and his wife fairly regularly. I was sometimes given to shocking people by my candour, and I actually discussed my wife's affair on more than one occasion when the four of us were together. I remember describing how devoted he was to her, and adding, 'Apparently he only has one fault: he's far too quick and has no sense of rhythm'. He was driving a car at the time and nearly collided with a bus, though it was only later that I realized the cause of this lapse.

When I discovered the truth, I was at first merely badly shaken by the duplicity involved and by the fact that he was somebody about whom I already had mixed feelings and with whom I probably had a strong but unacknowledged sense of rivalry. Over the years my wife had confided many sexual details of the affair and now proceeded to supply more in a spirit, so it seemed at the time, of trust, though in retrospect it appears to have been more a way of punishing me for my own misdeeds. I was also annoyed with and ashamed of myself; I should have been able to infer what was going on—the signs were patent. I recalled visions of my wife giving him tidbits from her plate in restaurants, and many other such indications. So obvious was the liaison, that a woman who knew all four of us remarked to me that Josie and the lout must be having an affair.

I had made an arrangement to go to the theatre with the lout and his wife and of course Josie. I telephoned him to say we were not going without giving any reason. He realized that I knew what had been going on and felt compelled to tell his own wife, who unlike me, said with great tolerance 'It shall be as though it had never been'. Josie and he rather reluctantly gave up seeing one another: Josie was mortified at having her one escape from domesticity removed, but I doubt if he would have had the courage to continue.

The reader may well ascribe some of what I have written to rationalization. However this may be, in recording my feelings I am in no way trying to justify either my breakdown or my jealousy. Indeed, I was ashamed of giving way to this loathsome emotion. Nevertheless, I managed to hold myself together after a fashion for a further two months. My natural inclination was to wreak physical injury on the lout, but my reason told me that such behaviour was uncivilized. So foolishly determined was I to be civilized that I eventually arranged to have a drink with him when I was passing through London. He proceeded to exculpate himself by saying that my wife had thrown herself at him, a statement that was markedly lacking in chivalry. My breakdown dated from that moment. I drove sixty miles home in a frenzy: I was fortunate not to kill myself. I had of course felt sexual jealousy before, but it is one thing to have twinges that can be suppressed by other interests; to be overwhelmed by this emotion to the exclusion of all other thoughts is different in kind.

My mind worked on two levels. I tried to comfort myself with the thought that there were elements of innocence in the affair. He was flattered beyond measure to find an attractive woman who liked him, whilst she not unnaturally enjoyed his attentions and such extravagant tokens of regard as being told: 'I had always known that there was something better in life'. Although such remarks are characteristic of the successful womanizer, I think in his case they came from the heart and the pair of them were swept away on a high tide of romance. I believed even then that he was sincere, and since the affair appeared to be good for Josie I felt I should have been able to rejoice on her behalf and accept it. Josie's motives were in fact characteristic of those of the housewife who has devoted herself to domestic duties and whose children are fast becoming independent. She needed romance. She told me that her pleasure began as soon as she got on the train to London, feeling as she did that at last she was free—free from the kitchen sink, the children and me. She was liberated from the boring cares of life and could for once take her own decisions. Once again, I beg the reader to remember that I am describing the affair as I saw it in my attempts to comfort myself. My description may not have captured its real flavour: it is intended only to reveal how I felt.

Although, even at my worst times, such ideas ran through the back of my mind, they did nothing to alleviate the more dominant cast of thought marked by the black passions of jealousy, hatred and panic. My anxieties were compounded by my own inability to forgive myself for being unable to behave rationally.

How I passed these early days of the breakdown, I find difficult to remember. I could not bear to be separated from my wife, and most of the time was spent in her company. I followed her around the house and on shopping expeditions: if I lost sight of her behind a row of soup tins in the supermarket, I would panic and think I would never see her again. I played tennis with her until the sight of her bare legs acted as such a spur to my jealousy that I had to give it up. It was as though only a single track in my brain was operating—whatever I tried to do led back to the same agonizing groove of jealousy. I was obsessed with visions of Josie's affair, and for hours on end my mind would be crowded with a succession of hideously detailed visual images of the sexual activities that she had so vividly related.

At times I did fight to regain some measure of control. I would drag myself into my office for two or three hours at a time thinking I was being very courageous. When I went to work, I could do none: instead I bored my colleagues with my troubles and telephoned home every half-hour. I was supposed to be examining a doctoral thesis, and for a fortnight I struggled with it morning and afternoon sitting in my garden. I tried to make notes on the contents, but I never succeeded in understanding a paragraph: my notes, penned with a shaking hand, turned out to be gibberish. From the outset of my breakdown, I tried from time to time to resume my normal activities. There was one book on psychology that I pathetically carried around with me and which several times a day I would attempt to read. In the ensuing five months I must have opened it several hundred times, but I never succeeded in getting past the first page. At the time it seemed like gibberish: when after my recovery, I was able to read it, I realized that like so many books on psychology it actually was gibberish.

There were three activities that gave me some slight respite. Two were pursuits that in my normal state I would have condemned as a waste of time: they were driving a car and doing *The Times* crossword. Perhaps I could concentrate on these tasks because in neither is it necessary to carry forward anything in memory from one moment to the next. I could not read because I could never remember the sense of what I had just read; to solve a crossword, however, one does not need to remember the answer to one clue in order to tackle the next, and I could find just sufficient gaps in my obsessive thought-processes to enable me laboriously to complete a puzzle clue by clue.

The third source of relief was talking. When they would listen, and at first many were prepared to listen, I bored my friends with the story of my woes. Provided this was the sole subject of conversation I could concentrate on what was being said and make intelligible replies. The relief was admittedly short-lived, since as soon as the conversation ceased I was as bored as ever. Moreover, repeating my troubles brought diminishing returns, and I eventually became almost as bored with them as did my friends. Breakdowns take many forms, and it is popularly thought that anyone who can talk about their problems cannot be in too bad a condition; in my own case 'getting it off my chest' did not provide any long-term relief. At that time, it occurred to me that one way of gaining relief would have been to leave Josie and divorce her. Although I contemplated divorce, I never took any steps for two reasons. First, I was incapable of undertaking any complicated course of action. Second, I thought it would be unfair to Josie, whom at the time I regarded as being the wronged one of the two of us.

The early days of my breakdown were marked by a further curious feature. I was seized by a compulsion to tell my wife of my own infidelities. I knew I should not do this, but as soon as I had divulged one, another would come to mind and I would shake with anxiety as I struggled not to reveal it. I would even force myself to go out and walk alone, hoping that the compulsion would die away, but it never did: until I revealed each affair as it came to mind, my anxiety level would go on rising, forcing me eventually to vomit it forth. Nobody who has not suffered such a compulsion can have any conception of what it is like.

My bizarre behaviour naturally upset my wife, and she alternated between tender concern and violent hatred. From moment to moment I never knew in which mood I would find her. She retained her customary charm and equanimity in her dealings with others, but her behaviour to me was almost as out of control as mine towards her. She would wake me in the middle of the night demanding to know more details of my most recently revealed affair and when I reluctantly supplied them she would release torrents of abuse about both me and the offending woman. She was herself on the verge of a breakdown and to make it worse the dramatic nature of my own ensured that I got all the attention from others.

The following incident illustrates the depth to which we were reduced. It is not typical of either of us—in normal circumstances Josie is a woman without rancour or malice—but I tell it here because it *is* typical of what can happen when things go wrong between two people with a deep involvement in one another. In a moment of anger, Josie insisted that I write an unkind letter to a woman with whom I had had a long-standing affair. I was hoping that the marriage would survive and indeed be strengthened by the revelations we had made to one another not merely about our infidelities but about our innermost thoughts and longings, but it seemed to me wrong to try to build our own happiness on writing an unkind letter. Nevertheless I had no choice but to write it with Josie standing over me. When it was completed, she seized it from me. I was in a desperate state and swallowed half a bottle of whisky. With the cunning of the trapped, I went into another room and addressed and stamped an empty envelope, which I pocketed. She sealed up the genuine letter and ran out of the house with me in close pursuit. I grabbed the letter as she was trying to post it and put it in my pocket saying: 'You can't post that'. Her anger flared, I put my hand in my other pocket, produced the empty envelope and handed it to her. She posted it. I later tore up the genuine letter and flushed it down the lavatory and out to sea. Over the next twelve hours, my anxiety about having deceived Josie built up to intolerable levels. Without telling her, I wrote out a letter that was as nearly as I could remember identical to the original and posted it. When I returned to the house. I related exactly what I had done.

During this initial phase of my illness, the phrase *folie à deux* came to have a new meaning for me. I could not help thinking even then that the extreme swings in Josie's attitude to me were reminiscent of some of the brainwashing techniques used to break down prisoners, and were likely to perpetuate my state of dependence, panic and misery.

After about ten days in this condition, I sought the help of a general practitioner, who referred me to a psychoanalyst.

2

Background

It may be wondered how it was that the rather commonplace events described in the previous chapter brought about a severe breakdown in someone who to all outward appearances had been fortunate in his lot in life. I can only say that the events in question, which I saw as a double betrayal of my rather simple-minded trust, still seem in retrospect to have been precisely shaped to unlock my inner uncertainties. I have always been afraid of terminal illness and death, but I assumed that short of such a prospect nothing could disturb my sanity. The world seemed so full of fascinating things to do and to observe that the idea that a trauma in one's personal relations could drain the interest from everything else would have seemed laughable. I could understand that death, illness, starvation or physical pain, whether my own or that of someone close to me, could cause me misery, but I never expected to be rendered wretched and useless by events that involved none of these banes. Sydney Smith spoke only for the sane when he wrote: 'If with a pleasant wife, a good house, many books and many friends who wish me well, I cannot be happy, I am a very foolish silly fellow and what becomes of me is of very little consequence'.

It is likely that we all have our breaking points, though what destroys one person may barely pierce the skin of another. We all have wishes, conflicts and uncertainties of which we are unconscious, but of what makes one crack under this misfortune, another under that, we know very little. Inherited factors may predispose to neurosis, but my own ancestors and relatives seem a singularly unneurotic, not to say phlegmatic, lot. As in all individual cases, one can only speculate about what—if anything—it was about my background that rendered me liable to a breakdown in middle age.

Before describing the bizarre events of my skirmish with psychoanalysis, I should outline something of my background, if only in order not to deprive psychoanalysts and other psychotherapists of the fun of tracing my breakdown to my life history [in the event several including Anthony Storr, were unable to resist this temptation].

My parents were the most devoted couple I have ever encountered. They were inseparable: indeed after retiring early my father even accompanied my mother when she was vacuuming. I was born at a time when middle-class parents were prone to follow current medical fashion about upbringing. The dogma was that babies should not be picked up when they cried and should be fed at set times. When I was nearly two years old my brother was born: the nurse told my mother not to see me for a fortnight. My mother obeyed the nurse rather than her own instincts and, so I am told for I have no memories of that period, I sat outside her locked bedroom door and howled for 14 days. Such an experience may be harmful or it may not.

My parents were upright but not overstrict, and were dutiful and in many ways self-sacrificing in the way they brought up their sons, sending us to prep schools that they could ill afford. They were distinctly Calvinistic in their attitudes towards drink, gambling, sexual licence and all other such indulgences that are today taken for granted. Their scale of values was greatly foreshortened, as in terms of wickedness they saw little distinction between rape and entering a pub.

My father was kind, sensible, placid and without ambition: he made a virtue of necessity and would have been genuinely contented with any lot in life. He was a retail pharmacist, but never made much money, as he gave medicines free to the poor and the rich never paid his bills. He was intelligent and well-read and inspired both his sons with an interest in literature, philosophy and science. My mother was more ambitious. She encouraged us to work hard and took great pride in our achievements. She was a hard taskmaster. When we came home from school, we were always greeted in her Glaswegian accent with the question, 'Were you top of the class today?' If the reply was negative, she would go on 'Who was top of the class? Why was *he* top of the class?' 'Why weren't you top of the class?', questions to which there could be no satisfactory answer. Furthermore, she often paraded us spruced and tidied up in front of her friends. She would embarrass us and annoy them by recounting such success as we had. Sometimes I felt I was being treated like a pet. On the other hand she taught me to read before I was three and when I was 'aged six years and seven months'—as she frequently told her friends—she encouraged me to write my first novel which to my annoyance was never published. Neither of my parents were given to self-questioning or moral doubts: they believed in the virtues of hard work and strict honesty and were surprised that not everyone adopted, let alone lived up to, the same standards. My relations with my younger brother were close, and untinged, as far as I can recall, with 'sibling-rivalry': the dark passions that Freud assumed to lurk within the family were unknown to me, though I may merely have succeeded in repressing them. You might say that for that day and age, I had a singularly normal and conventional upbringing.

We lived in Norman Road, Northfield, a suburb of Birmingham. Most of the houses were large, solid Edwardian buildings, but ours was one of the only pair of modern semi-detached houses in the street. It was very small, but the speculative builder had tried to redeem it by inserting mock Tudor beams and placing coloured and leaded glass in the front door. I often regret that my parents spent most of their lives in this tiny box.

Norman Road was the most middle middle-class street in Britain. The cars were thoroughly washed and waxed every Sunday and the children were scrubbed several times a day. It could truly be said of the mesh curtains that they were whiter than white: at the least sign of fraying caused by constant washing, new ones were substituted. Lawn mowers and rollers were in constant use (how I hated them) and both in the front and back gardens the grass was a clean-shaven bright green, while throughout the length of the street, there were roses, roses all the way. The inhabitants gave small dinner parties and politely discussed their new cars, the first crocus of spring, current news of the war and more occasionally politics. If mental illness ever occurred there, it would have been a grave solecism to mention it, such was its stigma.

Until I reached adolescence, I was cheerful, outgoing, gregarious and successful. Over the next few years, I became considerably less sure of myself and more introverted: by my late teens I was a clever but rather shy schoolboy. Once on the field, I enormously enjoyed playing rugby football, but I dreaded the train journeys to away games against other schools: I could neither enjoy the sexual and scatological banter of my team mates, nor approve of the sport of wrecking trains. I was a prig. I was particularly shy with girls: until I was 19, I had never been in the sole company of a girl of my own age. My awkwardness and lack of close contact with girls was to prey on my mind for some years to come. I despised my virtues and longed to develop some passable vices.

Up to the age of 22 I had led a sheltered life, and even then I was still partially dependent on the approval of my parents. I had attended an excellent grammar school and subsequently gone to Oxford where I read Greats (classics and philosophy). After a brief spell as a journalist, I was called up and went into the RAF. One of my friends had told me to 'Come on really strong' at the interview for a commission, which I was confident of obtaining, for I had played every ball game going and had an excellent academic record. My interview took place in a small office where a tiny pilot officer was seated. I saw he had wings on his arms, hence he must fly. I therefore greeted him in my best imitation of a moustachioed RAF squadron leader: Too bad. Tough on chaps like you to be grounded, what?' Unfortunately my aplomb (as I regarded it) was not received as well as I had expected. Indeed, I was the only one out of forty applicants not called for a medical examination.

My recruit training was the first contact I had had with the proletariat: it was both horrifying and fascinating. I had not realized there were sections of society who could construct sentences in which every other word was four-lettered and who, at least on their own account, seduced every woman they met.

Subsequently, I became an education sergeant, having paradoxically combined obtaining full marks for shooting and failing my examination in psychology. I asked for a foreign posting, but the Air Ministry with its extensive knowledge of geography sent me to the Isle of Man. I was terrified of entering the Sergeants' Mess, where everyone else had come up the hard way through the ranks. In fact they were the most genial, friendly and just group of men I have ever met. They called me Aristotle, explaining that they had called my predecessor Plato. Subsequently I annoyed my fellow dons at Oxford High Table by telling them how much more witty than they were RAF sergeants. My experiences in the RAF made me rebel against my parents" attitudes. I drank, I smoked and when I got the chance I fornicated or in my parents' terms 'indulged in free love'.

My character was undergoing a further change. I adopted, half con-sciously, a technique whereby I forced myself to behave in a confident and outgoing way regardless of what I felt underneath. In the matter of banter, which I continued to hate, I taught myself to give better than I got. I learned to hide my sensitivities, and soon few either dared to or could touch them. As often happens, the mask became the man, and I came eventually to feel as confident and extroverted as I behaved. At about this time I completely gave up listening to most music, since I found it too upsetting emotionally. I confined myself to Haydn and Gilbert and Sullivan.

I married at the age of 27. My wife was extremely attractive, but had run away from school at 14 and never developed an interest in ideas. I was priggishly horrified when I discovered she thought the sun went round the earth. On the other hand, she had a good eye for paintings, furniture and antiques, something that I sorely lacked. Mentally, we were incompatible.

Just before I married, I had taken up my first academic appointment. I taught and undertook research at the University of Oxford over the next 12 years, with the exception of two years spent working in the United States. I never fitted in to life at High Table, and my experiences there may have fostered some of my more intolerant attitudes. I came to abhor pretentiousness, pomposity, snobbery and hypocrisy—by which marks, along with cattiness, much High Table conversation was distinguished. As a junior fellow of a college, it would have required more courage and more disregard for my own career than I could muster to rebel openly. I therefore sat in silence whilst one or other of the senior fellows would expatiate on how and where the badge on his Rolls Royce had been stolen or would describe the dinner he had attended the previous evening where he was the only guest without at least an earldom. I was, however, never able to conceal my boredom. Subsequently I gave more open vent to my dislike of snobbery and pretentiousness, and even welcomed the opportunity of meeting people who displayed these qualities, in order to take delight in puncturing them. I saw my rudeness as a form of knight errantry, feeling I had a mission to suppress such pretentions. For example, when I was first introduced to the historian, Trevor Roper, he asked with what I thought was a slight sneer 'What is your subject?' I replied, 'Psychology. What's yours?' My abrasive remarks did me no good. When I applied for a professorship at Oxford, one of the committee solemnly told the others that I was not a suitable candidate because he had learnt that I hung my children up in a cage outside the window so that I could not hear them. He claimed, in addition, I fed them pellets of rat food through a dispenser that I had stolen from my animal laboratory. I had invented the story myself in order to shock someone whom I thought doted too much on her own children.

When I was 37, I became a professor of psychology at the University of Sussex. I had always worked hard, but I now plunged into a whirlpool of ceaseless activity that became a veritable vortex in the years before my breakdown: it may have been this vortex that finally sucked me under.

The popular stereotype of the leisured existence of university teachers has always mildly annoyed me. All professional people are busy and professors are no exception. In the pitifully exiguous hours of the day, I strove to find time to teach; examine; organize courses; attend university and government committees; travel to conferences; prepare reports; advise publishers; edit learned journals; interview students and potential students; appoint lecturers, secretaries and technicians; write references for students and staff past and present; and find sources of finance for the department I directed. In the interstices between these and other activities, I tried to pursue what I regarded as my real vocation—my scientific research and writing. I enjoyed almost everything I did, and of course many of the activities were voluntary, even though I told myself I had a duty to undertake them. I mention this hectic way of life only because it may have contributed to my ultimate breakdown. The pace of my existence had three further relevant effects.

First, I never allowed time to think about myself. Most people, I take it, occasionally ponder in the bath or while shaving. I bathed rarely and hastily; I shaved only in my car and, if I was lucky with the traffic lights several days running, would acquire a thick stubble. A former secretary recently told me, without rancour, that I used to dictate letters while seated on the lavatory: although I have no recollection of so doing, it sounds plausible. I therefore charged through life looking neither to left nor right, least of all inside. One or two of the numerous analysts and psychiatrists who subsequently treated me said: 'Don't you think that with all that activity, you were running away from something—perhaps from yourself?' This may be true, but it did not feel like that. I felt I was running towards something that was both useful and enjoyable.

Second, although I enjoyed organizing and administrating, I rather despised myself for spending so much time on it. Taking decisions came easily to me, and on the whole I think I showed good judgement in the staff I selected and in the direction in which I pushed my department. In the space of a few years, I built up a laboratory of psychology that was one of the foremost in Europe. Nevertheless, it all seemed too easy, and I could not help vaguely despising the skills involved. I continued to think of myself as primarily a research scientist making an original contribution to the subject; the ability to produce good original research was what I admired most in others. Amidst the welter of other activities, I found less and less time for my own research and I became less productive. It occurred to me, even at the time, that I was taking on all the extraneous commitments only in order to disguise from myself the fact that I was no longer capable of producing really satisfying work. The decline in my productivity was niggling at the back of my mind long before my breakdown. If one aspect of life is going really well that may be enough to help one to endure misfortune in the remainder: in my case a marital crisis occurred just when I was becoming increasingly worried about my work.

The third consequence of all my activity was its effects on the marriage. I devoted too little time and thought to the needs of my family. Indeed I worked throughout most weekends and usually spent some time in my office or laboratory even on Christmas Day. I have always loathed celebrating to order and found it difficult to make the moves appropriate to such occasions as birthdays, anniversaries and bank holidays. My habit of working at such times saved me from having to simulate the expected jollity: it was purely selfish. I used to think that everyone would benefit if people were more direct about their own wishes. How many wearisome dinner parties are going on at this moment because the hosts think it would be rude to say that they want to go to bed and the guests are afraid to give offence by leaving too early? I have always found pubs more congenial than homes. Dr Johnson summed it up:

> There is no private house in which people can enjoy themselves so much as at a capital tavern. In a man's house . . . there must always be some degree of care and anxiety, the master of the house is anxious to entertain his guests; the guests are anxious to be agreeable to him. Whereas in a tavern, there is general freedom from anxiety.

My predilection for pubs, my low tolerance of boredom and my restless urges made me a less than ideal husband and father. I admire people who can sit around a house and talk about nothing in particular, but I cannot emulate them, and it is difficult to describe the strangled feeling of being in a cage that made me contract every muscle of my body whenever I submitted myself to such situations. I tried to laugh off as eccentric my behaviour in leaving dinner parties (including my own) to visit the nearest pub. but my restlessness must often have given offence. Although my behaviour was selfish, I still do not understand how it could have been other than it was. I was and still am incapable of looking interested when bored.

Not only did I not give enough time to the conventional activities that make up most marriages, I did not devote enough thought to understanding my wife. Although I would always have acknowledged, I think, my dependence on her and my care for her, I took her too much for granted and never considered whether I was satisfying her needs or even what these needs were. [The last sentence suggests that my psychotherapists had influenced me more than I credited at the time—it could come straight from a psychological textbook. I now regard it as pure tosh—you don't have to *think* about others' needs, they are usually transparent.] Despite our underlying involvement, much of our life together was superficial. But is that not true of almost every couple?

It may be that I was at a time of life which makes it difficult to bear serious emotional upheavals. Many psychiatrists believe that middle-aged men are vulnerable and that they undergo in a milder form the equivalent of the female menopause. The experience is sometimes referred to as the mid-life crisis. According to Elliott Jacques, such a crisis is particularly common in creative workers, and if they survive their work is often improved. He claims that the death-rate among creative artists is particularly high in the late thirties, and instances Baudelaire, Chopin, Mozart, Purcell, Raphael, Rimbaud and Watteau. Statistical evidence, however, does not support this suggestion: there is no peak in first admissions to psychiatric hospitals between the ages of 35 and 45.

When my own breakdown came it was sudden and complete, although there may have been intimations in the form of irritability, sleeplessness, heavy smoking and anxieties about physical health. My health had been worse than usual in the preceding two years. I had caught a viral pneumonia which left me mildly depressed for a few months and I suffered several other minor but persistent ailments during this time. It is possible that at some level I knew more about my wife's affair than I acknowledged to myself. People who are subjected to great emotional stress are particularly prone to both physical and mental illness.

In summary, then, as in all breakdowns, so in my own case there was probably no one single cause. Josie's infidelity and the ensuing marital crisis were not on their own enough to account for the magnitude of my reaction and it is not possible to say how far the breakdown was induced by childhood traumas, my half-conscious decision to shut off many of my own feelings, the pace at which I worked or the fears of waning creativity, death, and the decline of sexual powers that accompany middle age. Intriguing though these possibilities are, I shall show later that it was in fact none of these things, but was determined largely by fluctuations in some of the chemicals in my brain, which were in turn caused genetically.

3

Psychoanalysis

When, a week or so after the onset of my breakdown, I sought help from my doctor, I insisted on taking my wife with me: I felt I could say nothing behind her back. The doctor seemed rather startled at my agitated condition. I pleaded for reassurance that I would recover, but he could give none. He advised us both to see a psychoanalyst who specialized in treating discordant married couples. I asked with touching naiveté whether the doctor thought Josie and I would be able to continue to live together or whether the passions let loose would force us apart. That was how it felt then, and was to feel for many months to come: I wanted only to live in peace and happiness with my wife, but there seemed to be strange forces within ineluctably driving us apart. He answered sensibly enough: 'Nobody can guarantee that you will be able to live together', and added with what I thought was unjustified optimism, 'Whatever happens will be for the best'. I interpreted this innocent remark as the pronouncement of a sentence worse than death.

In accepting the doctor's advice to see a psychoanalyst, I had considerable misgivings. As a psychologist, my own knowledge had made me scornful of the value of analysis, but in my despair anything seemed worth trying, and I agreed to go. I continued to see the analyst once or twice a week for the next six weeks. He lived about 40 miles away, and I used to drive to see him with hope in my heart—despite my intellectual doubts about analysis, at an emotional level I felt perhaps someone could help and I pinned my faith on him.

He lived in a quiet suburban house. He was a tall, thin, gentle and rather shy man in his forties. He warned me that he charged seven guineas a session, which was really a London price, but he always had more patients than he could cope with. He was, moreover, one of the best

known analysts in Britain. He allowed me to ramble on rather incoherently about my problems and my background and occasionally he made
a few interpretations. I had the feeling that he was slightly bored with
the whole proceedings: he seemed to spend most of his time either examining his wristwatch or gazing into the sunlit garden from which came
the noise of children playing. The very normality of such sights as
children at play came as a poignant reminder of times when I too had
been normal.

For several sessions he saw me together with my wife in an effort, as
he put it, 'to take the steam out of things'. He did his best to alleviate my
distress by pointing out the benefits to be derived from a breakdown ('better
understanding of yourself and others') and by applying the magic word
'collusion' to my wife whenever I blamed myself for having treated her
badly. 'Collusion' is a Catch-22 of much modern psychotherapy—if you let
someone else be nasty to you, you are colluding with them and just as guilty.
In general he tried to find something good to say about our situation. 'You
seem to communicate well together', he said, and he pointed out the benefit
of the flurry of compulsive sexual activity in which we were indulging. He
produced some mild alleviation in guilt, but my boredom and anxiety
persisted in as extreme a form as ever.

He was a genuinely kind and considerate man, and although he used some
Freudian interpretations he also used his common sense. I told him that
I was thinking of going up to London and beating hell out of 'the lout',
whom I felt like murdering. To my surprise, he said: 'That would be a much
more sensible thing to do than what you are doing at the moment—you
would be better to take it out of him than to go on taking it out of yourself.
I said: 'I never expected an analyst to advise me to go in for physical
violence' and he replied: 'You would of course have to make the violence
commensurate with the crime and be careful not to inflict any long-term
injury'.

Some of his dicta were more bizarre. It emerged that, despite my mental
pain, I had not shed tears since the onset of the illness. He implied that this
was regrettable: 'That means there is some underlying emotional disturbance of which you are not conscious; we must try to bring it to the
surface'. I went home and then and for the next week or so I used regularly to practise crying, but the tears would not come. However, I made
sufficient noise for others in the house to overhear, and my children would
explain to their guests: 'Don't worry—that's only Daddy practising his
crying'. When I told the analyst a week later of my attempts at tears, he
remarked: 'I was afraid that would happen'. I contemplated more serious
deeds than crying, and would open the bedroom window and climb out,
half-wanting to dash myself to death on the stones two stories below, but
I usually did this when other people were around. My suicidal gestures were
more a 'cry for help' than in earnest, though some of them were sufficiently
realistic to have imperilled my life.

Another of the analyst's recurrent themes was that: 'There is something puzzling about your case—you don't seem to want to get better. We must get to the bottom of that'. Needless to say, we never did. Of course one side of me desperately wanted to recover, but on the other hand I was so pre-occupied with my obsessions that I could not imagine them going away. The tendency to promise insights that were never vouchsafed was something common to all the therapists I encountered and I found it irritating. One's hopes would be raised in the course of a session by the therapist implying that next time we would try to get to the root of a particular problem, only to be dashed when further probing petered out with no new insights and no relief. I am, it is true, particularly impatient, but other patients whom I subsequently met also felt that they were often given false hopes. I should have realized better than most that there is no magic a therapist can offer to effect a sudden recovery. The analyst himself made some play with my impatience. He thought the suffering induced by my breakdown might help me to adopt a more stoical attitude.

My doubts about analysis and my knowledge of psychology probably made me a particularly difficult patient. I was prone to argue with any attempt at interpretation and to try to catch the analyst out in in-consistencies. The sessions often turned into arguments about the value of psychoanalysis and other forms of treatment.

After four or five consultations he announced that my problems were too complex to be treated in joint therapy with my wife, and suggested that I should undergo an individual analysis. He had accepted me as an acute case hoping to be able to produce some alleviation in a few sessions, but this had not proved possible: he had commitments to many other clients whom he saw two or three times a week for several years, and was not sure whether he could fit me in as a long-term patient. He agreed to see me on my own for a few more times, but then he went on holiday. At that point he referred me to another analyst in London. I put up only a feeble resistance to con-tinuing in analysis. I asked whether it would not be better to seek some form of drug treatment, but he scoffed at this: 'All that would do is to change your mood'. To anyone who has never felt real depression or anxiety, a change of mood may sound rather a trivial thing, but for many who are mentally unwell, it can be a matter of life or death.

The analyst whom he first suggested could not take me, since he also was too busy: he suggested another one who, he said, was 'perhaps a bit young for you, but he is extremely good and I think you will respect his intelligence'.

My new analyst lived in London. To reach him necessitated an hour's train journey along the stretch of railway line which had been used by my wife to reach the station hotel in London where she had made assignations with her lover. The train journey and the sight of the hotel at the other end reduced me to complete panic, and I would arrive at the second analyst shaking with terror. He occupied a small flat permeated by the smell of cooking. On my first visit he was late, and his wife showed me into a squalid consulting room where I lay down on a greasy couch and gave way to real tears for the first time in 30 or 40 years. I think he was rather gratified by my tears—transference had already begun before I had set eyes on him. He said: 'Did you think I had deserted you then?' He turned out to be a young man dressed in student dropout gear. I found his youth disconcerting, since it was hard to believe that anyone so young could understand the emotions that had attacked me in middle age.

Although in all questions of mental health it is difficult to assign cause and effect, I believe that the seven or eight sessions I had with him increased my distress by making me more anxious than ever. When I told my own doctor, who was himself a devotee of psychoanalysis, that analysis was making me worse, he said predictably: 'Maybe you had to be made worse before getting better'—another Catch-22 of the trade.

The young analyst was presumably anxious to be helpful, but he sometimes set about it in a heavy-footed way. He may have felt threatened by me, since I was a well-established psychologist and I had no faith in psychoanalysis. My doctor had been to great lengths telling me that I must be completely honest with the analyst. I accordingly gave him my views on the value of analysis, on the fact that he must have only recently completed his own training analysis, and judging by the poverty in which he seemed to live was not a great success. He countered this attack by telling me that he owned a large house elsewhere in London and had more would-be patients than he could take.

Although he tried to lift some of the load of guilt I was carrying, he made a number of remarks that I found very threatening. He said: 'It seems you have missed out on all the best things in life'. This may or may not have been true, but it was not a sensible remark to make to someone in my distressed state. Moreover, people differ over what are 'the best things in life' and he had no business to pass such an arbitrary judgement. At one stage he diagnosed me as a repressed homosexual, and in the course of my telling him some incident from my childhood, he leant forward and said something deeply shocking. I apologize to the reader, but to understand the nature of my reactions it is necessary to quote his actual words. They were: 'Did you not feel then as though you wanted your father to fuck you until the shit ran out?' If I had ever entertained any such notion, I had long since forgotten it, but I found the suggestion most upsetting.

Indeed around this time I read, in a lucid moment, a clinical case about someone who exactly fitted my picture of myself. He suffered from tormenting obsessions similar to my own, had like myself a deaf mother, and had been a compulsive womanizer. He had been under analysis for twenty years without showing any signs of improvement. He was diagnosed as a repressed passive homosexual, the womanizing being of course his way of disguising his homosexuality from himself. There seemed no hope for me. I should have realized, had my judgement not been impaired by the illness, that according to Freudian doctrine the only men who are not repressed latent homosexuals are unrepressed practising homosexuals. I recounted this clinical case history to one of my colleagues who happened to have a medical degree, and told him that I was apparently beyond all hope. He said: 'When I was a medical student, I used to think I had every disease under the sun. It is very easy to think you have all the aspects of a syndrome, but I don't suppose you really have. For example, were you ever a compulsive womanizer?' I said that I thought I had been at one time, and he said: 'How many women have you slept with?' I said, in jest: 'I can't remember—a few hundred'. He replied, wholly in earnest: 'Good God, you don't call that compulsive womanizing do you?'

It is characteristic of analysts and of many other psychotherapists to turn everything upside down. Going along with other people's wishes ceases to be an easy-going virtue, it becomes collusion; chasing women is a sign of homosexuality. When I tried to bolster the little that was left of my self-esteem by describing occasions on which I had not done things I wished to do for fear of hurting others, the young analyst said: 'You could interpret that as weakness rather than decency'.

I should not give the impression that he made no attempts to comfort me: he did, but sometimes in a rather bizarre way. He said, for instance: 'You know, I really admire you for breaking down'. When I asked him to explain this cryptic remark, he pointed out that many people charge through life without ever reflecting on their own behaviour and with no remorse for their misdeeds. Out of evil good might come: my breakdown had opened the possibility of changing myself. I was far from feeling this at the time, since the breakdown seemed to have occurred for entirely selfish reasons and was in itself demeaning. It is one thing to feel depressed and anxious because the world is full of people who are dying in agony, or starving or eking out a barren, lonely existence, but it is altogether shaming to break down through an insult to one's own *amour propre*.

In addition to making efforts to comfort me, the analyst also gave some sensible advice. I had told him about my behaviour at home, much of which was like that of a small baby. I would sit around moaning and holding my head, and although I seemed unable to stop myself I was aware that this was upsetting for my wife and children. He said: 'Your wife will be able to tolerate just so much of that kind of thing, but if you continue she will be tempted to leave you. Could you not just sit in a chair and feel like a little baby without giving outward expression to your emotions?'

I went home and tried to follow his advice, but it proved to be impossible. I continued to moan and groan out loud. Such behaviour was accompanied by very mixed feelings on my part. I felt that there was an element of faking about the outward expressions of my misery: they seemed partly simulated in order to gain sympathy and attention. Yet, although I thought some of my behaviour was sham, I could not stop myself from behaving in this way.

I merely added to my other worries the thought that even my breakdown was a fake. Was there nothing genuine about me?

He asked me to bring my wife to a joint session, and afterwards suggested that she was jealous of my being analysed and that the best way to cure this jealousy was for her also to become a patient of his. Being a sensible woman, she would have none of this. She pointed out that despite his own training analysis he fidgeted in his chair throughout the session and did not know what to do with his hands. Thereafter she rather unkindly referred to him as 'Pipsqueak'.

A theme that constantly recurred in my sessions with both analysts was the danger of leaving analysis prematurely: from the outset they both warned me that I would be tempted to break off treatment too soon. It would take many months or possibly years before my deep-rooted problems could be properly alleviated by analysis. It was indeed only these state-ments,which at the time seemed plausible enough, that kept me in a method of treatment that I now know was wholly unsuitable for my condition. After seven or eight sessions, I was so upset by the punishment the second analyst appeared to be handing out that I began seriously to think about consulting a psychiatrist and having myself admitted to hospital to undergo physical methods of treatment. When I mentioned this to the analyst, he was horrified; he said, 'Whatever else you do, you must never let yourself be admitted to one of those places'. He seemed indeed as prejudiced against mental hospitals as are some members of the general public.

My condition continued to deteriorate, but the decision about terminat-ing analysis was for the time being taken out of my hands, since my second analyst announced that he too was going on holiday. I was so annoyed with him for what I regarded as very unhelpful treatment that I did not pay his bill. When many months later, after I had recovered, I received a peremptory letter from his solicitors, I took legal advice myself and wrote to him saying that I had no intention of paying. I contested his claim on the grounds that his treatment had been incompetent and damaging. In the state of desperate anxiety in which I then was, his threatening remarks had only increased my problems: to accept such observations as that at some level of the unconscious mind one has homosexual proclivities, that one's virtues stem from weaknesses, or that one has missed out on the best things of life, it is necessary to be in a much more robust state of mental health than I then was. I also alleged that he himself felt threatened by my own knowledge of the subject and my doubts about the efficacy of psycho-analysis: consciously or unconsciously he had been attempting to punish me. Finally, I wrote that he had claimed to be able to make me feel much better within six months of commencing therapy, that this claim was fraudulent and I had entered therapy only through false pretences on his part. Such was my fury that I think I would have been prepared to contest a legal action, but it never arose. He telephoned me a few days after I had written, and was most solicitous and pleased about the recovery I had made.

It is small wonder that many analysts insist on being paid their fee, often in cash, at the end of each session.

[There was a sequel. Many years later I attended a party at the Freud museum and began chatting to someone, whom I thought was a stranger. It turned out it was my second analyst and after he had introduced himself, he said, I think in earnest: 'You know, you owe me £48'. I laughed.]

* * *

Since the two analysts and my doctor were now simultaneously on vacation, I was left in a therapeutic limbo. My wife was anxious to take the children to Naples for a holiday. I used to carry out research on vision in the octopus there every summer, and my children had fond memories of the place and longed to go back: they had been taking important examinations at school and my own illness had been a great trial to them. They deserved a treat. Moreover, my wife and I thought that if I got away from my normal environment it might help to break up the anguished pattern of my thoughts.

By this time I was desperately worried about money: we had lodgers in our house, and so terrible was my condition that I could hardly collect the rent, and when I did collect it I forgot to record it or to bank it. The roof was leaking and the problem of finding someone to repair it seemed insuperable. I forgot who was owing me money, and when with shaking hand I wrote a cheque, there was invariably a mistake on it. I sold a car for two pounds—admittedly it was not in prime condition, but it functioned. Since I could not face advertising it in the paper, I took the first offer from a dealer, and felt relieved that I would no longer have to bear the expense of running it. The children cried when they saw it go. I was convinced that I would lose my job and my family would be destitute. Naples was to be our last extravagance before declining into hopeless poverty.

As a university teacher, I was entitled to cheap student fares on foreign railways. I therefore booked tickets to Naples through a student travel agency for a twelve-day trip. The journey was feasible only because we had some very good friends in Naples who agreed to put up our children and to find a room elsewhere for me and Josie. I consulted a different doctor about whether I was in a condition to make the trip, and he thought I was. He had rather more faith in drugs than the other one and prescribed an antidepressant, sleeping pills and sedatives. I was convinced I was dying of lung cancer, and asked him whether I had club fingers: he examined them and replied, I thought very guardedly: They are within the normal limits'. I found this less than reassuring.

I dreaded the journey—36 hours on trains and boats with no possibility of alleviating the tedium by reading since that was totally beyond my powers of concentration. All I would have to occupy me were my obsessive thoughts.

I contemplated throwing myself off the cross-Channel ferry, but the train journey was much better than I expected. By good fortune, we obtained an otherwise unoccupied compartment for the night, and I took a massive dose of sleeping tablets and slept for 12 solid hours. We arrived at Naples through the ironworks on the outskirts with their chimneys belching flame, and were met at the Ferrovia Centrale by my friends. They had not seen me since the breakdown, and were upset by my condition whilst feeling powerless to help. The husband was himself in a medical profession, and reinforced my judgement that I must have done with analysis and seek psychiatric help.

I remember, on the first evening, all of us going to a brightly-lit open-air cafe for a drink, where in the past I had enjoyed the nostalgic sound of Neapolitan songs and the sight of the animated street life. I was now under such heavy sedation that I could drink practically nothing. The cafe was in a park along the front, and while the others sat at table I rolled around moaning in the dust. Such behaviour is disconcerting to others at first, but they quickly realize it is best ignored since there is little they can do to help. To my other worries was now added almost total impotence—induced partly by my mood, which was becoming more and more depressed, and partly by the drugs I was taking. With their aid, I obtained the blessed relief of nine or ten hours sleep each night, but waking brought back the pain.

I revisited many of the places I had once loved: the Museo Nazionale with its magnificent mosaics pillaged from Pompeii, Pompeii itself and Capri. None of them evoked a spark of interest—I stared listlessly and uncomprehendingly at the pictures in the museum with harrowing thoughts still racing in my mind. I could not guide the children round Pompeii, since I could not concentrate sufficiently to follow the plan. Capri had lost its beauty and charm. I could not even giggle at the vulgarity of the interior of Axel Munthe's villa, though the beauty of the formal garden and the magnificent view of the island and the sea from the belvedere evoked a slight response. The phrase 'See Naples and die" echoed through my mind: I was convinced I would never return alive to England, let alone ever revisit Naples.

I was poor company. My friends lived in an apartment on the fourteenth floor of a modern block of flats. While they were eating dinner, I would go out on the balcony and contemplate the drop. I even concealed myself in a corner of the balcony for half an hour in the hope that they would think I had thrown myself over—a shameful trick, though when they came looking I had enough sense to reveal myself fairly quickly. All this trip showed was something I should have known already: one takes one's depression with one wherever one goes.

On my return from Naples, I went back to my own doctor to tell him that I wanted to seek psychiatric advice and to attack my depression and anxiety with drugs. He was himself under analysis and was very much against this line of action. He said: 'You are going through a great emotional crisis, and drugs are not the solution. You owe it to yourself to have a prolonged analysis: if necessary you must mortgage everything you have to pay for the treatment'. So committed was he to analysis that when I suggested that giving up cigarettes and taking more exercise might help my mental state, he said: 'There is no evidence that exercise ever helped the mind'—a remark which, when I later reminded him of it, he regretted making.

In the end, I weakly agreed to have one more session with the first analyst for 'reassessment'. The reassessment took the form of advice to continue analysis in the hope of learning a new set of emotional responses: I had become preoccupied with the idea that I could never love anyone properly, and I asked him pathetically whether he could make me capable of love if I became his patient yet again. He said it would take time but he was sure this could be achieved. I asked whether I would be able to love my wife and he said: 'That I cannot guarantee: but I am sure you will be able to love someone'. Since I only wanted to love Josie, I became more upset than ever. I pointed out that new learning becomes more difficult with advancing years and doubted my capacity for it. The analyst retorted that he had recently been seeing a woman patient of 55 who after a year's analysis had 'seen a flower for what it was for the first time and had burst into tears'. I think it was the sheer idiocy of this story that finally decided me to abandon analysis and seek some other form of treatment.

4

The hospital

Having decided to seek help from a psychiatrist, I was of course anxious to find a good one. I had professional contacts with several psychiatrists and telephoned some of them for advice. I naturally did not want to be treated by a friend, and there was a consensus that one psychiatrist unknown to me was an excellent man. When I telephoned, he agreed to see me without an official referral from a doctor, though when I told my general practitioner that I had made this arrangement he reluctantly agreed to write the psychiatrist a letter outlining my medical history.

My first interview with the psychiatrist took a very different form from the inchoate ramblings in which I had indulged with the two analysts. He spent three hours taking notes on my life, broken into systematic topics —career, early family relations, marriage and friendships. He then said: 'You are suffering from an agitated depression. This is not uncommon in men of your age who have achieved professional success as a result of a great deal of hard work. Your depression is an illness and must be treated as such.' He advised me to become a voluntary patient in a psychiatric hospital, if only to break up the bad pattern of interaction into which I had fallen with those around me, particularly my wife. He also prescribed an antidepressant drug and warned me that it would have no effect for at least three weeks other than unwanted side-effects. He told me I would remain in hell for the next month or so but that ultimately I would definitely recover—an assurance that neither the doctor nor the analysts had been prepared to give.

My wife had accompanied me to the hospital, and he spent 20 minutes talking with her. He told her that I was in a condition where I was seeing everything in a distorted way as though I were looking at the world through darkened and buckled glass. He assured her that I would recover.

The psychiatrist saw me on a Friday, and I was to be admitted to hospital on Monday. Although I had more or less agreed to admission, I agonized about it over the weekend. I am not by nature a brave person. I was still in a state of extreme dependence on my wife, and although I could see it was not doing either of us any good I felt desperately that I needed her by my side. I thought at the time and I still think that entering hospital was the most courageous decision I have ever made.

My wife drove me there. Like all incoming National Health patients I was given a room of my own—cell-like but comfortable. The door had no lock and contained a window with a curtain *outside* so that nurses could observe the inmate at will. The young male nurse who admitted me was kind and considerate. He made sure that I was not carrying any drugs or alcohol, and for reasons I never fathomed he removed my electric razor, which was returned to me the day after. The reasons for retaining ordinary razors are obvious: they were issued before breakfast each morning and then recovered. Little attempt was made to explain the routine of the ward except for telling me the times of meals. It took me nearly three weeks before I discovered where and when to obtain clean sheets, though this was my own fault for not inquiring earlier.

While Josie waited on the ward, I was given a rapid physical examination by a consultant whom I never saw again. A few tests were made for signs of neurological disease, and my chest, blood pressure and rectum were checked. The drugs had made me so constipated that my stools were bloody, and the consultant assured me that I had neither bowel cancer nor piles. I rejoined my wife on the ward. After lunch I sadly watched her drive away into the sunlight and was left sitting in my little cell feeling sad, lonely and very anxious.

The ward was made up of two long wings, one for male the other for female patients, with a shared common room and dining room in the middle. Altogether there were about 60 patients on the ward. Each wing contained a corridor with private rooms opening off it and a dormitory at the end with about a dozen beds. As patients began to recover they moved from the private rooms to the dormitory. All the inmates were there on a voluntary basis and were expected to be 'short-stay'—less than 18 months.

The mental hospital was one of the best-equipped in England. It was set in extensive and beautifully maintained grounds and had facilities for almost every conceivable sport, including a gymnasium and swimming pool. It was free from much of the regimentation that pervades most hospitals for physical illness. Patients were up and about fully dressed in the daytime. Visitors were allowed at almost any hour. We were encouraged to attend occupational therapy, known as 'OT'—painting, dressmaking, typing, carpentry, yoga and so on, but no compulsion was brought to bear. Breakfast was at eight and supper at five-thirty.

Of more interest to most patients were 'tablet times'. The cry 'tablets' would echo through the ward at nine, one and six o'clock, and a fourth dose was obtainable from the night nurse before going to bed. Most of us who were taking drugs looked forward to our tablets and queued with alacrity. We swallowed them eagerly to the accompaniment of a draught of water from a plastic glass that each patient was responsible for rinsing and drying in readiness for the next. This was the only chore patients were expected to perform, apart from making their own beds.

While taking our pills, we were closely watched by a nurse. As it is well known that unless medicine is taken under supervision about 30% of it never finds its way to the patients' stomachs, it is remarkable that many hospitals still trust patients to swallow their own.

Almost all the patients who were seriously unwell found the six empty hours between supper and bedtime very hard to bear. The nurses did their best to help. They organized bingo, and they tried to lure any patient who looked particularly miserable into playing one or other of the 20 or so games —such as table tennis, snooker, Scrabble, Monopoly, or draughts—with which the ward was equipped. They also did their best to soothe anyone who was beside himself with anxiety. Despite these attempts to make the time pass, many patients found these hours very difficult and retired into their own miseries. There was a general feeling that not enough was being done to help us.

The ward contained three separate groups of patients, each under a different psychiatric consultant. There were alcoholics in the process of drying out, a group of patients with phobias, and the group to which I belonged, who were mainly suffering from depression.

The consultants were rarely in evidence. As in so many walks of life, as soon as they have proved themselves good at their own profession, extraneous calls on their time mount up: they practise psychiatry less and less and devote themselves instead to administering, teaching, and sitting on innumerable committees. Under each consultant was a senior registrar who in my group was a Sri Lankan with a permanent and cheerful smile. There was also a junior registrar allocated to each group, in whose direct charge the patients were. Also associated with each group were one or more clinical psychologists. All the doctors and psychologists had patients on other wards, and most also worked in other hospitals.

In the course of a week, patients spent on average about two separate periods of an hour or an hour and a half alone with a doctor or psychologist. The time between such sessions could feel terribly empty, and many patients saw themselves as existing in a vacuum with little being done to help. Any patient who had an appointment with a doctor or psychologist was treated by the others as being of great importance. On emerging from a session, he or she would be eagerly questioned about what went on; indeed. a patient's standing with the other patients came to be directly related to the number of occasions on which he was seen privately by the staff. The excitement generated by tablet times was also doubtless caused by the feeling that here was something that was actually being done to help.

Some of the doctors were careless about keeping appointments: they would say they would see a patient the next day and then fail to do so. This was bad for patients" morale, and some of the younger doctors were clearly unaware of the extent to which patients felt dependent upon them. To the plea that little was being done to help, the standard response of the medical staff was that everything that happened in the hospital was therapy—OT (occupational therapy), existence in a novel milieu, and the interactions with nurses and other patients were all therapeutic.

As patients, we were quick to resent lack of attention from doctors, but we were equally prone to suspect that the nurses were spying on us if they paid us too much attention. Part of their duties was to make reports on the patients' mental state. They sometimes seemed a little tactless in their attempts to draw patients out on, for example, how they fared during a weekend at home. Although the nurses were trying to be kind and sympathetic, many patients felt that such inquiries were being made with the aim of having something to report in the day-book. Reports were also sent back from occupational therapy workers and doctors, and we had the feeling that all our actions were known and recorded almost all the time. Whenever I was in my room, whether by day or night, the curtain would be removed from the window every two hours or so and a nurse would observe, replace the curtain and go away. No matter how much I told myself that such surveillance was for my own good, it was difficult not to feel that there was something sinister about it.

There was a further feature of life in hospital to which many inmates found it difficult to adjust. The younger doctors and nurses tended to treat patients as though they were insane, and this could be both infuriating and upsetting. Since all the patients were to some extent mentally ill, it may seem odd to be upset by being treated as such, but none of the patients was totally out of touch with reality, and their illness only affected part of their lives. Many, for example, knew better than the nurses what pills they were supposed to be taking. However, the doctors sometimes wrote up the drug sheets in such a hurry that nurses could easily make mistakes. It could seem very important to be given the right drugs, but when the wrong ones were handed out any attempt to argue with the nurse would be greeted with a bland smile and treated as part of the patient's illness to be recorded in the day-book. Because doctors and nurses could always shelter behind the belief that the patients were mad, they were in an impregnable position, and it was easy for patients to feel completely in the power of the hospital authorities. One of the alcoholics—an engaging con-man—had spent several years in prison in Dartmoor; he summed up his feelings: 'I'd rather spend a year in Dartmoor than a week here.' When I asked why, he said: 'At least you can get at the screws there: here there's no one to get at.'

I should stress that in describing the common grievances of the patients I am not imputing blame to the hospital staff: I am merely trying to describe what it feels like to be in a mental hospital. The point of substance is that even in a psychiatric hospital that is one of the country's showpieces and that is run in a most enlightened way at great cost to the taxpayer, patients could readily become apathetic and their feelings were easily bruised. The situation is much worse in most mental hospitals, which are run with fewer and less experienced staff. For long-stay patients, it becomes debatable how much of their incapacity to cope with life is due to their original illness and how much to being institutionalized.

I do not remember how I passed the first afternoon in the hospital. I think I talked to some of the other patients and I ate my dinner at five-thirty. The food was plain but, for institutional cooking, good and plentiful. On the evening of my first day there, my anxiety began to build up. Over half the nurses were coloured: I remember wondering how nurses with home backgrounds in Jamaica, India, Pakistan, Sri Lanka and many different African countries could have such sympathy with the absurd neuroses of the British middle and working classes. On my first night on the ward, an attractive and vivacious little African nurse was exceptionally kind to me. She chatted about my problems and inveigled me into playing table tennis and snooker with her: this distraction from my anxieties was extremely helpful. Many of the patients spent the evenings watching television, but throughout my stay in hospital I was far too agitated to concentrate on any programme, and although I once or twice entered the television room I was never able to sit there for more than five minutes.

The same nurse later upset me quite badly by crude but well-meant attempts to analyse my condition. I once explained that I could not join some of the other patients in a game of tennis because my motor co-ordination was badly impaired by my drugs. My statement was true: indeed so shaky was I that I had to concentrate very hard to cross a road. She said: "Oh you're always blaming your troubles on something else: if you're not blaming other people, you're blaming the drugs.' At the time this seemed very upsetting, and I was hurt for several hours: people in the state I was in are sensitive to the slightest suggestion of criticism.

At ten-thirty, the patients were allowed to make themselves Horlicks, and sweet biscuits were provided. I found the nightly glass of Horlicks, with its memories of protected childhood, a great comfort. The only other drink served on the ward was heavily stewed tea, though many patients kept in the kitchen their own supplies of coffee or cocoa. Although I much preferred coffee, I never got round to investing in a jar: I was determined to spend as little money as possible, partly because I believed I would never again be able to earn and partly because I had decided to do without any self-indulgence.

At 11 o'clock on my first evening, I went to the night nurse for my final dose of drugs before going to bed. I was horrified to find that the registrar who, under the consultant, was in charge of my case had not prescribed a sleeping tablet: I had been using sleeping tablets regularly for the last six weeks, and I was convinced that without them I would not sleep. I was by now in a desperate state of anxiety, and the prospect of going without sleep—the only thing to which I still looked forward—appalled me. The night nurse was sympathetic but could not find a doctor on duty and was naturally loath to rouse one from his bed. Although he could not give me a sleeping tablet, my prescription for sedatives was written in such a way that he was able to increase the dose without going against what was written on the drug sheet—nurses could not alter the drugs that were prescribed.

This particular nurse was an old-timer who had retired but still did occasional night duty as a part-time occupation. He was stocky, and possessed of demonic willpower. I talked to him from about midnight to one or two in the morning, and he told me how his only child had contracted poliomyelitis. The doctors had given up all hope of the boy ever walking again, and wished him to stay permanently in an institution. The father told me that he was determined 'to lick the doctors': he insisted on his boy living at home and by the sheer exercise of his own will he gave him the strength to live and to recover. I was talking of discharging myself the day after, since in my depressed and nervous state I had by now lost faith in the hospital and its staff. He told me that he had seen 'Many like yourself when they first come in. Those that run away too soon always come back.' He said I could lick my illness but I needed help: he claimed that he himself could lick the problem of sleep for me, and he ferociously willed me to sleep, seizing my arm in a vice-like grip. His faith and his will somehow enabled me to sleep. and when I woke again at four in the morning and stumbled into his office for comfort, he managed to will me back to sleep again. He was a most remarkable man, whom I was sorry never to see again.

The following day my anxiety gradually built up throughout the morning. After lunch there was a group meeting of the whole ward: these meetings occurred weekly and were attended by nurses, occupational therapists, psychologists and doctors, as well as by patients. I was unable to sit through the meeting—I began to wring my hands and moan and eventually I rolled on the floor. The male nurse who had admitted me took me outside and we walked round and round the grounds together. He allowed me to pour out the tale of my sufferings in an attempt to talk me down. For the rest of the afternoon nurses took it in turns to walk with me through the beautiful park in which the hospital was situated.

I would not have believed it possible to experience such extreme anxiety. My heart pounded, my body shook, my stomach felt as though all the blood had drained away, and my legs seemed too weak to carry me. My mind was occupied solely with my jealous thoughts: cruelly detailed and painful visual images succeeded one another in never-ending succession.

The Sri Lankan senior registrar had been summoned to see me, and I spent half an hour with him late in the afternoon. He tried to reassure me, telling me that I would feel very differently in a fortnight's time, and he prescribed a stronger tranquillizer—chlorpromazine. He described very exactly what the drug would do: 'It will act within half an hour of taking it. You will find that it will remove the physical feelings of anxiety so that your body feels calm. It will not stop your obsessive thoughts, but it will blunt their edge and make them less painful so that you can bear them more easily.' It worked exactly as he had predicted.

Although the new drug made life just bearable, I remained in mental agony: I was fortunate in one thing—I was now on such a dose of different drugs that I almost invariably slept well, and sleep was always something to look forward to and to sustain me through the fears and boredom of the day.

Over the next week I began to adapt to the drug, and obtained decreasing relief. The registrar reacted by tripling the dose, but I steadily adapted to the larger dose throughout the rest of my stay. The side-effects of the drugs I was taking were most unpleasant. Apart from having very poor motor co-ordination, I was now totally impotent. In addition I had severe constipation and it was agony to defecate: my stools were smeared with fresh blood spilt in the effort to pass them. I suffered from these pains unnecessarily, since it was only after I had been in hospital for a fortnight or so that I discovered from another patient that the nurses would issue Senocot tablets on demand at night. Even this did not solve the problem, since in my distracted state I usually forgot to ask. The reader may wonder why I did not mention the constipation to a doctor, but during the first fortnight in hospital I think I only saw a doctor once or twice, and there seemed to be more important things to discuss than constipation. A minor side-effect was difficulty in urinating, but the worst effect was dryness of the mouth: no matter how much water I drank, the feeling of a parched tongue and throat could not be shaken off.

Like most of the other patients, I went home for long weekends, leaving the hospital on Friday evening and returning on Monday morning. The idea of spending the weekend in hospital appalled me. The boredom during the week was bad enough, despite the fact that there were always other patients and nurses to talk to. occupational therapy classes to attend and a variety of games that one could play. There was also a chance that a doctor or a psychologist would summon one for an interview, something to which I, in common with my fellow-patients, always looked forward: not only did it break the monotony, I also felt it might actually be helpful. I developed a terror that the doctors would take my weekend leave away from me, and no amount of reassurance would convince me that they had no intention of so doing. When I left the hospital on Friday afternoons I often felt for a few moments free and exhilarated. But I carried my misery with me, and the weekends were as full of terror and boredom as the weeks. I tried not to admit this to myself and caught the train back on Monday mornings with sadness.

On my return to hospital, a nurse would always come across to chat with me. I was anxious not to reveal that at weekends the pattern of interaction with my wife was a bad as ever, since I thought that if the doctors knew how I behaved at home, they might stop my weekend leave. I therefore gave very guarded replies to the nurses' inquiries, and I remember saying once rather ungraciously: 'At least it's not as bad as this place.' In fact, most of the patients were actively encouraged to go home at weekends: the few who stayed did so either because they had no home to go to or because they could not face the prospect of meeting their family or friends, and preferred the tedium of a weekend in hospital.

Many patients had good reason to fear the prejudice of 'normal' people about mental illness. As they improved, efforts were made to obtain some sort of part-time work for them in the surrounding community. This usually proved difficult, since as soon as it was known that someone had been a patient in a mental hospital, potential employers lost interest. There is still much prejudice against the mentally ill, and I realized that one of the ways in which I was luckier than the majority of patients was that I could go home at weekends and talk to friends who would (usually) be sympathetic and understanding and who would not think that being an in-patient in a mental hospital was a great stigma. It was very different for many of the others: their friends would either try to be nice whilst concealing their embarrassment or they would be downright hostile or shun them altogether.

One of the patients—a middle-aged woman who lived in well-to-do suburbia attended one Sunday a religious ceremony connected with healing at her local church. She returned to her home with a woman who lived opposite her. The neighbour said: 'I suppose you will be moving away from here when you come out of that place.' When the patient expressed puzzlement, she said: 'Well, it would be much better for everyone in the street if you did—it would be very embarrassing to have you still around.' This was the attitude of a regular churchgoer, but to judge from the experiences of other patients it is common in the community at large.

Patients often felt they were a great affliction to their friends and family and should not trouble them with their worries. Some were so closed up that they found it difficult to talk to anyone. Many, particularly when they first came into hospital, found it a relief to be among fellow-sufferers in whom they could confide in return for listening to the confidences of others: they found it easier to open their hearts to complete strangers, whom after discharge they would probably never see again, than to those close to them. They also obtained some relief, at least at first, from telling the tale of their woes to doctors, psychologists and nurses, though the novelty of this usually wore off rather quickly, and patients began to find it a bore to go over their stories every time there was a change of doctors.

Although I was lucky in my friends, they too could be tactless. I remember being very hurt when, full of self-reproach, I asked a colleague of mine with whom I was on close terms what he had ever seen to admire in me: after a moment's thought he replied, 'I sometimes wonder'. After I had been discharged from hospital, whilst arguing with him in front of several other people over some intellectual issue I said: 'That argument doesn't make sense: you're mad', and he replied: 'At least I've never been a patient in a mental hospital.' I was desperately hurt, and this provides yet another example of how prone anyone in a neurotic condition can be to take offence. I later learned that his foolish behaviour was the result of attendance at encounter groups where he had been persuaded that he must always give vent to his 'true feelings'.

Visitors to the hospital could have a somewhat similar effect. They would often be bright and smiling and comment with surprise on what a nice place the hospital seemed to be, adding that they would not mind a few weeks' rest there themselves. Perhaps they had expected to see patients shrieking and in chains. After meeting other patients, they would say: 'I can't see what's wrong with him [or her], he seems quite normal', thus expressing the prejudice that someone who is deranged should behave in a mad fashion all the time. They did not realize that the girl who claimed that the hospital was trying to starve her, and who would constantly beg food items, was in fact suffering from anorexia and was in the habit of hoarding food in her room while eating so little that she was in danger of starving herself to death. Unless you have been acutely anxious or depressed yourself, it is difficult to realize that someone who is outwardly healthy and well fed, who is living in comfortable surroundings with what appear to be many pleasant recreations, and who is able to talk quite sensibly for much of the time, may be in mental anguish.

It is hard to know how to treat someone with a breakdown. The feeling that friends and family have that they can do nothing to help must be very frustrating. In my own case, I am sure that sympathy helped—at least temporarily. Being told, as I was by one friend, that my breakdown was a form of nemesis or, as some friends said, that it would do me good and help me to change myself, was distinctly unhelpful. The analysts also had a habit of saying that the breakdown was a chance to change myself, and I became very worried about how I was ever to change. I shall always be grateful to those friends who said: 'Don't attempt to change yourself—you were all right the way you were. And you'll go back to that when you're better'. If I were to sum up my own feelings on how friends and family should treat anyone mentally ill, I would say: 'Sympathize without condescension and never pass moral judgements. Try to find something to talk about to distract the sufferer.' The visitors who helped me most were those who could find something to discuss in the outside world that would take my attention away from myself.

In contrast to some visitors, patients were almost invariably kind to one another. They would go to great lengths to comfort or console any of their number who were in particular difficulties: the phrase, 'after all, we're all in the same boat' was frequently to be heard.

For almost the whole of my stay in hospital my anxiety would from time to time rise to quite uncontrollable levels. If I was on the ward at night, I would pace from one end to the other, pausing from time to time to screw up my body or to attempt to climb a wall or even to bang my head against one. This behaviour produced a mixture of consternation and amusement in the other occupants of the ward. I went out one evening with three other patients including Jimmy, a Glaswegian alcoholic. He worked on a building site and, although suffering from terrible anxiety himself, adopted a protective attitude towards me and was forever greeting me with: 'Och, ye'll be all rricht, Stuart, yell be all rricht.' On this particular occasion, I was far from all right: I was climbing lamp-posts and threatening to dash my head through shop windows in an effort to get rid of the tortured tenseness which permeated my body. Somehow they managed to get me on a bus and back to the hospital.

One of the thoughts that dogged me throughout my illness was envy of normal people going about their everyday business. When I went out to buy a few apples, I used to feel how lucky the greengrocer was to live a placid life not tormented by obsessional thoughts. I was particularly envious of the hospital staff when I saw them driving away to a normal life outside the hospital.

Given that the doctors and psychologists in the hospital could only spend at most two to five hours a week seeing patients individually, one of the greatest problems facing the hospital authorities was how to occupy the patients' time. It was generally agreed that nothing could be worse than letting patients sit around and brood. The main distractions were games and occupational therapy: nurses would constantly try to encourage patients to get off the ward during the daytime and occupy themselves by playing tennis or badminton, by swimming or by attending occupational therapy, which went on for three hours in the morning and two in the afternoon.

The head of the occupational therapy unit was a woman of great energy and faith. She tried to get to know patients and to discover their interests and talents. She constantly attempted to cajole them into taking part in play readings, poetry readings, giving or listening to lectures and musical recitals, and attending classes in dressmaking, pottery, woodwork, cookery and typing. She also organized expeditions to the local repertory theatre and to nearby exhibitions of art. Hers was a thankless task. Patients would volunteer to give talks to the others and then funk it at the last moment; they often simply forgot to come to a play reading, or the man playing the lead in a carefully rehearsed drama would be unable to appear on the opening night because he had just been given ECT (electroconvulsive therapy). She cheerfully survived such misfortunes and continued to infect patients with her own love of the arts.

When it was her turn to take yoga or relaxation classes, she often varied the routine by introducing exercises in touching and trusting. One patient would lie down and relax and then others would gently roll him or her on mattresses from one end of the room to the other. I could always relax sufficiently to offer no resistance to those rolling me, and I found the sensation quite pleasant. Another exercise was to pair the patients off in couples: one member of each pair was then blind-folded and was led round the room by the other. No verbal instructions were allowed: guidance was entirely by means of pressure applied by the hands and arms. Again I found this a pleasant enough diversion until I became bored with it, but lack of trust has never figured among my vices.

Since I could not do anything I was used to doing, being in hospital seemed a good chance to learn something new, and I attended pottery classes almost every morning. I progressed from a dish made in a mould to a mug shaped round a beer bottle, and then to a bowl built up by adding successive strips of clay. I was baffled by the complexity of the processes that went into making such simple objects—at how difficult it was to roll clay to an even thickness or to get rid of bubbles in it, to impose with the various implements provided any pattern upon it that was other than an untidy mess, or to press a layer of clay smoothly into a mould. To obtain an even glaze required a degree of skill that was completely beyond me. It was unfortunate that having made a pot it often took a week before the occupational therapy staff could fire it and another week to bake the glaze: a more immediate sight of the end-product of our labours would have been more encouraging.

Misshapen though my products were, I took some pride in having made them myself: no machine process could have produced objects of such total irregularity. The pottery instructress was possessed of unbelievable patience both with her pupils and with their pots: however crude one's efforts, she tried to find something to praise, and she was unsparing in the time she gave to repairing one's errors. I doubt if doing pottery taught me patience, and it certainly did not prevent my continuing obsessions, since it was possible to smooth away at the soft wet clay whilst thinking the most tortured thoughts. Despite hours of trying, I never learned to use a wheel: the trick of centring the clay cannot be imparted by words.

Patients were encouraged, though never forced, to put their former skills to use to help the hospital. A professional gardener on our ward trans-formed the appearance of the shrubbery beds by which it was surrounded. Since my own skills lay largely in writing and teaching, and I was in no condition to do either. I was hard pushed to find any useful task. Eventually my clinical psychologist gave me the job of preparing a card-index for a collection of several hundred scientific papers owned by one of the psychologists who worked in the hospital. Since the papers were heaped at random in cardboard boxes, and since the psychologist who owned them was in any case about to retire, I suspected that the task was useless and this disappointed me. Nevertheless, I was determined to prove to myself that I could do something that involved a little concentration, and I spent an hour or two a day on my own in a borrowed office writing index cards with a shaking hand. Although I could not read continuous prose, I was able to perform this task, because I did not have to carry anything forward from one card to another. I could write a card, or even part of one, such as the author's name, return to my brooding, and then go back to the task. Some of the articles appertained to cases like my own, and these I would occasionally manage to read or half-read in the process of cataloguing them.

During the daytime then, I tried to fill my hours with occupational therapy, progressive relaxation classes and the rather pointless indexing task. I also completed many more crosswords and wandered round the grounds with other patients. Many seemed to me to be in a much worse state than myself. They flitted through the ward like pathetic ghosts on the shores of Hell: some could do no more than mumble, and several were withdrawn completely from the real world and lived entirely with their inner miseries. Only the nurses, doctors and a few of the alcoholics who had already dried out seemed made of flesh. At occupational therapy, I met long-stay patients from other wards. Some had been in hospital for several years: others had been in and out for most of their lives. They were often sad, shambling creatures with slurred speech: their condition made me feel ashamed to be in hospital at all.

In subsequent chapters I shall describe in more detail how some of the other patients behaved and felt. At the time I was often touched by the pathos of their situation, and despite my own anxieties I sometimes felt an impostor in their midst. Their troubles often seemed to have arisen from nothing and to be quite outside their own control, but I felt that I was directly responsible for my own breakdown and blamed myself for collapsing and for allowing myself to succumb to my loathsome jealousy. At the same time, I experienced an almost directly contradictory feeling. Many patients had worries that were totally unreal: they were petrified by spiders or had paranoiac obsessions about the world plotting against them. In contrast, my own obsessions were about something that had really happened. If only some of the other patients could be persuaded to see the world as it really was, their problems would disappear: since my own obsessions were about a painfully real event, I thought there was no hope of ever overcoming them.

Early in my stay, I used to play chess with a young patient: like crosswords, chess involves little memory, and between my painful thoughts I could find just sufficient time to concentrate to make the next move. He was discharged soon after I entered, and this method of passing the evenings was taken away from me. As I spent only four nights a week in hospital, my dread of these evenings and my despair about how to make the time pass may seem unreasonable, but then so was the rest of my behaviour. I partially solved the problem by persuading my wife to visit me two evenings a week and by having friends to see me as often as possible on the other two. I would usually meet them in the local town rather than on the ward. In the evenings, I would sit sadly with my wife sipping ginger beer in a pub, since the least drop of alcohol interacted with my drugs and made me feel sick and dizzy. The interchange between us was often still bad. Yet no matter how much she had abused me early in the evening, by the time we came to part she was usually contrite and loving. We would make our way to the local station from which her train left, leaving ourselves time to consume watery hot chocolate in the squalid and crowded station buffet. That buffet came to seem like a Paradise from which I was cast out every evening to make my lonely way back to the terrors of the hospital.

I have now sketched the routine of the hospital, some of my own experiences there and the feelings that most patients had in common. We all felt disappointed that we did not receive more psychotherapy and more contact hours with doctors and psychologists. All incoming patients were disappointed not to see more of the consultant who had admitted them: they had often entered hospital only because of their faith in one particular experienced man, and on admission it was a shock to discover that he was so busy that he could in fact only see patients once every three or four weeks and then not on his own but in a case conference. The tedium of the evenings oppressed almost everyone, and the boredom at weekends afflicted those who did not take their weekend leave. We all felt we were very much in the power of the hospital authorities. Although we were free to discharge ourselves at any time, few were in a condition to do so, and so long as one stayed in hospital one had to agree to the conditions imposed: one woman was forbidden to communicate with her husband even by letter or telephone. This may have been good therapy for her—I never discovered why this condition was imposed—but it made the rest of us uneasy lest we suffer a similar fate. None of us liked the constant surveillance, and many of us felt oppressed because we could not deal on equal terms with nurses or doctors: because we were mad, they did not need to take us seriously.

These remarks should not be taken as a criticism of the hospital auth-orities or staff. Like the patients, they also are human, and the sensitivity needed to avoid offending the feelings of patients in our condition is beyond most human beings. Moreover, they were extremely busy—too busy some-times to grasp how dependent patients became upon them. Finally, there are limits to what can be done to help mental patients. Our ignorance of how best to treat them is profound. It may even be that in some cases hurt feelings are in the long run of therapeutic value, though I would like firm evidence before advocating it as a method of treatment.

Given that the patients had much in common, our behaviour was very different. The alcoholics tended after an initial period of drying out to be cheerful and sociable, though some remained desperately unhappy and reverted to secret drinking. If you used a spade to dig up a flower bed almost anywhere in the hospital, the chances were that you would unearth a bottle of gin or whisky that had been buried at night for subsequent consumption. Some patients were quiet and uncommunicative, occupying themselves with knitting or reading. One young woman, who was a medical student, had been in hospital for over a year and claimed to have read several hundred books but to have no memory of any. Some patients ran wildly round the grounds, or sat in a corner and sobbed. Others appeared superficially to be completely normal, though they were unable to function outside the hospital. I often admired the fortitude of some, particularly the women, who would sit patiently knitting or staring into space giving little outward sign of the boredom and agitation that dominated my own existence.

Only occasionally was there a scene—usually caused by one of the alcoholics returning to the ward totally drunk and shouting abuse at patients, nurses and doctors. Such offenders were often discharged at once, even when this happened late at night. They could be discharged from the hospital completely, given the option of moving to another ward, or if their condition was bad enough, detained under a compulsory commitment order. The outer doors were usually kept open. When they were found locked, a frisson went round the ward: either a patient had been expelled and they were locked against their unwelcome return, or a patient was thought to be in too bad a state to be allowed out.

I saw no physical violence during my stay, although several of the patients had in their ordinary life committed violent crimes. The most traumatic episodes were suicide attempts, usually made by swallowing fifty or a hundred aspirins—a desperately painful way to die. None of these attempts succeeded while I was there, but one girl twice had to have her stomach pumped out; much to the annoyance of the duty doctor she always chose the small hours of the morning and he was called from his bed to perform this unpleasant task. She would disappear for a day or two to a ward in a general hospital, and having recovered sufficiently would return quieter than before.

One final misery that all, except the few on the road to recovery, had in common was that we lived without hope: few of us believed we would ever get better and there was nothing in life to look forward to.

I am conscious that, perhaps because of an inability to sympathize now with my condition then, I have not conveyed the pathos of the situation in which I and other patients found ourselves. Our plight was better expressed in a letter written to me by a patient who had seen the articles I wrote on my illness, though she had clearly been in a less enlightened hospital.

I begged a nurse just to speak to me. 'Get back to bed we do not have to speak to you only to see you are in bed' were her words and to these words I have a witness. Hurt!!! I lay and cried for one hour—two hours — until the lights went on and it was day. 'May I go and phone my husband?' 'No—wait for the day staff . . . Dr Brown said she would see me at 4 o'clock, so I sat in Ward 4 lounge and fell asleep. Can you imagine how I felt when a nurse said that I was not there and was never there at all, in fact called me a liar? . . . The day dragged by and I kept asking to see the doctor who was in charge of my case ... I have attended meetings in hospital which are farcical and I told the doctor to stop looking at his watch and if he was too busy why bother . . . One night I woke at two in the morning and called and called for my husband. They would not call him. So I begged for a pill to sleep but no it was against the rules. So the nurse called the man in charge who also refused to make the call. I wrote my husband's name over and over again, on twenty-two pages. So I waited and at 7 a.m. when the day staff appeared again asked if I could make the telephone call. 'No. No calling'. 'Just a call'. 'No. No call'. So at 8 o'clock I begged someone to come with me to make the call knowing I must not leave the hospital: no—rules. So with all my strength spent I again lost confidence and had to go and phone alone, not knowing like an alcoholic I had taken the first drink—no more could I endure the silly rules and regulations made to break the will or laugh away the stupidity of it all'.

5

Treatment

Most of the psychotherapy I received in hospital was given by a clinical psychologist. Indeed I selected my consultant partly because he worked closely with this particular psychologist: although I had never met him before, I had corresponded with him professionally and he had a high reputation both as a therapist and for his research. He was about ten years older than myself, and the therapeutic techniques he practised had largely arisen out of discoveries made in my own speciality, experimental psychology. For all these reasons I was predisposed to trust and like him. He was tall, gentle, vaguely handsome, with a shock of grey hair, and his body tapered to unexpectedly tiny feet. He smiled readily and had a remarkable capacity for sympathizing with his patients' sillier fears and wishes as well as with their agonies. He treated all his patients with the gravest respect and was universally liked. It was a severe blow to many of them to be transferred to a different therapist.

I saw him for the first time a few days after I was admitted to the hospital. I was already talking wildly of discharging myself, and he observed that although I was free to do so I should give the hospital a fair trial. Staying there for a time might help to distance myself from my problems and hence to see them more in perspective. I should regard the hospital as a refuge from the cares of the outside world. I asked rather pathetically whether if I left they would relinquish all responsibility for me, and he said that I should not play ducks and drakes with them—another remark which though harmless enough I found most upsetting.

During the first few weeks of my stay, I had a constant fight with myself over remaining in hospital. Although my weekends at home were desperately unhappy, I told myself that they were not as bad as being in the hospital. I even thought of returning to psychoanalysis: despite my intellectual doubts, at an emotional level I still had some hankering after it and felt that I might have run away from it too soon. My wife's common-sense scorn for analysts did much to increase my resolve. Four things prevented me from discharging myself prematurely: the advice of the night nurse; the kindness of the clinical psychologist; the thought that by being kept out of the way of my family and friends I was avoiding distressing them unnecessarily; and, perhaps above all, the feeling that I must see something through.

The clinical psychologist explained that his methods of therapy were more pragmatic and empirically based than those of psychoanalysis, but he added that no method had received full objective validation, taking it for granted that as a psychologist I already knew this. Professionally I did know it, but emotionally I had been hoping for some magic that would lift my cares, and his honesty on this point came as a shock. He also explained that although some of my problems might stem from my previous history, he did not want to probe deeply into that. Despite the tenets of psychoanalysis, there is no reason to suppose that knowing the aetiology of a mental disorder is of direct help in alleviating it. He intended to investigate my current problems, and as they came to light to suggest methods whereby I might learn to change my behaviour: he believed that if people could be taught to behave in more appropriate ways, their feelings would undergo a corresponding change. This direct approach is characteristic of the method of treating the mentally ill known as 'behaviour therapy'. He added that any treatment he suggested could be undertaken only with my full agreement both as to its object and to the specific techniques to be used.

Much of his treatment was in fact based on common sense, though the common sense had been acquired only after years of experience. He said: 'It is going to be impossible for us to get to the bottom of your major problems overnight, but at least we can try to do something to help you in small ways.' He encouraged me to improve my physical health by losing weight, reducing smoking and taking more exercise. With the latter end in view, I attended yoga classes and went for walks: my motor co-ordination was too poor to allow me to play ball games. Of more direct help was his suggestion that I start doing the Canadian Air Force exercises, a graded series involving the daily performance of so many press-ups, sit-ups and so on, and finishing with jogging on the spot for a fixed number of steps. The exercises take only 11 minutes, and although I found them most unpleasant, I began to do them.

One of my main symptoms was the inability to concentrate. The clinical psychologist attempted to treat this problem by a simple and direct application of behaviour therapy. He directed me to take any book whose contents I wanted to master and systematically to go through the following routine at the same hour and place each day. First, I was to read for a period over which I thought I could sustain concentration—for example, for one minute; then spend the same length of time making notes on what I had read; and finally spend the same period checking that the notes agreed with the text just read. Having found a period short enough for concentration to be maintained, the length of each of the three periods in the cycle was to be raised by one minute at a time. In this way he hoped gradually to build up my ability to concentrate.

The method is based on a technique invented with animals and known as 'shaping'. Animals can be trained to perform very complex acts by rewarding them initially for making a response that is only vaguely similar to that desired; as they come to perform the initial response more and more frequently, the experimenter narrows the range of behaviour that will be rewarded, and so the animal's performance gradually comes to approximate the desired behaviour. Pigeons have been taught to play ping pong by this method, and it is the basic technique involved in much animal training. In more common-sense terms, if someone is unable to concentrate it will be frustrating to attempt lengthy concentration and fail: if they can concentrate successfully for short times, they are being rewarded (by success) for making the effort, and this will encourage them to practise concentration further.

The method appears to be successful with some patients. Moreover, as the psychologist pointed out, it sometimes produces a halo effect: when the patient's concentration returns, his other symptoms such as depression and obsessive thoughts are also reduced. In my own case, the technique failed: early in my stay in hospital I was too depressed and had too little faith in the advice I was given to settle down to practise concentration regularly; I tried from time to time but without success.

The psychologist tried to discover whether I had strong conflicting desires, in order to help me reconcile them; he also attempted to help me see my situation in a new and better light laying particular stress on the good aspects of my life. He proved as sharp at dialectic as the analysts, though he tried to use it to bring comfort. Unlike the analysts, who with their crazy logic put my guilt over my affairs down to latent homosexuality, he tried to assuage it, saying, 'There are always several ways of viewing things. Some people might say that anyone who does not have the odd affair is acting falsely and denying the animal side of his nature.' His ability to empathize with this side of my character was remarkable, for, as I well knew, he was himself a good family man. He also tried to convince me that it was not unnatural in my situation to feel jealousy and even homicidal impulses, but he always counselled me against the use of violence.

He administered a personality inventory based on a self-rating scale that reveals not what one is, but how one sees oneself. I scored very high ratings on three traits—'independence of thought', 'aggression', and 'need for suc-courance', in more everyday language a desire to be liked and accepted. He pointed out that if I was seeing myself as I really was, my need to be liked was in direct conflict with my aggression and refusal to be influenced by people and, other people being what they are, I could not for the most part expect both to be liked and to behave in too aggressive and independent a fashion. This dilemma—if it was one—was never resolved.

My most distressing symptom was of course my obsessional jealousy. In dealing with this, he repeated a pattern that I had experienced with both analysts, by promising an approach to it that was in fact never implemented. He told me that it might be possible to treat the obsessions by behaviour therapy, using a method known as 'desensitization', and I longed for the desensitization to begin. At first the feeling that there was a powerful weapon left in the therapeutic armoury was of some comfort, but as time went by and the weapon was never used I became more and more disappointed. I do not know why he never started desensitization—perhaps he was afraid it would not work, and wanted to keep it before my eyes to give me hope while the illness ran its natural course. It may be that in my impatience to recover I was being unreasonable: the psychotherapist has a tricky course to steer between giving the patient some hope that he can be helped and giving him expectations that, from the nature of psychotherapy, cannot be fulfilled.

In desensitizing obsessive fears or thought-processes, the patient rehearses the thoughts in question whilst in a state of relaxation. The clinical psychologist recommended me to attend relaxation classes in the hospital with a view to using this technique. He also pointed out that learning deep relaxation was useful in its own right: once the skill was acquired, I could use it myself to reduce tension and anxiety in moments of stress.

I zealously attended classes on progressive relaxation together with between two and a dozen other patients. At eight-thirty very morning, I would walk from the ward to the occupational therapy building where the classes were held. We lay on mattresses in a row on the floor in a darkened room, and the instructress made us systematically tense and relax all our muscles whilst breathing as deeply and regularly as possible. The instructions were given in a hypnotic tone of voice: 'When I say "Now" I want you to clench your left fist, as tightly as you can. Now. Make your fist tighter and tighter, feel the nails digging into the palm of your hand. It's a very unpleasant feeling; make it tighter and tighter until it hurts. Next, I want you to relax all the muscles of your fist—let your fingers spread out slowly. Feel the tension ebbing away through your fingers, leaving a pleasant relaxed feeling. Waggle your fingers very gently, and feel your hand growing warmer and warmer; feel it tingling and feel it becoming heavier and heavier as it grows more and more relaxed.' By the time I had systematically tensed and relaxed all the muscles of the body—hands, arms. feet, legs, thighs, stomach, torso, neck and face—I often felt as limp as a stuffed sack, and would sometimes fall sound asleep.

In addition to these classes, I attended once or twice a week special sessions of individual relaxation training given by trainee psychologists. I certainly learned how to relax my body, but no matter how relaxed it became it did not ease the torment in my mind even for a moment.

Although—so it seemed to me—none of the specific methods of treatment deployed by the clinical psychologist actually improved my condition, I continued to have faith in him. I believe that his grave acceptance of my tormented fears did relieve my unhappiness temporarily, but however much I looked forward to seeing him they would come back in full force within a few hours. He never remonstrated or recriminated, even when I failed to carry out a line of action that we had mutually agreed upon. It was at his suggestion that I embarked on the task of preparing a catalogue of a collection of papers, and I think I kept at it as much through a fear of letting him down as through fear of letting myself down. This is yet another instance of the dependence that neurotic patients develop on their therapists and doctors.

I found it very hard to bear when a week or so after my admission to hospital he went on a fortnight's holiday. I felt abandoned, and fretted that the intermission in my treatment would indefinitely postpone recovery. Although I did not acknowledge that the treatment I had so far received was of any help, I clung desperately to the belief that he would eventually be able to perform some miracle and make me whole again: I longed for the day when he would be ready to begin desensitization.

As well as seeing the psychologist twice a week, I had occasional sessions with doctors. Each Tuesday morning the consultant would appear to attend a case meeting with all the staff involved with his patients, including his senior registrar, his registrar, the clinical psychologist and the senior nurses and occupational therapists. At these meetings, the cases of patients in the group to which I belonged were reviewed, and in the light of reports from the different staff members it was determined how best to proceed. Every week, four or five patients would be summoned to attend the meeting. The consultant would listen to anything they had to say, ask a few polite questions, breathe a few words of encouragement, and possibly suggest some changes in treatment. How pathetically we looked forward to the summons to attend that performance, and how we envied those of our number actually privileged on a given occasion to enter. I remember week after week hanging round in the offing, hoping for a summons that usually did not come. Since the meetings were held in one of the common rooms, they were plainly visible through the glass with which it was surrounded. The doctors and nurses looked so composed as they sat around at ease crossing and uncrossing their legs while they discussed our fate.

As a new patient, I attended the meeting for a few minutes about a week after I entered hospital. I voiced my anxieties and told the consultant about my urge to discharge myself. He gently tried to dissuade me, but added that if I did decide to leave, the hospital would stand by me and give me all possible help as an out-patient. He repeated what he had said at our first meeting: the antidepressant drugs would in time take effect and bring about a change in my mood. He said: 'You have no faith in the hospital. in me or in yourself,' but he urged me to give things a chance. He also tried to reassure me about my fears that my weekend leave would be stopped. I complained about my boredom and the difficulty of passing the evenings, and he said solicitously that they must try to find something for me to do. I thought I might be able to write, and obtained his permission to take into my room a huge electric typewriter. I duly fetched it from home the following weekend, intending to record some of my experiences. It lay there unused for the remainder of my stay, a pathetic emblem of my inability to recapture my previous existence. He also pointed out that the hospital afforded many opportunities for recreation, and I rather ungraciously told him that even if I were well, the activities of a Butlin's holiday camp would have no appeal for me. It was not for a further four or five weeks that I again attended the weekly case conference. Although I would not acknowledge it, I was by that time in a slightly better state, and he cautiously said that I might soon be able to go home.

I also had sporadic individual sessions with the registrar in charge of my case. When I entered hospital, he was a most amiable young man with a slightly bemused expression, who took careful notes on everything I said, offered some solace and left it at that. I remember feeling very upset when he said: 'Would you say then that you have always been a rather difficult person?' How could he have got hold of such a preposterous notion? When I asked about my future treatment, he observed: 'At the moment we are using implosive therapy: later it will be explosive.' I never discovered the meaning of this cryptic remark. I complained periodically that the antidepressants were having no effect, and he always gave the same reply: 'Different antidepressants suit different people. If this one doesn't work, we'll try another one, and we'll keep trying until we find one that does. In the meantime, we must just wait to discover whether the one you are on at the moment does any good.' In retrospect, I think he saw me not to offer therapy but merely to keep abreast of my case in order to monitor my drugs.

I also saw the cheerful little Sri Lankan senior registrar from time to time. I liked him and used to try to waylay him on his way in or out of the ward. At one stage I was simultaneously taking two tranquillizers (chlorpromazine and Valium), an antidepressant (amitriptyline), and sleeping tablets. I asked him whether this was not too many drugs at once: I feared I could never be weaned from them. He said: 'We are well aware how dependent you become on people and things' (another threatening remark) 'but don't worry, none of them are addictive and we'll withdraw them from you gradually when you are ready for it.' Towards the end of my stay. I did in fact slop taking Valium, and since I felt none the worse for it, this was a considerable fillip to my confidence.

On another occasion, I was pacing up and down trying to restrain myself from telephoning my wife. I am not sure why I was so anxious to avoid telephoning: I think I felt I should not bother her too much. He told me to write out all my feelings about her and to show the result to the clinical psychologist who was treating me. I duly did so, but although many psychotherapist believe that writing things down is cathartic, it brought no relief to me nor has it ever. Some of the other patients did find it helpful.

In addition to individual therapy, there were twice-weekly group therapy sessions attended by my group as a whole. They were conducted by the registrar and were also attended by a senior nurse—a brisk but pleasant man from India, who was always neatly turned out. He had a ready smile, which was perhaps sometimes lacking in warmth, but he had considerable patience and rarely became ruffled, though he could be peremptory with recalcitrant patients. Each group session lasted for an hour: about half the time passed in complete silence, and we spent the remainder in sporadic discussion of what we ought to be talking about. Neither the registrar nor any of the nurses present offered guidance on this point.

The group meetings were boring and came to seem pointless. Since no compulsion was placed on attendance, only half a dozen or so of the patients out of the 15 in my group were normally present, and the same patient rarely came to two consecutive sessions. In addition, the composition of the group was constantly changing as old patients left and new ones arrived. In consequence, the group members never came to know one another at all well. Most were in fact reluctant to reveal their personal problems, and the group was rather fractionated. There were three women who formed a clique that I never succeeded in penetrating: they usually sat together both at meals and in the common room, but would fall silent when anyone approached them. Since we all had depressive illnesses, many of the group were withdrawn and did not relish meeting one another, though I did not fall into that category. One of our number was a rather extrovert young woman who said she found talking to the depressives 'too depressing'. Her social life revolved round the alcoholics, many of whom were much more cheerful than us. so she rarely attended the group meetings.

I am not sure to this day what were the avowed aims of the group therapy, or even whether it had any, other than as a way of passing the time. It is usually held that to be successful it should involve sessions lasting about two hours, with the composition of the group remaining unchanged: neither of these conditions was fulfilled. The alcoholic patients had two-hour group sessions on almost every weekday, usually attended by the consultant as well as the registrar, and many of them thought them very helpful. Through these meetings the alcoholics certainly came to know one another much better than we did. and they found support in discussing methods of coping with a problem they all had in common.

When I had been in hospital for about three weeks, the registrar announced at a group session that he was leaving and was being succeeded by a 'lady doctor'. The last group meeting before her arrival was devoted to a discussion of how we felt about being treated by a new doctor who was a woman. Most patients were upset by the feeling of discontinuity—just as one doctor had got to know their problems, he was leaving, and they now had to start anew with a stranger. In addition almost all the women present felt it difficult to trust a woman doctor.

When the new doctor arrived, the patients became very upset. Although this is a characteristic reaction, some of her behaviour appeared to exacerbate the problem. She was dark-haired and small, and she moved and spoke in a busy, efficient way. Although slightly masculine, she was not unattractive. Her dealings with patients often seemed authoritarian and provocative: she may well have believed that such a stance was of therapeutic value. When I raised a query about my drugs she silenced me: 'I prescribe the drugs here; I'm the doctor and I am wholly responsible for your drugs.' Again when I quoted to her something the clinical psychologist had said concerning the possibility of discharging me she said: 'I'm in charge of your case and I take all decisions about your discharge."

She suggested I was behaving like a child of seven, and produced from my case notes instances of childish behaviour, asking whether I did not think they were 'unbecoming for someone of your status'. However correct her observations were, they seemed very threatening at the time. She also upset many of the other patients: she announced to one that she was not going to handle her case with kid gloves, and was critical of the neurotic behaviour of others. Several of the women patients emerged in tears from their first interview with her. One claimed that the doctor had slammed the door in her face: when this was brought up at a group meeting the registrar replied that she had done no such thing, the door was difficult to close because it had just been painted.

Although I usually found sessions with her upsetting, I still longed to be summoned to her office and would be disappointed when I asked a nurse: Is Dr Bloggs seeing me today?' only to be told that she was too busy. I remember being touched and even cheered by one act of kindness on her part. As I was walking out of the hospital to go home for the weekend, she drove in through the gates and stopped her car to ask me how I was feeling and wished me a pleasant weekend. Here was a doctor actually treating me as a person not a mentally disturbed patient.

Her arrival transformed the atmosphere in group meetings. The doctor attacked the patients and the patients attacked one another. In every session one or more women would burst into tears and flee from the room. The first time this happened, nobody paid much attention, and the doctor rounded on the patients and said: 'Why do none of you go after Sue when she's in so much distress?' Sue's two closest friends explained that she often walked out of group meetings, and that in her present mood she would be unapproachable. A new patient who had done almost all the talking and was clearly an experienced professional in group meetings said she would go after Sue, whereupon Sue's friends urged her not to follow, saying it would only upset her more than ever. The new patient left the room and came back crying ten minutes later, having been severely rebuffed by Sue. Bad feelings were provoked between Sue's friends and the new patient, who appeared to them to have interfered unwarrantably in something she knew nothing about; things were not made any better by the doctor putting her arms round the new patient and saying: 'I'm very proud of you: you're a brave girl.'

This incident was typical of the way in which emotions boiled over because of trivial incidents in the group sessions. A further instance was a long discussion about a woman patient in another group who was alleged to be a gossip and to have other undesirable but unspecified habits. The registrar wanted the patient who had criticized this woman to arraign her in front of a full meeting of the whole ward, but the patient who was complaining was not unnaturally reluctant to do so.

Although I and other patients were upset by this doctor's behaviour, she may well have thought that some patients would be helped by being provoked, and indeed it is quite possible that some of us, including myself, were in fact helped.

In addition to the group therapy given to the three separate groups of patients, the ward met as a whole once a week in a session attended by doctors, nurses. OT workers and clinical psychologists. Again, everyone was puzzled about the function of this meeting, since once the quality of the food had been discussed, and some comments made on what games had gone missing and why the swimming pool was not open on Friday afternoon, there appeared to be nothing else to talk about and much of the meeting would pass in complete silence. Some of the nurses would use this meeting as an opportunity to castigate patients who had misbehaved. For example, one young woman who was not herself an alcoholic had on several occasions come back to the ward very drunk, thus upsetting the genuine alcoholics. The charge nurse on the ward was a buxom African woman with beautiful white teeth and a skin of ebony. Although she often smiled, we were all scared of her tongue. She gave the offending woman a public dressing-down at a ward meeting, and the woman promised in floods of tears to behave better in future. A patient who had unsuccessfully tried to commit suicide was berated for this antisocial behaviour, which had put the medical staff to a good deal of trouble in the middle of the night and had upset other patients.

Although a few other patients would usually give verbal support to anyone subject to public vilification in this way, it seems unlikely that the experience would be helpful to them. Most of the patients and particularly those with suicidal tendencies already held themselves in very poor esteem: to be publicly shamed could only lower their self-regard further, and might delay recovery. I was myself in danger at one stage of being denounced before the ward meeting. A woman patient approached me and said she wanted to raise a rather delicate problem. I am unfortunately sometimes given to belching. My eructations had not gone unmarked by some of the women patients, and this particular woman gently warned me that some of them intended to raise the subject at the next group meeting. I thanked her for her courtesy in forewarning me, and promised to try to bring my wind under better control. I think I succeeded: in the event no more was heard of the matter (in either sense of 'heard').

I am afraid that the picture I have drawn of the treatment administered in the hospital is somewhat gloomy. Later in the book I will discuss in more detail the general issue of the aims and effectiveness of psychotherapy. My professional knowledge and scepticism about the value of most methods of treatment may have made me a particularly difficult patient. Moreover, during almost all my stay in hospital I was in such a state of panic that it is doubtful if any psychotherapy could have had been helpful. Indeed the treatment I received was probably intended less to effect a recovery than to provide some comfort until such time as the storm of my anxiety would abate either spontaneously or through the action of the antidepressants: one of the doctors said as much to me. The nurses usually behaved with great kindness and patience; the clinical psychologist provided comfort and suggested methods that, within my limited powers, I could pursue in order to help myself. If I saw less of the doctors than I would have liked, that was because they were all overworked. Some of the younger ones may have been lacking in sensitivity to the feelings and needs of their patients, but it may require more experience than they had to develop such sensitivity when confronted with people so very readily upset. The group therapy was perhaps the weakest point of treatment: I had a feeling that it had been introduced because it was fashionable rather than because anyone had much faith in it, and I doubt if any of the staff involved had had any training in this method of treatment.

I was in fact extremely lucky in being able to use my own professional knowledge to select the hospital to which I was admitted. It was one of the National Health Service's showpieces, run at great expense to the taxpayer. Most mental patients both in Britain and America find themselves in incomparably worse surroundings; they are frequently housed in ugly ramshackle buildings and herded together in overcrowded dormitories. The number of nurses and doctors is often wholly inadequate for the number of patients. In such circumstances it is more difficult to control patients without strict regulations, and their freedom is correspondingly curtailed. Had it not been for the gloom of the patients themselves, the atmosphere in which I found myself was more like that of a holiday camp than a hospital. Moreover the renown of my hospital ensured that it could attract nurses and doctors who were among the best in the country. The staff certainly felt that something could be done to help the patients, and their optimism communicated itself to us. How much more terrible is the plight of those incarcerated in long-stay wards with inadequate facilities where the doctors and nurses have no more hope of improving the patients' lot than do the patients themselves.

6

Recovery

When I first entered hospital it was midsummer. It was an unusual English summer with prolonged fine weather, and many of my memories of my sojourn there are anomalously tinged with the glow of that continuous sunshine. Even on that second afternoon when, in the extreme of my anxiety, I was walked round the grounds by one nurse after another, I remember noticing the beauty of the hospital's park: the majestic trees, the flowering shrubs, the scented lawns were all enveloped in the same summer calm, in complete contrast to my own mood of torment. I remember being surprised to come suddenly on a freshly-mown cricket pitch and wondering who if anyone ever played there. In the last fortnight of my stay, summer was turning to autumn, and the early stages of my recovery were associated with a paler sun and with the crisp air and heavy dew through which I walked each morning to my ritual relaxation exercises.

On his return from holiday, the clinical psychologist devoted a whole session to a discussion of how to help me give up smoking. Among my other fears was that of killing myself through cigarettes: I had been a heavy smoker for 20 years, and in hospital my consumption was around 50 cigarettes a day. I was so intensely miserable that I thought that to stop smoking could hardly make me worse: it therefore seemed a good time to try. I had made many previous unsuccessful attempts to give up, and had studied the literature on the problem with some care. I knew that there was no objective proof that any method worked, but I was sufficiently desperate to wish to use something as a crutch. If I succeeded, I thought it might restore some modicum of self-respect.

We discussed and rejected many methods. The psychologist suggested that I should put aside the money saved by not smoking and use it to reward myself with some self-indulgence like occasional expensive meals.

Unfortunately, I was so depressed that I could think of no treat I would enjoy. He rejected the possibility of punishing me for smoking with electric shocks as both unethical and inefficacious: smokers so treated soon cease smoking in the situation where they are going to receive a shock, but smoke just as much at other times. Committing a large sum of money repayable only after a period in which one has not smoked may help in the short term, but I had so little faith in my ability to stop that I was not prepared to put up the money. Arousing anxiety by showing smokers films of lung cancer operations or wards of patients suffering from emphysema or chronic bronchitis is also known to be ineffective. As one smoker said at a time when the newspapers were full of reports about the harmful effects of smoking: 'It has made me so scared I've stopped reading the papers.' I was also not prepared to be locked in my room without cigarettes for a fortnight: this might extinguish the smoking habit in my room, but as soon as I emerged and found myself in other surroundings, I thought I would go straight back to it. Nor was there any point in taking tranquillizers to help me through the first stages of nicotine withdrawal: I was already taking massive doses of such drugs. [In those days neither the nicotine gum or patch had been invented.]

Eventually we decided that on a prearranged date I would simply stop smoking. The clinical psychologist would give me as much support as he could. Such is the human desire for praise that verbal support—praise for success in stopping for a period and sympathy for any failures, together with an exhortation not to be dismayed by a single lapse but to keep on trying to give up—could well act as the most potent form of reward. Moreover, it could help one to persevere rather than abandoning the attempt at the first failure. The clinical psychologist added something I thought very helpful: he said that smoking was a physiological addiction, and it was only possible to give up if I was prepared to be miserable for a period of up to a year. On stopping, I simply had to regard myself as suffering from an illness and over the period of convalescence I must accept that it might be impossible to work or function efficiently, or indeed to be happy. Any work well executed or any happiness experienced after giving up could be welcomed as an unexpected bonus, but to give up successfully one should be prepared to accept the worst. He also suggested circulating my friends and relatives with a letter asking them to treat me gently while undergoing the pangs of withdrawal, but this was never carried out.

It was agreed that when I went home on the next weekend, I would have a chest X-ray to establish that my lungs were currently all right. I had an extremely sympathetic chest physician in my home town who arranged for the X-ray: the few minutes waiting for the results were, as always, agonizingly anxious, but I returned to the hospital with the knowledge that there was nothing showing on the X-ray.

On the following day, I saw the clinical psychologist and agreed to give up there and then. Over the next few days, I fought constantly to prevent myself cadging cigarettes from other patients, and on about five occasions my resolve broke down: I also smoked outside the hospital one evening when I went out for a meal with a visiting friend who was a heavy smoker. None the less, I persisted in the attempt. Instead of smoking, I consumed vast quantities of apples—about thirty a day. When I went home the following weekend, I knew I could not smoke since there was no possibility of doing so without my wife seeing me, and she was determined that I should cease. By the time I returned to hospital I was convinced that I would never smoke again.

Although I had managed to stop smoking, I still felt as depressed as ever, though during that week I did manage to read a complete novel and even derived a little enjoyment from it—I think it was Peter de Vries's *The Cat's Pyjamas*. However, I would not admit either to myself or to anyone else that I was any better, though both my friends and the clinical psychologist told me I was behaving more normally. He said that in his experience there were usually three stages in the recovery from depression. First, outward behaviour improved and this could be observed by others; second, the patient himself came to see that his behaviour had improved; the final symptom to disappear was usually the patient's own agonizing feelings—another example of a change of feelings being dependent on a change in behaviour.

My actual recovery—if it was a recovery—was as sudden and dramatic as the breakdown itself. After spending a week without cigarettes, I returned home for the weekend. Friday evening, all day Saturday and most of Sunday were passed as usual in a state of anxiety and depression. In the morning I lay in bed trying to sleep for as long as I possibly could, since it was only in sleep that I could obtain forgetfulness. I mooched around the house by day, doing the odd crossword puzzle, and I accompanied my wife shopping. In the evenings I would meet friends in a pub, though I could only risk a single pint of shandy myself.

At six-thirty on the Sunday evening my mood changed dramatically. I was upstairs finishing off the *Sunday Times* crossword puzzle, when I heard a record being played in the sitting room beneath me. The tune was at that time 'top of the pops', and I had heard it over and over again while in hospital. It was called 'Eye Level', and was an orchestrated piece with a good thump to it and a dying fall. Banal though it was, it seemed to combine joy and sadness. I suddenly found myself enjoying it, rushed downstairs and turned it up full volume. I can now appreciate that it is not in fact a great piece of music, but at the time I thought it the most inspiring composition I had ever heard. It filled me with happiness and hope. That evening I not only read the Sunday papers with some interest, but for the first time in five months I did something that looked towards the future: I made a note of several books reviewed that I wanted to read.

The following day, instead of taking a train to hospital, I persuaded my wife to drive me. I was convinced that I was better and that the woman registrar would see this and agree to my discharge: I would load my belongings into the car, drive off home and be happy ever after. I had an appointment that day with the clinical psychologist, and told him that I was much better, thanking him profusely for all his help. He said that if I wished to discharge myself there was no point in my staying, but since the woman registrar (under the consultant) was in charge of my case, I must also see her. I told all the nurses excitedly that I was better, though I behaved in a less exuberant fashion in front of the other patients, since I did not want to compare my own good fortune with their sad lot.

I attended a group therapy session after lunch, in which I fell into an argument with the woman registrar over how far one should exercise tact in apprising people of their faults: I think she was on the side of honesty, I of tact. I grabbed her after the session to explain that I was better and wanted to discharge myself. She promised to see me later that afternoon, and I hung about the ward waiting for her. After supper, I discovered from the nurses that she had gone home. I was crestfallen. Discharging myself from the hospital had itself become an obsession. I was of course free to pack my belongings and drive off, but it had been impressed on me, as on all patients, that we must take our drugs exactly as prescribed, and by spending the night at home I would miss my night and morning doses: the nurses were not allowed to issue drugs to take home except on the instructions of a doctor.

I discovered from the nurses that there was another registrar still on the ward: he had only just taken up his post at the hospital and was in charge of a different group of patients. I went up to him as he came out of his office, explained that I was better, and that through no fault of my own I had not been seen by my own registrar: he was a benevolent-looking young man, and much to my surprise agreed to prescribe drugs to tide me over the night. I returned joyfully home with my wife and came back to the hospital the following day. I gathered from the nurses that the senior registrar, the woman registrar and the clinical psychologist were having a case meeting, and since the clinical psychologist had said he would discuss me with the woman registrar I assumed that one of the topics for consideration would be my discharge. By lunchtime, I had still not seen the woman registrar, but I caught her coming out of her office with the clinical psychologist. I approached her and said: 'Is it all right? Can I go home?' She said: 'I cannot agree to your discharge.' When asked whether she would prescribe drugs, she was evasive.

My hopes were once again dashed, and I had a miserable lunch: I felt it probable that my change of mood had been in part due to the antidepressant drug, and I did not feel I could take the risk of returning home and abruptly withdrawing from all my drugs.

When I was called to her office after lunch she said: 'You have always been too impulsive—now you want to spoil your chances by acting impulsively yet again and discharging yourself prematurely.' I tried to explain that I felt better and there seemed no point in staying in hospital:

I also pointed out that the clinical psychologist had agreed with me. She said: 'You are not to play him off against me. It is my decision whether to prescribe drugs.' She picked up a note that was lying on her desk, read it and then said: 'I have decided not to withhold your drugs if you do not follow my advice. I advise you to stay in hospital, but if you discharge yourself I will prescribe your drugs. I want you to promise to attend the next case meeting with the consultant: he is ultimately in charge of your case. You should also continue to attend the hospital in the daytime and to come to group therapy.' I readily agreed to these conditions, and that afternoon I packed my belongings in the car, including the huge electric typewriter that had sat unused for five weeks in my room.

I attended the case meeting two days later: the consultant was most affable. He agreed that I should live at home, implied that I should soon start tapering off my drugs, and wished me success in my marriage and a speedy return to work. He recommended me to continue to attend the hospital once or twice a week to see the clinical psychologist and the registrar: he thought I should go to group therapy only if I found it helpful. In practice, I gave up the group therapy almost immediately.

At my next meeting with the woman registrar, I asked her when I should begin to reduce my drug dosage. She said that it would be a good idea to begin soon, and, wrongly, I formed the impression that she wanted me to reduce them of my own accord, so I cut down the tranquillizing drugs that I was taking. Although I was now cheerful, I was still given to bouts of anxiety and was hyperactive and sleeping less than usual: it seemed to me that it would require considerable self-control to reduce my drug intake. When next I saw her, I told her with pride that I had succeeded in reducing the dosage of tranquillizers, but instead of bestowing the praise that I had expected, she said: 'You have no business to go in for self-medication: you must take the drugs I prescribe in the exact doses I specify.'

My sessions with her had now turned into a series of heated arguments often unconnected with my own condition: for example, we spent half an hour in a fierce dispute about the character and habits of Americans. The interaction between us was painful to me and exasperating for her. She said: 'You treat me not as a doctor but as a woman'; when I discussed her with one of the nurses he said: 'Ah, I expect you are in love with Dr Bloggs and possibly she with you.' He may have been right. The breaking point in our relationship came when I smuggled a tape-recorder into her office and recorded a complete session. In my exuberance, I regarded it at the time as a piece of harmless mischief, but my judgement was sadly lacking. When I told her what I had done she offered to let the consultant hear the tape, but I thought it best to destroy it. It was decided that further treatment should come not from her but from the consultant. I continued to see both him and the clinical psychologist every few weeks for the next year.

Two questions can be asked about my recovery. First, what was it that brought it about? As usual in such cases, it is impossible to give any certain answer. Was it the antidepressant? The support of the clinical psychologist? Giving up cigarettes? The realization that many others were much worse off? Was it being needled by the woman registrar that restored some fight and spirit? Or was it merely that most depressions are self-limiting, and restorative processes usually occur even without medical intervention? This illustrates the difficulty of testing methods of treatment: all cases are different, and in the individual case one can never be sure of the factors that bring about recovery.

Whatever the cause, my mood had altered drastically, and within 24 hours I had moved from a state of hopeless gloom in which I could see no future for myself to a mood of optimism and fascination with the world around me. My external situation had also completely changed: I was back with my family and I returned to work immediately.

The second question that may be asked is whether I had really recovered. Although I did not realize it at the time, I had not. I had bounced from a mood of deep depression to one of great elation, and although this was fun for me it was as upsetting for those around me as was my depression.

7

Aftermath

I was asked to revisit the hospital periodically for several weeks after my discharge, doubtless so that my manic state could be assessed, though I did not realize the reason at the time. On one of these visits a curious incident occurred. The pleasant senior registrar from Sri Lanka asked me if I would do him a favour. Would I spend half an hour with a trainee psychiatrist and chat with him? In my manic state I was greatly flattered by this request, for I thought the registrar wanted me to teach the young man the nature of depression. We went into an office where I sat in front of the trainee, while the registrar placed himself in the background. I chatted amiably to the young man, outlining my depression, answering a few questions and assuring him with gusto that I had made a full recovery. Later I met the registrar in the corridor. I asked him whether the trainee had learned anything. 'I hope so', he said. 'You see, it was part of his examination.' I asked whether he had passed and the registrar replied with a smile 'I'm afraid not.' Presumably the poor examinee had failed to realize that I was hypomanic. He was not the only one to make this mistake, for I did so myself: throughout my hypomania I had no idea that my behaviour and feelings were abnormal. [It was only years later that I realized that the woman registrar had wanted me to remain in hospital to prevent me from damaging myself through the folly of hypomania.]

Shortly after discharging myself, I telephoned one of my psychiatrist friends to tell him that I had made a complete recovery and that I was grateful for his advice to seek proper psychiatric care and for his suggesting the name of an excellent consultant. I was full of praise for the medical treatment I had received and I happily informed him that the breakdown had been one of the best things that had ever happened to me, that I now had a new lease of life and was working with great energy and effectiveness.

He thanked me for telephoning and said that it was rare for someone who had taken the sort of advice he had given to express their thanks. He also asked whether I was continuing to see the consultant, adding: 'Depressions are funny things, and they rarely disappear suddenly without after-effects.' I thought at the time that his concern about whether I was still receiving treatment was a little sinister, but I was so elated that I put it to the back of my mind.

In fact I acted for the next three months or so in a way that was every bit as mad as my behaviour during the depression. My mood was characterized by a complete lack of shame or reserve, wild optimism about the future combined with reckless spending of money in the present, a fascination with the external world of people, objects and books, an inability to stop talking and a tendency to indulge in pranks.

I visited a private art gallery in Bond Street, where there was an exhibition of Magritte, an artist in whom I had always delighted. I looked at the pictures with an enthusiasm normally reserved only for love making. There was a young lady at the desk, whom I approached asking 'How many are there in the sale? She replied with remarkable poise considering that I was no doubt my usual unkempt self, clad in a worn out velvet jacket: 'There are ten in the sale, sir. Would you like me to call a director?' I had just sufficient caution to ask how much the pictures cost to which she answered that they started at £150,000. She then asked 'Shall I call a director?' Forgetting my cautious approach I said 'Call the director.' A moment later a suave and handsome young man immaculately dressed introduced himself to me. He conducted me round the ten pictures that were for sale explaining for each its provenance, the period when it was painted, its significance, balance and relationships to other pictures of Magritte. After each of these fascinating lectures, I would say 'How much is it?' '£250,000', he would reply. Whereupon I would thump him on the shoulder and say 'Come on. Surely you can make it a 150,000 for cash.' Despite being treated like a second-hand car salesman, he remained imperturbable and would pass without comment to the next picture.

Some of my japes were less decorous. I purchased in a sex shop on the Tottenham Court Road an object known in the trade as a 'tickler', and invented, I believe, by the Arabs: it consists of a ring of goatskin with the hairs still attached. The salesman's promise that it would give my wife 'ecstasy' was not borne out by the event. Next time I was in London, I made a point of passing the shop with Josie and pulled her in before she realized the nature of the establishment. I accosted the salesman, pulled the tickler out of my pocket, and said: 'Look here, I bought this from you last week and it's virtually useless.'

He replied politely: 'What seems to be the problem sir?'

'You said it would really turn my wife on, and it's done nothing for her. Has it darling?'

She confirmed my opinion, and I continued: 'Not only that but it's far too small: it's practically chopped my penis in half.'

'I'm sorry about that sir, we could find you one in a larger size.'

'Even if you have an outsize one in stock, that's not going to help my wife, is it?'

'We like to give satisfaction to our customers, sir: if you care to look around, maybe we can exchange it for something else.'

I accepted his offer and chose for fun some other device that looked as though it would be no more helpful than the original tickler. On being shown it, he said: 'I'm afraid that costs £4, sir, whereas the tickler was only two: perhaps you wouldn't mind paying the £2 difference.'

I slapped him on the shoulder and said boisterously: 'I'm one of your best customers—you're surely not going to haggle over a mere £2.'

He said helplessly: 'Take it away.'

By this time I had accumulated a considerable audience. Sex shops are for the most part frequented by furtive-looking men in raincoats, who keep their hands in their pockets and by examining the objects on display out of the corners of their eyes are able to keep up the pretence that they are not really interested in the wares. I now turned to the salesman and said in a voice of thunder, thinking to discover how far his shop catered for all tastes: 'By the way, do you happen to have any canes or whips?'

At this point my wife sought refuge in the street. The salesman replied: 'I'm sorry, sir, we used to stock them, but we no longer do. If you like to come with me to the bookshop next door, they occasionally keep them under the counter.'

I followed him into a sex bookshop. Up to this point he had been talking rather after the fashion of an assistant in a Savile Row tailor's, but when he accosted his friend behind the counter of the bookshop he reverted to his native cockney.

'Got any kines in at the moment, George?' he asked.

'Sorry, Fred, we're outa stock: 'ad a big consignment in only last week, but they sold like 'ot cakes and we're fresh out of kines.'

I expostulated: 'I really don't know what this country is coming to: one week there's no sugar to be had, the next everywhere is out of lavatory paper, and now it's virtually impossible to buy a cane in the whole of London.'

I do not normally engage in pranks of this kind, and the story illustrates the extent to which hypomania can abolish all reserve. Apart from thinking that my own jokes were funnier than they were, my judgement was sapped in ways that could have been more dangerous. I whisked my wife into a furrier's in South Kensington and bought her a fur coat more suitable for a tycoon's mistress than for the spouse of a comparatively penurious professor. I also ordered a car that was large enough and expensive enough to have bankrupted me, but fortunately Rolls Royces were in short supply, and by the time it was available I had sufficiently come to my senses to cancel the order, albeit with some financial loss.

I was convinced that I would make a fortune by writing a highly successful introductory textbook on psychology: a successful text of this sort can net its author several hundred thousand dollars in royalties if it is widely adopted in American universities. It seemed to me that I was just the person to write such a book, though I overlooked petty details, like when I would find the time to do it and how I would actually manage to gear it to the interests of teachers in some of the less well-known American universities of which I had no experience. I fired off letters to six American publishers pointing out my pre-eminent qualifications for writing a work of this kind and asking for a $25,000 advance; I did not scruple to inform them that in addition to being widely adopted for the teaching of intro-ductory courses to undergraduates in psychology, the book would un-doubtedly be 'the best and most popular account of modern psychology for the general reader'.

Even in my elated condition, I was a little disappointed at the publishers' response. One of them politely declined my offer on the grounds that his publishing house was too small to be able to afford me, but wished me every success in my dealings with other publishers. Others used phrases such as 'the economics of book publishing have become rather restricted' and 'the heightened competition plus increased splintering of the market, make it more difficult to achieve sales figures of the sort you have in mind.' One of them went so far as to ask to see a synopsis and a specimen chapter with a view to negotiating a contract, but I was so restless and excited that I could not sit long enough at my desk to produce such tedious details: I was convinced that once a contract was signed and an advance safely in the bank, the book would somehow write itself with the minimum effort on my part.

In my elated state, I was receptive to new ideas provided they could be understood without lengthy concentration. I established a friendly relation-ship with an assistant in a men's clothing shop who had a distinctly gay manner and was prepared to put up with my volubility. In my previous existence, I had been, to put it mildly, careless about my appearance, but I was now anxious to acquire smarter apparel as behoved a potential millionaire. He selected new clothes for me, including an expensive velvet jacket that I could ill afford, though this did not deter me. He also taught me how to tie my ties with a Windsor knot and my shoe-laces with a 'tennis' knot: in the past I had done up both ties and shoe-laces rather casually, and they were as often untied as tied. It is odd how one can remain ignorant for so many years of useful tricks such as these. He also suggested changes in my hair style, including the growing of sideburns, and referred me to a good hairdresser—'Don't forget to ask for Lennie: I wouldn't let anyone else touch my own hair', he said, giving it a pat.

I was without reticence, shyness or reserve. I tried to seduce an attractive woman in my own drawing room in the presence of my wife and her husband. I found I could lead community singing in pubs and could buttonhole strangers and tell them the story of my life, whether or not they wished to hear it. Every book I read, every film I watched, every play I attended and every painting I saw were the greatest works of their kind there had ever been, and in my attempts to communicate my enthusiasms to others, I was often puzzled at how rarely they came to share them.

I also discovered a hitherto unsuspected ability in myself to 'camp things up' and from time to time made mock passes at homo- and hetero-sexual men alike, much to the alarm of both. My behaviour in this respect would doubtless have delighted my analysts, and I felt I was a credit to them, though whether I was giving vent to suppressed homosexual urges or acting out of mere bonhomie neither I nor anyone else can know. As a Peter de Vries character put it: 'My unconscious was now doing a magnificent double-take. I was defending myself against defending myself against latent homosexuality by pretending to be one."

In my previous existence, I had always had a taste for the bizarre and was gratified when, as I sometimes did, I found myself in curious situations. In the state of supremely elevated confidence in which I now found myself, however, I discovered a facility for making the bizarre occur to order. One illustration must suffice. It is drawn from the period when I went through a second high phase about a year after the first, by which time I had resumed smoking. I was returning home from London on a late-night train, when I found I was out of cigarettes. I went down the corridor looking for someone smoking, and the first smokers I encountered were ensconced comfortably in a non-smoking first-class compartment. They were two rather attractive young women and a man, none of whom was likely to have bought a first class ticket. I entered and said: 'Give me a cigarette or I'll call the guard.' They kindly offered me cigarettes and I stood and chatted.

It turned out that one of the women worked in a massage parlour in my home town. The massage was strictly for men, and was of the variety that in the terms of the trade offers 'relief'. She received £2 for each half-hour session, and the owner of the parlour also pocketed £2. If she provided services beyond the expected massage and manual masturbation, she could make her own terms for additional payments. She had for many years made a good living at this profession: she was able to provide her small daughter with two ponies and to maintain her and her own parents in some comfort in the country. She told me how fond some of her clients, many of whom were lonely and old, became of her and of the gifts they brought her. She varied her activities by working the trains back from London in the evening, where she found many businessmen were glad to avail themselves of her services in the lavatory at £10 a time. She approached only first-class passengers and always picked on shy-looking men, since in her experience they were the most likely clients.

When we were about 20 miles from our destination, she suddenly got up, put her arm through mine and said: 'I've taken a fancy to you: come into the lavatory and you can have it off for nothing.' I put in a polite plea of *nolle prosequi* on the grounds that my wife was fast asleep in the next coach, and should she wake I might have difficulty in explaining any joint occupation of the train's toilet facilities. She kindly invited me for a free visit to her massage parlour, an offer I could not refuse, though it turned out to be rather sleazier than I expected.

Having failed to secure a contract for an introductory book on psychology, I was seized by the idea of publishing a detailed account of my breakdown in a Sunday paper: I had read that one paper had recently paid someone a vast sum for publishing extracts from an extremely frank book on his mother's life. I now told everyone that I was going to make my fortune by divulging sensational facts not about the dead but about the living.

Several of the living did not share my enthusiasm for the project. Indeed I received a stern letter from a doctor who had been a friend of mine and who was in the same firm as the doctor who had persuaded me to embark on analysis. It began by saying that although I might not like the letter, it was written primarily out of concern for myself. Despite this disclaimer, what followed suggested he was at least as much concerned for himself as for me. He pointed out correctly that I was in a hypomanic condition and warned me not to publish an account of my medical treatment while in that state. He concluded by threatening to resort to the Medical Defence Union if I in any way impugned the professional skills of his colleagues or himself. This doctor was also a devotee of psychoanalysis, and his claim that the letter was written primarily out of concern for me suggests that the insight psychoanalysis gives into one's own motives is not necessarily very deep.

Several of my friends were also concerned lest I publish an account of my breakdown. They were afraid it would harm me—such is the taboo against admitting that one has been through a period of mental instability. When I asked a friend what harm it could do, he thought for a minute and answered: 'Suppose you ever want to join the Athenaeum: they would never admit you after publishing something like that.' I replied that regardless of my mental disorder, the possibility of my being admitted to the Athenaeum was remote in the extreme. My major concern was the reaction of my own family. Had I not been hypomanic at the time, I think I would have been more reluctant to make public some of the intimate details of my life and of my relationship with my wife. Despite my elation, I had sufficient insight into my condition to realize that I was not my normal self, and I had already decided that whatever I wrote would need careful vetting to make sure that I was not recording anything too damaging either to myself or to others.

The elation could be interpreted as a way of covering up a continuance of my original anxiety state and depression. I slept little, waking very early in the morning: when I woke it was as though a searchlight illuminated my mind, and I began going over exciting plans for the future which precluded any return to sleep. Moreover, although I was now reading and writing a great deal, I was not able to concentrate in the way I could when normal. My mind wandered when I attended talks on psychology, and although I wrote at great speed I found it difficult to undertake the more tedious and painstaking process of revising and systematizing what I had written. I was given to sudden bouts of anxiety which would come on for no apparent reason and leave my heart pounding and my body weak. Finally, several times a day I was still attacked by obsessive and harrowing thoughts which I could overcome only by burying myself in activity.

It is of course a standard psychoanalytic tenet that elation is a defence put up to conceal from oneself unresolved conflicts and anxieties. Despite the underlying anxieties, most of my elation was enjoyable to myself if not to others. I had completely lost the fear of death that had occasionally assailed me in moments of inactivity. I can remember when I first discovered that everyone had to die: I was about eight years old at the time and was being driven up a hill in an old Rover car by a friend of my father's, and I can still visualize the dashboard of the car and the appearance of the road. He imparted the dreadful news that everything ends in death: at first I was incredulous, but then I realized he must be right. While elated, I could accept the inevitability of death, but it had ceased to worry me: the phrase 'Fate cannot harm me' echoed through my mind.

I was comparatively lucky with my hypomania: I did not take any irrevocable rash decisions, although I emerged from my elated state considerably more impecunious than when it began. Since hypomanics usually have little or no insight into their condition, some behave in recklessly extravagant ways that can lead to bankruptcy or the alienation of all their friends and relatives. We know as little of the causes of elation as of the causes of depression. My psychiatrist told me that my own elation was 'a rebound effect of the depression' and had not been caused by the drugs I had taken. Indeed I managed to give up all drugs within a month of leaving the hospital. States of abnormal elation sometimes occur with no preceding depression, and the sufferer may be reluctant to seek psychiatric help unless pushed to it by relatives or friends.

My hypomania lasted for three or four months, and then I gradually descended into a further prolonged depression. It was very unpleasant, although it did not have the quality of agony that accompanied my previous collapse, in which I was totally unable to concentrate. I now tried to escape from reality by lying in bed dozing fitfully until noon or one o'clock; I was once again unable to take much interest in the external world. I was told by both the clinical psychologist and the psychiatrist that I must force myself to get up in the morning and to fill my day with normal activities. With a great effort I managed to teach, read and write, though my writing was unsatisfying and lacking in verve. I again became a prey to anxiety and obsessive and painful chains of thought. After seven months without cigarettes, I found myself entering a tobacconist, and I added the shame of having reverted to smoking to my other worries.

Over this period, I managed to complete a revision of my newspaper articles on the breakdown. I eliminated the more highly personal material, and wherever I was in the slightest doubt of the veracity of what I had written, I deleted it. After much further delay, the pieces were published: nine months had elapsed since my second depression, and I had been in a mentally abnormal state for over a year and a half.

I wrote from a mixture of motives: I thought that publishing the details of my depression and showing that, as I then thought. I had made at least a partial recovery might help comfort others who were depressed, particularly as many of my symptoms were common to all depressives. I felt the articles might help to remove some of the stigma attached to mental illness by showing that someone with a moderately successful life and career had been subject to it—and was not ashamed of it. My account of what it was like to undergo a breakdown might also be of some interest to the general reader. I wanted to inform the public about mental health and the different types of treatment adding warning notices to some. I was also fascinated, in retrospect, by my own bizarre experiences and by the subject of mental health in general, and I wanted to communicate some of this fascination. More selfishly, but perhaps above all, I greatly enjoy writing and here was a ready-made topic that might be of interest to many readers. Finally, as an American friend remarked to me some years later, 'You're the only person I've met who goes into a mental hospital and comes out with a fortune in his pocket.' Little did he know: *Breakdown* has been widely read, but seldom bought.

I was anxious about how readers would respond. Perhaps my more cautious friends were right and I should not expose myself publicly in this way. I was open to the charge of washing dirty linen in public in return for money or notoriety; although I felt no animus towards anyone who had been involved in my treatment, I had in all honesty to reveal that not all the treatment had been helpful, and I could be accused of taking a petty revenge on people of whom I had run foul. The attitude of some psychoanalysts to patients who write about their treatment is summed up by the quotation on this book's flyleaf. Worst of all, perhaps the articles were not sufficiently interesting and would merely bore the reader.

I have spelled out my feelings at the time the articles were published in some detail, since I think it was the reception of the articles, at least in some quarters, that brought me back to a more normal frame of mind. Many people whom I scarcely knew came up to me in public places and thanked me for having written them: they would often reveal that they too had been through similar experiences and that it was some comfort to see it all set out in print. For example, Spike Milligan kindly invited me to have dinner with him in a London restaurant. He spent the first half hour saying how terrible it was to be a public figure: he was tired of people coming up to him to shake his hand or demand his autograph. About half-way through the meal someone did approach our table. Milligan's eyes lit up, but the chap approached me asking, 'Aren't you Stuart Sutherland?' Milligan looked crestfallen.

Many people wrote to me to say that their own experiences, particularly in the hands of analysts and in psychiatric hospitals, had been so similar to mine that they could hardly believe I was writing about myself not them. I was surprised at how many of my acquaintances told me they too had had breakdowns: it is an experience to which most people do not readily admit except to fellow-sufferers. I was gratified at the number of people I encountered who had actually read the articles with some interest. In short, I was immensely relieved by the way they were received, and not a little flattered.

Not everyone approved: the doctor who had first referred me to an analyst thought it very sad that I had published them, but then he would, wouldn't he? He added that I had not done myself justice, a remark that an analyst might have interpreted as projection. My psychiatrist colleagues had divided opinions: some thought that what I had written needed saying, others did not like the implicit criticism of some members of their profession and thought it wrong to inform the general public of the difficulties and dangers inherent in some methods of treatment. It was the unexpected stir created by the articles that led me to expand them into the present book.

I am conscious that both in this book and in the articles I may have failed to convey the full agony of my own experiences. I consider I was lucky to recover and it is hard to recapture the mood of torment. I quote below some further extracts from the letters written to me: they both express the feeling of pain better than I can and also demonstrate that my own experiences were by no means atypical:

These terrible nervous feelings and the awful sense of isolation, of being boringly, frighteningly alone—a spiritual isolation.

The words' [quoted from my articles] 'an event tailor-made to cause me the maximum possible hurt' carried such meaning for me. The degree of pain not only went right off the scale of previous experience but far exceeded anything I could describe or imagine. I know the torment of disintegration, and the 'irrevocable and cataclysmic'—words which often fall on uncomprehending ears—the self recrimination, and the incredible loss of the previous personality, leading to self-unbelievable behaviour and tortured impairment of function.

Bed was my sanctuary where I could shut the world out for a few short hours.

Where I am going or what will happen I do not know, I need help desperately, but seem to fall victim to all the wrong things ... I do not want to see my children because I cannot bear the reproach in their eyes.

The articles read, in parts, like a carbon copy of my own experiences during the seven years in the 'living hell' of depressive anxiety.

I was very much reminded of my own similar experiences. So many of the points the professor made struck me as being very pertinent and typical of one's feelings at being an in-patient of a psycho-therapy unit.

I should perhaps trace out the forms of therapy I have received since I left the hospital just over two years ago. During my first period of elation and the subsequent depression, I visited the clinical psychologist almost once a week. Over part of this time he saw me together with my wife and attempted to encourage us to improve our behaviour to one another. We still often harped back on past wrongs, and although we could both see this was childish and pointless, we did not have sufficient self-control to avoid painful and boringly repetitive recrimination. Her jealousy vented itself in anger, mine usually in sadness. We would repeatedly vow to the psychologist to behave better to one another, only to reappear next week admitting that we had not kept our promises. He eventually said ruefully that if anyone were to ask him whether he had been able to help Josie and Stuart he would have to admit that he had not: he was an honest man. Towards the end of my second depression he again began seeing me alone and at last introduced the long-awaited desensitization treatment for my jealous obsessions, but my depression turned once more to elation, and the jealousy abated of its own accord.

About this time the consultant in charge of my case decided to refer Josie and me to another psychiatrist who specialized in 'marital therapy'. We saw him together with a woman social worker: the presence of therapists of each sex avoids the problem that a single therapist may be in sympathy with only one of the couple. The psychiatrist was pleasant and anxious to be helpful, and I am grateful to him for the time he spent with us. He had the restrained manner of one who has been to one of the better English private schools, and I thought he found it difficult to empathize with my own tempestuous emotions.

For entirely different reasons Josie and I were difficult patients. She has more pride than I do, and she found it difficult to reveal herself to comparative strangers. On one occasion she mentioned some intimate thoughts to me and I said: 'You ought to tell that to the psychiatrist,' to which she made the magnificent rejoinder: 'That's much too personal to discuss with a psychiatrist.' She was also given to claiming that she was too ill to see a doctor. She found it difficult to accept the artificiality of some of the exercises we were asked to perform, through a fear of looking ridiculous. The psychiatrist, for example, suggested that to encourage mutual trust she should place her hands in mine and let me support her. We were also asked to perform another standard therapeutic trick, namely to take it in turns to let our bodies go plastic whilst the other arranged the body in a pose characteristic of the way he or she saw the partner. Such games were not for Josie.

Although rather more willing to give things a try, possibly because I was more desperate, I shared much of her cynicism about the possible benefits of marital therapy. Moreover, my own knowledge often led me to ask for a justification of any step the psychiatrist proposed, and it cannot be much fun for any therapist to be called on by the patient to account for every move he makes. When he suggested some procedure, I would say 'What is the evidence that that helps?' leaving him without reply. I would then continue, 'Do you know the article by Harris and Harris in the *British Journal of Psychology,* 1971? It shows your idea is counterproductive.' I was anxious that no misunderstandings should occur, and I had an annoying tendency to correct what I regarded as any errors of interpretation or verbal slips made by the psychiatrist. Although I was genuinely anxious to keep the record straight, such insistence on precision could well have appeared to be gratuitous hostility on my part.

Moreover, it is difficult for therapists seeing a couple once a fortnight or so to come to know and understand them: the occasional remark would reveal how deep such misunderstandings could go. For example, at one point the social worker suggested that my wife, not having a career, might be jealous of her. This rendered Josie speechless with embarrassment, since although she might relish the thought of being a successful couturier, actress or dealer in fine art, the idea of being a social worker lacked sufficient glamour for her to feel anything but mild good will towards anyone undertaking such work.

Perhaps to avoid misunderstandings, the psychiatrist at one point suggested that we should sit down and say exactly how we felt about him. I went over some of the material reproduced above, and added that I thought that underneath he probably felt real concern, but that his approach was rather intellectual and that, perhaps because of his upbringing, he might have difficulty in revealing his feelings. I suspect such frankness is rarely helpful in personal relationships, and no matter how much a therapist may try to put down hostility from patients to projective or other mechanisms, they are themselves just as vulnerable as the rest of us.

Some of the psychiatrist's sayings and advice were not a little bizarre. At one point, and for no clear reason, he wrote on the blackboard the details of our family trees. Since Josie's mother was a bastard, the identity of Josie's grandfather was lost in mystery. On learning this he remarked: 'Ah, so your maternal grandfather is just a faceless penis to you.' We were both sane enough at the time to disregard this remark, but had we been more distressed we might have been deeply puzzled by it and spent agonizing hours trying to fathom its significance. As it was, I assumed we had reduced the psychiatrist to a state of incoherence, in which he was desperately trying to say something clever no matter how meaningless.

For some time, one of the worst aspects of my own jealousy was that it was provoked most strongly in sexual encounters with my wife. The sight of her bare body re-evoked my worst jealous imaginings, and at times I could not bear her to touch me. He suggested that she should do everything she could to titillate me, whilst we were to debar ourselves from actual inter-course for a fortnight: I was adamantly to resist her advances. We were also to put aside set times of day for recriminating against one another: I was to shout and she was to throw things, four times per diem before meals. Although encouraging patients to practise habits they wish to he rid of is a currently fashionable method of treatment (known as 'paradoxical intention'), the theoretical rationale behind it is obscure: it is vaguely described as an effort to bring unwanted behaviour under one's own control, but there is nothing to suggest that it is actually helpful. Both for this reason and because neither of us could accept the artificiality of these techniques, my wife and I were unable to carry out the advice proffered.

I am grateful both to this psychiatrist and to the social worker for their persistence in trying to help two such difficult patients. It may be that it is easier to help married couples whose problem is lack of communication than people like ourselves who suffer from too much communication of the wrong kind. There was little about our behaviour that an outsider could point out that we had not been over together *ad nauseam*. We knew or thought we knew how we should behave: our problem was that we could never put such knowledge into practice.

Our encounter with marital therapy lasted in all for about nine months, though we only fitted in about twenty sessions during this time. I continued to see the original consultant in charge of my case, at first two or three times a month but latterly at much longer intervals. He was always relaxed, sane and helpful: like the clinical psychologist, he treated even my silliest thoughts and fears with seriousness and gravity, never recriminated and never made silly jokes.

It would be pleasant to be able to report that having recovered from my second bout of depression my mood remained stable and I lived happily ever afterwards, a better and wiser man for the experiences I had undergone. Unfortunately, this did not happen. I underwent a further spell of mild euphoria and then descended into a more prolonged period of mild but miserable depression. I am of course incomparably better off than during the acute phase of the breakdown. My jealous imaginings no longer dominate my life to the exclusion of everything else, and I am able to work and concentrate.

The emotional tone of my life has, however, at least for the time being, changed out of recognition. Whereas previously I always seemed to be choosing between a multitude of fascinating things to do, at the moment I cast around between unappealing alternatives in the vain hope of fastening upon something outside myself and my own situation that will capture my whole-hearted interest. I long for a return of the uncomplicated and uncontrived zest with which I used to pursue my daily activities, but no matter how much I force myself to engage in this or that pursuit, the zest does not reappear. Although many might envy my external situation, I can often find nothing in life to which to look forward, a feeling that characterizes depression. I suppose that I was once lucky and no longer am. I sometimes long for a return of the falsely optimistic and fragile mood of elation; it both annoys and puzzles me that I cannot think of a way of attaining a stable balance at the mid-point between the slow swings of mood that have dragged me in their wake since the breakdown. When I asked the clinical psychologist about the possibility of a complete recovery, he said: 'Most people get better, but they often have the feeling that there is something missing in their lives.' Despite the unstinting efforts of some of the most distinguished members of the helping professions, I have been unable to work out my salvation.

My wife and I have stayed together. In our joint encounters with psychotherapists, the one thing that never failed to unite us was their suggestions that we should 'seriously consider separating, at least for a time: try not to fantasize about it, but consider it very carefully'. Although we have often speculated about it, we do not know what invisible bonds have held us together through the storms of the last few years. Is it love? Hate? Pity? Unconscious masochism? Fear of the unknown? Or are we just clinging to the creature comforts with which we reciprocally supply one another?

People often ask me whether I have learned anything from my breakdown or whether it has changed me. I can certainly understand the agony of mental distress in others in a way that I previously could not. If a woman student failed to produce an essay on time pleading that she had just broken up with her boy friend, in the past I would say, 'What's that got to do with it?' Now I am more understanding and say, 'Too bad—but you ought to distract yourself by writing essays.' I may have more insights into myself, but the insights have brought only pain, since I do not like what I see. The main insight is that I am more dependent on women that I thought and more vulnerable to their fickleness. I still, however, believe in my previous maxim that all women are replaceable: but I now acknowledge that finding a replacement is not easy and if one is depressed, it is impossible. Psychoanalysts would doubtless allege that the insights do not go deep enough to be helpful, but I remain sceptical of the idea that self-knowledge is a precondition of happiness and effective functioning. Periods of high endeavour such as the Renaissance, Elizabethan England or Ancient Greece have often been characterized by a singular lack of direct concern with the hidden springs of behaviour except in so far as they can be obliquely externalized in drama, verse and painting.

In my own case it is too early to know what will be the final outcome of the breakdown. In gloomier moments I repeat to myself the Greek proverb:

'Call no man happy until he is dead," but such are the vicissitudes of human fortune that at other times I continue to hope and to strive.

The previous paragraphs were written two months ago: since then I have become immersed in writing the remainder of this book. I let the paragraphs stand as a reflection of what a minor depression feels like, but I am currently revising the book in a better mood than that in which some of it was first written. I seem to have found a quiet harbour from the restless ocean of despair and elation on which I have been tossed for the last few years. I wish I could feel that the haven was anything other than a temporary refuge.

8

Sequel

It is nearly 12 years since the previous sentence was written [this chapter was added to the updated edition in 1987]. The 'haven' to which it refers was indeed only a temporary refuge. To be more specific, it was the beginning of a second bout of hypomania. I had entered into an annual cycle in which for over a decade I became depressed every summer and was abnormally elated every winter. Between these highs and lows, there was usually a spell of two or three months when I was 'normal'. With the exception of my final period of depression, which took place five years ago, none of the depressions had quite the agonizing quality of the first, nor was I ever again quite so ebullient as during my initial high.

After my first depression, none of my swings of mood were triggered by external events. I could be engaged on a piece of research or writing that fascinated me, with my home life running smoothly, or—perhaps more accurately—as smoothly as it had ever done, and then, one day in the spring, I would begin to feel gloomy. The project on which I was working would lose its appeal, and the savour would gradually disappear from food and from all other aspects of life. Over a period of a few weeks I would grow increasingly gloomy and anxious, and although I always fought to go on working, I would eventually have to stop, since it became impossible, however hard I tried. I was simply unable to concentrate on anything except my harrowing thoughts, none of which were now concerned with jealousy.

I would seize on unreal worries. One year, I became obsessed with the idea that the trees on the strip of land next to my house were growing roots so powerful that they would bring the house down. They were admittedly very large trees, and indeed most of my morbid obsessions had an air of plausibility. (In fact this worry was more than plausible—it was more realistic than the views of those who scoffed at it: as I later discovered the trees created a real risk of subsidence. The pessimism of the depressed is often more accurate than the optimism of the normal.) I would feel that I would lose my job and face financial ruin, again a fear that was not wholly unrealistic. Most of the depressions contained a period of a few days or a few weeks during which I could not concentrate sufficiently to read, nor *a fortiori* to work. I was lucky in that these periods usually fell in the summer vacation when I had no teaching commitments and few administrative duties. Sometimes, however, they occurred in term-time and thus imposed a strain on my colleagues, who undertook my duties for me. At first they bore this burden cheerfully, but, perhaps not surprisingly, some of them became extremely resentful towards the end of my protracted illness and, despite the fact that they were themselves psychologists, accused me of faking depression. Nobody would willingly fake the mental torment I went through, but unlike me, my colleagues had no direct experience of it.

My emergence from each depression was even more gradual than my entry into it. I would discover that I could read a novel, slowly and laboriously and with my current obsession intruding every paragraph or so. After a few weeks, I would resume my normal activities but without enthusiasm and at the cost of great struggles to concentrate. Eventually, I would find myself functioning normally and this would continue for two or three months, at the end of which time I would move slowly into a state of extreme elation.

None of my bouts of hypomania were as extreme as the first, during which I thought I could do—and often did—anything I put my mind to. Apart from indulging in pranks, I was of course absurdly optimistic. I was extremely lucky this optimism did not lead to the financial ruin that I feared in my depressions, as has happened to so many other sufferers of hypomania. To give one example, when high I fancied my judgement as a wine connoisseur and borrowed money to invest in considerable quantities of first-growth clarets. Through pure good fortune, the demand for good claret increased so much that I was subsequently able to subsidize my own drinking by selling off at a considerable profit some of my stock. One of my therapists had impeccable taste in these matters and became my best customer. As a prank, I even sold wines of lower quality to *restaurateurs* in Brighton. Josie, however, did not see my excursions into the wine trade in the same light as myself, and thought that my extravagant behaviour would shortly ruin us.

If recurrent depression is agonizing and hypomania dangerous for the patient, they are extremely difficult for family and friends to bear. For ten years my wife heard me declaring that we were about to go bankrupt and must get used to living on bread and margarine, only to find me entering the house a few months later with a dozen cases of Chateau Margaux. Despite my hypomania, I eventually learned sufficient sense to smuggle my cases of wine down to the cellar when she was out. When depressed I used to think of myself as boring in the extreme, and of course when high I regarded myself as the life and soul of the party. This was not the reaction of my wife and friends. They have told me that I was in fact much more tolerable when depressed than when hypomanic. At least I would listen to others in my depressions, even if I did not have much to say myself, while the absolute conviction of being right and the egocentricity induced by hypomania made me almost intolerable to others.

During the whole of my illness, I saw my psychiatrist regularly, particularly when I was depressed. He was always courteous and sensible, and would listen to me gravely and with sympathy. He prescribed a series of different antidepressant drugs. To my mind they made no difference—the depressions would always last for about three months. When I remarked on this, he said 'You can't tell how much worse you might have been if it hadn't been for the antidepressants', a pronouncement that it was impossible to gainsay.

About six years ago, he did something that almost certainly saved my life. I had been experiencing severe pains in the chest when taking the slightest exercise, even when walking slowly. My general practitioner had diagnosed a hiatus hernia, but like myself, my psychiatrist suspected angina. I made an appointment with him out of concern for my physical health. So convinced was I that I needed hospital treatment that I took pyjamas with me. He telephoned a cardiologist at the hospital where he worked and I was immediately admitted. I underwent various tests, including the insertion through the groin of a small camera attached to a tube, which was threaded through an artery up to the heart. The following day I was told that unless I had a coronary by-pass operation, I probably had less than three months to live. The surgeon added that I had a 7% chance of dying during the operation: it would have been more encouraging if he had said I had a 93% chance of survival. Apart from its dangers, the operation is moderately painful, but neither beforehand nor afterwards did I experience the mental agony that accompanies depression. Indeed, Josie and my daughters suffered far more stress from the operation than I did. Faced with a choice, I would very much prefer to have that operation again than endure another bout of severe depression: throughout the operation and its aftermath I had hope, in depression all hope for the future is lost.

The person for whom my mental illness had been most gruelling was of course Josie. Although he did not say so for many years, my psychiatrist seems to have concluded that Josie and I might be better off apart. He eventually began to suggest that we try a trial separation. As far as I can remember, he did not use the old psychiatric cliche 'The only people who can live together are those who can live apart', but when I queried the outcome, he said with what I regarded as naive optimism that whether we decided to separate for good or come back together, all would be for the best.

Between us we made as bad a job of our numerous separations as we had of the marriage. I resisted the idea for some time, and it would have required more ruthlessness than she possessed for Josie to leave me when I was in the depths of a depression. Moreover, she was indecisive, since dealing with my illness had reduced her, as she put it, to a zombie. She had nowhere to go and was lacking in confidence. For my part, I was still very dependent on her when depressed and in that state I could not have gone anywhere else except into a mental hospital. But when I became high, I began to see the attractions of a temporary separation. Hence, our separations always occurred when I was hypomanic and of course I never took them seriously, as the following episode illustrates. An American friend recently reminded me that on a visit to my department, he gave a talk after which a group of us went off for a drink. I had invited them home for dinner, but on arrival there was no sign of Josie. I picked up a note, read it and announced 'Ah, I see Josie's left me again. Don't worry, she's prepared the meal. Do be seated.' She had not only prepared the meal, but left detailed instructions on how to serve it.

Sometimes it was I who left. I would go to Oxford, where I spent my time writing, but I would have to return to Brighton to carry out my duties there every fortnight or so. I greatly enjoyed these breaks, secure in the optimistic belief, induced by hypomania, that Josie would always have me back and, indeed, she always did. During one of my expeditions to Oxford, I began to have the premonitory signs of depression. It began unusually early, in late February. I had no alternative but to go home. Josie was not at all pleased to see me and made it clear that my return was interfering with other arrangements she had made. This hint aroused the jealousy that had lain dormant in me for nine years. I saw my consultant and he advised me to come in to hospital. The main reason he gave was that he wanted to put me on a different drug, lithium, but even at the time this seemed to me more of an excuse than a reason, since it is possible to assess the correct dose of lithium without the patient being admitted to hospital.

Lithium is more fully discussed in Chapter 25. In brief, it is a drug which is effective in the treatment of what is known as bipolar manic-depressive disorder, that is an illness in which periods of depression alternate with periods of hypomania. It is unique among drugs for mental illness in that it often not merely alleviates symptoms, but can abolish them. Since it had long been obvious that I was suffering from this condition, it is puzzling that my psychiatrist had not insisted on my taking lithium long before. There are several possible reasons. First, it was not easy for him or indeed any other doctor to insist that I did anything. He had occasionally suggested my taking the drug and I had always been resistant to it. I had read about lithium extensively and had come across papers purporting to show that it sapped creativity; in addition, I knew it had several undesirable side-effects. Second, it is not clear that the consultant was fully aware of the extent to which I became hypomanic, for he rarely saw me in that condition and, when he did, I could put up a tolerable show of sanity for an hour or so. Indeed when I was hypomanic Josie would sometimes write him furious letters beseeching him to do something to calm me down. Third, lithium is a drug which has to be taken virtually for the rest of one's life if one is to avoid a relapse into the cycle of violent mood changes, and he may have felt that I would not persist with it unless I was really ready to take it. In the event, he regretted not having put me on lithium earlier. Although I would not have taken it when hypomanic, I believe I would have done so readily enough when depressed: if in that condition I could clutch at the straw of psychoanalysis, I would have been only too ready to avail myself of the prop of lithium.

Unfortunately, the psychiatrist had changed hospitals. His ward was full and I had to wait for nearly two months to be admitted. I spent most of this time in bed, bored beyond measure, once again clinging to my wife who was now reluctant to be clung to, and thinking that I would never recover. This belief is a typical symptom of the illness—I had after all experienced and emerged from nine other depressions, but I refused to see that this one would not be permanent.

Eventually I received the summons to go into hospital. Together with my other necessities I packed a razor blade, which I hid on top of a door lintel in my ward, the one surface that is never cleaned. In practice, I would never have had the courage to kill myself.

The men's dormitory was tiny, but contained ten beds in two rows of five, placed head to head. The sides of the beds were separated by only a few feet, and there was barely enough space to squeeze between the bed ends and the inadequate wardrobes lining the walls. The common-room was dirty and its furniture decrepit. The canteen food was nauseating. It was, nevertheless, one of the most renowned mental hospitals in Britain.

Apart from its extreme squalor (which was made worse by the fact that it was being redecorated at the time), there were several features of the ward that distinguished it from the previous one. The other patients appeared to be much more disturbed than those in the previous hospital, the majority of whom had been either alcoholics or patients with reasonably circumscribed phobias. Moreover, the patients in the second hospital defied the tidy classifications beloved of psychiatrists. None of them were clear-cut cases of schizophrenia, yet they would exhibit schizophrenic-like symptoms. Others were depressed, but they sometimes added outbursts of rage to their depressions. I could not understand what one pleasant elderly lady, who bore herself well and talked rationally, was doing on the ward—until she disappeared to a closed ward after a suicide attempt. There were several very sad cases. One was a woman who was normal much of the time, but would have hysterical fits in which she talked about God and wailed that she would roast in hell. Again, there was a man of about 60 who had held an important administrative position in the trade union movement. Although he could often talk rationally, he could not concentrate and would suddenly produce bursts of abuse for no reason. John Ogdon, the pianist, was in the same hospital, but on a different ward. He would talk to me incoherently about

P. G. Wodehouse. Although none of his conversation made sense, he would go round the wards playing the piano in each with brilliance. He even went out of the hospital under supervision to give concerts.

My psychiatrist had warned me that on that ward I would see what human misery was really like. We made a sad spectacle as we shuffled aimlessly around, trying somehow to fill the weary hours. As in my previous stay at a mental hospital, I felt somewhat of an impostor, since although I was miserable and unable to help myself, most of the others were clearly in a far worse state. Although I did not always recognize it at the time, they had less grounds for hope than I did.

Apart from the psychiatrist, the main staff that I encountered were the senior registrar whom I thought cold; an amiable junior registrar; a clinical psychologist who applied psychological theories in too doctrinaire a way and appeared to have little intuitive understanding; and a bland social worker. They were all male. The consultant had told me that there was an excellent sister on the ward and, in so far as one can look forward to anything when depressed, I had looked forward to meeting her. She turned out to be rather cold (perhaps out of shyness) and she rarely made eye contact with patients. Although I was in no position to judge, I could not see what was so excellent in her. She greeted most remarks with a prolonged silence, rather like psychoanalysts. The more junior nurses were sympathetic but bemused. It was a doctrine of the ward that everything that happened on it was therapeutic—one's interaction with other patients, occupational therapy, and one's dealings with nurses. The nurses were encouraged to spend a great deal of time in tête-à-têtes with patients. They admitted that they had no idea what was expected of them. When I complained that my wife was about to leave me, none of them made the obvious comment that that was very upsetting, but that once I was over the current depression I would recover some of my previous determination and be able to cope with the loss, if only by finding someone else.

Looking back it seems to me to have been a ward in which common sense was for the most part lacking and in which, although the orientation was not entirely psychoanalytic, an effort was being made to help patients discover hidden truths about themselves. I found no such truths and I doubt if anyone else did either. However, the mentally ill are not the easiest people to deal with and I am grateful for the time, patience and sympathy that the nurses lavished on me.

The group meetings were more frequent and seemed even more artificial than on the previous ward. Most of them would be passed in silence, but some sort of discussion would sometimes start towards the end, only to be terminated by the senior registrar saying 'Time's up.' When asked why a discussion so often started near the end of the meeting and why he always cut it off on time, he would give the stock psychiatric response. 'Ah. You should think about that yourself.' At the first group meeting I burst into genuine tears, doubtless feeling mildly proud that I had been able to fulfil the dictates of my first analyst. I was reproved by the ward sister, who stopped me from talking about myself, for reasons that still escape me. Perhaps she thought it was too tedious for the other patients, but the boredom I might have induced could hardly have been worse than the ten minutes' silence that followed.

Occupational therapy helped to pass the time, but as soon as one got up sufficient determination to embark on a project, the occupational therapist responsible for it would be absent from work. Having wandered timidly down to occupational therapy, one would have to shuffle disconsolately back to the ward. I vainly tried to draw faces and I made another four misshapen pots. The head of occupational therapy had been at the previous hospital. Her dedication and enthusiasm were remarkable and were rightly rewarded with an OBE. She used to go round the wards collecting patients for her play-readings, which I attended regularly. It took us several afternoons to get through *Blithe Spirit,* a title that ill-consorted with the spirit of those reading it. I was always disappointed at the smallness of my part, but it was in fact a piece of judicious casting, for my concentration was so poor that she usually had to read my lines herself. The patience of the occupational therapists was admirable, and apart from proffering a much needed distraction, they provided relief by treating us as people rather than as patients, for they had not been indoctrinated with the half-baked ideas that underlie most brands of psychotherapy. It is tragic that the National Health Service cannot afford more of them.

I have now briefly described the nature of the second hospital and I return to my own story. To my dismay, I was confined to the hospital on the first weekend. This procedure was a dogma and was applied to all new patients for reasons that remain obscure. It may have been that patients allowed home soon after admission would be unwilling to return. Everyone in the ward had gone home except for a rather pretty young woman with whom I played Scrabble. She was extremely unwell and tended to snap savagely at me, something which I now recognize was a symptom of her illness, but which at the time I found upsetting. I do not know how I got through the boredom of that weekend. I remember one afternoon sitting watching the hands of the clock dawdling their sluggish way from four-thirty to five-thirty, at which time eating would provide a few minutes' distraction. The hour seemed endless. I would sometimes deliberately avoid looking at the clock for what I judged to be five minutes, only to find that less than a minute had gone by.

My wife, I suspect rather against her will, visited me during the weekend and alternated kindness and taunting. I was upset to learn that she would like to go to bed with three men at once, an ambition that was never realized and has, I imagine, long since been abandoned. I developed the obsessions that go with depression—jealousy and the fear that the hospital would forcefully prevent me from seeing my wife.

The clinical psychologist appeared to me less helpful than the one in the other hospital. He told me that the only point in having me in hospital was to separate me from Josie. When I told him of my sexual jealousy, he said he would get the male social worker who was seeing my wife on her own to find out whether she had been sleeping with anyone, and persuade her to tell me all about it in a meeting with him and the social worker. (My memory tells me that what he actually suggested was that he would persuade them to make love in front of me, adding 'It can't take more than an hour', but this seems such a curious idea, even for a psychotherapist, that for once I feel I cannot trust my memory and have preferred a tamer version.)

This plan seemed somewhat contrived. Moreover, although he was doubtless following the psychological principle that if one is sufficiently exposed to a stimulus the emotions it arouses die down, I thought he had failed to take account of another equally valid psychological principle—namely, that the more one is exposed to an emotion-provoking stimulus, the more intense the emotion becomes. Much psychology is like the Bible—it can provide support for almost any conceivable view.

During the first week or so in hospital, the consultant also told me that I should not spend the weekends with my wife, since the whole idea was to keep us apart. Since weekends in hospital were unendurable, I spent them with those friends who were loyal enough to put up with me. One woman, who was no more than a friend, was particularly kind and tried to distract me by driving me around the countryside. We would keep passing places I had visited with Josie, and in my maudlin and melodramatic way, I was overcome by the thought that for the rest of my life I could never pass those spots without bursting into tears at the thought of her. My friend nearly achieved what I had failed to do with my razor blade: she came out on to a main road in front of a car that was heading straight for me, but to my regret it screeched to a halt. She took me up Box Hill, where I tried to induce a heart attack by making the steep ascent as fast as possible.

I was very proud of my firmness in not going home for weekends, even though it was negated by the fact that I continued to see Josie fairly regularly in the week. I found it difficult not to be constantly on the telephone to her. When I rang, I would pray that she would be in, since any absence from the house would fuel my jealousy. On evenings when she did not visit, I would try to have other friends at hand. I had complained to the junior registrar about the antidepressant I was taking, since it was causing impotence. To my surprise he genially prescribed another, which reduced this effect and which was compatible (at least in my eyes) with drinking. I limited myself to two or three pints each night, but I was reproved by the ward sister for coming back smelling of beer ("You shouldn't get into the habit of relying on drink to reduce anxiety.'). After that, I took pains not to breathe in the direction of night nurses.

The clinical psychologist had upset me by his candour in saying that the reason I had been admitted to hospital was to separate me from my wife.

As I would be living on my own when I left the hospital, he suggested I took cookery classes there. The suggestion was no doubt meant kindly but I was insulted: I may not be a Cordon Bleu chef but I can boil a palatable three and a half minute egg and on occasion rise to higher things. He also drew a touching description of life after our separation, with Josie coming round to my house to watch television and my going round to hers from time to time for a meal. I barked, 'I don't own a television set and she's a rotten cook', only half of which was true.

Regardless of Josie's decision, he kept urging me to separate. Nothing was further from my mind. Meetings were set up once a week with the social worker and the ward sister, in which Josie and I were supposed to discuss in public whether we wished to separate. At one meeting she alarmed me beyond measure by announcing that she had decided to separate. This destroyed my resolve not to go home, and the following weekend I did go home in order to dissuade her. I apparently succeeded since at the next meeting she said she had changed her mind. I doubt if it had been my piteous pleas that affected her: in fact there had been a change in the liaison she was having at the time—she had discovered the man in question was impotent.

Although I derived considerable satisfaction from Josie's change of mind, the social worker and the nurse looked aghast. Between us, Josie and I had thwarted the main point of my being admitted to hospital and since I was feeling a little better I discharged myself. I agreed to stay long enough to attend that piece of psychiatric ceremonial known as a ward round. At a duly appointed hour, I was led to a room in which were seated the consultant, his registrars, the clinical psychologist, the social worker, an occupational therapist, the ward sister and one or two others who may or may not have been involved in my treatment. It reminded me of the end of a play when the cast appears in order to receive their applause.

Psychiatrists may occasionally push patients in a given direction, but they are (or at least should be) scrupulous about allowing them to make up their own minds, Instead of remonstrating with me for returning to an un-satisfactory marriage, the consultant said benignly that he hoped Josie and I would be happy. He added (or was it someone else?) that he hoped I would not trouble the psychiatric services again with my marital problems, which were no worse than those of many others who solved them on their own. I was extremely annoyed at this remark, for I had been pushed into entering hospital, and as will shortly be apparent I had unquestionably had a manic-depressive illness which had nothing to do with the marriage.

I had begun to take lithium in April, and I discharged myself from the hospital in June. Although I was still very shaky, I went straight back to teaching, with, according to the students, some success. There was one incident which illustrates the ignorance of laymen about mental illness. Two days after I had come out of hospital, the Dean of the faculty within which

I worked came into my office and told me that I should resign my post. Although the suggestion, given my past history, was not unreasonable, the manner of making it, and the time at which it was made, were.

I waited to see whether I would become hypomanic the following winter. I did not—the lithium was working. Moreover, I was lucky in its side-effects. It gave me nothing more than a slight tremor and a massive thirst. Indeed I adopted the habit of carrying a gin bottle full of water, to my own lectures, to talks given by others, on trains and in my car; not everyone believed my account of the bottle's contents. I still drink at least 20 pints of water a day, a habit which, though highly pleasurable, is inconvenient, particularly on long car journeys, since the water has to be expelled. This could lead to awkward situations. As I was driving through Guildford with Josie on our way home from Oxford, I had an overwhelming urge to urinate. Josie wanted me to stop at an antique shop, and I thought I could gain relief there. I explained my predicament to the proprietor, but he refused to allow me to use his lavatory. Fortunately, J located a room at the back, in which I filled a large Delft vase almost to the brim. I have to get up several times in the night, but all this is a small price to pay for freedom from those slow swings of mood that disrupted my life and that of those around me for ten years.

Thus ends the account of my mental illness: over the last five years I have been free from the agony of depression and the folly of hypomania. It is, however, perhaps worth telling the sequel, for it illustrates the difference between depression and ordinary human misery.

The story stops almost where it began. On my return from a trip to the States, Josie seemed particularly distant. Eventually she told me of the abortive affair she had had with someone who was impotent. Then she said 'Do you mind if I tell you something worse?' She said she had developed an infatuation for her boss, and it subsequently transpired that she was sleeping with him. People are unpredictable. Here was this woman, who espoused conventional middle-class values, expressing a craving for someone who had once run one of Brighton's seediest night-clubs and who, as Josie well knew, had killed his own wife out of sexual jealousy. He had been sent to jail on a charge of manslaughter. Moreover, he was a member of the National Front, a Fascist organization.

Not unnaturally I was upset. Indeed for the eight weeks or so that passed before the issue was resolved, I was extremely miserable. At first I condoned the affair, although Josie, as though confiding in me out of friendship, taunted me with details of their sexual activities. My unhappiness was, however, utterly different from depression. I could read and I could work, though perhaps not quite as effectively as usual. I even gave talks at other universities. Fearful of entering a real depression, I saw my psychiatrist, who said 'A man must be master in his own house.' Clearly no feminist he. He added some advice, which I was already in the process of executing 'Find yourself another woman.'

I did not think my despondency would last for ever; somehow a solution would be found. I told Jose that if she wanted to continue the affair we must separate. We agreed that as soon as the university term ended I would live in Oxford for three months, at the end of which time she would move out of the house and live elsewhere. I went to Oxford determined to go on working and determined to seek distraction elsewhere. I was lucky in both respects: it only took two or three weeks for my mood to lift. I was sufficiently recovered to give my wife a bullet-proof vest for Christmas.

I had feared that my house in Brighton would be so reminiscent of Josie that I would be unable to live in it. A woman friend had driven me there from Oxford, but the house was too much for me and I returned with her to Oxford in a shaky condition. During that time, I had a number of enjoyable liaisons, the most intense of which was with a 28-year-old German woman who, ironically as a result of reading *Breakdown,* had come to England partly in order to meet me. She had been miffed at not finding me in Brighton, but we met by chance in the common room of the Oxford Department of Psychology. I have recounted our four-year relationship in fictional form *(Men Change Too).* When eventually I returned to Brighton with her, my house bore none of its previous upsetting associations: the furniture and the bric-a-brac evoked no twinge. A 27-year-old marriage had been dissolved without undue pain to either of us. Despite occasional cause, I have felt little in the way of sexual jealousy over the last 14 years. Perhaps the clinical psychologist was right and it is an emotion that burns itself out.

I am convinced that without the lithium the break-up of the marriage would have thrown me into a deep depression, which would eventually have been succeeded by extreme hypomania. But more importantly, what happened to me suggests that there is a real difference between misery and depression. The difference is partly that misery is less agonizing, and partly that unlike depression it can be accompanied by the retention of hope for the future and by the feeling that one can do something to help oneself. But it should be borne in mind that the two-way interaction between the events of one's life and the biochemistry of the brain is complex and poorly understood. I had suffered many depressions and many bouts of hypomania for no external cause: apart from the first and last depression, absolutely nothing happened to explain my severe mood swings. I feel certain that had Josie's original affair never taken place some other event would have triggered a depression. I find it extraordinary that psychiatrists and psychotherapists should have been so presumptuous as to attempt to separate Josie and me, particularly as I have been diagnosed as manic-depressive. There is no change of scenery, job or partner that has ever been found to alleviate this condition. My own depressions had nothing to do with Josie—they were caused by my illness, and, not surprisingly, it was largely my illness that made Josie unhappy. My mood swings were almost certainly biochemically caused, but this does not mean that the feelings accompanying them were not real. The jealousy, the anxiety, the fears, the boredom, the self-hatred, the despair, even the spasms of elation—all were real. They represent aspects of myself that I normally control rather better than during that grim decade.

The fact that I entered and emerged from so many depressions for no external reason reinforces my belief that it is useless and hurtful to say to someone who is severely depressed 'Come on: snap out of it.' There is little or nothing that he or she can do to help themselves, a fact that people who are lucky enough not to have experienced depression find hard to understand.

9

Postscript

The previous chapter appeared in an updated version of the first edition written in 1987. A few years earlier I had signed a contract with the playwright, Simon Gray, giving him the dramatic rights to *Breakdown*. He had now written the play, entitled *Melon,* which was about to be produced. I thought that the new edition could ride on the back of the likely success of *Melon:* I did not of course have the conceit to think that the republication of *Breakdown* could increase Gray's box office sales, though I had the temerity to suggest this to him. He agreed to provide a foreword for the book, which is a most handsome encomium and—like all his prose—brilliantly written.

In the play. Gray turned me into a publisher, not my favourite profession, but his characterisation of myself was not that wide of the mark, though I like to think I am not as unpleasant as Melon. I was superbly played by Alan Bates, whom I congratulated on his performance. I could not resist adding, 'There is only one problem. When you roll over and over on the ground you do not look like a man in mental agony, you look like someone who doesn't want to get his suit dirty.' I have always admired Gray's plays and I thoroughly enjoyed *Melon.* Several friends have asked me how it felt to watch myself being portrayed on the stage. In fact, it was like watching any play: despite the similarity, I did not identify with the principal character.

For many years after my wife's departure my life continued comparatively undisturbed and certainly without depression. My psychiatrist commented that I was a living testimony to the efficacy of modern psychiatry and surgery. I had no doubt that my stable and cheerful mood was permanent. I was lucky in my women friends; I continued to teach; I published the occasional article in learned journals; I wrote a dictionary of psychology and a book on irrational decision making, as well as two novels and a play. After ten good years, my cheerful existence was marred by a six month period in which I woke early and could not get back to sleep, because for no apparent reason I was attacked by anxiety. After a few months, the anxiety passed away as suddenly as it had appeared, again for no external reason. I concluded that this mild but unpleasant episode was caused by my manic-depressive illness: this was confirmed by what happened next.

My original psychiatrist had retired. When I saw his successor in order to discuss my lithium dose, he was amazed to learn that for over ten years I had had neither depression nor hypomania. I thought at the time that his surprise was rather sinister. Medical fashions change and, as I well knew, the recommended level of lithium in the blood had been reduced by more than a half since I started taking it. We agreed to halve my own dose. Subsequently we halved it yet again, largely because it can damage the kidneys. Six months later, I entered the first depression I had experienced in 11 years. It was mild compared to the previous ones: I could still read and write, but slowly and laboriously. I could take no pleasure in anything; the future looked bleak; and I could not settle to performing the most routine tasks such as checking bank statements, paying bills or even shaving. I found myself unable to prepare a talk for a prestigious lecture to be given in California. I had very much been looking forward to it and was extremely disappointed to be obliged to cancel it.

Exactly a year later, and sadly without any intervening bout of hypomania, I went into a similar depression. As in the past, I found a spurious cause for it—worry over a letter I had written that I thought might be libellous: I was convinced I would be sued. In fact it was harmless and it eventually brought me an apology and a cheque for £75. I have been mildly depressed on and off ever since, though the rhythm is completely different from in the past: it has become diurnal. I wake feeling quite cheerful, but within a few seconds, there is a feeling of constriction in my throat and anxiety seizes me. Compared with the agonies of severe depression or panic attacks from which so many suffer, these symptoms are a minor unpleasantness. I dread the daily struggle to forego the security of bed and face the world. I feel I should be able to control my mood and should force myself to get up. As the day goes by, my mood lifts and by the evening I am normal or almost normal, for as old age approaches I feel less ebullient than in the past. My salvation has lain in work.

Since the above words were written, my mood has lifted. Is it the extra lithium my psychiatrist prescribed? Is it part of the cycle of manic-depression? Or is it that I have striven to accomplish something? Unfortunately, I no longer have compensating spells of hypomania. My life is very different from what it was four years ago, when I was convinced I could never again suffer the disabling pain of depression. I now feel that once a manic-depressive, always a manic-depressive, and look forward to the future with mild foreboding.

It is worth comparing my manic-depressive illness with that of Kay Jamison, herself a clinical psychologist, who describes her own in her highly readable book, *An Unquiet Mind*. Her bouts of hypomania were similar to my own, except that they were more intense: she spent money much more recklessly than I did and was given to extreme irritability, whereas as far as I can remember I was no more irritable than usual. Unlike me, however, she developed fully psychotic mania, a terrifying experience. She writes, 'I knew I was insane. My thoughts were so fast that I could not remember the beginning of a sentence half way through. Fragments of ideas, images, sentences, raced round and round in my mind ... I wanted to slow down but could not . . . Sex became too intense for pleasure, and during it I would feel my mind encased by black lines of light that were terrifying to me . . . The screams [of dying plants] were cacophonous. Increasingly all my images were black and decaying.' She had hallucinations, in one of which she saw herself being whirled to pieces in a centrifuge with blood all over her room.

Her depressions were not dissimilar to my own. She would wake feeling tired and wondering with dread how she could get through the day: she was preoccupied with 'death, dying and decaying' not just her own, but that of everything around her. She was bored and sometimes extremely agitated. She felt the same sense of shame and worthlessness that afflicted me. Although while depressed she often chose not to read, it is not apparent whether she could have read or watched television if she had decided to do so. Despite her depressions, which began much earlier in life than mine, she managed to obtain a sufficiently good degree to gain a much coveted award which enabled her to attend graduate school at the prestigious University of California in Los Angeles. Moreover, when she subsequently joined the academic staff there, she appears to have been able to continue lecturing and treating patients throughout her depressions. On the other hand, she did something I would never have had the courage to attempt—she tried to commit suicide.

Although she was a clinical psychologist, she repeatedly gave up taking lithium, plunging herself back into mania or depression; she missed her hypomanic moods and, like many people, felt it wrong to live on drugs which 'make you not yourself. Moreover, she believes that in many people, including herself, hypomania is associated with creativity; in consequence she does not regret her illness, particularly as it is now controlled by lithium. This seems to me rather a sentimental reaction: one doubts whether, if given a choice between normality and full blown manic-depression, she would be prepared again to undergo the misery of her illness, her terrifying hallucinations and her bouts of psychotic mania.

As for me, I would give all I had to avoid experiencing again the anguish and hopelessness of my ten depressions. I would also give a very large sum to escape the present mild depressions, which drag heavily upon me and impede my enjoyment of life. Moreover, mental illness affects others besides the patient. My children were taking important examinations at the time of my first breakdown. Neither my own absurd behaviour nor the quarrels between myself and their mother could have been pleasant for them, though they seemed to bear it all with some stoicism. Although when hypomanic I saw myself as vastly entertaining and interesting, this opinion was not shared by my friends, who found me better company when depressed. As for Josie, I reduced her by my uncontrollable moods to the verge of breaking down herself. Unlike Jamison, I found the experience of depression merely demeaning and I learned nothing from it except to sympathize with those who were in a similar plight or who were experiencing the normal un-happiness caused by misfortune. Nor do I believe that my manic-depression has added to—or subtracted from—my creativity, such as it is. In short, I would rather not have been a manic-depressive, not merely for my own sake, but for that of those around me.

I am reluctant to end my account of my mental illness on a pessimistic note, if only because I would like to encourage other sufferers. As one of my psychiatrist friends remarked: 'Depressions are funny things.' They come and go unpredictably. My present slightly low moods are more bearable than most of the afflictions from which the human race suffers. I am dissatisfied with this chapter, partly because it is rather self-centred, though if I am to convey the inward feeling of mild depression that has to be so. Moreover, I am lucky to have escaped the horror of severe manic-depression which would have been impossible before lithium came into use. Finally, I am no worse off—indeed rather better off—that most others. Everyone has serious problems, which they conceal from all except their intimates.

Maybe I will gain the courage to fight harder, feeling with Ulysses and his aged crew:

> Tho' much is taken, much abides; and tho'
> We are not now that strength which in old days
> Moved earth and heaven; that which we are, we are;
> One equal temper of heroic hearts,
> Made weak by time and fate, but strong in will
> To strive, to seek, to find, and not to yield.

This comparison should not be taken too seriously, for I lack Ulysses' courage, nor do I have the 'many wiles' that Homer attributed to him. And I hate boats.

PART II

Mental illness: its nature, origins and treatment

Who's who

The second section of this book provides a general introduction to mental disorder for the layman or for beginning students of the subject. It excludes some specialized topics, like mental disorder in children and forensic psychiatry (the application of psychiatry to the law).

There are a baffling number of different professions involved in the care and treatment of the mentally ill. Particularly in Britain, even the educated often find it difficult to distinguish the roles and beliefs of psychiatrists, clinical psychologists, psychotherapists, psychoanalysts, psychiatric social workers and counsellors. (Only the other day the *Sunday Times* confused psychoanalysis with psychotherapy.) I shall therefore provide a cast list, but first it is necessary to distinguish two different kinds of treatment.

The first is physical methods, which include the use of drugs and electro-convulsive therapy. The second is psychotherapy—talking with the patient, a method described by R. D. Laing as: 'A conversation between two people, one of whom is by mutual consent declared to be sane.'

Psychotherapy covers a multitude of different approaches ranging from psychoanalysis, through Gestalt therapy to behaviour therapy. Broadly interpreted it has four aims. First, to make a diagnosis and to decide the best method of treatment; second, to support the patients through their disorder, which is more important than it sounds both because of the misery of mental illness and because of the risk of suicide; third, to help patients to behave in such a way as to ameliorate their illness, even if this merely means persuading them to take their drugs. Finally, psychotherapy can be an attempt to bring about a long-term improvement in the patient's condition.

Physical methods, including drugs, can be used only by psychiatrists or other doctors. Psychiatrists have a comprehensive medical training and normally must pass the examinations and practical tests needed to become members of the Royal College of Psychiatrists in Britain or the American Psychiatric Association in America. Because the symptoms of mental disorder can be produced by physical illness, for example by a brain tumour or by poor functioning of the thyroid glands, a knowledge of general medicine is needed in order to diagnose such illnesses.

In mental hospitals the ultimate responsibility for the patient always rests with the psychiatrist, though he usually works with a team that includes all or most of the other professions to be discussed below. The power of the psychiatrist is a frequent source of annoyance to psychologists, who may have their own plan for treatment, which the psychiatrist forbids them to execute.

All psychiatrists diagnose, support and advise their patients. In Britain, and even more so in America, many also provide psychotherapy with longer-term aims. The type they use depends on where they were trained and on their personal predilections.

The second most important profession is clinical psychology, although some of its practitioners might query my use of the word 'second'. Their skills overlap those of psychiatrists: indeed some wag asked to explain the difference between them said 'A hundred dollars an hour.' Clinical psychologists must have a degree in general psychology and must thereafter have taken a higher degree in clinical psychology, which necessitates both passing examinations and treating patients under supervision. Many of the public on meeting a 'psychologist' think that he or she broods over people on couches or, at the very least, treats mental patients. In fact, there are many other kinds of psychologists. Many teach or do research on normal people or on animals, investigating such topics as vision, language, memory, reasoning and so on. Some (educational psychologists) are employed to deal with the psychological problems of school children, others (applied psychologists) work for firms, government or the military, attempting to improve management structure, or to adapt products to their consumers' needs, or to boost morale.

Like psychiatrists, clinical psychologists have to be accredited by a recognized institution—The British Psychological Society or the American Psychological Association. Both bodies have the right to strike members off their list for malpractice and both earn fat fees for registering clinical psychologists. Anyone who can legally call themselves a clinical psychologist will have had a training in diagnosis and in some form of psychotherapy. Most behave better towards their patients than some of the more maverick unregistered psychotherapists, if only for fear of losing their licence.

Clinical psychologists are better trained in mental testing than psychiatrists: indeed, in Britain until about forty years ago psychologists were not allowed to treat patients under the National Health Service (NHS)—they were restricted to giving tests to help in diagnosis or to assess improvement or deterioration. This was also true in America until the Second World War when, because there were not enough psychiatrists to give adequate treatment to servicemen, psychologists were permitted to give psychotherapy. Clinical psychologists are usually well trained in research methods and it is probably true to say that more research on mental disorders is carried out by psychologists than by psychiatrists.

Psychotherapy is a catch-all term for the attempt to relieve mental distress by talking with the patient. It is practised by many different professions and there are many different varieties of it. One among these different breeds of psychotherapists is psychoanalysts. Unlike psychiatrists and clinical psychologists, they are not recognized by law and anyone can attach a brass plate to their front door reading 'S. Freud, psychoanalyst'. Although all psychoanalysis stems ultimately from the ideas of Freud, the movement, as we shall see, split into many different factions, each of which departs from Freud's beliefs in fundamental ways. Most analysts belong to one of the various organizations representing the school of analysis in which they believe. To become members, they must usually undergo a training analysis, which may take many years, and must treat patients under supervision. In the USA, the main bastion of Freudian analysis only allows doctors to join. Until recently one American psychiatrist in ten was also a psychoanalyst, but with the emergence of new and more effective types of psychotherapy, the figure is now very much lower.

In mental hospitals, patients may see a senior or junior psychiatrist two or three times a week and a clinical psychologist perhaps twice a week. The front-line workers are psychiatric nurses who are trained both in diagnosis and treatment. They can administer drugs and injections under a psychiatrist's prescription. They also keep detailed notes on the behaviour of their patients, which are passed on to the psychiatrist. The therapy given by nurses is usually dictated by the psychiatrist or clinical psychologist. The more recent forms of treatment, such as behaviour or cognitive therapy, require little time to learn and can readily be administered by nurses particularly if they are equipped with some common sense. Nurses should be encouraged to provide such therapy if only because psychiatrists' time is expensive and (at least in Britain) there are far too few clinical psychologists. Since the main contact of patients in mental hospitals is with nurses, their current mood and future prospects probably hinge more on the quality of nursing than on their dealings with psychiatrists or clinical psychologists (if we omit the importance of drugs). Community psychiatric nurses visit patients in their homes. They make sure they are taking their drugs, give supportive therapy and report their condition to the doctor in charge of their case.

In Britain about two-thirds of patients consulting GPs (general practitioners) have some form of mental disorder; in half the cases the disorder is not diagnosed and therefore goes untreated; serious cases are referred to a psychiatrist. To the rest he doles out psychiatric drugs as he is usually too busy to give psychotherapy himself, but he may refer the patient to a clinical psychologist, counsellor or social worker if he thinks it would help. In practice 80% of the mentally disordered are treated only by their GP.

Until recently a general medical training was woefully inadequate in psychiatry according to a report by the Royal College of Psychiatrists. Moreover, the report concluded that psychiatrists themselves were often poorly trained. The problem was confounded by the fact that other medical specialities held psychiatry in poor repute so that the calibre of doctors entering that speciality tended to be low. Aubrey Lewis, one of the most distinguished psychiatrists of the age referred to 'The withering effect upon students of prominent and admired teachers of other branches of medicine [who] adopt a frankly derisory attitude towards psychiatry.' Although the training of psychiatrists has improved and their status risen, prospective GPs are not taught enough about the subject.

No special qualifications are needed to become a counsellor and these days there are counsellors for almost all activities, ranging from marriage counsellors to 'leisure counsellors', who presumably advise their clients on where to go on holiday and which television programme to watch. There is no specific training for counsellors and anyone can claim to be one. They are employed by local authorities and by some firms, though many operate privately. Some specialize in psychiatric care and offer psychotherapy. In this connection, it has been found that untrained counsellors produce as good results as trained ones. The reason is almost certainly that dealing with the mentally ill requires common sense and many if not most of the different schools of psychotherapy provide rigid approaches that depart widely from common sense. If you subscribe to psychoanalysis, Reichian therapy or the primal scream you will focus on one aspect of the patient and may become blind to his or her other problems. All professions want to claim some knowledge or techniques that the general public lacks, if only to justify their own existence.

Social workers are an outgrowth of the welfare state. They can un-doubtedly help people to understand their rights, such as disability pay-ments, old-age pensions, unemployment benefits and so on, and they can also assist by providing and filling in the bureaucratic forms needed to obtain these rights, many of which would baffle a chartered accountant. Both in the US and in Britain there are bodies that certify authorized social workers on the basis of a recognized training, which is either a university degree in social work or a two-year diploma. In America, but not in Britain, people cannot call themselves a social worker without such a training. Even in Britain, however, many employees now insist that all but the most junior social workers should have a degree or diploma in the subject. Some of the main employers are local authorities and hospitals. Social workers specializing in mental health have usually taken a three month course on the subject, which supplements any knowledge of psychology they may have acquired during their university work. Residential psychiatric social workers are to be found in community homes for mental patients. Since 40% of such patients are schizophrenics it might be thought they would be better cared for by a psychiatric nurse who has a fuller training in mental illness. Psychiatric social workers also work in the field, where their role is largely to go to patients' homes, both to deal with practical matters, and to assess the conditions under which the patient is living and their relations with their family; this information is passed on to the doctor in charge of the case. A scathing book entitled *Can Social Work Survive?* reports that 83% of social workers prefer discussing their clients' emotional problems to performing mundane tasks such as finding ways to pay the rent. Needless to say, their clients take exactly the opposite view. Many psychiatric social workers give some form of psychotherapy. Unfortunately the types of psychotherapy taught to social workers are often among the zanier kinds ranging from psychoanalysis to encounter groups.

Social work is amorphous and social workers who specialize in psychiatry may, not without justice, feel they are subservient to other professions. They are sometimes seen as being interfering busy-bodies, many of whom are Marxists or extremely left-wing. Their political beliefs may stem in part from their university education, which usually includes courses on sociology, a vague subject that became fashionable in the sixties, when its teachers had a strong bias to the left. It is unclear why studying the abstruse ideas of Talcott Parsons or Ernst Gellner should enable social workers to help their fellows.

Some social workers do not believe in drugs for mental disorders and may even discourage their patients from taking them. In their zeal to do good, they sometimes do considerable harm. For example, social workers falsely accused four sets of parents in the Orkneys of child abuse and had their children removed (for a fuller account of the search for child abuse, see Chapter 28). Their behaviour can be crass in other ways. In Britain there has recently been an outcry against social workers' politically correct policies for child adoption. In considering whether a couple are fit to adopt a child, they have insisted that the prospective parents and the child be of the same race and have the same language. In one instance, they made it a condition for the adoption of a Chinese child that the parents learn Mandarin. Since the demand for adopted children vastly exceeds the supply, this policy has left tens of thousands of children needlessly being brought up in institutions and has deprived many suitable parents of rearing a child. They have also refused to let children be fostered by parents who wish to send their child to a public (in the US private) school, on the grounds that they would 'push the child too hard'.

Here is an anecdote, which one hopes is not typical. A friend of mine had a mastectomy in one of the most prestigious hospitals in Britain. Soon after the operation a 25-year-old social worker arrived at her bedside and, having sent away the woman's husband and grown-up children, sat herself down. She said 'I'm your social worker. Tell me, what does it feel like to have lost your femininity?' After the death of Diana, Princess of Wales, social workers descended on schools to comfort the mourning children. Whether they made them more or less disconsolate is open to question.

It may be wondered why I have singled out social workers for criticism: after all the sins of psychologists are often just as egregious, but because their errors are much better documented, they cannot be fitted into this chapter, but will be analysed at some length later in the book. There are doubtless many sensible and dedicated social workers as well as the idiotic ones, though one wonders whether we need quite so many given that until fairly recently we got on perfectly well with none at all.

The dogmatism of some social workers may be explicable as a reaction to being at the bottom of the pile of carers both financially and in terms of esteem. Doubtless, there are many social workers who are less doctrinaire and who exhibit some common sense. I have had to rely mainly on anecdote because there are so few studies of the efficacy of social work.

One such study compared the effects of having school truants visited by social workers with having their parents repeatedly brought to court with the threat that their children would be placed in care if they continued to play truant. The group looked after by social workers played truant much more often than the other and committed five times as many crimes.

Apart from psychiatrists and doctors, none of the professions I have mentioned existed until recently: it might be wondered how the mentally disordered survived without them. One answer is that the parish priest performed the functions of all the specialities named. Another is that, at least in Britain, there used to be less geographical mobility and people may have received more help from members of their community and from their immediate family. Many, of course, survived only under appalling conditions. They were locked in lunatic asylums, manacled in chains and kept in order by cold douches.

Relations between the professions reviewed are not always easy. In the 1940s and 1950s clinical psychologists battled with psychiatrists to be allowed to give unsupervised psychotherapy. By the late 1950s they had won and in the US patients could refer themselves direct to a clinical psychologist. The loss of one of their rights had a severe effect on psychiatrists. With remarkable honesty the president of the American Psychiatric Association remarked: 'If we are not different from and superior to clinical psychologists, psychiatric social workers and nurses, who are being increasingly licensed for independent practice, is not our financial security and professional integrity going to be increasingly at risk?'

Since clinical psychologists are much cheaper than psychiatrists, American health insurance companies now often insist on their clients being treated by them rather than by a psychiatrist. In consequence between 1975 and 1990 the number of American psychiatrists increased by a mere 10,000 whereas the number of clinical psychologists rose by 27,000 and that of clinical social workers (who also give psychotherapy) by a staggering

55,000. In America there are now more clinical psychologists than psychiatrists and their numbers are doubling every ten years. There are now about 20 clinical psychologists per 10,000 American citizens: the corresponding figure in Britain is about two. They have achieved considerable status in the US, with some holding chairs of psychiatry or being directors of psychiatric clinics. In Britain under the NHS, there is invariably a long waiting list for clinical psychologists. Because newer forms of psychotherapy are effective, there is a strong case for increasing the number of clinical psychologists in Britain.

Clinical psychologists are now attacking another of psychiatrists' prerogatives—they want, after a brief training in psychopharmacology—to prescribe drugs, a change that needless to say is strongly opposed by psychiatrists on the spurious grounds that psychologists would not understand the biochemistry of the brain nor the often harmful interactions between psychotropic drugs—that is, drugs for the mind—and also with other drugs. In fact there are now so many drugs that even psychiatrists frequently have to look up the possible interactions before prescribing. Clinical psychologists are now themselves under threat from social workers, counsellors and even nurses, all of whom are capable of giving psychotherapy at considerably reduced rates, but psychologists are reluctant to allow these other professions to give such therapy without being supervised.

As we have seen, amateur therapists are on average at least as good as professionals so there is no reason whatever why social workers and nurses should not be allowed to practise therapy. Both psychiatrists and psychologists will have to give way. Since psychiatrists are paid much more than psychologists and since social workers earn less than psychologists, if doctors and psychologists give up their privileges, the treatment of the mentally ill would become considerably cheaper, an outcome that is surely both inevitable and desirable. The spectacle of the different professions fighting over their privileges is unedifying, particularly as they usually claim it is for the good of the patients when in reality it is for their own financial gain.

* * *

We must not lose sight of the patients served by these professions. In Britain the majority are cared for solely by their GP. The rest fall into four categories. First, patients who are either a danger to themselves or to others can be committed (sectioned) to reside in a mental hospital. Psychiatrists have a difficult choice. They are loathe to section patients, because if they are admitted to hospital voluntarily they are more likely to co-operate. Psychiatrists are bound to make mistakes, either by sectioning someone unnecessarily or by failing to section someone who needs to be in hospital. One psychiatrist I know had for several weeks been trying to persuade a depressed patient to come into hospital voluntarily. Eventually, the patient agreed and an ambulance was sent to collect him. He asked the driver to stop so that he could urinate, ran off and committed suicide by cutting his throat. The psychiatrist was admonished by the coroner.

Sectioned patients can be kept in separate quarters where they are under constant surveillance. Even voluntary patients can wind up being sectioned if their behaviour warrants it. On both the wards I was in, the section was one of the greatest fears and many, probably apocryphal, stories of its miseries were bruited around. It was said that even when a patient was parched (a common side-effect of many psychotropic drugs) it often took hours to persuade a nurse to fetch a glass of water.

The laws governing compulsory commitment are complex and will be examined later. Basically, such commitment can only occur if someone is deemed to be a danger to themselves or to others. In practice psychiatrists may resort to more devious means of preventing voluntary patients discharging themselves, when they believe it is in the patient's best interest. Junior psychiatrists may plead with a patient to wait until he is seen on the consultant's weekly ward round, or they may refuse to supply a prescription for the drugs patients need if they leave hospital. I once visited a student of mine who was undergoing a mild schizophrenic episode and had voluntarily admitted himself. He wanted his discharge but could not leave because his clothes had been removed. Had he walked out naked, the diagnosis of schizophrenia would of course have been confirmed. When I was thinking of leaving the hospital during my first stay, my clinical psychologist told me, 'You must not play ducks and drakes with us' and the junior registrar did her utmost to persuade me to stay. It was unclear—at least to me— whether my drugs would have been prescribed had I left of my own accord, though a prescription was forthcoming when my discharge had been agreed.

A second category of patients are those who admit themselves to hospital voluntarily. Such an admission has several different functions. It can remove patients from a stressful background and the ordinary cares of life in order to give them a breathing space. It can help the psychiatrist to form a better judgement of their condition through their observations and those of other doctors and nurses. It ensures that patients take their tablets and it provides the opportunity for more intensive psychotherapy (including group therapy) than is normally possible for patients living at home. And in theory it may convince the patient that he is not too bad because he is likely to meet others who are much worse, though in the case of severe depression such as mine it would take a lot to produce this conviction. Finally, electroconvulsive therapy is usually administered only to in-patients.

Long-term stays in hospital have the danger of 'institutionalizing" patients. They may become apathetic and lose interest in life because they do not have to fend for themselves. Partly because of this problem (and partly to save money), in both Britain and the US the number of psychiatric beds has been drastically reduced over the last 40 years, a reduction that was facilitated by the introduction of effective drugs for schizophrenia and depression.

For humanitarian reasons and in order to cope with patients released from hospitals, both in Britain and the US, another method of caring for patients has been developed known as 'Community Mental Health Centres". Such centres are located in the patient's community, each with a catchment area of about 100,000 so that the patient can keep in touch with friends and relatives. They provide several different services, the first three of which are residential.

So-called 'half-way houses' were originally designed to house patients discharged from hospital in order to rehabilitate them sufficiently to return to their own homes. Inevitably, many of them had to return to hospital and reappeared after each discharge—a process known as 'the revolving door'. The hostels are run by a warden, but the inmates are visited by psychiatrists, clinical psychologists, social workers and community nurses, with their GPs also involved. A second kind of accommodation, known as 'group homes', is intended for the chronically mentally ill—often schizophrenics—who do not need supervision but are not well enough to live on their own. About five or six of them live together usually in a house in a residential area: by pooling their skills they should be able to cope with the day-to-day business of living. They are visited regularly by psychiatric nurses and social workers. In addition to these hostels, there is often a nearby psychiatric ward intended for short-stay patients.

Another aspect of community care is a clinic where non-residential patients can be seen by members of the different mental health professions. There is also a day centre, in which patients who live at home can spend their day-time hours and undergo rehabilitation. Apart from caring directly for patients, the clinics keep in touch with other helping organizations such as the local churches and branches of Alcoholics Anonymous, the Samaritans, and even RELATE.

The Community Mental Health Centres set up in America have focused less on residential accommodation and more on 'crisis intervention' than have those in Britain. As the name implies, the latter deals at an early stage with people who have had a crisis in their life in the hope of preventing it developing into a mental illness. The crises in question include bereavement, loss of a job, separation or divorce, leaving home for the first time and so on. Brief psychotherapy is given that focuses entirely on the nature of the crisis and the patient's reaction to it. One study reviewing research on community care came to the dismaying conclusion that the effect of the interventions was very close to zero.

The establishment of Community Health Centres in the 1960s was for many reasons a humanitarian step. They avoid the institutionalization that occurs with a long stay in hospital; they enable the patient to see friends and relatives easily; they avoid the stigma attached to mental hospitals; they encourage co-operation and the exchange of ideas between the members of different mental health professions; they make use of local voluntary services; and they give the patients greater freedom, less feeling of powerlessness, and a less boring and more varied life than do mental hospitals.

Furthermore patients like them and are more likely to seek help if it is on their doorstep. With the exception of the severely ill, patients do about as well in these centres as in mental hospitals. It has also been found that community care is slightly cheaper than mental hospitals, though hospitals will still be needed for some psychiatric patients. Unfortunately, the services offered by existing Community Centres are often limited by lack of funds: a single psychiatrist may have to cope with 500 patients of whom about 50 are in-patients and the rest out-patients.

One disadvantage of Community Care is that it is not popular with the public, who especially dislike group homes, which are normally placed in residential areas and which can lower the value of neighbouring houses. Recently in London, residents jointly bought a house in their street to prevent it being used as a community home. Schizophrenia can often be controlled by drugs, but patients who stop taking them may occasionally resort to violence: there have been several episodes in Britain recently. A report by the Royal College of Psychiatrists criticized the lack of adequate care for patients in the community and blamed 13 out of 39 recent killings by psychotics on a failure to supervise them adequately. The then Minister of Health concluded that the more dangerous patients should be kept in mental hospitals. The root cause of such problems is that neither in Britain nor the US are there enough Community Care Centres to cope with the exodus of patients from hospitals. One investigator wrote that in Bayshore, Long Island, discharged patients were 'Frequently found wandering across neighbours' lawns in the middle of the night. Several appeared on the main thoroughfare directing traffic. Many of the derelicts and alcoholics in New York City who sleep in the doorways at night and panhandle in the daytime were formerly patients at Central Islip Hospital.' This only strengthens the case for more and better serviced Community Health Centres.

Finally, patients may live at home, looked after by their GP, sometimes with visits from social workers or community nurses. They may also attend out-patient clinics run by psychiatrists or clinical psychologists. In Britain 95% of the mentally disordered are in fact treated solely by their GP and are not referred to a psychiatrist. Given that most GPs only have a rudimentary knowledge of psychiatry and that they appear to be already over-stretched, this figure should almost certainly be reduced.

In the unlikely event of the different professions giving up the exclusive rights to some of their privileges, psychiatric services could be improved and their costs reduced.

11

The nature of mental illness

This chapter describes the symptoms of the commoner forms of mental disorder. There are so many different kinds that some, such as disorders of childhood, have had to be omitted. The difficulty of making accurate diagnoses will be discussed in the following chapter.

The major categories of mental illness are usually taken to be the psychoses and neuroses, but even here there is a great deal of overlap and it is not clear how far they should be regarded as lying on a continuum. One authoritative manual stated: 'The distinction between so-called psychotic depressions and depressive neurosis appears to many psychiatrists artificial and sometimes impossible.' In general, the psychotic is out of touch with aspects of reality, whereas the neurotic, however badly incapacitated by anxiety or depression, is in contact with the environment and is aware of what is going on.

The psychoses are divided into 'organic' and 'functional'. The organic psychoses are due to known malfunctioning of the brain. This does not mean that the functional psychoses are not also due to physical disorders of the brain: we are merely less sure what the physical disorder if any is. The organic psychoses include mental illness caused by general atrophy of the brain (senile dementia), one form of which, Alzheimer's disease, is marked by memory loss for recent events, irritability, and inability to think coherently. It is caused by a specific type of degeneration in the nerve cells of the cortex, but the symptoms are so similar to other kinds of senile dementia that its presence can often only be established by a post mortem. Patients may sink into a prolonged coma and the average length of life after onset is about ten years. Other organic psychoses can be caused by infection of the brain, as in syphilis, by poisoning or nutritional deficiencies, and by overindulgence in drugs such as alcohol, barbiturates or amphetamines.

A wide range of symptoms may be produced by such causes, and they may be short-lasting or persist for long periods of time. Drugs that cause hallucinations, like LSD, sometimes lead to a long-lasting psychosis whose symptoms are similar to those of schizophrenia. Prolonged use of amphetamine (speed) can also produce a condition indistinguishable from schizophrenia.

Alcohol poisoning can cause Korsakov's psychosis, a chronic and incurable condition characterized by an inability to retain anything in memory for more than a minute or so: the patient usually fills in the gaps in his memory by confabulating imaginary events. Withdrawal from alcohol can produce delirium tremens, an acute condition which rarely lasts more than a week: the patient is disoriented and confused and may have bizarre visual hallucinations, though pink elephants are seen less often than is popularly believed.

It is possible that poisoning, faulty nutrition or atmospheric pollution is responsible for more mental illness than can currently be traced to such causes. Ergot, a disease of rye, has caused outbreaks of mental illness in previous centuries. Throughout the history of civilization, drugs have been used to produce bizarre mental states akin to psychotic conditions. Witches smeared their broomsticks with an ointment made from such plants as deadly nightshade and mandrake: they rode their broomsticks naked, and the ointment was absorbed through their vaginas. Some of the substances it contains, when administered to volunteers, have been found to produce an illusion of flying and sensations of panoramic vision.

The organic psychoses will not clear up unless the underlying cause is removed, whether it be a brain tumour, vitamin deficiency, poisoning or abuse of drugs. The symptoms of organic psychoses closely resemble those of the functional psychoses, and it is therefore essential to determine at the outset through a medical examination and a life history whether the symptoms are produced by any of these physical causes.

* * *

The two categories of functional psychoses are schizophrenia and the affective psychoses (pathological changes of mood). The onset of schizophrenia tends to occur early in life, with a peak in first admissions to hospital of people between 20 and 30. Roughly one in every hundred suffers from it at some point in life. It is a common misunderstanding to suppose that schizophrenia refers to cases of multiple personality. It means the patient is cut off from reality rather than that his personality is splintered into separate components. Although schizophrenics usually retain a clear state of consciousness, they may experience marked feelings of unreality. They often believe that their inmost thoughts are open to the inspection of others and even that their thoughts are under others' control. They are usually subject to delusions, including paranoia—a complex and systematic set of false beliefs in which patients are convinced either that they are being persecuted or that they are much grander than they really are (for example, the belief that they are Napoleon). Hallucinations are common, and they may hear voices commenting on their every thought and action. They may be unable to follow any coherent train of thought, and have inconsequential and meaningless speech. They tend to seize on irrelevant aspects of a situation or take everything literally: in one hospital there was a door bearing the notice 'Please knock', and one schizophrenic patient carefully knocked every time he passed down the corridor. The outward display of emotion may be flattened and shallow or emotions may be trivial or inappropriate; the patient may giggle meaninglessly or laugh when he hears his father has died. In some cases, artificial poses of the body are maintained for long periods of time and the patient may sink into stupor: this may alternate with severe but pointless spells of excitement.

The affective disorders are marked by abnormal moods either of extreme depression or elation and excitement or of an alternation between the two. The terminology is thoroughly confusing. Manic-depression was (and sometimes still is) used to refer to three distinct kinds of illness. In 'unipolar manic-depression' patients have episodes of mania or depression but not both, while in 'bipolar manic-depression' they have both kinds of mood swings. Nowadays, the term manic-depression is sometimes used to refer only to cases in which the patient swings between the two extremes, but I shall use it to mean any severe disorder of mood whether bipolar or unipolar. When manic-depression causes completely disturbed thought processes, with accompanying delusions or hallucinations, the illness is classified as a psychosis. Usually patients who are sometimes psychotic also experience milder attacks of depression or mania, in which they remain in touch with the external world. Psychotic affective disorder is much rarer than the milder kinds.

The account of my own depressions conveys some idea of what they are like: although they were not psychotic, they were agonizing enough. Apart from feelings of utter despondency, worthlessness, guilt, inability to concentrate and loss of self-regard, depression may be accompanied by extreme agitation and anxiety. In addition there is usually a loss of appetite for both food and sex and there are difficulties in sleeping. In some depressives, thought-processes and bodily movements are greatly slowed down: they may adopt a glazed facial expression, and reply to questions only after a long interval and then in an almost inaudible voice. They may have delusional ideas and think that they are shunned by others, or in extreme poverty: if depression lasts long enough such ideas may come to correspond to reality.

I have also given a description from my own case of what it is like to be pathologically elated. I underwent periods of hypomania (mild mania, though the term 'mild' is misleading), but in psychotic mania, behaviour can be much more extreme. Patients may exhibit flights of ideas connected by only superficial links such as the sound of a word, which may produce a pun or a rhyme resulting in a complete change in the direction of thought. The excitement may be so uncontrollable that speech becomes wholly incoherent, and terrifying hallucinations may occur, such as those of Kay Jamison which were described earlier.

There has been considerable controversy over how to divide affective illness into sub-categories: although many hundreds of papers on this problem have been published, no general agreement has been reached and the consensus of opinion changes almost from year to year. It is however, agreed that bipolar manic-depression, with its spells of depression alternating with mania or hypomania differs radically from unipolar. Apart from its different symptoms, the evidence for its being a discrete diagnostic category comes from three sources. First, there is a strong genetic predisposing factor—there is usually a high incidence of manic and depressive episodes in the ancestors and other blood relatives of patients suffering from clear-cut bipolar illness. Second, the levels of certain substances in the spinal canals of bipolar manic-depressives differ from those of both normal people and of unipolar depressives: this indicates that the biochemistry of the brain also differs. Third, a particular drug (lithium) can prevent the recurrence of bipolar illness but has little if any effect on other forms of depression.

Within the unipolar group of depressive illnesses there are many different possible ways of categorizing. Until recently it was common to divide them into endogenous and reactive depression it was assumed that the latter was set off by a personal misfortune such as bankruptcy or the loss of a spouse, whereas the former arose spontaneously, probably through constitutionally determined fluctuations in brain biochemistry. It was also thought that endogenous depressives have difficulty in sleeping in the morning whereas the reactive depressive finds it hard to get to sleep at night and that unlike reactive depressives, endogenous ones feel less depressed later in the day than in the morning. Some psychiatrists believe that antidepressant drugs are more effective for endogenous than for reactive depressions. Despite a vast amount of research it is still not established with any certainty that there is a consistent difference in the symptoms of those placed in each diagnostic category. Furthermore, so-called endogenous depression seems to be as often triggered by a personal misfortune as reactive depression. My own psychiatrist told me: 'It does not matter whether we call your illness reactive depression or endogenous depression, the treatment is the same.'

All the kinds of depression so far discussed are known as primary depressions. Secondary depression is caused by other forms of mental disorder, such as schizophrenia, or obsessive-compulsive disorder. In addition, it frequently accompanies or follows some kinds of physical illness such as viral pneumonia, influenza and glandular fever (mononucleosis).

Depression is also a normal consequence of severe misfortune like bereavement, divorce or loss of a job. Provided the person recovers in reasonable time and provided it does not degenerate into the incapacitating illness from which I suffered, the misery attendant on personal misfortune is not regarded as a disorder or illness. In practice, the borderline between 'normal' and pathological depression warranting treatment is hard to draw, despite the existence of clear-cut cases like my own where the reaction was out of all proportion to the triviality of the precipitating event. In fact, it is becoming increasingly common, particularly in the US, for people suffering merely from grief to seek psychotherapy or drug treatment. Oddly, the standard story that grief helps one overcome severe loss, like the death of a spouse, is not upheld by recent research, which suggests that the less one grieves and the more one distracts oneself, the faster recovery takes place. I have already called attention to the difference between sadness and depression. About 8% of the population will suffer a serious depression at some point in life: women are more prone to the disorder than are men.

* * *

As we have seen, the distinction between psychosis and neurosis depends on how far patients remain in touch with reality and have insight into their own condition. Apart from the less severe forms of manic-depression, the most commonly recognized categories of neurosis are as follows.

Most of the mentally ill suffer from anxiety, but there is a sub-group in whom anxiety or fear is the dominant symptom. Anxiety disorders can be broken down into six types. In 'generalized anxiety disorder' the patient suffers severe anxiety not caused by any current stress: the condition tends to be long lasting.

The victims of 'panic disorder' experience repeated attacks of total panic, with pounding heart, a tight feeling at the bottom of the throat, laboured breathing, and so on. They feel extreme terror and may believe they are about to die.

In 'simple phobias', the person has an unreasonable and intense dread of approaching a given situation or object. Many otherwise normal people, particularly women and children, have mild circumscribed phobias. Some of the commonest are fear of blood, worms, snakes, insects, mice, thunderstorms, public speaking, air travel, and taking examinations. A severe phobia can be completely disabling. One girl on my ward, pale-faced and thin, had developed a terror of spiders. She was in continual distress, and so great was her fear that wherever she went she clutched to her bosom a tin of insecticide. She was unable to go to bed at night for fear of finding spiders in her room, and would tearfully entreat the nurses to enter it before her to make sure it was spider-free. She lived in a private Hell populated only by spiders, but as far as could be ascertained she had never had an unfortunate encounter with one.

'Agoraphobia' is usually counted as a different disorder from the simple phobias. It is, like them, much more common in women than men. Unlike other phobias, it is usually accompanied by panic attacks. Sufferers will not venture into public places, not so much because they are afraid of them but because they are afraid of having a panic attack in public: they do not want to create a scene and they may be afraid nobody will come to their assistance. They prefer to stick to the security of their homes. Agoraphobia is usually accompanied by general anxiety and by depression. It is not clear whether there is always a precipitating event, but here is one not atypical case. A middle-aged woman was out shopping when she found herself violently attracted to a man standing next to her. The man made an indecent proposition; she panicked and ran out of the shop in distress. Subsequently, she developed a phobia of entering any shop, and found that the nearer she approached a shop the more terror she felt. She naturally avoided going near shops. Every time she withdrew from their vicinity she became calmer: hence, since it made her feel better, her avoidance of shops was rewarded and she learned to stay further and further away from them until eventually she could not venture out of her house.

'Obsessive-compulsive disorder' also involves extreme anxiety it can be illustrated by another patient on my ward. He was a pleasant but shy and soft-spoken man of about 45. He muttered to himself, usually about things he feared he might have left undone or articles that he might have left out of place. It took him several hours to get into bed: he could not stop himself from checking the exact position in which he had left each item of clothing, and as soon as he tried to climb into bed he would feel over and over again a compulsion to go back and check in case he had overlooked anything the previous time. Many obsessive-compulsives are terrified of dirt and, like Lady Macbeth, repeatedly wash their hands. Normal people often develop annoying but not disabling compulsive rituals. They may systematically avoid walking on the cracks in the paving stones, or feel that ill luck will befall them if they fail to tie up their left shoe before the right.

The final anxiety disorder was recently given the name 'post-traumatic stress disorder' (PTSD): in the First World War it was called 'shell shock', in the Second 'combat neurosis', but it is now recognized that anyone who has experienced a horrific event may suffer from it, particularly if they have an existing disorder such as depression or some form of anxiety. They become extremely anxious, and have difficulty sleeping. They may dwell on the details of the traumatic event and have severe nightmares about it. Some try to put it out of their mind: they may avoid encountering anything connected with it, and appear numb with flattened emotions and an inability to take an interest in others. PTSD appears to be on the increase, particularly in America where vast sums can be obtained through suing when the calamity that set off the disorder was caused by negligence. Amazingly, even in Britain policemen who assisted at the Hillsborough football disaster, where many spectators were crushed to death, sued the authorities for the PTSD caused by this event.

* * *

Thanks to Freud, perhaps the most famous example of neurosis is 'hysteria'. In 'conversion hysteria', some bodily organ fails to function for psychological not physical reasons, or the patient may feel aches or tingles that have no organic basis. Such patients may develop paralysis of a limb or contorted postures; they may even have seizures that mimic those of an epileptic. They may also develop partial or complete blindness or deafness or lack of sensation in a limb. The principal way of distinguishing such conversion symptoms from similar symptoms caused by organic damage to the nervous system is that, in hysteria, the symptoms correspond to the patient's ideas about anatomy. The patient may develop total lack of feeling in the area covered by her (most hysterics are women) gloves or stockings, but the region of skin involved was thought not to correspond to a part served by a single nerve that might have suffered injury. A related disorder is 'psychalgia'—feeling pain in a part of the body with no physical cause.

In a further kind of hysteria, 'dissociative states', the patient's consciousness may be limited to a single realm of experience. She may walk round in a trance paying no attention to the external world. It is common for patients subsequently to have no memory for what occurred in such fugue-like states. Some patients may forget large segments of their lives to the extent of wandering off, unaware of their own names and previous identities.

Most of Freud's patients were hysterics and it is often said that hysteria is much less common today. In fact in a lifetime about five women in a thousand and rather fewer men will be diagnosed as hysterics. Moreover, many of the symptoms of hysteria can be caused by brain damage and advances in our understanding of the brain and our investigative methods make it much more likely that neurological causes of hysteria-like symptoms will be correctly diagnosed today than in Freud's time. It is now known that even the classic symptom of hysteria— numbness in the region of skin covered by a glove—can be caused by carpal tunnel syndrome, in which the nerves are pinched as they run through the wrist. Considerable misdiagnoses still occur: one study of patients diagnosed as hysterics found that over 62% of them had neurological damage, which was probably the cause of their symptoms. In addition, it should be remembered that the form psychiatric symptoms take is to a considerable extent dependent on fashion (as will be demonstrated in connection with multiple personality). The young middle-class women in Vienna who were Freud's patients had plenty of opportunity to copy one another's symptoms.

The hysterical defects in sensation or memory have no apparent physical cause, but psychological problems can produce genuine physical illnesses, such as peptic ulcers. Over-ambitious men (Type As) who are always watching the clock and are impatient of delay are thought to render themselves prone to coronary disease, though the evidence is somewhat conflicting. There is, however, no question that prolonged stress renders people liable to allergies, such as asthma, and through its effects on the immune system to infections including 'flu and the common cold. Such illnesses are known as psychosomatic—there is a clear chain from the psychological cause, through a physical reaction like acid in the digestive system to the ultimate physical symptom.

Like hysteria, neurasthenia appears to have been commoner in Victorian women than it is today. It is characterized by extreme lassitude and irritability and is often accompanied by headaches. It may have been replaced by mylencephalic encephalitis—ME or 'yuppie flu', now renamed 'chronic fatigue syndrome'. It is not known whether this condition, which affects predominantly the moneyed classes, has psychological or physical causes: a report by the Royal College of Physicians in Britain recently stated that it almost certainly had no physical cause, much to the annoyance of those suffering from the disorder who would prefer to have a physical rather than a psychiatric illness, presumably because of the stigma attached to the latter. As will be shown, it is possible that this illness and many others are modern forms of mass hysteria, which have simply been given a more specific name.

Eating disorders appear to be becoming more prevalent among young women. I have already described an anorexic patient on my ward. The sufferer is unable to eat and may starve herself to death. Some are unable to keep food down: they often have extreme fluctuations in weight and may at one time have been obese. The illness is usually accompanied by amenorrhoea and severe depression or anxiety. It is possible that there is some underlying physical pathology. The condition is very hard to alleviate, though it sometimes remits spontaneously. Another eating disorder is bulimia in which the patient gorges herself periodically, subsequently making herself vomit up the food.

* * *

It is usual to distinguish 'personality disorders' from neuroses, but the dividing line is difficult to draw. In general, they are less marked by anxiety or depression, and behaviour is less bizarre. They are attributed to those who are excessively sensitive, too aggressive, too gloomy, too exuberant, too shy. very aloof, over-conscientious, too dependent on others or too passive. Indeed one could almost define personality disorder as the possession of any trait of which the psychiatrist disapproves.

Personality disorder should perhaps be regarded as lying midway between normality and an incapacitating neurosis, but many psychiatrists would like to dispense with this category. Some personality disorders have been given high sounding names, such as 'schizoid'—a person who is emotionally cold, withdrawn, and incapable of forming normal social relations. Many people, particularly journalists, attracted by the flavour of the term, misuse it, believing that it means schizophrenic. Psychiatrists do agree on one category of personality disorder—psychopathy or sociopathy, now renamed 'anti-social personality disorder'. As this name implies people with this disorder are antisocial and frequently criminal; characteristically they are not restrained from illegal acts by any fear of punishment. This diagnosis is only given if antisocial tendencies, like lying, theft, vandalism, or truancy, have been present since early adolescence. The disorder was recognized in the nineteenth century when people who were 'irredeemably depraved' were said to be suffering from 'moral insanity'. Psychopaths do not respond to treatment.

Taking any form of illegal and addictive drug is treated as a mental disorder when it is a danger to the person's health or welfare. Alcoholism is only recognized as a disorder when so much is drunk that the drinker is damaging their own physical or mental health or is disturbing their relations with others.

* * *

Exact figures on the frequency of different kinds of mental illness are hard to obtain: they will in any case vary with changes in diagnostic fashion. A survey undertaken in London found that in the year 1962, fourteen people in every hundred consulted their family doctor at least once for some form of mental illness. Over twice as many women as men consulted for this reason: since half the patients complained of disturbances lasting for over a year, most of the problems were not of a trivial nature. Nine out of each hundred individuals surveyed were diagnosed as neurotic.

About 3% of the population will experience a psychosis at some period of their lives. Depression and anxiety account for 80% of chronic neurosis, and over a lifetime about 15% of people will suffer severely from one or both. Nearly three times as many women as men suffer from unipolar depression, but bipolar manic-depression is equally common in men and women. About 3% of chronic neurotics have phobias or obsessive-compulsive disorders. Put like this, it sounds rather few, but in absolute numbers it represents a formidable total of human suffering. In Vermont, two per thousand members of the population were found to be suffering from severely disabling phobias, of whom less than half were receiving treatment. If we generalize these figures, it would mean that in the USA alone there are at any one time over 400,000 people whose lives are crippled by a phobia. Amazingly, 3% of the population, both in Britain and the US, are psychopaths and almost all of them are male.

Although different estimates are made, depending on the criteria applied, in countries like Sweden, Britain and the USA between 13 and 30% of the population will at some time in their lives undergo a neurotic breakdown and over 4% at least one psychotic episode. A report from the American National Advisory Health Council estimates that in any one year over 20% of the population has one or more neurotic episodes, while nearly 3% will have a severe mental illness, such as schizophrenia. Over a lifetime 8% will suffer severe depression, 1.5% schizophrenia, 1% bipolar manic-depression and 19% addiction to drugs or alcohol.

There is one thing on which all investigators of the frequency of mental illness agree. When its prevalence is estimated by screening members of the population rather than by using figures based on the number in treatment, it is always found that a vast number of cases, indeed the majority, go untreated. Four massive North American studies, each of which screened about 10,000 people to assess their mental health, produced results that are roughly in agreement. The first two were conducted in the 1960s, one in Manhattan, the other in a rural area of Nova Scotia, while the more recent ones, undertaken in 1984 and 1994, each took place in several different towns in the US. The early studies found that about 20% of the population were seriously impaired by mental disorder, while as few as 18% were judged to have good mental health; the remaining 62% exhibited at least one usually severe neurotic or psychotic symptoms. The more recent studies yielded similar results. In each it was calculated that in a lifetime about one person in three would suffer at least once a seriously disabling mental illness and many would suffer more. It is a matter for debate how severe a mental disorder should be in order to merit clinical treatment, but such figures give some idea of the misery and loss of effective functioning attributable to mental problems.

Diagnosis

The classification of mental illness is a furiously contested topic. Although all classification must be based in the first instance on symptoms, its main point is to decide the most helpful treatment. In physical illness, classifying according to the causes of the illness, for example, a bacterial infection, a vitamin deficiency or a tumour, normally indicates what treatment should be given. We still have little certain knowledge of the causes of most psychiatric disorders, and only in recent times has it become apparent that different constellations of symptoms respond differentially to different methods of treatment. Hence, classification is largely based on the clinical discovery that a particular group of symptoms tend to occur together and are associated with a particular life history. Diagnostic fashion varies from country to country and within a country from one psychiatrist to another: it also changes over time. Guidelines suitable for international use have been laid down by the World Health Organization: the tenth revision of its International Classification of Diseases (ICD-10) appeared in 1993. The US is guided by its own Diagnostic and Statistical Manual (DSM) of which a major revision (DSM-IV) appeared in 1993; British psychiatrists tend to use DSM rather than ICD.

Successive editions of DSM have radically changed their nomenclature, possibly influenced in part by political correctness: 'mental retardation' is in, 'mental deficiency' is out and the term 'learning difficulties' is to some extent taking over from mental retardation in diagnostic usage; the word 'neurosis' is no longer used, though admittedly it covered an exceptionally wide range of disorders; 'mental illness', which carries considerable stigma is abjured, with 'mental disorder' being substituted. Moreover, each new edition of the manual drops some categories of disorder, while—with the increasing en-croachment of psychiatry on human affairs—adding others. Homosexuality was counted as a mental disorder by DSM until 1968 when it was removed from the manual, only to be replaced in 1980 by 'ego-dystonic homosexuality' which refers to homosexuals who are distressed by their proclivities. This term was in turn abandoned in 1993. In that edition there is a special category for 'exhibitionists' but none for rapists.

The boundary between mental illness and other behaviour is hard to draw. Both rape and exhibitionism should only be classified as a mental disorder when the person has an irresistible compulsion to commit these acts. I have described my own compulsion to reveal my infidelities to my wife: I could not possibly have resisted it and have never suffered anything similar before or since, I am in no doubt that it was part of my illness. How to decide whether someone who exhibits himself in a public park does so from a compulsion or voluntarily is a difficult question, which I shall discuss later. DSM lists as disorders a variety of sexual practices that are common: for example, fetishism, that is deriving sexual excitement from a part of the body not connected with sex such as a foot or from an object, like fishnet stockings. Fetishism would only be diagnosed where it caused distress either to the fetishist or to his partner (most fetishists are men). Among other newly introduced disorders are over 200 caused by substance abuse. These can be either long-lasting 'withdrawal symptoms' including psychoses or temporary 'intoxication' or related side-effects, such as "alcohol-induced sexual dysfunction', a condition recognized by Shakespeare himself. In pursuance of political correctness, even 'nicotine-related disorder' is now included.

* * *

As an example of the difficulty of agreeing on diagnostic categories, consider schizophrenia. Until recently this diagnosis was about twice as common in the United States as in Britain, and the diagnosis of affective illness was correspondingly less common. When a team of British and American research psychiatrists agreed with one another on a set of explicit criteria for diagnosing schizophrenia, and used them to assess patients admitted to hospitals in New York and in London, there was good agreement between the diagnoses made by the different teams. Moreover, the difference in the percentage of patients in London and New York diagnosed as schizophrenic largely disappeared. Many of the New York patients thought by their own doctors to be schizophrenic were not so classified by the research workers, but were diagnosed as manic-depressive. The group of patients admitted in New York with a diagnosis of schizophrenia but reclassified as manic-depressive is of particular interest. It was found that they had many more relatives who had suffered from manic-depressive disorder than the patients who were agreed by both hospital and research psychiatrists to be schizophrenic. Of more practical importance, they were not helped by being given drugs widely used in the treatment of schizophrenia, but they were helped by lithium, the most efficacious drug for preventing episodes of bipolar manic-depression. This is a nice example of the way in which refining diagnostic categories can improve the treatment of the mentally ill.

The story does not end there. Over the last ten years, research workers have distinguished schizophrenia with positive symptoms from schizophrenia with negative symptoms. Among the positive symptoms are severe disturbance of thought-processes including delusions and hallucinations. The negative symptoms are withdrawal, passiveness, and lack of initiative. Schizophrenia with positive symptoms tends to start suddenly, while that with negative symptoms has a slower onset. The prognosis for the former is better than for the latter, although both kinds of symptom may appear in the same person, patients with positive symptoms tend to respond to the drugs most commonly used for schizophrenia whereas the other group does not, but the distinction is not included in the latest edition of the American Diagnostic Manual (DSM IV) despite the fact that it is important for treatment, as we shall see. We cannot be sure that schizophrenia is a single entity. In contrast, DSM now divides manic-depressive disorder into no fewer than forty-eight categories, most of which have no relevance for treatment.

* * *

Several different methods are used in diagnosing mental illness. The most obvious is an interview by a psychiatrist in which the life history and current condition of the patient is recorded. Instead of such an open-ended interview, the psychiatrist may use a 'structured interview' in which the questions are prepared in advance by research workers. Depending on the answers the patient gives, the psychiatrist may be instructed to branch to different sets of questions, zeroing in on the information needed to make a diagnosis. Such schedules of questions are often scored automatically so that no clinical judgement is needed. A second method is to ask the patients themselves to complete an inventory of questions. For example, some of the questions may probe how far they are suspicious, aloof, guarded, sensitive and prone to worry: a high score on these questions would suggest paranoia. Finally, there are methods of assessment invented by psychologists, known as 'projective tests'. The most famous, or perhaps one should say infamous, is the Rorschach. Patients are shown an inkblot and asked what they see in it. The idea is that they will project their own unconscious worries on to the inkblot and that their condition can be diagnosed from their responses. For example, they might see one part of an inkblot as their brother's face with a wicked smile, whereupon their psychiatrist would infer that they were jealous of their brother—'sibling rivalry' as it is called. In fact it has been shown that the standard method of scoring the results of the Rorschach is useless —the diagnoses bear no relation to those given by other methods.

Despite these findings, in the USA tens of thousands of Rorschach tests are still administered every year by psychologists and psychiatrists, a prime example of human folly.

Even when psychiatrists are trained on the use of a diagnostic manual, agreement on the correct diagnosis is poor. According to one authority, 'Experienced diagnosticians using DSM-II . . . found they could not agree with one another. In some instances inter-judge reliability was so low as to make a diagnostic category functionally useless.' The same authors point out that more recent studies on DSM-III-R (1987) were so badly flawed as to be completely unreliable. Psychiatrists were not prevented from discussing their own diagnoses with others so that the diagnoses compared were not independent. Moreover, each psychiatrist was allowed to make several different diagnoses which increases the probability of his making at least one that is the same as his colleague's. Finally, if two psychiatrists made different specific diagnoses that came under the same more general disorder, they were deemed to have made the same diagnosis. Thus if one diagnosed 'panic disorder' and the other 'obsessive compulsive disorder', they would be counted as agreeing with one another since both are examples of anxiety disorder. Although the dice were, therefore, heavily loaded in the psychiatrists' favour, agreement between them was poor.

Psychologists and sociologists have had the bright idea of pretending to be mentally ill and having themselves admitted as 'pseudo-patients' to psychiatric hospitals in order to observe what is going on. The most famous of such studies was undertaken by Professor Rosenhan of Stanford University in the early 1970s. He and seven collaborators set out to gain admission to psychiatric wards. They presented themselves at eight different hospitals complaining that they had been hearing voices. When asked what the voices said, they replied that they were often unclear but they seemed to be saying 'empty', 'hollow' and 'thud'. They assumed that the interviewing psychiatrist would interpret this to mean that their lives were empty and hollow. Throughout the remainder of their initial psychiatric interview and during the whole of the rest of their stay in hospital they behaved completely normally. They gave the psychiatrist detailed and accurate accounts of their life histories, including their relationships with their parents, their immediate family and their friends. All eight were admitted to psychiatric wards, and all but one were given the diagnosis 'schizophrenia'.

Whilst in hospital, they behaved normally except that they took detailed notes on everything that happened: at first they did so in secret, in order not to arouse suspicion, but when they found that their 'compulsive writing behaviour' (to quote from the case notes) was accepted as part of their illness, they wrote out their observations in public. Each pseudo-patient remained in hospital until the psychiatrist agreed to their discharge: their average stay was 19 days, with a range of 7 to 52 days. None of the hospital staff saw through the deception, though about one-third of their fellow-patients did. Indeed, on discharge their case notes were marked not 'recovered' but 'schizophrenia in remission'.

Their experiences show that it is difficult for psychiatrists and other hospital staff to distinguish between the mentally ill and the malingerer. This is scarcely surprising. In the case of voluntary admissions, it is understandable that psychiatrists should err on the side of admitting people who do not need to be admitted: the risk of suicide must be for ever present in their minds, and with the exception of a few malingerers, and the occasional research worker, it is inconceivable that anyone should voluntarily seek admission to a psychiatric ward unless he were in a dire mental condition. What is surprising is that, even after observing the pseudo-patients for up to 52 days in hospital, no psychiatrist changed their initial diagnosis, despite the fact that throughout their stay they presented no symptoms whatever, and claimed that they felt fine and no longer heard voices.

Professionals are often unwilling to acknowledge their own defects. At one American hospital, a computer program was devised that on the basis of patients' answers to a set of questions classified them on admission as psychotic or neurotic. As judged by the final diagnosis made after the patients had spent some time in hospital, the program was more accurate than were the psychiatrists who interviewed patients on admission. So great is professional pride that the program was shortly abandoned.

* * *

As an example of a diagnostic fad, consider multiple personality disorder, a condition in which the patient, usually a woman, exhibits two or more different personalities, one of which normally appears most frequently. The personalities tend to be very different, for example, one might be prim and another skittish. While in one personality the patient may not remember events that happened in another. The condition used to be extremely rare, so rare indeed that the diagnosis did not exist in the American Diagnostic Manual until it was added in 1980. At that time one of the diagnostic criteria was that 'each individual personality is complex and integrated with its own unique behaviour pattern and social relationships'. This stipulation was removed in 1987, thus considerably enlarging the number of people who could be diagnosed as 'multiples'.

Until 1973 there had been less than 100 known cases of this disorder in the whole world. Now there are tens—possibly hundreds —of thousands in the US, with whole hospitals devoted solely to their treatment. How can this be? Do American psychiatrists suffer from a form of mass hysteria? Has there been a sudden change in the symptomatology of their patients? Or are they merely finding what they are looking for?

It is likely that all three elements have played a part in the surge of multiples. There is massive evidence that people find what they seek. It is not so long ago since psychiatrists were convinced that the now wholly discredited insulin therapy (reducing the patient to a coma by insulin injections) alleviated schizophrenia. When multiple personalities were comparatively rare, discovering a new one would raise the psychiatrist's prestige, for it would merit an article in a learned journal. The diagnosis snowballed, but it also affected the patient's symptoms. Because the patient is always anxious to please her doctors and therapists, she is likely to respond positively to leading questions put by them in their search for multiples. Indeed, tape recordings of sessions with patients reveal that some psychiatrists have browbeaten their patients into acknowledging that they have more than one personality. Some American psychiatrists even use hypnotism to induce a trance, which they can then interpret as the appearance of a different alternative personality ('alter'), although it is known that false ideas can be readily implanted under hypnosis.

Moreover, in the US from the 1950s onwards, multiple personality received vast publicity—in the press, in books, on television and in films. In 1954 the book *The Three Faces of Eve,* and the film based on it, caused a stir. Over the next few years the number of 'multiples' in the US began to rise, but it was not until nearly twenty years later that a psychiatrist, called Cornelia Wilbur, collaborated in the publication of an even more influential book about a multiple called Sybil. Her technical account of the case had been rejected by medical journals because at that time few psychiatrists took multiple personality seriously. She therefore allowed a journalist, Schreiber, to publish a sensational popular account of the case, which claimed that in over two thousand hours of therapy, she had extracted from Sybil horrifying details of sexual abuse suffered as a child: she had used hypnotism and sodium amytal (a sedative drug), although neither technique helps people to recover buried memories. In due course it was accepted by many psychiatrists that the cause of multiple personality was child abuse. The proposed mechanism by which abuse produces multiples is wrapped in gobbledygook: the child develops different alters 'in order to compartmentalize overwhelming affects and memories'. The idea that multiple personalities were a result of child abuse intensified the search for them, since every diagnosed multiple provided one more instance of child abuse, much to the satisfaction of those engaged in the witch-hunt for child abusers.

An immensely popular self-help book, *The Courage to Heal,* brought the alleged link between sexual abuse and multiple personality home to the general public. It encouraged a frenzy of self-examination, leading people to believe that they had suffered child abuse and to diagnose themselves as multiple personalities. It also outlined ideas for self-treatment. The diagnoses of the malady rose from a stream to a torrent. Consciously or unconsciously, people copy the actions of others: not only does the suicide rate go up after a suicide is shown on television, but the method of committing suicide is copied. The epidemic of multiples may be compared with that of people claiming to have experienced Satanic abuse: over half the mental patients in one hospital in the US said they had taken part in

Satanic rituals, including torture, human sacrifice and cannibalism, at a time when these practices were much featured in the media. Three separate studies in Britain and America failed to find a single case of Satanic rituals. Even less plausible—if that were possible—were claims made by a similar number of patients that they had been kidnapped by aliens and sexually assaulted.

People had strong motives for assuming multiple personalities. They gained attention, not merely from psychiatrists but from the media, and the disorder could be used as an excuse for misdeeds. How was it possible to punish one personality for a crime committed by another? This plea successfully exculpated, on the grounds of diminished responsibility, one multiple charged with rape: it has also been used several times in the US as a defence against murder.

In fact one study found that multiples had not suffered sexual abuse more frequently than patients with other mental disorders, such as hysteria. Again, it was found that whereas 46% of female multiples claim to have been sexually abused (including indecent exposure which most women experience at least once), the corresponding figure for a control group of women with pelvic pain was 64%. There is therefore no evidence to link multiple personality to sexual abuse.

It was not long before someone invented a questionnaire to diagnose multiple personality, the 'Dissociative Experience Scale' (DES), which was completed by suspected multiples and used to screen them. An investigation in six hospitals concluded suavely that 'the DES data collected in this study were unrelated to the diagnostic process"; in other words, although the scale was and still is widely used, it is useless.

Two psychiatrists argued that because of the publicity, one cannot be sure of any diagnosis of multiple personality made after 1953: patients might merely be copycats, and psychiatrists too influenced by fashion. They therefore examined all diagnoses before that year for which there was adequate documentation. They concluded that some so-called multiples were in fact suffering from bipolar manic-depression, a condition in which the personality differs vastly from one phase of the illness to another; in other cases, the patients' psychiatrists had actually told them that they exhibited completely different personalities and even when they denied it pressed them to give a new Christian name for their 'alter'; many of the patients had brain damage; others appear to have fantasized when children that they were someone else and merely recovered this fantasy as adults. The article concluded that, 'It is likely that MPD [multiple personality disorder] never occurs as a spontaneous persistent natural event in adults.' The tenacity with which some psychiatrists cling to unsubstantiated myths is equalled only by that of businessmen, financiers and politicians. The epidemic of multiples in the States has not occurred in Britain. Although some psychiatrists there have begun to diagnose the condition, most have been sceptical of this bizarre import from America.

I have used multiple personality to illustrate the problems of diagnosis, but it has to be admitted that the example is extreme. There are other forms of mental disorder that are limited to one society. In South-west Asia, some men exhibit acute anxiety because they are convinced that their penis will retract into their abdomen *(Koro)*. In Malaysia there is a disorder called Amok in which men start by brooding and then become for no apparent reason extremely violent, often using weapons. In Arctic hysteria, Eskimo women tear off their clothes, scream, cry and run wildly about in the snow, endangering their lives through cold. These are almost certainly cultural variants of respectively phobic, schizophrenic and hysterical disorders: they suggest not that different societies have different forms of mental disorder, but that the way a disorder expresses itself depends on cultural beliefs. No man could worry about his penis retracting unless the concept were current in his society, anymore than Westerners could become anxious about the prospect of going to Hell if Hell had never been invented.

However this may be, it is clear that diagnosis is uncertain and subject to fashion. Yet another example is that the diagnosis of attention-deficit hyperactivity disorder is more than ten times as common in the US as in Britain. This recently identified disability (originally called 'minimal brain damage', a term discarded when no damage could be found) is said to occur in children who are extremely restless, over-active, distractible and unable to pay attention. The American tendency to diagnose this condition so frequently is almost certainly a fad, possibly strengthened by the fees psychiatrists are paid to treat such children—usually with Ritalin, an amphetamine-like drug whose long-term effects are not known. Finally, there is always the danger of ascribing symptoms to a psychiatric disorder when they are in fact caused by brain damage. This mistake is particularly likely to be made for hysteria: as explained in the last chapter, 62% of diagnosed hysterics in fact have brain damage.

It may well be that hysteria is just as common today as in the past: it simply takes a different form—or forms—in the late twentieth century from that in earlier times. Multiple personality, chronic fatigue syndrome, belief in having been abducted by aliens or sexually abused and possibly Gulf War syndrome, anorexia and bulimia could all be hysterical in origin. Epidemics of mass hysteria are particularly likely nowadays because the media not only sensationalize such maladies but spread information (or disinformation) about them far and wide. This thesis has been ably put forward in a recent book by Elaine Showalter. It should be added that whether these disorders are of physical or psychological origin, does not alter the genuine suffering of those who have them.

Although then the classification of disorders is often wrong, it is necessary: it will lead—and indeed has led (consider the example of manic-depression and schizophrenia)—to better understanding and treatment of mental disorders, but it can only become a science when we know more about the causes of mental disorder, a topic to which I now turn.

13

The origins of mental illness

Despite over a hundred years of thought and research devoted to the problem, the origins of most mental illness remain obscure. The possible causes include physical pathology in the brain, heredity, constitutional defects caused by physical trauma or infection in the womb, nutritional defects, poisons, dangerous drugs, the unnatural mode of living imposed by modern society, the stress of poverty, maternal deprivation, childhood trauma, and personal misfortune. These factors are not alternatives: some could and do operate simultaneously, and they play different roles in the aetiology of different kinds of mental illness.

* * *

Although all mental illness must be caused by abnormalities in the brain, it is important to distinguish two very different kinds. The first is the formation of unusual connections between nerve cells brought about by faulty learning. To take a crude example, a woman might learn that she can gain attention by exhibiting hysterical symptoms and hence become a genuine hysteric. Direct study of the brain would not reveal this kind of abnormality for it would involve small undetectable local changes in the connections between different nerve cells. The other kind of abnormality is on a larger scale: I shall refer to it as 'gross malfunctioning of the brain'. It can be caused by too much or too little activity in a particular region or regions of the brain or pathological changes in the activity of one or more neurotransmitters, the substances that pass messages from one nerve cell to another. Improvements in techniques for studying the brain, including several kinds of brain scan and sophisticated biochemical assays, enable us to detect some kinds of gross malfunctioning, either while the person is alive, or sometimes at post mortem. Moreover, if an illness can be alleviated by a drug, that is presumptive evidence that it is caused by gross malfunctioning of the brain, for there is no known drug that can improve behaviour and mental functioning in normal people except over very short periods.

Where a genetic factor increases the predisposition to mental illness, it must do so by producing a gross abnormality in the brain. It is not, however, true that an abnormality can only be produced through inheritance. It can be caused by poisons, illegal drugs, tumours, and probably by psychological trauma or stress, which are known to increase the activity of certain biochemicals (corticosteroids) which affect the brain. The interaction between environmental events and brain biochemistry is ill understood. As an example, it is likely that depressing events produce the symptoms of depression only in those who are innately susceptible and the depression so induced in turn affects the centres in the brain that can produce depression, so that a vicious circle results.

There is now conclusive evidence, set out in the previous chapter, that both schizophrenia and bipolar manic-depressive disorder are caused by gross malfunctioning of the brain. Both can be ameliorated by the appropriate drugs, both have a strong genetic component, and both are associated with gross biochemical abnormalities. One recent and exciting finding has revealed an area of the brain whose activity directly correlates with depression and mania. Activity in nerve cells in a region of the prefrontal cortex was measured. It was significantly lower than normal both in unipolar and bipolar depressed patients and it was higher in bouts of mania (all the patients studied had a family history of depression). It was already known that damage to this area (caused, for example, by a stroke or a tumour) tends to produce flattened emotion, particularly in interactions with other people.

Until recently, it was thought that most neurosis was not caused by gross malfunctioning of the brain, but recent findings suggest that two disorders, previously classified as neuroses, are actually the result of gross abnormalities. Several studies suggest that obsessive-compulsive disorder (OCD) is caused by abnormal functioning of a particular area of the brain, namely part of the basal ganglia which are situated just below the cortex. There are five lines of evidence. First, parts of this area show abnormally high activity in obsessive compulsives. Second, OCD tends to occur in people with known damage to the same area. Third, the disorder is ameliorated by drugs that increase the activity of a particular neurotransmitter, serotonin. Fourth, damage to this area can produce repetitive and excessive grooming in animals, which may be an analogue of OCD. Finally, the basal ganglia are involved in motor movements and the disorder appears to result from a defect in the motor system which leads to constant repetition of certain complex movements, like grooming or washing. This account does not explain one of the primary symptoms of OCD—the patients' declaration that the reason for the repetitive behaviour is that they are afraid they have not properly completed the task on which they are engaged: they repeat their actions to make sure everything is in order. My own explanation is that the patients have to explain to themselves why they are driven to repeat the action. They therefore confabulate an explanation, namely, that they are worried that they have left something undone.

Another recent report presented at a conference provides evidence that gross brain malfunction may also be the cause of anorexia. There is unusually high activity in certain regions of the brain, one of which is involved with vision: anorexics see themselves as fatter than they are and this is one of their reasons for not eating.

The findings are important in that they suggest that at least some so-called neuroses are caused not by faulty learning or bad upbringing but by gross pathology of the brain. With further refinements in our techniques for examining the brain and increasing our knowledge of it, we shall almost certainly discover that gross brain pathology is responsible for some other mental disorders.

* * *

One of the reasons why it is so difficult to tease out the causes of mental disorder is the interaction between one's genes and one's environment. Exactly the same genes may produce one result in one environment and a totally different result in another. If Ghandi had been British, it is unlikely that he would have become an Allied hero in the Second World War, whereas if Churchill had been Indian he might have been merely a rather outspoken rickshaw carrier. Nevertheless, there is increasing evidence for the importance of genes both in shaping personality and in producing a predisposition to specific mental illnesses.

Since identical twins have the same genes, one would expect that, if inheritance plays a part in producing schizophrenia, when one such twin has the disorder, the other will have it more frequently than it occurs in the population at large. In studies of twins in which one twin has an illness, the percentage of co-twins having the same illness is known as their 'concordance' for that illness. There have been over a dozen studies of schizophrenia in such identical twins and all agree that when one has the illness the chances of the other having it too are greatly increased—in fact it develops in about 50% (the "concordance") of co-twins; in non-identical twins and in pairs of ordinary brothers or sisters (who have half their genes in common), the corresponding figure is about 10%. Since only about 1 % of the general population are schizophrenic, anyone who has the same genes as a schizophrenic twin is fifty times as likely to develop the illness as somebody with no close schizophrenic relatives; anyone having half their genes in common with a schizophrenic relative is ten times as likely to become one. These studies suggest that schizophrenia has biological causes, a theory supported by recent findings: brain scans have revealed differences in the brains of schizophrenics from those of normal people. Among other abnormalities are more very rapid brain waves and changes in the size of the ventricles (cavities in the brain filled with fluid).

Studies in Denmark, where very complete records of adoption are kept, show that these figures are not produced by the twins having been brought up in the same (damaging) way. Adopted children whose *biological* mother is schizophrenic have an increased risk of schizophrenia (and of other psychiatric disorders). Moreover, the chance of developing schizophrenia is not increased by being adopted by a schizophrenic parent. It follows that genes play a major role in the development of schizophrenia. Another striking finding is that when one identical twin diagnosed as schizophrenic has spent at least two years in a mental hospital, 77% of the other member of the pair is also schizophrenic. One can ask why the figure is not 100 %. The answer is not known, but it suggests that the environment may play some role and indeed it is known that episodes of schizophrenia can be induced by personal misfortune in those with a predisposition to it. Studies of the parents of schizophrenics suggest that they have a slight tendency to be unstable and given to drug abuse, but these traits could be caused by their having some of the genes that predispose their children to schizophrenia, rather than by the parents causing schizophrenia in their children through an inadequate upbringing. It has, however, been found that the environment can play a role in preventing relapse in schizophrenics discharged from hospital. Those living in a 'low-expressed emotion' family—that is one given neither to aggressive behaviour nor to being too solicitous towards the patient—are less likely to relapse. Patients living in such families do even better if they continue to take the appropriate drugs.

Since schizophrenics are likely to produce fewer viable children than others, the question arises of why the genes have survived. It may be that only a rare combination of the relevant genes produces schizophrenia and that some of these genes on their own favour the evolutionary fitness of the individual. A number of studies suggest that the children of a schizophrenic mother who are not themselves schizophrenic are exceptionally creative. According to one author, they have 'more colourful life histories', hold 'more creative jobs', and follow 'more imaginative hobbies'.

The use of the same techniques as those described for schizophrenia suggest that inheritance plays a considerable role in affective disorders. For severe bipolar disorders the concordance rate for identical twins is about 70%, regardless of whether they have been brought up together or apart. In first-degree relatives (siblings, parents or children), if one member has bipolar disorder the other has either bipolar or unipolar disorder in 20% of cases, suggesting that some of the genes involved in bipolar disorder can also cause unipolar illness. Inheritance seems to play a smaller part in severe unipolar depression, though its frequency is eight times that of the general population in adopted children, one of whose biological parents has suffered a major depression.

The strong hereditary element in both schizophrenia and affective illness has been confirmed by studies of human DNA, the material passed from parents to children that carries the blueprint for the next generation. For both schizophrenia and manic-depression local stretches of DNA containing a gene raising the disposition to develop the illness have been found. In the case of schizophrenia five such genes are thought to have been discovered on 5 of the 23 different chromosomes (the paired strands that carry the DNA). As to unipolar depression, not only has one of the individual genes responsible been identified, but the composition of its DNA sequence is known. It is clear from the pattern of inheritance that in both cases several genes are involved, and this makes it more difficult to isolate the individual genes.

As in the case of schizophrenia, it is puzzling that the genes for affective illness have survived—severe depression not only reduces the sex drive but deprives the patient of the energy and motivation to find a partner. In manic-depression, periods of hypomania may compensate for this. Many manic-depressives and unipolar depressives have been exceptionally creative in the arts: in a fascinating book, *Touched with Fire,* Kay Jamison lists about 250 poets, artists and musicians who have had affective disorder. An analysis of biographies of famous people in this century made by A. M. Ludwig comes to the same conclusion on the relationship between artistic creativity and manic depression. He found that in scientists on the other hand the incidence of mental illness was no higher than in the general population. Moreover, an exceptionally high percentage of famous people of all kinds have been sickly as children—perhaps that drove them back on their own resources. But why artistic ability should have survival value is unclear, unless those possessing it were at one time afforded special privileges by society.

It has been suggested that depression originated in our distant ancestors as a defence against being low in the dominance hierarchy (pecking order). Since depressed people withdraw into themselves, they are unlikely to offend more dominant individuals and therefore would escape attack. This theory is implausible if only because physical injury does not normally lead to depression. The evolutionary origins both of schizophrenia and affective disorder remain a mystery.

In the neuroses, heredity is less important. One study, however, found that identical twins had a 40% concordance for all anxiety disorders, while non-identical ones only had a 15% concordance. Moreover, the location of one gene (on chromosome 17) contributing to the tendency to feel anxious has been discovered. A recent study shows that obsessive-compulsive disorder, already known to involve gross malfunctioning of the brain, has a considerable genetic component.

There is evidence that inheritance is more important in determining criminal behaviour (which is allied to psychopathy) than is type of upbringing. In a study on adopted children diagnosed as having a conduct disorder (being antisocial), it was found that their biological parents tended to be antisocial but none of their adoptive parents were. In another study, adopted children did not commit more crimes if their adoptive father had a criminal record than if he had not, but they were twice as likely to commit crimes if their biological father was a criminal. It seems likely, then, that genetic factors play a role not only in mental illness (though their importance varies with the type and severity of the disorder), but in most human character traits. They are also known to influence personality and the tendency to become an alcoholic.

Since concordance between identical twins for mental illness is never complete, some other factor must be at work. It is not necessarily psychological: there is some evidence that mental illness can be caused by damage suffered in the womb, for instance through lack of oxygen or a virus infection, like 'flu.

Almost all human behaviour depends both on the environment to which the person is exposed and on their genetic inheritance, but nowadays, as a result of recent discoveries, most workers in the field stress the importance of genetics. Many, like Michael Rutter, place much less stress on the importance of the environment than they once did. Although he has modified his position, he still defends the importance of experience, for example, in an article that begins with an alarming piece of psychiatrese: 'The time has come for an explicit research focus on the forms of interplay between genes and environment and on how this interplay is involved in the causal mechanisms for the origins of antisocial behaviour and for its persistence or desistence over time.' Being translated this means that the interaction between genetic factors and the environment is an important topic for research, an unexceptional sentiment. A nice instance of such interaction is that the genetically fractious child may alter its environment by causing adverse reactions in its parents, which may have further effects upon it. In one study on adopted children that Rutter cites, it was found that less than 3% of children whose biological father was not a criminal and who had a good upbringing committed petty crimes. Of those with a poor upbringing but a respectable father, 6% also committed crimes as against 12% (twice as many) with a criminal father and a good upbringing. Finally, when the biological father was a criminal and the upbringing poor, 40% became criminals. In this particular study genetic effects were larger than environmental: it suggests that they create a predisposition to crime, which is actualized if the environment also does so.

Although the importance of genes for criminal behaviour is well established, the whole topic is extremely controversial and cannot be pursued here. Indeed I have already said enough to risk my neck.

It is true that in the West five times as many crimes are committed today (at least according to official statistics) as fifty years ago and this must surely be due to a change in environmental fashion not genetics. The way in which given genes express themselves in behaviour varies with the environment, but it is likely that if crime were less fashionable, those with the appropriate genes would find other forms of malfeasance. Moreover, although Rutter is right when he argues that inherited deviance may possibly be ameliorated by intervention, the effects of correction are usually fairly minimal and, in the case of psychologists, non-existent. Massive attempts in the US to improve the intelligence and prospects of deprived children under projects like Head Start were only partially successful. The children whose lives were enriched in infancy did better at school than other deprived children, but not as well as the average undeprived child.

Nevertheless, it is important to remember that the way in which genes express themselves in behaviour can sometimes be altered by psychological means: the amelioration of major depression and of obsessive-compulsive disorder by cognitive-behaviour therapy are cases in point.

To sum up: both character traits and many forms of mental illness are at least in part determined genetically. It seems likely that people would not develop a severe mental illness unless they had a genetic predisposition to do so. In most cases environmental factors (including physical disease or injury) may determine whether a given illness develops; they also determine how a genetic character trait expresses itself. (The reader is warned that I have not discussed the technical point that the measurement of both genetic and environmental factors depends on the variability both of genes and environments in the population studied.)

* * *

There is no evidence whatever to support the view that mental illness is caused by the way of life adopted by modern Western civilization. Research on its prevalence in different communities is hard to interpret because the rates found vary with the criteria used to decide what counts as illness. Where comparable criteria have been employed, however, little variation has been found from one country to another. For example, in a study already mentioned, it was found that in a single year fourteen people in every hundred in one district of London consulted their family doctor for some form of mental illness, of whom nine out of every hundred were diagnosed as neurotic. A study of the inhabitants of an Ethiopian village produced almost identical results. Fifteen in every hundred consulted a doctor for mental disorder over a twelve-month period: again, nine in every hundred were thought to be neurotic. The prevalence of psychiatric illness among Ugandan university students was found to be virtually the same as among students at Belfast or Edinburgh.

It is true that there are wide variations in the rate of suicide from one country to another, but they are caused largely by the attitudes of the different societies, being high in Japan where suicide is often seen as an honourable gesture and very low in Islamic countries where it is condemned by the Muslim religion. The availability of an easy means to commit suicide is also important. The suicide rate dropped in the US when barbiturates ceased to be prescribed as sleeping tablets and in Britain when a less toxic form of gas—natural gas—was introduced. The availability of guns partially accounts for the high suicide rate in America.

The popular belief that there are simple societies living in harmony and free from mental disorder is a myth. To give but one example, two investigators set out to study one such society—the Hutterites—who live in North America. They are an almost entirely self-sufficient farming community leading a simple life far removed from urban civilization. Anecdotal reports had suggested that they were an exceptionally happy, stable and well-adjusted people; in 75 years, there had been only one divorce and three separations in their community. The research workers therefore expected to find very little mental illness, but these expectations were not confirmed. Despite the absence of mental hospitals or psychiatrists, the rate of psychosis was found to be higher than in most urban communities.

It is more difficult to obtain evidence that bears on changes in the rate of mental illness over time. One might expect an increase in rates of hospitalization brought about by the increasing availability of psychiatric services. The state of Massachusetts has kept particularly careful statistics on hospital admissions going back to 1840. When these were examined, it was found, against all expectations, that between 1840 and 1940 there was no increase in first admissions for functional psychoses in the young and middle-aged. There is no good evidence on whether the incidence of neurotic illness has changed from the distant past. Nevertheless, on reading the biographies of those who have lived in former ages, whether it be Dr Johnson, Newton or van Gogh, one cannot help being struck by the number who have exhibited the irrational and self-destructive character traits that would nowadays be classified as neurotic.

In recent years the picture has changed. In the West there has been an alarming rise in depression. One study estimates that the chance of a major depression in a lifetime for Americans born between 1905 and 1914 was just over 1%, whereas the rate for everybody living now is more like 6%. The increase is particularly marked among the young: those born between 1945 and 1954 have ten times the likelihood of becoming depressed by the age of 34 than those born between 1905 and 1914 do in a complete lifetime. Moreover, depression in childhood, which was virtually unknown 50 years ago, is now becoming common. The same trends are evident in many other countries including France, Italy, Germany, and the Lebanon. Some of these changes may be attributable to the increase in the members of the helping professions combined with the general public's greater awareness that help may be forthcoming, and to changes in diagnostic fashion, particularly a reduced tendency to diagnose schizophrenia and an accompanying increase in the diagnosis of depression in America.

There has, however, also been an increase in suicides, again especially in the young. Both in Britain and the US, the rate for young people (aged from 15 to 25) has risen steeply over the last 30 years and the risk for that age group is now about three times as large as for the rest of the population. The cause of the disturbing rise is not known: the increase in drug taking may be partly responsible, together with the break-up of the nuclear family. Since the vast majority of suicides is caused by depression, the increase in suicide rate strongly suggests that there is also a genuine rise in depression among the young.

Certain mental disorders have markedly increased in recent years, for example, anorexia and chronic fatigue syndrome. Such sudden changes cannot be caused by genetics. They are in part the result of fashion, both on the part of the patient who unwittingly copies illnesses that appear in the media and the psychiatrist who likes to be à la mode with his diagnosis. There may be more to it than that: the ingenuity of the chemical industry ensures that we are exposed to a vast range of new poisons, whose long-term effects cannot be predicted.

It is debatable whether bad living conditions caused by poverty can affect the incidence of mental illness. In general, rural areas tend to have slightly higher rates of psychosis than urban and slightly lower rates of neurosis, but the differences are not large. The lower social classes, particularly in urban areas, do exhibit more psychiatric illness of all kinds than do the middle and upper classes, but it is not known how far this is the direct result of poverty. Those afflicted by mental illness tend to move down the social scale and to drift into urban slum areas. To the extent to which mental illness is inherited, the same considerations will apply to their children. Hence, a pool of the mentally incapacitated is likely to accumulate in lower-class districts.

* * *

For many years, going back to Freud, psychologists believed that infancy and early childhood formed people's personality and emotions. This view was based not on evidence but on a hunch. More recent scientific studies have shown that neglect and verbal cruelty (excluding physical brutality) have no detectable effect on adulthood. I shall consider here only the effects of maltreatment and neglect: sexual abuse will be dealt with later.

Many, including Laing and Bateson, have held that a faulty upbringing can produce schizophrenia: in particular it was suggested that parents who make conflicting demands on their children, by for example saying one thing while meaning another, can induce schizophrenia. For example, a mother may say to her child, 'I love you darling' and then stiffen and reject the child if it tries to embrace her. Careful studies of interrelations in the families of children who have subsequently developed schizophrenia have failed to provide support for this notion: it is hard to detect any clear differences in the upbringing of children who become schizophrenic and normal children. Laing himself failed to find any difference between the families of normal children and those of children who developed schizophrenia: dishonestly he refused to publish his results. Any differences that exist are small.

Moreover, no theory based on parental behaviour can explain why it is so unusual to find more than one schizophrenic son or daughter in a family. It may well be that any slight abnormality in the behaviour of the parents of schizophrenics is caused by the unusual behaviour of the child affecting their attitudes rather than the other way round or by the parents themselves possessing some of the genes that predispose to schizophrenia. Laing's ideas on this problem were particularly unfortunate in that they added to the misery of a parent with a schizophrenic child the guilt of feeling personally responsible for its condition.

George Vaillant, of Harvard University, has undertaken a particularly interesting study on the influence of the child's environment on personality and mental health in later life. In the early 1940s, he recorded detailed information on the life history and personality of 199 male students at Harvard University. Thirty years later, he succeeded in locating most of these men and investigated their subsequent development. Although there was a very slight tendency for a good childhood to be associated with good mental health in adult life, his findings contain some surprises. There was no association between childhood factors and successful marriage or a happy sex life. Nor did those who had what would conventionally be thought of as a good and happy upbringing have more successful careers than others. Indeed, only 5% of the men rated as having the best childhood appeared in *Who's Who in America* or in *American Men of Science,* whereas 27% of the remainder figured in one volume or the other. This could be taken as supporting the Freudian notion of sublimation, but it could equally well merely mean that the impatient or aggressive child grows up to be an ambitious adult.

Both this study and several others have found that there is little or no association between neurotic traits in childhood and the development of neurosis in later life. The child who wets his bed or sucks his thumb and the child who is fractious or painfully shy and withdrawn are just as likely to grow up to be normal well-adjusted adults as the child who is happy, good-tempered and reasonable. Indeed, according to my mother, admittedly a biased witness, I was myself an exceptionally well-adjusted child, at least until adolescence.

In sharp contrast to the lack of connection between *childhood* adjustment and adult happiness, Vaillant discovered that good adjustment as a *student* was highly correlated with both happiness and success in later life. It seems likely that personality and the ability to cope with life may change violently from childhood to late adolescence, but that there is little change after that.

The importance of a close bond with the mother (or mother substitute) has been much disputed. There is no question that such a bond is the natural state of affairs both in human beings and in apes and monkeys, and this suggests that it is important for the well-being of the infant. It is known that infants of between six and eighteen months who are separated from their mothers for a prolonged period go into a depression: they become apathetic, lose weight and are prone to physical illness. However, the effects of bad upbringing, including maternal deprivation, on mental illness in adult life are not established. Indeed, children in kibbutzim were separated from their mother but grew up normally, as do Guatemalan children who receive almost no attention from their parents.

The findings of the few studies that at one time appeared to support this idea have been disproved. For example, G. W. Brown earned considerable applause for his discovery that women living in a poor district of London who had lost their mother before 11 years of age were three times as likely to be depressed as comparable women who had not lost their mothers. Several further studies, including one by Brown himself, failed to confirm this finding.

There are now many recent studies that refute the idea that hardship or neglect in early life causes permanent psychological damage. Some children reared under appalling conditions can be perfectly normal as adults. One pair of twins was brought up in a children's home until the age of 18 months and then confined in a cellar, where they were beaten, malnourished and deprived of all other company. When they were discovered at seven years of age, they were unable to walk or speak and were terrified of ordinary objects like mechanical toys and television sets. They were placed in a foster home and by the age of 14 were normal in intelligence and in most other respects. Infant monkeys brought up without a mother but with the company of their peers grow into normal adults.

A group of orphans who spent their first few years in a Nazi concentration camp grew up to be normal adults, as did infants made homeless through war. One study on deprived children concluded that 'As we watched these children grow from babyhood to adulthood, we could not help but respect the self-righting tendencies . . . that produced normal development, under all but the most persistent adverse circumstances.' Provided the environment improves, it would seem that deprivation in childhood has little or no permanent effects. Martin Seligman, a cautious but wily theorist, in a review of work on child abuse concludes 'The major traumas of childhood may have some influence on adult personality, but the influence is barely detectable . . . There is no justification . . . for blaming your adult depression, anxiety, bad marriage, drug use, sexual problems, unemployment, beating up your children, alcoholism or anger on what happened to you as a child.'

The idea that a child who is abused or neglected will grow up to be a bad parent and to have antisocial tendencies—'a cycle of disadvantage' as Michael Rutter named it—has been called in question. Although some studies show a relationship, most have relied on the word of their subjects on whether they had been abused in childhood. Regardless of whether such abuse occurred, violent people are more likely to claim that it has, if only to exculpate themselves. Some studies have failed to find an effect, and the effect is usually small in those that do. For example. Kathy Widom followed up 2,600 children whose parents had court records for neglect or abuse. 18 per cent of them were arrested as adults for violent offences, as against 14 per cent of children of normal families matched for socio-economic status. This small difference may well have been caused by genetic factors rather than by ill-treatment as a child.

Nor is it true that parents who were badly treated as children automatically treat their own children in the same way. The long-standing belief that they do is attacked by Belsky who writes of the myth 'There are few in the scientific community who would embrace [it].'

There is a caveat. Physical brutality can have long-term consequences. Moreover, regardless of the effects of a cruel or disturbed home on adulthood, children should obviously be treated with kindness for their own sakes—and also, as it happens, for the sake of the parents themselves, as it has been found that children who are not subjected to threats and punishments behave better than children who are.

* * *

We have now considered the influence of society and of upbringing. There is a third way in which the environment may affect the individual. Here the results are clear-cut—personal misfortune may precipitate all forms of mental illness, including schizophrenia and affective disorder. The most convincing way of establishing this is to investigate the number and severity of 'life events' that a person has experienced immediately before the onset of their illness. Normal people are presented with a list of potentially stressful events and asked to rate them in terms of severity. Death of a spouse was deemed to be the most severe, followed by divorce or separation, but some events often regarded as fortunate were also thought to be stressful, particularly getting married or being promoted. The list is exhaustive- even Christmas is included. Winning millions of pounds on the British lottery may seem lucky, but it brings stress to many and disaster to some. It has been repeatedly shown that the onset of schizophrenia and depression tends to be preceded by an unusually large number of such life events. Moreover, because stress has an adverse effect on the immune system, it is likely to be accompanied by infections and other physical illnesses.

Apart from stressful circumstances, general unhappiness may contribute to mental disorder, but this is hard to establish because the unhappiness may reflect the disorder's early stages. In the study already mentioned, Brown found that women who had someone to confide in were less likely to become depressed than women who had no close confidant: unlike his other results, this finding has been replicated several times. Like so many other findings in the field of mental illness, this result is hard to interpret. People prone to depression do not make good company, and it may be that it was for this reason that women who became depressed lacked confidants rather than the other way round.

Post-traumatic stress disorder is by definition brought on by witnessing or taking part in a horrifying event, though those vulnerable to the condition usually have a history of anxiety. In a study of American soldiers in the Second World War, it was found that the incidence of mental illness in a given army unit varied directly from week to week with the number of casualties suffered by that unit. Vulnerability to stress varies greatly: an event that may break down one person may leave another untouched. Normal reactions to bereavement resemble those of depression. Usually it is followed by a phase in which the person feels numb and cannot acknowledge that someone close to them has died. In the second phase, the bereaved person feels sad, they may sleep badly, weep, and lose the ability to concentrate. Some feel they are in the presence of the dead person and about one in ten have hallucinations. In the third phase, these symptoms gradually subside and the person becomes reconciled to their loss. Bereaved people are less likely to lose their self-esteem or to have suicidal thoughts than those who are depressed. It is a moot point whether mourning helps.

* * *

A further possible cause of mental disorder is faulty learning or faulty cognition. I have already shown how phobias could be explained by faulty learning: until the phobic patient (usually a woman) actually approaches the object of which she is afraid, she cannot learn that there is nothing to be afraid of. Every time she withdraws from the object or situation, her anxiety is reduced and hence the tendency to withdraw is strengthened. Another anxiety disorder—panic attacks—can be explained by the patient's mis-interpretation of her bodily feelings, as portending death.

There are two recent theories that attribute depression to faulty thinking, which are entirely consistent with one another. The first was discovered by accident. At random intervals some dogs were given electric shocks from which they could not escape. A day later they were placed in a box that had two compartments with a barrier in between. Shocks were again delivered but the dogs could now escape from them or avoid them altogether by jumping the barrier into the next compartment. Dogs not given prior shocks learned in about four trials to avoid shock at the second stage of the experiment. Those who had been previously given inescapable shocks did not learn: at first they jumped about randomly but then became entirely passive often lying down and accepting the shocks. Presumably while they were receiving inescapable shocks they had learned that there was nothing they could do to avoid them, a condition known as 'learned helplessness": even when they by chance successfully escaped by leaping the barrier they did not repeat this response. Similar effects have been found in people: if they are given insoluble tasks (like looking for non-existent anagrams), they perform less well on other problems than do people who have not been discouraged by failure.

Not everyone who fails at some activity becomes depressed. It has been shown that people who blame themselves for their failures are more prone to depression than people who do not: if you fail an examination you may either think it was because of your own stupidity or put it down to bad luck over the questions set. In one study, people's tendency to blame themselves was measured: when followed up over the next five years, it was found that those who blamed themselves were more likely to become depressed than those who did not. It would appear, then, that depression is partly due to failure and partly due to attributing the failure to oneself rather than to circumstances.

An alternative but similar hypothesis is the cognitive theory of depression, put forward by Aaron Beck, a disenchanted psychoanalyst who became a renegade. In essence, he believed that depression is brought on by taking too gloomy a view of oneself, one's experiences and one's future. Depressives blame themselves for their failures and misinterpret their experiences: for example, if someone they are talking to excuses himself, they may think they are boring him rather than that he has had a call of nature. Beck points to a series of errors in thinking made by potential depressives. They over-generalize bad happenings—if one person dislikes them, they come to believe that everyone will dislike them. If someone praises them but includes a small amount of criticism, they will remember that but not the praise. Told that they are a brilliant cook but use too much salt, they remember only the latter phrase. Because they feel they are worthless, they give up trying. The less they try, the less success or pleasure they have and the more miserable their life becomes: they sink into gloom and depression.

Both these theories seem to be sensible accounts of minor depressions though it should be remembered that not everyone with low self-esteem becomes depressed. Moreover, the therapies to which these theories have given rise have proved highly successful as treatments for moderately severe depression. There must, however, be more to depression than merely negative thoughts. These cognitive theories cannot explain why the depressed person loses their taste for food and drink, has difficulty sleeping or becomes agitated or anxious. The answer is almost certainly that psychological events interact in both directions with states of the brain and in particular with the activity of neurotransmitters, the substances that are secreted by one nerve cell to excite or inhibit another. Again, a vicious circle may be set up—depression induced by miserable experiences or thoughts may affect the brain and this effect may in turn exacerbate the person's low mood.

* * *

Both Freud and most of today's psychotherapists have put forward yet another cause for mental disorder, unconscious conflicts originating in childhood, a view that, as will be shown, cannot be sustained.

14

Freudian theory and practice

Psychoanalysis presents yet one more account of the cause of mental illness. It was created by Freud, an immensely imaginative man: indeed until recently all psychotherapy ultimately derived from his ideas. Such was the appeal of his bizarre theory that it blinded people to less inventive but more effective ways of treating mental disorder. It could be argued that Freud held back progress in psychotherapy by 100 years.

He recognized explicitly that people often act from motives of which they are unaware. Others, such as Pierre Janet and William James, had recognized the existence of unconscious mental processes before Freud, but they had not constructed a detailed theory of them. Moreover, the idea is used implicitly by many writers including Shakespeare and also in everyday life: for example, someone may be spiteful out of jealousy without recognizing their motive. It is one thing to use an idea implicitly, another to recognize it explicitly and to build a vast theoretical system upon it.

Freud's second insight was that there must be an explanation for irrational or self-destructive actions. He concentrated entirely on such activities—mistakes, dreams and neurotic symptoms. He tried to explain them by showing that they were in fact rational in that they released wishes of which we are unconsciously ashamed. If someone makes a slip of the tongue, it is not enough to say he did so because he was tired, we should explain why he made this particular slip and not that slip. Freud's answer was to suggest that the form that mistakes take, the dreams we dream and the symptoms the neurotic develops, all release unconscious wishes: to prove this point he produced many instances that could be more or less credibly explained in this way. Oddly, Freud never realized that rational behaviour stands in as much need of explanation as irrational behaviour. What are the mechanisms that enable people to play chess well, to find their way home, to understand their native language or to recognize a familiar face? All these tasks require a vast number of unconscious mental operations: we are conscious at any one time of only a fragment of what is going on in the mind. The existence of such unconscious processes is recognized today by almost all psychologists: it was first clearly enunciated by Hermann Helmholtz in the year before Freud's birth. Freud, then, not only limited his explanation of behaviour to its irrational aspects by trying to show that they were really rational, but he did not see that rationality itself needs to be explained.

Summarizing Freud's theory is not easy since he altered it many times, but here is an attempt to give its essence. He divided the human mind into three parts—id, ego, and superego. People are unconscious of the mental processes in the id, the part from which basic drives spring, though aspects of these drives may appear in the ego, the realm of consciousness. The instinctual drive, on which Freud concentrated, he termed 'the libido', which is the sex drive broadly interpreted: it includes not merely sexual desire, but in infancy the urge to suck from the mother's breasts and the pleasures to be derived from expelling or withholding urine and faeces. The superego represents the prohibitions placed by parents or society on giving free release to the unconscious wishes buried in the id. It censors these wishes by allowing into the ego (that is into consciousness) only those that it regards as permissible, through a series of 'defence mechanisms'. Some of these mechanisms almost certainly exist and Freud was canny enough to spot them, but in so far as they exist they apply not merely to libidinal wishes but to all motives of which we are consciously or unconsciously ashamed. Freud's concentration on the sex drive to the exclusion of all others was perhaps his biggest error.

For Freud, the most important defence mechanism was *repression,* by which those unconscious wishes and their associated memories that are prohibited by the superego are not allowed to enter the ego from the id. Men cannot for example, acknowledge consciously the wish to sleep with their mother or to kill their father. According to Freud, repression on its own is unsatisfactory since the repressed wishes still exist and the fact that they cannot be fulfilled causes anxiety and neurosis. There is no evidence for the existence of repression, though people do sometimes unconsciously try to push unpleasant thoughts out of their mind. But such thoughts are not necessarily ones of which the person is ashamed—it is common for people who have witnessed a disaster to try not to recall the horrific details; moreover such thoughts often intrude into the mind and they can be consciously recalled at will.

Most of the remaining defence mechanisms either allow repressed wishes release in a form that disguises their true nature from the ego, or they support the superego in its attempts to disguise the wishes of the id.

In *projection,* traits of which one is ashamed are ascribed to someone else. The mean person sees other people as being mean to disguise from themselves the fact that they are too. Although this sounds plausible, it has been found that people tend to think that others are more similar to themselves than they really are in all respects, including good as well as bad qualities. Projection applies, *pace* Freud, to all traits not just bad ones.

Reaction formation is the adoption of an attitude that is diametrically opposed to one's unconscious wishes. For example, someone with a secret lust for pornography may spend time condemning it and even hunting it down and examining it with horror, while unconsciously obtaining pleasure from it. Allied to reaction formation is *denial*—people deny with exceptional vehemence that they have traits of which they are ashamed. Both these mechanisms may exist, but they are often used consciously by people who are aware of their discreditable drives. Moreover, they are not limited to the libido: a lazy person may hotly deny that they are lazy. Whether they are used to defend the ego against the id is altogether another question.

In *displacement,* the shameful wish is released but with a different object. A person with an unfulfilled desire to hoard their faeces may become a miser and hoard money instead.

Rationalization is the production of spurious but plausible reasons for one's actions or beliefs. For example, the hypochondriac may without knowing it be feigning illness to avoid work or other responsibilities. A person may associate with prostitutes believing that he is saving them from a life of vice, whereas he is really releasing a repressed sexual urge. There is secure evidence that this defence mechanism exists. People who make a choice over-value the object chosen: they cannot bear to admit even to themselves that they have made a mistake. And people who cannot get something they want often under-value it ('sour grapes'). Once again, however, rationalization is clearly not limited to libidinal drives.

Intellectualization is a vague mechanism by which the person strips off all emotion from buried wishes. Its mode of operation is unclear. Often it is merely an accusation made by psychoanalysts confronted with a patient who is cleverer than they are.

The final defence mechanism worthy of mention is *sublimation*. According to Freud all art and all human endeavour that does not have some practical goal are attempts to release the libido in disguised form. The painter depicting lush landscapes is releasing his desire to peer at his mother's pubic hair, while the curiosity of the scientist arises from the infant's curiosity about the sexual behaviour of its parents. It is of course true that someone frustrated in one sphere of life may throw themselves into another hoping to find some alternative satisfaction, but this is far removed from alleging that all curiosity stems from repressed childhood wishes. In fact all mammals, particularly monkeys and apes, exhibit curiosity and a desire to master their environment. Surely they cannot all have suffered from the parental prohibitions that according to Freud repress aspects of the libido, which burst forth in the form of curiosity.

A second strand in Freud's theorizing is his idea that the libido develops in phases. In the oral stage the child's libido is centred on the mother's breast from which it derives pleasure by sucking and which it may bite or chew if insufficient milk is forthcoming. Freud believed that people could become 'fixated' at a given developmental stage if they had experienced difficulties there. Such fixation could either lead to a particular kind of personality or to a neurosis. According to him, anyone fixated at the oral aggressive stage (in which they bite the breast) because of receiving insufficient milk will become an impatient, aggressive, envious adult.

The second stage, termed the anal, lasts from about one and a half to two years of age, when Western children are normally being toilet trained, thus focusing attention on their faeces. Freud thought they obtain pleasure both from expelling and retaining their faeces, which activities may lead respectively to a generous, pliant personality or to a stingy meticulous one.

Most of Freud's attention was focused on the third stage, the phallic, at which masturbation begins. One of Freud's most central—and most bizarre—ideas was that at this stage all young boys want to possess their mothers; naturally enough, the fathers are not enamoured of this wish, and the boys come to fear them in case they take vengeance on them. In his later writings Freud thought that their fear of their father took the specific form of anxiety lest he cut off their genitals ('the castration complex'), whereas little girls hate their mother because she has not given them a penis and long for their father because only he can give them one. Small boys may wish to kill their father, but because he is so powerful they may disguise this wish from themselves by identifying with him. By imagining they are he, they can sleep with their mother in fantasy and obtain vicarious gratification whilst at the same time taking over his morality. The young boy's conflict over his father is the famed 'Oedipal complex'. Yet another way to resolve it is for the child to identify with the parent of the *opposite* sex. Putting oneself in the position of this parent results in making love in fantasy to the parent of the same sex: this in turn disguises the jealousy felt of that parent, but at the expense of giving rein to the homosexual side of the person's nature. According to Freud everyone is bisexual.

It is, to put it mildly, unlikely that a three- or four-year-old child could entertain such complex thoughts about sex. How at that time of life could they know anything about sexual intercourse? Moreover, studies of children, such as those of C. W. Valentine, a British psychologist, who was originally a believer in psychoanalysis, suggest that girls of this age are actually more attached to their mothers and less to their fathers than are boys, thus refuting the Oedipal complex. Freud postulated two further developmental stages—latency which lasts until adolescence and during which the sex drive is absent; finally there is the genital stage, in which the libido is focused on another person and unselfish love can arise—if all goes well.

* * *

Freud's evidence for his theory comes from his analysis of dreams, mistakes and free associations. His belief that all dreams fulfil repressed wishes cannot be sustained. Indeed, almost all the examples he cites deal with the emergence of fully conscious wishes in dream form. For example, his own daughter Anna dreamt of eating strawberries after she had been forbidden to eat them the previous day. Freud argued that the superego censors and distorts the repressed wishes so that they appear in dreams in disguised form unrecognizable by the ego. This helps to preserve sleep since if the wishes appeared in their original form the sleeper would be woken by anxiety. This view takes no account of nightmares, which often waken the dreamer and it is as logical to argue that all dreams express hidden fears as that they express repressed wishes. Moreover, many people, including myself when under analysis, have dreamt about sleeping with their father, mother or siblings, actions that Freud would presumably expect to appear in dreams only in heavily disguised form.

Freud's use of mistakes and free associations is just as tendentious. For example, a slip made in quoting Virgil by a travelling companion of Freud's led through a chain of about 20 associations to the companion's eventual confession that he was afraid that he had made his mistress pregnant. Freud cleverly but unconvincingly relates all the associations to this fear, but once again the fear is fully conscious: it is not a repressed wish. With sufficient ingenuity any chain of associations or any dream can be interpreted in any way one wants. When a patient entered Freud's office without closing the door to the waiting room, Freud thought the patient was unconsciously trying to show him that he was not a very eminent doctor since he had an empty waiting room, but it could equally well mean that the patient wanted to show he could easily escape or simply that there was no point in closing the door when the waiting room was empty. According to Freud many objects are phallic symbols—indeed it is hard to think of anything that could not symbolize either the male or female genitals or both. Jung remarked mockingly that 'After all, the penis is only a phallic symbol' and Freud himself is reputed to have said 'Sometimes a cigar is only a cigar.'

Freud was never clear about the precise causes of neurosis. He repeatedly asserted that it arose from repressed libidinal desires, but since he thought everyone, whether neurotic or not, had such desires they are clearly not a sufficient cause. Perhaps for this reason, he instituted the notion of an unspecified constitutional defect as part of their cause. The very experiences that turned Leonardo da Vinci into a great artist and scientist could have rendered someone with a different constitution a neurotic or a sexual pervert. For the most part, the unfortunate experiences consist of departures from the methods of child-rearing current in Vienna around the turn of the century: mothers can wean both too early and too late, they can be too loving or not loving enough, toilet-training can be commenced too soon or too late.

Freud's views on child-rearing, on which his whole theory is based, do not stand examination. Throughout most of history, child-rearing practices have been very different from those current today. In the sixteenth century, the mortality rate among young children was so high that no mother or father could afford to become too emotionally involved with them. The survivors were often savagely beaten, locked up in the dark, taken to see hangings and corpses, and even mutilated by having their teeth ripped out to provide dentures or being castrated to supply testicles for magical potions. For lack of toilet-training children often lived in their own excrement. In many periods of history, childhood masturbation was not frowned upon. Courtiers kissed Louis XIII's penis when he was a young child, and he was encouraged to explore the vaginas of ladies-in-waiting with his fist. The Ancient Greeks practised infanticide on a grand scale, and had anal and oral intercourse with young children. In Victorian times, British upper-class children were breast-fed by wet-nurses and often had only the most formal and occasional contacts with their fathers. Neither the Elizabethans nor the Victorian upper classes were noticeably more neurotic than anyone else.

According to Freudian theory, the phallic stage is succeeded by the latent stage, in which the libido is quiescent. The genital stage follows in adolescence: if all has gone well, the other stages are fused with it and the person is capable of loving someone of the opposite sex.

On reading Freud it is quickly apparent that whenever he starts to deal with neurosis, his writing becomes opaque and his arguments more difficult to follow. If he is unclear about the origins of neuroses, he is equally unclear about the method of cure. Freud believed that psychoanalysis worked by bringing the repressed libidinal urges into consciousness: once the patient recognizes that his libido is stuck at an oral or anal stage, or that it is fixated on inappropriate objects such as the mother or father, it is somehow freed to move on to a more adult stage or to fasten on more appropriate objects. To be effective, recognition of unconscious urges involves more than merely conscious assent to what the analyst says: a cure can be achieved only if the patient accepts his own psychodynamic make-up at some deeper level.

Freud pictured psychoanalysis as a battle to overcome the patients' own resistance to recognizing their repressed wishes. Since these wishes are repressed precisely because people are afraid of them, it is natural that they should unconsciously strive at all costs to avoid recognizing them. In overcoming such 'resistance', the analyst acts as the ally of the patient and tries by encouragement and sympathy to bring them to light. In this endeavour, the mechanism of 'transference' plays an important role. Freud noticed that most patients become very interested in and dependent on their analyst: they fall in love with him. In so doing, they act towards him in the ways in which they have responded towards other important figures in their lives, particularly their own parents. Hence, what occurs in transference can reveal patients' unconscious feelings about their parents. Moreover, the patients' love for the analyst can be turned to good account, since they will try to please him, which provides a strong motive for uncovering and accepting their own unconscious wishes. Freud himself described transference as a neurosis that supervened on the original neurosis, and it was only when the transference neurosis was in turn resolved that the patient would recover. It can only be overcome when the patient himself recognizes the nature of the transference: with such understanding he ceases to be dependent on the analyst.

Most patients, like me, also undergo phases of 'negative transference' during which they hate the analyst: this is yet a further form of resistance —by despising the analyst, the patient is able to reject his interpretations and thus avoid admitting to his own desires. In negative transference, patients are again repeating attitudes, this time hostile ones, to earlier figures of importance in their life—particularly, towards the parent of the same sex.

The reader should by now have formed some impression of what to expect on embarking on a traditional Freudian analysis. The first few sessions are usually devoted to an assessment of whether the putative patient is a suitable case for treatment. Freud himself believed it was useless to treat psychoses by analytic methods, and he thought that depression ('melancholia' as it was then called) was also resistant to psychoanalytic treatment. He rightly stressed the importance of making sure that there was nothing organically wrong with the patient.

He emphasized that two qualities are needed in a patient if psychoanalysis is to have any hope of success. The first is intelligence: presumably unintelligent patients would be unable to follow the contortions of their own psyche, as envisaged by Freud, and this would render attempts at interpretation ineffective. Secondly, many analysts only accept patients with high 'ego-strength'. By this is meant patients who are in touch with reality and give evidence of a certain amount of willpower. One can readily agree that determination is a *sine qua non* of a successful analysis: it is a protracted, expensive and painful process. Nevertheless, a patient with a strong ego cannot be very disturbed. Everyone agrees that a determination to recover is clinically a hopeful sign, and it could be thought that in selecting such patients analysts are in fact treating only those who will recover of their own accord.

Traditional Freudians insist on the patient lying on a couch. Its use arose from a historical accident. Freud's first essays into psychotherapy were based on hypnotism, conducted while the patient was lying down and relaxed. Freud gives several reasons for continuing the use of the couch. He writes that he disliked being stared at for eight hours a day, but is quick to add clinical reasons which, had they been adduced by one of his patients, he would doubtless have described as rationalizations. He believed that for transference to be put to the best possible use the analyst himself should remain as shadowy and indistinct as possible: by so doing, he would encourage patients to respond to him in the way they had previously treated important figures in their life. Patients are thus enabled to project on to the dim figure of the analyst the characteristics of their own parents or siblings. In addition, the couch encourages relaxation, and thus helps the patients to think dreamily and to voice irrational trains of thought.

As we have seen, Freud was interested only in irrational thought-processes which he thought were the clues to the unconscious workings of the mind. Freudian analysts will at an early stage in treatment instruct the patient to withhold nothing, however trivial or irrelevant it seems. They concentrate on the patient's dreams and free associations. Most patients find it difficult to capture and reveal their stray thoughts, and may require several sessions before they learn what is required.

Analysts usually ask the patient to be completely open in voicing his or her opinions about them, but it is difficult to state in all honesty such feelings. They are bound to contain hostile elements, and one assumes that even analysts have their *amour propre:* most of us are loathe to hurt others' feelings except in anger. In addition, as I always felt, apart from the altruistic motive of not wanting to be beastly to one's analyst, there is a more selfish reason for not saying exactly what one thinks: he is normally in a better position to hurt you than you are him. The doctrine that patients should be completely honest in reporting their feelings about their psychotherapist is widely held even by non-Freudian therapists: it is rarely observed.

Evaluation of Freud

No brief description of Freudian theory and practice can hope to capture the full range of his thought: he covered every realm of human life from belief in God to wetting the bed. He himself, particularly in the *Introductory lectures,* is much his own best expositor. It should be remembered that he revised his theories many times and never attempted a careful synthesis. I have ignored much of his wilder theorizing developed later in life, when he became very pessimistic about mankind and laid great stress on Thanatos, the death wish, the unconscious attempt to die or to hurt oneself. The addition of such a motive to the operation of the libido makes interpretation easier but even more vacuous, since these two major motives can clearly explain *ex post facto* any human action.

One must ask what is the standing of Freudian theory and practice today: I write 'theory and practice' advisedly, since it is important to separate the two. It could be that Freud's theories about human motives and the development of the personality are correct while the therapy has no value: it is also possible that his theories are nonsense while the therapy works - neurotics might, just possibly, be helped by being presented with mythical stories about the origins of their feelings and actions. Freud himself was well aware of the dichotomy: he thought that he would be remembered more for his insights into the development of personality than for his therapeutic methods.

In the previous chapter, I argued that there is some plausibility in Freud's defence mechanisms, with the exception of repression, though apart from rationalization they are difficult to demonstrate. Moreover, they apply to all shameful motives, including ones of which the person is conscious and not merely to the libido. I criticized his theory of dreams and suggested that not all human endeavour nor, come to that, not all human error can be ascribed to the libido. It is worth stressing this point. There is no reason to suppose that ambition or the desire to form friendships have anything to do with sex, but they may well be determined by the drive to master the environment and the drive to socialize, which appear in other primates not subjected to the demands of the superego. Some neuroses may be based on sexual anxieties but others are triggered by events that have nothing to do with sex such as witnessing a disaster, flying 25 bombing missions in the last war, or becoming unemployed. It is perhaps because most of Freud's patients were comfortably off women living in Vienna, who had little to think about except finding a husband, that Freud concentrated on the sex drive. Some neuroses clearly revolve around sexual anxieties, but to conclude that all do. no matter how disguised the libidinal problem, is unjustifiable. It is truc that neurotic anxiety—or indeed anxiety of any kind -is inimical to normal sexual functioning, but it also impairs all thought-processes and can play havoc with one's appetite for food.

Freud's theories are so flexible and imprecise that it is difficult to have faith in any of his detailed interpretations. In both dream symbolism and in neurotic symptoms, one thing can always be replaced by its opposite. 'An element in the dream which is capable of having a contrary may equally well be expressing either itself or its contrary or both together.' The mother can stand for the father, the breast for the penis, the scrotum for the womb. An Oedipal complex can be resolved by identification with the same-sex parent. which in later life may manifest itself either by rampant homosexuality or in the disguise of severe disgust at homosexuality. Freud also allows the opposition of many psychic forces: id and superego, Eros and Thanatos, the masculine principle and the feminine principle, self-love (narcissism) and love for others. What are we to make of passages such as the following?

'. . . the life instincts or sexual instincts which are active in each cell take the other cells as their "object" . . . they partially neutralise the death instincts . . . while the other cells do the same for them, and still others sacrifice themselves in the performance of this libidinal function.'

When you read a Freudian case history, it all sounds very plausible, but if you stand back from the material it immediately becomes obvious that the same case could be interpreted in many different ways even in Freud's own terms.

A few brave souls have attempted to validate Freudian theory objectively. According to Freud, age of weaning or age of toilet-training can be related to later personality: early weaning or early toilet-training should result, respectively, in oral or anal characteristics. The 'passive' oral personality (as opposed to the 'aggressive' described above) is marked by such traits as love of eating and drinking, pessimism, guilt and dependence in contrast to the anal personality, which exhibits obsessional traits such as orderliness, cleanliness, meanness and obstinacy. The majority of studies find no relation between personality and age of weaning or toilet training: some have yielded results directly opposed to Freudian predictions, and about the same number have produced findings in the predicted direction.

Many experimental studies have been performed to test the Freudian concept of repression. Both neurotics and normals have been exposed to material that on Freudian theory might be expected to arouse anxiety, and subsequently tested for whether recall is less good than for neutral material. One survey of this field concluded: 'In view of the amount and consistency of the data accumulated to this point... the continued use of the concept of repression as an explanation for behaviour does not seem justifiable.' Another reviewed five careful studies of repression and concluded that it had nothing to do with mental disorder. It is of course open to Freudians to say that the processes underlying repression are so complex that they cannot be uncovered in artificial situations: in other words, the theory cannot be tested.

One of Freud's less important hypotheses has recently been put to the test. He argued that in order to compensate for their frustrated libido people who have little sex will have more sexual fantasies than those with a fuller sex life. In fact, a series of studies, undertaken by psychologists with time on their hands, show the opposite is the case: the more sex you have, the more you fantasize about it. Trivial perhaps, but a straw in the wind.

A few years ago, it looked as though some support for Freud might be forthcoming from studies on the effects of disturbed homes, but as we have seen most deprived children make a good recovery. Even if they did not, this would not confirm any of the details of Freudian theory. Moreover, in many periods and for many classes of mankind, parental affection was the exception rather than the rule.

Freud claimed that psychoanalysis was a science, but this is clearly untrue. Not only did he fail to collect systematic data, his case notes were based on his memory: he never made notes during a clinical session, since he thought that would distract him from listening to the patient. On his own theory of mistakes, this procedure would be likely to produce severely distorted accounts, which would be in line with his own wishes. His interpretations are more akin to the methods of the historian, except that historians (unless influenced by Freud) infer conscious motives, while Freud inferred unconscious ones. His untrammelled methods of interpretation, no matter how ingenious, could be made to explain any dream, mistake, free association, or neurotic symptom. A theory that can explain anything is one that explains nothing.

As we shall see Freud was extremely dogmatic: he insisted that his followers should have complete faith in his ideas, and if they differed from him they were expelled from the fold. In orthodox Freudian analysis the dogmatism continues. At the Freudian bastion. The British Institute of Psychoanalysis, trainees are required to buy the complete works of Freud.

If Freudian theory is too narrowly conceived, too ambiguous about the effects of childhood experiences, and too lacking in any kind of empirical support to be acceptable, there is a presumptive case against the therapy derived from the theory. It might be expected that it would be a simple matter to find out whether neurotics who undergo psychoanalysis fare better than those who do not. In practice, this is not easy to discover. It is particularly difficult in the case of psychoanalysis because analysts have been extremely reluctant to have the efficacy of their methods tested. For example, the Tavistock Clinic refused to allow a clinical trial of its therapy to be conducted by some of its own staff and independent research workers. The American Psychoanalytic Association did undertake a survey of the effects of psychoanalysis. The results were so poor that they withheld them from publication, an act of gross dishonesty. Moreover, analysts argue that the aim of analysis is not to remove symptoms, but to enable the patient to gain self-knowledge. Freud himself believed that it was useless merely to remove symptoms since the elimination of one symptom would simply be replaced by the appearance of another, a belief that has been found to be wholly false. If one symptom such as obsessive thinking can be alleviated others like anxiety or sleeplessness are also diminished. In one study, analysts themselves were questioned about their own success. Although they claimed that 80% of patients who completed analysis had been helped by it, they admitted that they had removed the symptoms for which treatment was sought in only 23% of cases.

If analysis does have beneficial effects, they are at best slight and un-certain. David Malan, a prominent British analyst and a member of the leading British centre for Freudian analysis, wrote: '[Research on] the most influential and ambitious of all forms of psychotherapy, that based on psychoanalysis, has yielded almost nothing—a matter for shame and despair —until it has been saved at the last moment by the Menninger Foundation's report.'

Malan's last remark is extraordinary, and is hardly borne out by the contents of the report. The Menninger Foundation is one of the main centres of psychoanalysis in the United States, and the report in question summarizes the effects of psychoanalysis on forty-two patients over a period of eighteen years. On turning to it, we find that the authors display a commendable candour. They write that they found it impossible: 'to list the variables needed to test the theory [of psychoanalysis]... to choose and provide control conditions which could rule out alternative explanations for results; to state the hypotheses to be tested; or finally to conduct this research according to the design.' Their main conclusion is that patients with a sound personality ('strong ego-strength') will prosper regardless of the method of treatment, whereas patients with weak ego-strength will not benefit from psychoanalysis. The authors even write that their findings 'raise the question to what extent psychoanalysis may be considered the ideal treatment for patients who need it least, that is for those with initial high ego-strength.' In other words, it may be that analysis is unhelpful regardless of whether a patient's ego-strength is high or low.

The Freudian cult

Many analysts are themselves sceptical of the value of psychoanalysis in speeding recovery from neuroses. Why then do they continue to practise? When I challenged my own analysts with figures on recovery rates, they both made the same reply. One (the posh one) said: 'For every shrink in the south-east of England making people better, there are six in Manchester fouling people up.' The other answered: 'There are only six good analysts in London—the rest often make people worse.' I was clearly fortunate to have chosen against all likelihood two analysts who were among the *crème de la crème.*

There is some evidence (reviewed in Chapter 18) that it is helpful for psychotherapists to display empathy and warmth to their patients. Although these qualities may to some extent distinguish good psychotherapists from bad ones, psychoanalysts are the least likely to possess them. The master himself wrote: 'I cannot advise my colleagues too urgently to model themselves during psychoanalytic treatment on the surgeon, who puts aside all his feelings, even his human sympathy.'

The second line of defence on which analysts fall back is that the lack of success of analytic treatment is the fault not of the analyst but of the patient. Only some patients are suitable for psychoanalytic treatment, and at present we do not know who they are. To quote again from Malan's article: 'I am also convinced that what analysts have never faced up to is that there are many types of patient, whom we continue to treat with never diminishing hope and ever increasing denial, who are not helped by our methods.' Again, the Medical Director of the St Louis Psychoanalytic Institute wrote: in many individuals the limitations of their own psychopathology or the therapeutic capacities they bring to the treatment situations make it necessary for other [i.e. non-analytic] approaches to be introduced.' In other words, it's all the fault of the patient, poor thing, the analyst's never to blame.

A third reason given by analysts for ignoring the evidence on their inadequacy is that they are not merely interested in effecting cures, they are trying to bring about some character change, including the acquisition of self-knowledge: the nature of this character change is so elusive that it cannot be specified, much less detected, by the use of objective methods. This argument is unacceptable. Anyone who is in the desperate state of misery that I endured when depressed does not want to have their character changed, they want to recover and to be able to function normally. Unless analysts believe they can achieve this, they should not practise on neurotic patients, though there would seem little harm in continuing to offer analysis to normal people who have sufficient time, money and fortitude to understand and possibly change themselves by examining their libido.

Indeed, both in Britain and in North America, there appear to be many more normal people undergoing analysis than there are neurotics. Analysis is much more widely practised in America than it is in Britain, particularly in large urban centres such as New York and Chicago. It has been suggested that much analysis is akin to prostitution, in that instead of paying for sex, the patient buys synthetic friendship—'Rent-a-Friend'. Anyone seeking treatment for this reason would again do well to avoid traditional Freudian analysts, and should perhaps bear in mind the reply of one analyst to the question of what would happen if a normal person came to him: 'Even though he were normal at the beginning of the analysis, the analytic procedure would create a neurosis.' In fact, both in America and Europe. psychoanalysis is decreasingly fashionable: other forms of therapy, some sensible, many bizarre, have been replacing it. Indeed, in the 850 pages of *The Handbook of Psychotherapy and Behavior Change* (the bible of research workers studying clinical psychology), Freud is referred to only 14 times, whereas a Dr Howard, although unknown to the general public, receives 66 mentions. Contemporary psychotherapists, unlike the *literati,* have largely lost interest in Freud, except curiously in France, though whether Lacan is a cause or a symptom of the recrudescence of psychoanalysis there, it is hard to say.

It is not surprising that many analysts continue to believe in the efficacy of a method of treatment for which there is no good evidence. The history of medicine abounds with examples of treatments that were worthless—and often lethal, but were employed for many decades by practitioners with an honest but misguided faith. Many once widely accepted treatments for mental illness, such as insulin therapy or prefrontal lobotomy, are now known to have been useless or even harmful.

For psychological reasons analysts are more likely to cling to their faith in their techniques than are most doctors in theirs. First, they will have submitted themselves to the expense, time and pain of analysis. There is abundant evidence that anyone who has made a sacrifice to attain some object comes to over-value it: people cannot afford to admit to themselves that they have made the sacrifice in vain. Hence, to abjure analysis, the psychoanalyst not only has to give up a profitable method of making a living, he must admit to himself that he has made a costly mistake. It is small wonder that few are prepared to do so—though some, to their credit, have, and are now practising better attested forms of psychotherapy. Although doctors also have a long and arduous training, they are less likely to be committed to one particular method of treatment: if a drug is found not to work, it requires less moral courage to admit the mistake and substitute another than it does for an analyst to forswear his whole procedure.

The analyst's faith in his own theories is confirmed by his patients, who produce the material he most wants to hear, that is material that agrees with his view of the origins of neurosis. By expressing interest or approval, analysts reward their patients for talking about topics they think are important. Many go much further than this: Freud himself writes, 'We give the patient the conscious anticipatory idea (the idea of what he may expect to find) and he then finds the repressed unconscious idea in himself on the basis of its similarity to the anticipatory one.' In his writings, Freud repeatedly stressed that it was only with the help of suggestions made by the analyst that the patient could hope to uncover his unconscious desires. 'There are some patients who need more of such assistance and some who need less; but there are none who get through without some of it.' It seems likely that far from discovering the contents of their unconscious, all patients do is merely to rediscover material implanted by the analyst, and then embroider it in ways pleasing to him. For these reasons Freud's patients may well dream (or at least report) Freudian dreams, Jung's dream Jungian dreams and Adler's dream about power suitably symbolized. The patient shapes himself in the image of his analyst:

> The Aethiop gods have Aethiop lips
> Bronze limbs and curly hair,
> The Grecian gods are like the Greeks
> As tall blue-eyed and fair.

Each analyst gets the patients he deserves.

It could be argued that psychoanalysis was designed to protect the analyst rather than to help the patient. The lack of eye contact and Freud's injunction not to show sympathy save analysts from being emotionally involved in their patients' troubles. In addition, psychoanalytic theory acts as an ingenious device for propping up the therapists' esteem. All analysts can and do ascribe critical remarks made by the patient to an expression of hostile impulses towards their parents or other figures of importance in their early life. Analysts frequently extend this notion into everyday life, and are so busy thinking up the psychodynamic reasons why other people say things that they rarely take what is said at face value—particularly if it is threatening to their own beliefs. Freud himself was guilty of this irritating trick. He frequently said that he would not reply to his critics because no rational argument would convince them: he maintained that the only reason anyone could have for not accepting psychoanalytic theory was their resistance to acknowledging their own shameful wishes. This argument is of course self-defeating: if one takes it seriously, one can only speculate about the traumatic events in Freud's early life that led him to uphold such a bizarre body of beliefs as an adult. The unconscious motives, Freudian or otherwise, for holding a given belief are wholly irrelevant to its truth or falsity. Good ideas stand—and bad ones fall—in their own right, whether they are produced out of a love of knowledge, a desire to be promoted, a longing for the Nobel prize, the wish to prove a colleague wrong, or the displaced infantile lust to examine one's mother's genitals.

Most episodes of mental disorder remit of their own accord, and the fact that the majority of the analyst's patients therefore show some recovery fortifies them in their faith that their method works. If they abide by the principle that only patients with high ego-strength are fit to be analysed, the probability that the patients will recover—with or without analysis—is greatly increased. Moreover, those who fail to recover will sooner or later drop out of analysis, and the analyst can close his case notes by writing 'terminated analysis prematurely'.

Finally, all professions want to believe that they have knowledge or techniques not available to the general public. Each clings to its own mystique. Management consultants subscribe to Total Quality Management, which is an unsubstantiated collection of managerial techniques akin to common sense, but dressed up in fancy terms; lawyers draft wills in unnecessarily opaque language; and so on. The analyst's knowledge of Freudian theory (and the fact that they have themselves been analysed) justifies them in charging for their services. If psychoanalysts had no theory of which to boast, patients might just as well discuss their problems with a friend.

* * *

It is small wonder, then, that analysts themselves have retained their faith in their methods. More surprisingly, it is hard to think of any theory (except possibly Marxism) that has had so much influence on twentieth century Western thought as psychoanalysis. It appears in novels, plays, biographies and everyday conversation. Perhaps the main reason for Freud's popularity is that there is simply no other theory of human personality and motivation that is of any intellectual interest. None covers so broad a range of human behaviour and none is constructed with such imaginative flair. If you read the works of psychologists on personality, you will find them for the most part not only dry but mere restatements of commonplaces in rebarbative language. One American psychologist rose to fame in his profession by making the great discovery that people (particularly Americans) have a 'need for achievement' ; numerous followers got together, christened the need 'N.Ach' and went to work preparing questionnaires to measure it. This is not the stuff that captures the imagination of the public nor indeed that of any sane psychologist. Perhaps the only interesting rival theory to Freud's is that of sociobiology which offers explanations in evolutionary terms for such aspects of human nature as the differences between the sexes, or altruism—the latter a concept which Freud had difficulty in explaining: he put it down to culture but how it arose in culture he does not explain. Given the interest people have in themselves and given that there is no rival theory, Freud's ideas were eagerly embraced—and still are by some.

Many of his beliefs fit in with the current *Zeitgeist*. They can be and often were—by, for example, the Bloomsberries—taken as providing a licence for unbridled sexual activity. If the most basic aspects of personality derive from the sexual urge, and if a frustrated libido causes neurosis, the remedy is obvious. Freud himself often warned against this interpretation of his theory. Although he took a censorious attitude towards so-called perversions in which he included many kinds of sexual activity, including oral sex, that are today regarded as normal, his theories can be seen as justifying all forms of sexual deviation: if our upbringing is responsible for the direction our sexual urges take, why should we hold ourselves responsible for them? It should be remembered that Freud started publishing towards the end of the Victorian age, when many suffered guilt about masturbation and extramarital sex. He helped both to lift the taboo on talking freely about sex and also to remove some of the guilt associated with sexual urges. It is difficult to know how far he is popular because his ideas fitted in with a changing climate of opinion, how far he actually helped to create this climate.

A further reason for Freud's popular success is the sheer imaginative power of his theorizing. As Hans Eysenck elegantly puts it:

> Freud was a great novelist and dramatist himself; his theories are like a medieval morality play, with heroes, villains and monsters rushing about in all directions. Here the 'ego', 'id' and 'superego' have their three-cornered fight; there the censor battles with the forces of the 'unconscious'! Watch the celebrated 'Oedipus complex' burrowing its way to the surface! See 'sublimation' and 'displacement' at work! Watch Eros battling against Thanatos! There is a tremendous cast, and their antics are astounding. The whole action of the play is centred on sex—what could be a greater draw than that?

Much of Freud's own writing has the compulsion of a detective story. In case after case, we watch the great sleuth hunting down the clues to the wicked activity of the unconscious mind. Close on the trail of the id, he follows the same tortuous paths of reasoning as Sherlock Holmes or Hercule Poirot, and despite the many bafflements *en route* we can read happily on, secure in the knowledge that in the last chapter he always gets his complex.

Apart from his talent for drama, Freud was a remarkably persuasive expositor of his own ideas. He was particularly good at anticipating his critics, and took great pains to disarm them: indeed there are few criticisms that can be made of his theories and methods of reasoning that he did not explicitly set out himself. The following passage is typical:

> But you will now tell me that, no matter whether we call the motive force of our analysis transference or suggestion, there is a risk that the influencing of our patient may make the objective certainty of our findings doubtful. What is advantageous to our therapy is damaging to our researches. This is the objection that is most often raised against psychoanalysis, and it must be admitted that, though it is groundless, it cannot be rejected as unreasonable. If it were justified, psychoanalysis would be nothing more than a particularly well-disguised and particularly effective form of suggestive treatment and we should have to attach little weight to all that it tells us about what influences our lives, the dynamics of the mind or the unconscious. That is what our opponents believe; and in especial they think that we have 'talked' the patients into everything relating to the importance of sexual experiences—or even into those experiences themselves—after such notions have grown up in our own depraved imagination. These accusations are contradicted more easily by an appeal to experience than by the help of theory. Anyone who has himself carried out psychoanalyses will have been able to convince himself on countless occasions that it is impossible to make suggestions to a patient in this way. The doctor has no difficulty, of course, in making him a supporter of some particular theory and in thus making him share some possible error of his own. In this respect the patient is behaving like anyone else—like a pupil—but this only affects his intelligence, not his illness. After all, his conflicts will only be successfully solved and his resistances overcome if the anticipatory ideas he is given tally with what is real in him. . . . We endeavour by a careful technique to avoid the occurrence of premature successes due to suggestion; but no harm is done even if they do occur, for we are not satisfied by a first success.

Note the skill with which Freud makes concessions to his opponents—'the objection . . . cannot be rejected as unreasonable'—only to trounce them at the expense of taking for granted the very point he is trying to prove. 'After all, his conflicts will only be successfully solved and his resistances overcome if the anticipatory ideas he is given tally with what is real in him.' Note the disarming cunning of that 'After all'—so reasonable, so persuasive. And then, the *coup de grâce;* 'Anyone who has himself carried out psychoanalysis will be able to convince himself.' In other words, no one except a practising psychoanalyst can possibly judge the theory—a theme that recurs repeatedly in Freud and his successors: it sounds plausible but it is a shabby argument, for we should resist taking anyone's word on trust. whether he is a lawyer, a doctor, a historian or a psychoanalyst. Finally, observe the subtle reference to technique: 'We endeavour by a careful technique'; it sounds scientific but it is not—Freud's techniques are nowhere spelled out in detail, and indeed he says himself that they could only be learned by experience.

Moreover, Freud made a brilliant use of telling analogies—possibly more so than any other advocate of a cause.

> Now, however, you think you have me at your mercy. 'So that's your technique.' I hear you say. 'When a person who has made a slip of the tongue says something about it that suits you, you pronounce him to be the final decisive authority on the subject. 'He says so himself!' But when what he says doesn't suit your book, then all at once you say 'He's of no importance—there's no need to believe him.
>
> That is quite true. But I can put a similar case to you in which the same monstrous event occurs. When someone charged with an offence confesses his deed to the judge, the judge believes his confession; but if he denies it, the judge does not believe him.

Again, Freud was a great synthesizer: he rests his case not merely on his experiences with patients on his couch, but on many acute observations about incidents from everyday life, particularly dreams and mistakes, on evidence from anthropology, myth, and drama, and upon a re-examination of the lives of famous figures such as Leonardo da Vinci. He was somewhat of a polymath, and appears to have had a retentive memory for everything he read. He tries in fact to understand in his own terms almost all of human existence, and there is a temptation to be awestruck by the size of the edifice at the expense of failing to notice whether it is built of bricks or cardboard.

Finally, the ideas are for the most part easy for the layman to follow, since the arguments are couched in everyday language and the few technical terms are no obstacle to understanding. Anyone can quickly learn how to interpret the actions of those around him in Freudian terms, and the reasoning involved is so elusive that nobody can prove them wrong. Making such interpretations has become a parlour trick for novelists, biographers and literary critics, and the trick has much the same fascination when well done as Freud's own detective work in his case histories.

Perhaps one is surprised at Freud's popularity only because in any age there is a tendency to believe that currently held beliefs are rational. They are not. In this respect we are little different from our forefathers who believed in alchemy, necromancy and phrenology. In the Victorian age it was widely held that masturbation led to insanity, and this is stated as a self-evident truth in medical textbooks as late as the early years of the twentieth century. Indeed, the persistence of such myths is startling. The government of the People's Republic of China circulated its citizens with a tract condemning masturbation and explicitly stating that it leads to weakness of the nerves, while a survey conducted as recently as 1960 showed that 50% of the medical students in Philadelphia thought that masturbation led to insanity. Almost all the largest companies in continental Europe (and 3,000 in the US) employ graphology, a technique that has been shown to be useless.

* * *

Given that there are no sound reasons for believing in the dogma of psychoanalysis, we can still ask how far Freud's influence has been for good, how far for harm. On the credit side, the psychoanalytic movement played a role in opening up important areas of human behaviour for discussion and investigation, though there were others, unconnected with analysis, such as Havelock Ellis, who were also instrumental in bringing this about. Moreover, by attempting to specify the causal origins of mental illness, Freud and his successors may have reduced the stigma attached to it.

On the debit side, are the experiences of all the poor wretches who have endured to no purpose the pain of an analysis. It has moreover fostered a false approach to human motivation among all the arts disciplines, including not only practitioners but critics. But maybe in that world it is more important to believe an entertaining lie than a boring truth. In addition, with its emphasis on upbringing, it has imposed unnecessary suffering on the many parents of mentally disturbed children, who have been persuaded or bullied into believing that they were to blame.

Many analysts exhibit unusual arrogance and self-righteousness, as displayed for example in the words of a chairman at the International Psychoanalytic Congress held in Vienna in 1971: 'Psychoanalysts have a unique contribution to make owing to their privileged access to the psychological processes of human functioning. 'Such arrogance is merely a source of irritation to many, but it can be the cause of agony in some. Most hospitals both in Great Britain and North America have had cases of women who were treated for frigidity by analysts only to discover eventually that they had a vaginal lesion; or of men who underwent the pain and expense of an analysis to cure depression or agitation, when the real cause was that their thyroid glands were not functioning properly. Anyone in doubt about this aspect of analysis should read *The Victim is Always the Same,* a book written by a neurosurgeon, I. S. Cooper. It describes the fate of four children suffering from a rare neurological complaint known as dystonia musculorum deformans, which produces horrifyingly painful muscular contractions that force the sufferer into hideously contorted postures. All four were unfortunate enough to fall into the hands of psychoanalytically oriented psychiatrists.

One of these patients was a boy called David. His right hand was so contorted that he could not use it for masturbation, and this was interpreted by the analyst to signify castration anxiety; his illness forced him to stick out his stomach whilst he walked, and this was taken as an imitation of his mother when she was pregnant with his younger sister; he walked with his bottom stuck up in the air, and the psychoanalyst naturally saw this as an invitation for a sexual assault from the rear. David was told that he identified himself with women and was attracted to men. In time he came to believe all the nonsense with which the analyst fed him. This must surely be a classic case of how easy it is to interpret any symptom in Freudian terms—and how easy it is to be wildly wrong. Despite the fact that without an operation the brain disease would become progressively worse, he was discharged from the psychiatric hospital with the diagnosis 'Conversion hysteria: condition—much improved. 'Some of the other cases were even more horrifying.

It is of course true that anyone with a misplaced faith in his own methods can produce suffering of this sort. Many surgeons have made the reverse mistake of operating on patients presenting hysterical symptoms. Nevertheless, some analysts seem peculiarly prone to extreme arrogance, despite the fact—or perhaps because of it—that there is no reason to suppose that analysis is helpful.

Perhaps, however, the worst effect of psychoanalysis is that its mystique has until recently prevented psychologists from developing more effective, if less recondite, methods for alleviating mental disorders.

The wars between the analysts

All analysts share the belief that neuroses are the outward expression of frustrated and unconscious urges and that neurotic patients can be helped by giving them insight into their unconscious mental life. Each of Freud's main successors emphasized a different set of unconscious wishes, and although this has resulted in a rather broader view of neurosis, many analysts practising today are just as dogmatic about the importance of the particular set of motives on which have seized as was Freud himself in his insistence that sex was the root of all evil—and good.

The most renowned of Freud's associates was C. G. Jung, a Swiss Protestant who had in fact developed many of his own ideas before he met Freud. He was at first warmly welcomed into the Freudian fold if only, as Freud put it, to save psychoanalysis from 'the danger of becoming a Jewish national affair'. Having informally appointed Jung as his chosen successor, Freud broke with him in 1913, mainly because Jung rejected the libido as the underlying cause of all neurosis and the motive force behind all human endeavour. In 1910, Freud had told him, 'Promise me never to abandon the sexual theory . . . We must make a dogma of it, an unshakeable bulwark', adding 'I cannot risk my authority.' The development of psychoanalysis has perhaps been marked by more doctrinal schism and intolerance than that of any other movement in history, with the exception of Christianity. Freud, however, did not have the power to burn Jung at the stake, and contented himself with never letting his name cross his lips again. It is not without irony that Jung, who downgraded the importance of the sex drive, was a great womanizer whereas Freud, who thought it was all that mattered, was a chaste family man (as far as we know), who gave up sex at an early age. Maybe, there is something in the psychoanalytic principle of 'compensation' after all.

Unlike Freud, Jung wrote badly and obscurely. Moreover, he made little attempt to build systematic theories but threw in new ideas as they occurred to him. His writings are marked by a strain of mysticism: he believed that dreams could foretell the future, and he claimed to have had many paranormal experiences himself. For example, when he had a heart attack, he dreamt that his doctor would die in his place and the doctor obliged by doing so. He accepted other paranormal phenomena, such as clairvoyance and psychokinesis, attempted to prove the truth of astrology, and derived inspiration from the writings of alchemists and Gnostics, an early Christian heretical sect. He also believed in God.

Despite his mysticism, Jung had some important ideas. Although he did not invent the method, he saw the potential value of word association as a technique for arriving at 'complexes': he showed that if patients were asked to give associations to a list of words, the time taken increased if the word was emotionally laden for them. He even used this method to trap criminals, and was one of the first to experiment with measurements of changes in the electrical resistance of the skin for the same purpose. He can therefore be credited with the invention of the lie-detector. He was also the first to distinguish clearly between introversion and extroversion. The introvert has 'a hesitant, reflective, retiring nature that . . . shrinks from objects, [and] is always slightly on the defensive.' The extrovert on the other hand has 'an outgoing, candid and accommodating nature that adapts easily to a given situation, quickly forms attachments and will often venture forth with careless confidence into unknown situations.' Nowadays, extraversion-introversion is widely accepted as one of the most important dimensions of personality.

Jung anticipated three recent developments in therapy. First, he developed the concept of individuation—harmonizing one's wishes and fulfilling one's talents. Second, he concentrated on the patient's present conflicts and largely ignored childhood. And third, he broadened the concept of the Freudian unconscious to include a great many motives other than the sex drive.

Jung fractionated the mind into many more components than Freud himself. Every man was supposed to contain an 'anima': the feminine part of himself, and every woman an 'animus': her masculine tendencies. Falling in love, according to Jung, results from projecting the anima (or animus) onto the beloved: people in love are in fact in love with a part of themselves and are blind to the true qualities of the object of their love. Again, everyone has their 'shadow', the personification of everything that is evil within them, of which they will normally strive to remain unconscious. In an attempt to disown one's own shadow, it is projected on to others —preferably on to people unlike oneself—and this results in prejudice towards outgroups, for example racial prejudice. Everyone develops a 'persona', or mask, which is the image they exhibit in public as a result of the roles they play: if this differs markedly from the true self, much psychic energy can be used in maintaining it, and neurosis can result.

Jung referred to these aspects of the mind as 'archetypes'. He thought that many of our ideas and images were derived from 'the collective unconscious': we are born with them. Jung developed this notion because he was much impressed by the similarities between some of his patients' dreams and the myths of other civilizations. For example, an uneducated patient asked him whether he could see the sun's penis, from which a great wind came, and Jung subsequently discovered that exactly the same image appears in the Mithraic religion, a cult emanating from the East and practised in the Roman empire. He thought that a child's images of its parents derived at least in part from archetypes of the good and the bad mother as typified by the Virgin Mary and an evil witch. The animus, anima, and shadow were all, at least in part, archetypal, and derived from the collective unconscious of humankind. The archetypes could affect our conscious ways of thinking but they appear more directly in dreams, when they may give us good advice.

Jung was vague about how far archetypes could be modified by experience: he thought they moulded the way people interpreted their own experience, but he also wrote that experience could be 'poured into' the archetypes. The general idea is not so silly as it appears at first sight: we do have inherited instincts like the maternal instinct and the ability to recognize certain facial expressions (like anger or happiness); probably the male's idea of what constitutes an attractive woman is partially innate. But most of the specific archetypes Jung describes cannot be justified. Why these and not others? Furthermore, Jung was vague about the interaction between archetypes and conscious thought processes and the concept of archetypes has no predictive power. He was equally unclear about the origins of neurosis, but he thought it partly arose from the conscious mind being out of touch with the archetypes.

Jung believed that modern man had lost touch with his archetypes, which in previous civilizations were directly represented and accepted in the form of myths. To be healthy and to discover the true self, one has to get in touch with the unconscious elements of the self and in particular with the archetypes. Jung quotes with approval a letter from a patient describing how he came to his true self:

> By keeping quiet, repressing nothing, remaining attentive and by accepting reality, unusual knowledge has come to me and unusual powers as well, ... So now I intend to play the game of life . . . accepting my own nature with its positive and negative sides.

Jung himself suffered a mental crisis in his thirties when he felt that life had no significance, and much of his subsequent thinking seems to be a search after a meaning for existence. Some of his latter-day followers have tried to strip his ideas of their mystical elements, but when they are so stripped most of them appear rather banal and they fail to provide a reason for living.

Anthony Storr, an analyst with a Jungian training, has pointed out that Jung's beliefs about the development of the self can be seen as egocentric. For Jung, salvation lay in obtaining access to the unconscious parts of oneself rather than in satisfactory personal relationships: even love is devalued to the projection of one's own animus. Notwithstanding his mysticism and his egocentricity, however, he should be given credit for widening the scope of analysis.

The idea of accepting all sides of one's nature, discovering the true self, becoming an individual ('individuation' in Jung's terms) or a 'real person', reappears in more recent therapeutic movements, particularly in Gestalt and existential therapy. It has of course also appeared often enough in the past, from the Greek motto 'Know thyself' to Polonius's injunction 'This above all, to thine own self be true.' I have recounted how I rejected the more emotional and more feminine sides of myself—my 'anima': had I been treated by a Jungian analyst, he would doubtless have seized on this aspect of my life. Whether it is desirable or even possible to know all aspects of one's own mind remains an open question.

The techniques of Jungian analysis (often known as 'analytic psycho-therapy' rather than 'psychoanalysis') are similar to Freud's particularly in their emphasis on the use of dreams. They differ only in the kind of inter-pretation made and the concepts used, such as archetypes. Nevertheless, despite his woolly mind, his mysticism, and his failure to become a cult figure, Jung has influenced modern day psychotherapy almost, if not quite, as much as the master himself.

* * *

Adler's system is more eclectic than those of Freud or Jung, but it is also nearer to common sense. One psychiatrist reproached Adler after a lecture by remarking, 'You're only talking common sense', to which Adler replied, 'I wish more psychiatrists did.' He thought of people as being always engaged in the mastery of some task involving the pursuit of goals usually not far removed from consciousness. The neurotic had either picked the wrong goals, adopted poor means of achieving them or was in some way misperceiving reality, for example by seeing everyone as hostile to him. Adler is best known for his concept of 'the inferiority complex'. In an effort to master social relations, people often want to feel superior to others. In areas where they may have reason to feel inferior, they frequently overcompensate, the short man by chasing women and boasting of his sexual exploits, the unintelligent by loudly despising intellectual activities, and so on. Compare Freud's concept of 'reaction formation'.

Much Adlerian theory has a modern ring to it, and in some ways it resembles a recently developed method—behaviour therapy. Adler saw the therapist's task as giving the patient insight into his own goals and attempts to achieve them—his 'life-style'. Insight alone, however, is not enough: the patient must learn with the therapist's help to change his goals when they are not attainable, and when they are, to adopt better methods of reaching them based on a more realistic perception of the world. Adlerian therapy is more directive than either Freudian or Jungian. The therapist may set his patients tasks and may train them to behave more appropriately by, for example, showing more—or less—aggression in dealing with others. Adler thought it important to recognize one's own strengths and weaknesses in order to select suitable goals. He also stressed the importance of interpersonal relations and of seeing other people as they are. His ideas may not sound very exciting, perhaps because they are so near to our everyday modes of thinking, but it is no small achievement to have pursued a common-sense approach to the problems of the neurotic at a time when Freud and Jung were creating their spectacularly implausible theoretical edifices. Freud offered the universal lure of sex, Jung imaginative but opaque ideas; Adler offered neither, but he was much nearer the mark and has been sadly neglected.

* * *

More directly in the Freudian tradition were his daughter, Anna Freud, and Melanie Klein, both of whom worked in London. They undertook the analysis of children as well as adults: since they thought they saw neurosis in very young children, they attached more importance to the pre-Oedipal stage than did Freud, that is, to events in the first two or three years of life. In America, Reik also thought this the most important period for the formation of the personality and concentrated on the way in which the patient had been mothered. Neurosis could be induced both by negligent mothering and by a surfeit of mothering. In particular, Reik thought the 'Jocasta' mother a prime cause of neurosis: such mothers are characterized by having an unfulfilled love life with an adult, so that they direct all their love and concern to their child, whom they will not allow to become independent. The Reikian therapist attempts to uncover the complex of repressed material and emotions centred upon the mother.

Freud himself had taken an unflattering view of women: he regarded them as castrated men, and thought they all suffered from penis envy. Hence, as adults they look up to men and adopt a passive role when faced with the possessors of this powerful organ. One of the first to challenge this view was not surprisingly a woman analyst, Karen Horney. She originally worked in Berlin but emigrated to the United States in 1932 and was so impressed by the cultural differences between Germany and America that she came to believe that neuroses were the product of society's expectations of the developing person. At that time, in the USA boys were expected to be aggressive and ambitious and girls to be meek and compliant. According to

Horney, the neurotic rigidly adopts the ways of behaving expected by society, instead of responding flexibly as the occasion demands. The neurotic is unable to act spontaneously and there is a conflict between society's expectations and the true self.

Horney believed American women aspired to be the ideal wife and mother; failure at this difficult task caused anguish and loss of self-esteem. She also pointed out that the American ethos of success was bound to produce many neuroses, since it is in the very nature of success that not everyone can attain it; those who try and fail become a prey to envy of others and hatred of themselves. Neurotics resist having their false picture of themselves stripped away, and find it difficult to accept themselves as they really are, but only by so doing can they hope to 'actualize' themselves. The therapeutic process therefore attempts to overcome this resistance, to persuade the patients to accept their real self and to develop the best aspects of it.

Hornevian therapy became immensely popular in the United States— 23,000 applications for treatment were made to the Karen Horney clinic in 1972. Horney started two important and subsequently influential trends. She saw neurosis as being caused by society, and she believed that there was some good in everyone; all that was needed to be happy and mentally well was to discover one's own virtues and to develop them. Her ideas contain the seed of the concept of alienation, which today has become a cant word in therapy. It is likely that there are elements of truth in all these theories, but this does not mean that the proposed methods of treatment are effective.

In my account of different schools of analytic therapy, I have omitted many important figures. For example, Eric Erikson made a name for himself in America by concentrating on the ego and the importance of social relations. He is best known for inventing the identity crisis said to afflict adolescents and for beating Freud's five stages of development by three. All his eight stages involve conflict between different emotions, winding up at the age of 65 with that between integrity and despair. Furthermore, I have said little about the neo-Freudians (except for Horney), who while adopting a basically Freudian position put more emphasis on interpersonal relations and less on the dynamic processes occurring within the id.

All these latter day analytic camps arose and flourished almost entirely in the United States for reasons that are obscure, for it seems unlikely that Americans are either more gullible or more neurotic than other nations. One has the impression that many WASPs lack close friends, but the real reason is perhaps that there were a great many Americans wealthy enough to afford the indulgence of being analysed. On a more positive note, many Americans seem to believe in the perfectibility of mankind and particularly of themselves, a need for which Dale Carnegie catered before the analysts arrived on the scene.

I hope I have given some idea of the diversity of the different approaches and of the flavour of each. Many of the practitioners of all schools follow

Freud in believing that nobody should write about a particular brand of analysis unless they have experienced it, but if this precept were followed it would make comparison impossible, since it is upsetting enough to undergo one type of psychoanalysis, let alone several.

It should be apparent that most schools of analysis offer not merely the promise of a cure for neurosis but a view of the nature of our species. Each strives to interpret human existence in terms of its own, usually rather narrow, conception of the meaning of life. Moreover, analytical theories from Freud onwards reflect the preoccupations of the middle classes, who form the great majority of analysts' patients. All schools—except for those that are merely barmy and those that are so mystical as to be virtually unintelligible—may have captured aspects of the truth about the human condition, but no school begins to grapple with the true complexity of humankind. By fastening on only a few features of personality, each presents a caricature, and none grapples with the richness of human existence. Indeed, it is likely that the reasons for breaking down are as multifarious as the goals that different people pursue, and it is curious that, perhaps with the exception of Adler, no analysts have recognized this possibility.

It is perhaps a mark of the intolerance of the different schools of analysis that each refuses to have anything to do with the others and that the series of schisms has continued. Jung, Adler, Rank, Reich and others were expelled from the Freudian camp. In the US Alexander and Grinker broke away from the main Freudian bastion, the American Psychoanalytic Association, and founded their own institute, keeping its name (the American Academy of Psychoanalysis) as similar as possible to that of the body from which they had seceded; Karen Horney also founded her own institute, from which in turn her associates Sullivan and Fromm duly departed.

The different analytic factions agree on only two points. First, to become a member it is necessary to endure a training analysis, supplemented by lectures on the dogma to which the particular school adheres. Second, for the sake of the patient it is essential to charge high fees; only thus will patients recognize the value of analysis and stick to it, for fear they have spent their money in vain.

It could be argued that all forms of analysis are elitist and self-indulgent: with the exception of Adlerian therapy and possibly Hornevian, they concentrate solely on the patients while ignoring their interactions with others. Some analysts have themselves commented that analysis may have untoward effects on the patient's spouse and children.

Both in America and Britain, the number of analysts is declining, but the therapy is still practised. I believe that there will come a time when analysis will be regarded as one of those curious aberrations of the mind—ranging from astrology to leeching blood—to which humankind is periodically prone. Each age invents its own delusional systems.

Psychotherapeutic sects

Although the couch, along with orthodox psychoanalysis, has largely disappeared, psychotherapy is one of the most flourishing industries of the twentieth century. It permeates every aspect of human life. Psychotherapists descend like vultures on the scene of all major disasters, such as the murder of school children in Dunblane, Scotland or the massacre at Waco in Oklahoma City. Whether you are lacking in self-esteem, not sufficiently assertive, dissatisfied with your marriage, too fat or too thin, there is an army of psychotherapists and counsellors who will help or at least claim to help. There are workshops on almost every human activity -Lesbian workshops, feminist workshops, orgasm workshops, and workshops for alcoholics, drug abusers, deviant adolescents, smokers, and pregnant women. There are psychologists who specialize in treating members of the Stock Exchange and other financial institutions and others who deal with 'bench stress', an affliction of judges. Camelot, which organizes the British National Lottery, provides counsellors for winners. University students are no longer expelled for not working, they are sent to one of the many resident psychotherapists (at my own university it was a standing joke that if a student went to the doctor with a sore toe, the first question asked was whether his mother had trodden on it when he was an infant). Finally, there are psychotherapists who specialize in helping one another to deal with the stress imposed by their patients, proof that therapists themselves believe in the efficacy of their techniques. We are not in the age of computers, aeroplanes or space travel, we are in the age of the psychotherapist.

At the last count there were over 400 types of psychotherapy, each with its own brand name. In this chapter I list four of the more respectable, in a later one some of the wilder, though admittedly it is sometimes hard to make the distinction. Because nowadays most therapists deal with people who are not mentally ill but are merely disturbed by their lot in life, they usually refer to those they treat as 'clients' rather than 'patients'.

One puzzling phenomenon is that despite extreme doctrinal differences. the different psychotherapeutic factions live in harmony. They do not on the whole disparage one another, unlike the analysts who used every available weapon to crucify other schools including character assassination based on employing their own analytic methods on their opponents. Parties thrown by psychoanalysts are terrifying, since anything you say is likely to be used as evidence against you, or rather against your unconscious. Psychotherapists on the contrary seem to believe that the more schools the merrier: if you are inveigled into one psychotherapy, you may well try another when you become fed up with the first.

Most psychotherapists subscribe to 'dynamic therapy', the attempt to examine people's motives. Freud's belief in the overriding importance of the libido has been dropped, but his emphasis on unconscious motives is usually retained. By helping people become aware of these, it is assumed (without evidence) that they will be better able to deal with them. Therapists may also try to help people to sort out conflicts between different motives, to attain their aims in life or to relinquish them if they are impossible to achieve.

The belief that to be a good therapist one must have had psychotherapy oneself has survived; this is remarkable, as the few studies undertaken on this question have shown that therapists' effectiveness is either decreased or at best not influenced by having been in therapy themselves, but objective evidence means little to most therapists. According to Sol Garfield, a leading American psychotherapist, budding therapists select which therapy to practise on bases 'other than research evidence', which include whether they find some therapies boring and others 'interesting and exciting'. In fact many psychotherapists are eclectic, using ideas and techniques devised from several different approaches.

* * *

Almost all therapists believe that neurotics lack personal esteem. It is true that one of the few secure results in the field of psychotherapy is that recovery from a breakdown is associated with improvements in self-regard. Hence, most therapists will attempt to build up their clients' self-esteem, if only by showing that they are genuinely concerned for them.

This approach to therapy was carried to its extreme by Carl Rogers in the United States. In the late 1940s he founded a new movement called 'non-directive' or 'client-centred' therapy, in which the therapist merely listens to his clients and reflects back what they say: the therapist expresses his or her concern but does not make interpretations, nor give any direct guidance. Rogers was one of the first clinical psychologists to break with the psychoanalytic tradition and develop his own therapeutic style. He also departed from the medical tradition, regarding neurosis not as an illness but as on a continuum with the difficulties that affect us all.

Client-centred therapy has a complex theoretical superstructure, though many of the ideas appear to derive from such predecessors as Jung, Horney and Reik. Rogers thought that the primary human drive was towards self-actualization (individuation in Jung's terms): throughout life people have a need for deeper and more creative experience. Out of the need for richer experience, the growing person comes to develop the concept of himself as distinct from the outer world. His self-concept is enriched when others have a high regard for him, and hence the need to be liked stems from the need for self-actualization. This drive for approval can distort the perception of the self: in order to please others, people may suppress aspects of themselves that are unacceptable, and strive to develop a more likeable but false front. Neurosis arises because neurotics distort both their behaviour and their perception of themselves in directions calculated to obtain esteem. Hence they are prevented from actualizing their true selves, and anxiety arises.

Rogers thought that successful therapy was based on three crucial factors, all of which are aspects of the therapist's attitude to the client. First, the therapist must accept his clients unconditionally as they really are, by providing 'unconditional positive regard'; in this way, clients are helped to accept their true self. Next, the therapist must be completely genuine and honest in everything he says, in order to demonstrate that it is possible to accept one's true feelings. Finally, he must understand and empathize with the clients' feelings. Since the aim of the therapy is to make the client accept and develop his true self, and since only the client can know that self, the therapy is 'non-directive' and is centred on the client. The three qualities of the successful therapist have been summarized in the acronym 'CARE', standing for Communicated Authenticity (genuineness), Regard (warmth) and Empathy (understanding). Rogers believed that the actual therapeutic techniques used were of little consequence. All that mattered was for the therapist to display CARE. He even wrote that his own client-centred technique was 'by no means an essential condition of therapy'.

Rogers's views pose a number of problems. He is not very specific about what constitutes self-actualization, perhaps because different people may actualize themselves in different ways. He adopts a distinctly Panglossian view of human nature: everyone is good at heart if only they can discover it. But cultivation of the self can be regarded as an elitist and selfish doctrine. Most people do not have the leisure for self-actualization—they are too busy trying to earn enough to pay the rent. Finally, the therapy can presumably only be practised by those rare individuals who, like Rogers himself, can be totally accepting of others and who believe that at heart everyone is good.

Rogers would also ask his patients to be honest and display their emotions, a request that could lead to contretemps as when a woman client flung herself into his arms and kissed him announcing, 'I love you, I love you.' Because he was such a passive therapist. Rogers has been wittily described as 'a cheer-leader watching the client engage in self-help'. He was, however, an honest man, being one of the first therapists to encourage objective tests of his ideas and of the extent to which his therapy was helpful.

The results of these studies are not encouraging. Therapeutic sessions were tape recorded and the degree to which the therapist displayed warmth, genuineness and empathy towards the client was assessed. Some studies showed that therapy was more effective with one or other of these qualities, but which quality was important varied from study to study. Moreover, other studies showed that some of these qualities actually produced disadvantageous results and that therapists high in one quality, for example warmth, were likely to be low on another, for example, genuineness. More recent research suggests that therapists who are warm and supportive do marginally better than those who are not. The discrepancies in the results obtained are hardly surprising. First, some of the three qualities may be incompatible with others. For example, if a therapist dislikes the client, he can only show warmth at the expense of failing to be genuine (sincere). Second, It may well be that the failure to find that the more empathy the therapist displays the more likely is the patient to benefit is that there is an optimal level of empathy. If there is too little patients will be alienated, if too much they may feel their problems are worse than they are: moreover, nobody likes gush. It is unlikely that this type of relationship between empathy and successful therapy would have been discovered, using the standard methods of analysing data. Third, the optimal degree of each of these qualities is likely to vary from patient to patient.

Since non-directive therapists do little in the way of interpretation, it is possible to simulate with a computer program, albeit in rather a crude fashion, the way in which they talk. Such a program was written at the Massachusetts Institute of Technology. On one occasion, it was left loaded on the computer in error and a computer salesman wishing to access it from a remote terminal found himself conversing with it through a teletype, without knowing what had happened. He wanted to demonstrate the computer's performance to potential customers. The following dialogue ensued.

Salesman:	Do you think I can use the computer this morning?
Computer:	Why do you ask?
Salesman:	I might be able to make some additional telecomp sales.
Computer:	Why aren't you sure?
Salesman:	My prospective customers have never seen a demonstration of the system.
Computer:	Does this mean very much to you?
Salesman:	Of course it does.
Computer:	You seem very positive about that.
Salesman:	This is ridiculous.
Computer:	What do you mean this is ridiculous?

Salesman: Is there any reason why I can't use the computer now?
Computer: Tell me more about your prospective customers.

The program was of course marginally more obtuse than most non-directive therapists, but it does catch the flavour of their technique.

*   *   *

Gestalt therapy is one of the first and best known of the new schools. As one verse has it:

> That brings us round to Frederick Perls
> Whose penchant for pinching the bottoms of girls
> Made lechery a therapeutic style . . .
> When has there ever before been a doctor
> Who charged his patient while he foctor?

Perls, the founder of Gestalt therapy, took a medical degree and then trained as a psychoanalyst in Germany and Austria, where he subsequently worked with brain-injured soldiers. He emigrated to South Africa, becoming a psychiatrist in the British Army, and in 1946 moved to the United States to work in private practice.

In an attempt to gain credibility, Gestalt therapy borrowed its name from a movement in experimental psychology that studied vision and reasoning: in fact the two schools have little or nothing in common.

Perls' theorizing is so vague as to be worthless, and the application of Gestalt terminology to personality and emotion is a gimmick. He believed that neurosis arises because the personality is fragmented and is no longer an integrated Gestalt (that is, a whole). The healthy person can form good Gestalten: he can organize his experiences in meaningful ways. When someone is reading they are conscious only of the meaning of the text: it stands out against a background of other sensations of which the reader is only dimly aware. Neurotics are unable to organize their experience meaningfully into figure and background in this way, and are unconscious of large areas of their experience. Perls placed great emphasis on being aware of one's environment, both the appearance of objects in the world and the feelings of others. Gestalt therapists also attempt to train patients to become aware of their own feelings and bodily sensations. Great stress is laid on the 'here and now', on concentrating on what is happening within and around one in the immediate present: neither the past nor the future exist, only the present.

Perls was suspicious of verbal expressions, and like Reich tried to make the patient aware not just of what he was saying but of the tone of voice used, the expressive movements of his body, the presence of bodily tensions and so on. He thought there were five layers within the neurotic personality. The outward layer consists of 'game-playing': the neurotic plays games or roles, and attempts to live up to a false conception of himself. If this layer is stripped off, the 'phobic' layer is revealed, in which the patient is afraid of his true self, concerned about his failures and governed by moral imperatives ('shoulds' and 'should-nots'). Beyond this is the 'impasse' in which the patient feels empty and without meaning in his life. Next comes the 'implosive' layer in which the neurotic turns his thoughts inwards: he uses his psychic energy to examine himself instead of interacting with the world. The final layer, which when uncovered signifies a return to health, is the 'explosive'. The patient reassesses his own feelings and can express himself openly and spontaneously whilst interacting fully with the world around him. There is no evidence for any of these stages.

The emptiness of Perls's theorizing, much of it based on verbal puns and silly analogies, can best be illustrated by a quotation:

> What is the opposite of existence? The immediate answer would be non-existence, but this is incorrect. The opposite would be anti-existence, just as the opposite of matter is antimatter. As you know, scientists have managed to create matter out of energy. What has this to do with us in psychology? . . . There are no 'things'. 'Nothingness' in the Eastern languages is 'no-thingness'. We in the West think of nothingness as a void, an emptiness, a non-existence. In Eastern philosophy and modern physical science, nothingness 'no-thingness' is a form of process, ever moving.

There is little new in Perls's thought—he borrowed ideas from Freud, Reich, Sullivan, the existential psychologists and many others, and then applied the window-dressing of a terminology partly invented by himself and partly borrowed from the Gestalt psychologists.

Perls himself was a bombastic bully. He often abused and ridiculed his patients, some of whom, including one who doubled up as his mistress, committed suicide. He used his position as a psychotherapist to have sex with those of his women patients whom he fancied 'in the here and now'—namely his consulting room. In this way he doubtless tried to help them strip themselves down to the explosive layer. Some of his followers appear to have inherited these traits—a tendency to bully and exploit patients for their own ends. Gestalt therapy is often very aggressive: the therapist challenges everything patients say in an attempt to make them concentrate on the present and dig down to their true feelings. The therapist tries to strip away the patient's defences and to prevent them acting passively. He may forbid them to use the word 'it' and other detached verbal expressions, and will constantly accuse them of playing games in order to hide their true self. An outbreak of anger or tears from a patient is taken as a sign that they are beginning to recover their feelings.

Although Perls and his followers were vague in their theorizing, they did invent a number of specific tricks to help the patient develop fuller awareness. Patients may be told to talk to a pain in their body, act out parts of their dreams, pretend to be an inanimate object or address an empty chair while imagining their father or some other important figure in their life sitting in it. I shall instance further ploys of this sort when I describe the encounter group movement, in which Gestalt therapy has been highly influential.

No effort has been made to test the efficacy of Gestalt therapy; the emphasis on subjective experience as the measure of all things has made its practitioners reluctant to submit their techniques to objective testing. Its aggressive nature and its emphasis on self-actualization can make it very threatening to anyone at all seriously depressed or anxious. At such times it is particularly difficult to live up to someone else's idea of what you should be like.

Indeed at one point in my own depression I attempted some of the exercises recommended by Gestalt therapists. I tried to 'make up sentences about what [I was] immediately aware of, beginning them with "now" or "at this moment" or "here and now" ', but I continued to be depressingly aware only of my own jealous obsessions. I tried thinking of 'pairs of opposites' and reversing the roles of everyday objects; I tried attending to my own bodily feelings—itches, aches and tensions. I was, however, unable to see the world in a new way or to feel empathy with inanimate objects like stones and tables; in my depressed condition I thought to myself that my failure signified that I was an even more hopeless human being than I had imagined. I recalled that I had always had great difficulty recognizing people. (Indeed, I once followed a singularly attractive woman in the street, only to find on overtaking her that she was my wife, a discovery that induced a strange mixture of pleasure and disappointment.) The result of my brief brush with Gestalt methods merely made me feel more inadequate than ever.

* * *

Another therapy that concentrates on the present rather than the past is 'existential therapy' or 'existential analysis' as it is sometimes known. It stems from the obscure philosophizing of Heiddeger and Sartre and was introduced in the US in the 1950s by Binswanger, a Swiss therapist. His works do not make easy reading, as is illustrated by the following not atypical extract about a young girl called Lola, who caught typhoid and subsequently developed various phobias including the fear that something terrible would befall her:

> It is self-evident and follows from the total mode of existence that, in the case of Lola Voss, her existence had deserted itself and had succumbed to an alien power . . . It does not maintain itself any more in designing its own authentic potentialities, but is constantly sucked into the whirl of inauthentic possibilities of being, that is, such as have not been chosen by it but imposed upon it by a power alien to the self. It exists only as something 'thrown', or in the state of 'thrownness'. But thrownness is

still part of existence. Hence, the 'alien power', although alien to the self, cannot be considered as alien to existence.

When one of Binswanger's patients committed suicide, it was claimed that the therapy had been successful because it had enabled her to make a dramatic choice. Not all existential therapists are so extreme, but it is difficult to understand their ideas, let alone to encapsulate them in a few words. Much stress is placed on our freedom to choose and on trying to make patients accept that they are responsible for their actions but are always free to act wisely. The person you are depends upon the choice of actions you make, and depending on your choices you are always in the course of becoming another person. Existentialist therapists emphasize the totality of current experience without trying to interpret it: they encourage patients to accept their own experiences. Everyone is said to be 'thrown'—as in a die, meaning that certain aspects of their existence are determined for them by the circumstances of their birth and environment. It is everyone's task to find their 'authentic self, and much play is made with the concept of self-actualization: failure to live up to one's authentic self results in inescapable guilt and neurosis. Everyone has to realize that fundamentally they are alone in the world and must face up to events over which they have no control including the certainty of death.

Most existential analysts believe that therapists must never deceive their client in any way; like Rogers they must act with genuineness, spontaneity and love. To someone in the throes of a severe breakdown, however, existentialist doctrines can be very threatening—particularly the emphasis on self-actualization and taking responsibility for one's own actions. The existentialists believe that anxiety is produced because people seek meaning in their life, but they must accept that life has no meaning. Their very state of 'being-in-the-world' produces 'existential anxiety' and the only relief comes from accepting it, without attempting to combat or explain it. They must also be true to their 'authentic self, though no guidance is given about what is authentic and what is not.

* * *

The paramount importance of the quality of one's own experiences and of universal love formed the basis of yet another movement, humanistic therapy, which was introduced in America mainly by Abraham Maslow, an avowed totalitarian who opposed equal votes for everyone on the grounds that 'The taste or judgement of one superior person can and should outweigh 1,000 or a million blind ones', a view that curiously was shared by his arch-opponent, the behaviourist, B. F. Skinner. In 1967 he tried to dignify his ideas by setting them out in 28 propositions which combine pomposity, silliness and vagueness in about equal proportions. Some extracts follow:

Proposition I. Self-actualizing individuals (more matured, more fully human), already suitably gratified in their basic needs, are now motivated in . . . higher ways, to be called 'metamotivations'.

Proposition II. All such people are devoted to some task, call, vocation, beloved work.

Proposition V. At this level the dichotomizing of work and play is transcended.

Proposition X. Less evolved persons seem to use their work ... as a means to an end.

Proposition XII. These intrinsic values are instinctoid in nature . . . The illnesses resulting from deprivation of intrinsic values (metaneeds) we may call metapathologies.

As Braginsky and Braginsky point out, few people can aspire to meta-motivation: The assembly line worker who is bored with his job (not "devoted to beloved work"), who looks forward to weekends when he can go fishing (he "dichotomizes work and play") who, nonetheless, works as much overtime as he can in order to earn enough money to send his oldest daughter to college (he "works as a means to an end") is suffering from "metapathology".' They might have added that he is presumably a 'less evolved person' than someone who devotes himself to the 'beloved task' of writing bunkum.

Humanistic therapy has developed considerably since Maslow and is by now perhaps the most popular form of therapy, particularly among lay therapists, both in Britain and America. It embraces several different approaches but originally its supporters had a vague belief in the dignity of humanity, which they regarded as threatened by science, particularly psychological science. Nowadays they tend to think that everyone has a right to happiness, which can be achieved by 'self-actualization' (also called 'change' or 'personal growth'). They usually take it for granted that all change is for the better, but a cynic might argue that, at least after the age of 30, most people only change for the worse, becoming more not less selfish. Unlike the existentialists, humanistic psychologists take a singularly optimistic view of the world. As one of its practitioners remarked, 'You can . . . achieve . . . anything you want out of life . . . your state of mind determines what you can and can't do . . . Reprogram your mind in minutes. It's the new science of personal achievement.' Dale Carnegie strikes again. Never mind that you may not have the talent to fulfil your aspirations: just think positively and all will be well. The cult word of modern psychotherapy is 'personal growth'. It reminds me of a story about a therapist who said to his patient 'You must learn to grow', to which the patient replied, 'But I'm six foot three already.' It is presumably the promises held out by recent humanistic therapy that have made it so successful, but there must be many disappointed customers. There is no question of coming to terms with yourself, as many other therapies advocate; you have no limitations provided you are prepared to 'change'. The main technique appears to be exhortation and encouragement, though humanistic therapists borrow ideas and techniques at will from others ranging from psychoanalysis to Gestalt therapy.

Great emphasis is usually laid on self-esteem, but as Aric Sigman notes, 'Feeling bad about feeling bad about yourself contributes little to self-esteem.' Can't phrases like 'you must learn to love yourself or nobody else will' are used. It does not seem to have occurred to anyone that it is possible to have too much self-esteem. One outcome of depression is low self-regard, but when I was hypomanic, I had dangerously high self-esteem and became a pest to those around me and a danger to myself. As far as I know, no one has taken the trouble to discover whether criminals have high or low self-esteem. Certainly many have no sense of shame and it seems likely that a successful bank robbery or even snatching an old woman's purse is one way to boost self-regard. Some governments of American states are taking part in the effort to raise self-esteem. For example, California has established 'The Californian Task Force to Promote Self-esteem and Personal and Social Responsibility'. Nobody asks whether people with low self-esteem make better or worse citizens. It is known that most people have an exaggerated view of their talents as compared with judgements made by their friends; it is true that this will enable them to persevere with the attempt to achieve their ambitions, but it will also make them aim too high and hence fail in their endeavours. It seems likely that humanistic therapy's concentration on personal growth and on the self is merely rendering people unpleasantly selfish and unhealthily introspective.

The view that everyone is potentially good has had some undesirable consequences. There is a tendency not to punish offenders: their crimes are the fault of their upbringing, their poverty or their race. The result has been case after case in Britain where violent behaviour results in a disproportionately small sentence or even no sentence at all. Adolescents with dozens of convictions are sent by social workers on safari in Africa, though just why a sojourn in that continent should promote 'personal growth' is unclear. This lenient sentencing policy has produced howls of protest from the victims of the crimes: a desire for revenge is instinctive, but the victims are not supposed to feel it: instead they are advised to attend 'anger workshops', in which psychotherapists will help them cope with their fury.

Psychology, particularly humanistic psychology continues to invade new domains. There are now dozens of schools in America and a few in Britain where children are taught 'emotional intelligence'. They are systematically observed and are counselled on how to identify their feelings and those of others, on exercising self-restraint, on delaying gratification, and on reducing stress. Indeed, almost the only desirable quality not taught is a sense of humour, but that might be beyond the powers of their earnest teachers. Even big corporations have fallen victim to the prestige of psychologists, who offer a range of workshops with high sounding but meaningless titles like 'Dimensional Management Feedback', 'Cross-functional Team Building' or 'Intensive Interviewing Skills'. It is not known whether such workshops do any good, but it is known that they are extremely lucrative for those who run them. In fact, psychologists know no more about personality and emotion than the man in the street: their claim do be 'experts' is bogus as Ellen Herman demonstrates in her fascinating history of the use of psychology by the US government. For years the American government has hardly dared take a decision without consulting psychologists on its likely effects: since they invariably receive conflicting advice, they do what they would have done anyway.

The popularity and diversity of therapeutic groups, particularly in California, has led to the introduction of many entertaining new expressions. If you want to get your act together, learn how to relate, work through your hostility, get to know where you're at, get on the right wavelength, or stop acting out, you'd better join a personal growth group, a consciousness raising group, a human potential group, or even an aromatherapy one. If your problem is more specific, then it may be that the answer is a flirting workshop or a creative divorce group. After all, according to the human potential movement, there is no such thing as an insoluble problem.

Group therapy

Group therapy is now practised by therapists of almost all theoretical persuasions, with the exception of orthodox Freudians, for whom it is not a suitable method because of their emphasis on uncovering the history of the individual. This therapy began in the 1930s under the neo-Freudians, who stressed the importance of social interaction. The optimal number of patients in a group is usually thought to be about eight. Many practitioners believe there should be two therapists present preferably male and female: apart from giving two points of view, they can observe and interpret one another's behaviour in the context of the dynamics of the group.

Group therapy uses a variety of techniques and has little place for theory other than the belief that the group will induce personal growth in its members. There are two exceptions, which will be dealt with briefly. In the 1950s, Moreno invented psychodrama, in which clients perform the roles of themselves or others. They each take it in turn to be the protagonist, who acts a given role, for example that of spouse, child, or friend: the people with whom the person interacts are played by other members of the group. The therapist directs the brief 'drama', and afterwards everyone discusses it. The protagonists are encouraged to play their roles in different ways in the hope that they will discover a method of behaving that is more adaptive.

Berne, the inventor of the other therapy transactional analysis—believed that everyone was composed of parent, child, and adult. The aim of his therapy was to bring parent and child under the control of the adult, while leaving the child free to produce spontaneous and creative behaviour and the parent to exhibit caring behaviour. The therapy has the unusual merit that it encourages the client to care for others' happiness as well as their own: one of its slogans is 'I'm OK, you're OK.' Berne believes that most behaviour is simply an attempt to please, impress, dominate or manipulate others. People play games with one another and the content of what they say should not be taken literally. He gives as an example of a game a woman who encourages a man to pursue her by dressing provocatively or lifting her skirt and then when he falls for the act rejecting him—all done to boost her ego. Berne points out to the members of his groups the games they are playing and encourages them to act towards one another with sincerity and intimacy. Although both psychodrama and transactional analysis are highly ingenious, nobody has any idea whether they actually do any good and both are now on the wane.

* * *

One obvious advantage of group therapy is that it saves the therapist's time, but a plausible rationale has been developed for supposing that at least for some patients it may be a better method of treatment than individual therapy. Irvin Yalom of Stanford University, one of its leading exponents, lists ten advantages of group over individual therapy, of which the most important are as follows.

Most neurotics are pessimistic about their future: only if they can be given hope will they begin to strive towards recovery. By including within the same group patients at different stages of recovery, those who are most seriously disturbed may see directly by observing others that recovery is possible. The success of Alcoholics Anonymous may in some measure be due to this factor.

Many neurotics feel that their wretchedness is unique: they become isolated and lonely and then compound the problem by blaming themselves for their own sorry state. Once in a group, they can see that they are not that much out of the ordinary. They can also share their miseries more readily with others who are equally unhappy, since they do not run the risk of being looked down upon. It will be recalled that patients in the hospital I attended did not dare to confide their problems to their friends. Yalom found that many normal people, as well as neurotics, harbour secrets that they feel would make them despised if they revealed them to others. He requested normal people to write down anonymously their most guilty secret. He was struck by how commonly the same secrets were produced —feelings of inadequacy, worries about being unable truly to love anyone or to feel deeply, and shame about deviant sexual longings or actual sexual practices. Any therapist knows that everyone has committed cruel or dishonest acts of which they are ashamed, but the demonstration from other patients that we are all guilty of the same sins is surely a much more effective way of relieving guilt than any reassurance from a therapist.

In a successful group, patients help one another both by sympathy and by interpreting each other's behaviour. Feelings of uselessness and worthlessness predominate in most neurotics: helping other patients may go some way to restoring their own self-esteem.

Most neurotics have poor relationships with other people. They may lack social skills, and misinterpret the behaviour of others particularly when it is directed at themselves. In the course of group therapy, they may learn from other members that they avoid looking people in the face, or that they are bores or overbearing. Yalom instances a patient who in conversation went into endless minute and often irrelevant detail in everything he said: until the group pointed this out, he had been unable to understand why people shunned him.

Within the safety of a group, patients may also be able to experiment with new ways of responding that they would not risk trying on their own friends. Most people, particularly neurotics, are often afraid to show their true feelings for fear of making fools of themselves. If patients can give expression to their feelings before the group and are still accepted, the experience can be both cathartic and liberating. Yalom refers to this as 'the corrective emotional experience'. He asked patients who had recovered if they could recall an incident in group therapy which for them formed a turning point. Two kinds of incidents were commonly mentioned. In the first, the patient had expressed anger or had condemned something said by another patient; he had been surprised that his forthrightness, instead of provoking a catastrophe, had been calmly accepted. He had learned that his previous avoidance of saying anything that might give offence was irrational. Secondly, some patients recalled incidents in which they had openly expressed liking for other members of the group and were surprised to find that they were not derided or rejected. The group, then, makes possible the open display of previously concealed thoughts or feelings: if these are accepted, the experience can be beneficial. Yalom administered a questionnaire to his patients in which they had to place 60 possibly helpful items in order from most helpful to least. They judged the factors listed above to be the most beneficial.

Although a case can be made for the potential benefits of group therapy: the question remains how often these benefits are realized in practice. Some groups may function along the ideal lines indicated by Yalom, with members being supportive towards one another while at the same time accurately appraising each other's good and bad points. In many other groups, however, the members are hostile towards each other: they use the group as an opportunity to dominate or to vent their own aggression, and far from supporting one another's weaknesses they may actively disparage them. It is common for a member of a group who disagrees with the rest or who is merely different from them to become a scapegoat. The reader will recall that the group therapy I attended in hospital bore little resemblance to the ideal depicted by Yalom. It is not a suitable method of treatment for those who are very disturbed—when I first entered hospital I was unable to sit through group sessions, since I could not control my anxiety.

Yalom claims that groups can be wrecked if one member monopolizes the conversation, or is boring, silent, or self-righteous or who consistently complains while refusing help from the group. It would be difficult indeed to pick eight people none of whom had any of these attributes. According to Yalom, groups are also disrupted if their members have affairs with one another.

Yalom found that patients popular with the group in the sixth week of therapy had a better prognosis than unpopular patients: group therapy may help you if you are likeable, but not if you are not. Most of Yalom's ideas are based on his own observations of groups, though some have been confirmed by more systematic research which suggests that successful groups are cohesive, they provide an opportunity for catharsis, for learning how to deal with other members and for gaining insight into oneself.

On one point all are agreed: group therapy can make many of the participants worse not better. In one study the casualty rate was 30%, while about another 30% dropped out, many of whom presumably did so because they felt the therapy was harming them. One would of course expect group therapy to be more hazardous than individual therapy, because the participants are exposed not merely to the therapist but to the other members of the group who may be less sensitive than the leaders, though to judge by my own experiences some therapists can be less understanding and less caring than members of the public. Some people, including Yalom, despite his doubts, continue to believe that group therapy can be beneficial overall, at least when conducted by caring therapists. The evidence suggests that, if drop-outs are ignored, it does about as well (or badly) as individual dynamic therapy, but the results of this research are unconvincing, since none of the studies took into account all the problems of testing therapy that are discussed in Chapter 23. It should, moreover, be noted that the groups on which these findings are based were run by the most respectable leaders. Maverick therapists will normally not allow investigations by outsiders and they are almost certainly the ones that are least successful and do the most damage.

* * *

The basic techniques of group therapy are now widely used with people who would not be classified as neurotic. In business, the method was known as 'T-groups' or 'sensitivity training groups', which were attended by members of companies in order to learn how to improve their skill in dealing with others: the theory was that they would learn how others saw them, modify their own bad habits, become more sensitive to others" feelings, and hence be more effective in their jobs. When a businessman returns from such a group, he is sometimes at first rated as more effective by his colleagues, but any beneficial effects seem to dissipate rapidly, and no effect is measurable after six months or a year. Nobody has attempted to assess whether T-groups produce more or less short-term benefits than other changes in routine like a skiing holiday, a weekend in the country or an ocean cruise:

most such alternatives have the merit of being cheaper. Almost as many who attend T-groups are harmed by them as are helped: the biggest organization conducting such groups is the National Training Laboratory, whose headquarters are in Washington, and they report that 1% of their clients suffer 'serious stress and mental disturbance' as a result of attending such groups. Many more suffer less serious emotional upset.

Another derivative of group therapy is encounter groups until recently enormously fashionable in the United States, where it was estimated that one adult in three participated in this craze. In general, encounter groups encourage more extreme interactions than their predecessors, T-groups. There are now a great variety of these groups, and people have diverse motives for attending. They may wish to explore themselves, to improve the ways in which they relate to others, to experiment with methods of behaving that they do not normally use, to make friends, to feel part of a group, to use the group as a chance to take out their aggression on people whom they will not see again, to obtain a sexual kick, to find a marriage partner, or to satisfy their curiosity about what happens in such groups.

The founders of the encounter movement were Rogers, Perls, and another clinical psychologist called Schutz, and its Mecca was Esalen, at Big Sur, California. Although all kinds of encounter groups exist, the movement tends to be dominated by the ideas of Rogers and Perls. Great emphasis is placed on the expression of the emotions, however transient or trivial; on becoming aware of one's own and others' true selves—often achieved by aggressively telling other members of the group what one thinks of them, whether it be good or ill; and on the value of opening oneself up to immediate experience and feelings. Participants are taught by the leaders to ignore the verbal content of each other's remarks and to concentrate only on the feelings behind them. Intellectual remarks expressing opinions, as against the expression of feelings, are anathema to most leaders of encounter groups, and are regarded as a defence against one's true feelings—'mindfucking', in the schoolboy language adopted by Perls. According to him, 'a good therapist does not listen to the bullshit the patient produces, but to the sound, to the music, to the hesitations.'

Numerous techniques have been developed to persuade the members of encounter groups to wean themselves from mere verbalization and to act out their emotions. Schutz starts off the proceedings by asking members to say whom they like and dislike and why. Members may be asked to spread themselves out on the floor and try to experience sensations suggested by the leader; they may be instructed to feel one another's bodies, concentrating on the nature of the sensations obtained. They are encouraged to confront one another—at first perhaps just by standing in pairs staring into one another's eyes, or- -through the use of Gestalt techniques—by occupying the "hot seat" or 'making the rounds'. A patient in the 'hot seat' is told by each of the other members in turn exactly what they think of him. In the reciprocal process, making the rounds, when a member has made a remark about the group as a whole, he may be asked to make it individually to each member of the group in turn, showing in what way it is applicable. Another method is the 'stay-with-it' technique: a member who expresses some unpleasant feeling, for example disgust at the sight of someone else's body, may be asked to stay with the feeling—to preserve the disgust as long as possible and to talk about it: by so doing he is supposed to assimilate his unpleasant feelings and learn that they are part of himself, instead of running away from them.

In some encounter groups, nudity is *de rigueur,* and the participants are ordered to hug one another. Some use drugs to heighten sensory awareness of the here and now, others encourage group sex. One Gestalt encounter group devoted to 'marriage enrichment' at a respected Canadian university became a simple vehicle for wife-swapping. Many encounter groups are not counted as successful until all the members have at one time or another been reduced to tears; others involve physical punch-ups. Even that relatively staid body RELATE (which changed its name from 'The Marriage Guidance Council' in deference to the growing number of unmarried couples) has faith in tears. It insists that its counsellors attend encounter groups as part of its so-called training. A woman friend of mine training with RELATE was ordered to attend a group made up of strangers, who hysterically poured out their troubles to one another. Because she was the only one not to cry, she was subsequently told that she must have a year's psychotherapy before rejoining the course. One would have thought that the last thing couples in distress would welcome is the sight of a counsellor bursting into tears over their problems. In Britain many universities run courses for social workers which include compulsory encounter groups. The student's performance at such groups is assessed—'Cried well: 100%'. One student at my own university failed a course for not crying.

The American Psychiatric Association's Task Force on Encounter Groups found evidence of many instances of physical injuries. Marathon encounter groups lasting for 48 rely on sheer fatigue to break down normal methods of reacting, feeling and sensing. Perhaps the best known such group is EST (Erhard Seminar Training). Erhard hired large halls which he filled with his adherents, who were forbidden while there to eat, drink or smoke or even, so it is said, to relieve themselves, though how this could be is unclear given that the sessions lasted for 24 hours. His assistants circulated among the crowd often insulting its members, while he would present the simple message that 'Your self is fun'. Every attempt is made to whip up mass hysteria, but whether you would be better off attending a football or baseball match is not known.

Most encounter groups do not claim to offer psychotherapy, but inevitably, many disturbed people attend: if you are neurotic and have been brainwashed by current psychotherapeutic fads into believing that neurosis results from the inability to express your feelings and to relate intimately to others, encounter groups may seem a quick and easy solution to your problems. They can, however, be disastrous for the mentally disturbed: not everyone reacts well to being told exactly what others think of them. Many encounter groups are led by charlatans with no training in psychotherapy: they may be in the business for financial gain, as a means to express their own aggression, to exploit group members sexually, or because their own existence is emotionally shallow and they need the synthetic emotional highs provided by the encounter game.

Bruce Maliver, a clinical psychologist with wide experience of the encounter movement, wrote: To my knowledge, not one of the current encounter game stars holds a certificate from a program specializing in conventional psychotherapy.' The American Psychiatric Task Force concluded: 'If encounter were a drug, it would clearly be banned from the market.' If a comparatively reputable organization like the National Training Laboratory itself admits to producing psychotic reactions in 1% of its clients, it can well be imagined what is the risk of psychosis or breakdown for participants in groups run by less skilled leaders openly encouraging aggression between members. Many suicides are on record directly produced by attendance at encounter groups. Whether or not they were caused by the methods used, there have been at least three at Esalen.

The available evidence suggests that even the mentally robust gain little or nothing. The most thorough study to date was undertaken at Stanford University by Yalom and his collaborators. In evaluating the results, it should be remembered that all the leaders were reputable and that there were observers present at all sessions: hence, the leaders were likely to be on their best behaviour. The investigators compared personality changes over the same period in students who attended groups with changes in students who did not. They estimated that 12% of students attending suffered serious psychological damage as a direct result: the proportion was higher in those groups run on the highly aggressive lines favoured by Perls. When interviewed immediately after participation, three-quarters of those attending thought they had been helped by the experience, but six months later only about a third believed they had profited. These figures do not mean much, since, as already remarked, anyone who voluntarily undergoes a time consuming or distressing experience reconciles themselves to it by exaggerating its benefits. Moreover, as seen by their friends, fewer changes for the better and more changes for the worse were noted in those who had attended encounter groups than in control students who had not attended.

In summary, attending encounter groups can harm you: they may make you think you feel better for a short time, but they are likely to make you obnoxious to your friends.

The encounter movement emphasizes the value of experiencing strong and unusual sensations and emotions, and tries to manufacture them by synthetic means in situations where they may be totally inappropriate. As Braginsky and Braginsky write:

By providing, as Koch notes, a convenient psychic whorehouse for the purchase of a gamut of well advertised existential 'goodies', authenticity, freedom, wholeness, flexibility, community, love, joy, encounter groups simply distort and coarsen our sensibilities. Manipulative gimmicks, a simplistic lexicon and psychic striptease replace the intelligent, sensitive struggle of man attempting to come to terms with himself, with others and with the world.

Encounter groups can be seen as purveying the group emotions experienced in other countries and other times through fertility rites, military rallies, wakes, public hangings and religious ceremonies. They differ in that they serve no extraneous aim: the spurious emotions are directed from one member to another rather than being focused on some external purpose. It may or may not be true that in the Western world most people give too little expression to their feelings, and that they lack the opportunity that intimate friendship provides for unburdening their souls. There is in fact little evidence in literature that people in other ages felt the need to discuss their innermost thoughts with those around them, though some religions, like Catholicism, have a place for institutionalized confession.

The atmosphere of many encounter groups resembles the hysteria of some of the revivalist sects that flourished in America in the 1920s and 1930s. Such sects appear to have had a recrudescence. Billy Graham relied on mass hysteria to achieve religious conversion, while in North Carolina Jim Bakker persuaded his flock to give $158 million to Christ, of which at least S4 million found its way into his own pocket. It is not without significance that both psychotherapy and revivalist sects are more popular in the US than in Britain. Both hold out promises of a happier life—or after-life.

At their best then encounter groups provide a harmless source of diversion, at their worst they produce suicide, psychosis, and divorce. Moreover, they encourage authoritarian and intolerant attitudes in that in the hysteria of the moment the leader and most members are unwilling to tolerate the opinions and wishes of the minority who do not subscribe to the same set of beliefs: members not prepared to enter into the spirit of the group are often treated with derision and spite. Baring one's soul to strangers or taking part in group sex may be agreeable for some, but this does not excuse the bullying of members reluctant to participate in such activities.

One has the impression that, with the exception of their use by some organizations like RELATE that cling to the past, encounter groups are on the wane. They foster a synthetic and artificial approach to human relationships, the cultivation of which outside the context of a group with common aims and interests seems a desperate and pointless undertaking. Moreover, the intimacy generated within groups is likely to be shallow and irresponsible compared with normal friendships evolved through close and continued association with those with whom we live, work or spend our leisure hours. Finally, the encounter movement underestimates the intellectual and creative side of humans. It may be that some people can feel fulfilled merely by giving vent to the expression of the self, but many undoubtedly need to follow goals outside themselves, and the apostles of encounter offer no such goals.

Encounter groups have begun to acquire a bad reputation. They have largely been replaced by 'Personal Growth Groups' or 'Experiential Groups'. Although the change of title makes them seem less threatening, it is doubtful whether it has led to a significant change in practice. Much depends upon the outlook and skills of the leader, who will import into the group setting the techniques and ideas he espouses for individual therapy. The psychoanalyst will interpret interactions within the group as revealing unconscious motives (libidinal ones if he is a Freudian), a Rogerian will try to persuade members of the group to confront their emotions honestly, while a Gestaltist will try to make them live in the 'here and now'. Many leaders are eclectic and will use any technique or idea that comes to mind.

One further change is that there are an increasing number of groups that are directed to specific classes of people, who are likely to have problems in common or to people who wish to achieve a specific aim rather than vague personal growth. There are Lesbian groups, feminist groups, drug abuser groups, self-assertion training groups, social skills training groups, groups whose members have post-traumatic stress as a result of witnessing the same disaster, groups for women with breast cancer and so on.

If realizing that others have feelings or problems in common with yourself is helpful, then such groups are sensible. Moreover, they give the group members a chance to air worries that are common to all the members without being contradicted. There is, however, one danger for such groups which would, for example, apply to feminist groups: it is known that when the members of a group all have the same opinions, those opinions become exaggerated by mutual interaction, leading to smugness and intolerance. Listening to and providing arguments only on one side of a case irrationally strengthens the individual's faith in their beliefs because they do not hear opposing viewpoints. On the other hand, the members of groups facing a common problem can often provide one another with useful information.

Some of these groups use the technique of 'role playing'. In assertion training and social skills training a client may be asked to show how he would request a pay rise from his boss or how he would approach a woman sitting opposite him in a train. He may even be asked to play the boss himself to gain an idea of how he is likely to react. The earliest group formed for a specific purpose was Alcoholics Anonymous: according to members it has a remarkable success rate—40% abstain from drinking. There is no evidence about the success of other such groups.

The wilder shores of therapy

Along with the growth of the encounter movement, there have recently appeared several zany forms of individual psychotherapy; this chapter provides some light relief by describing some of the dottier schools, many of which were derived from psychoanalysis. Rank, one of Freud's apostates, believed that all neurosis originates in the 'birth-trauma'. The pain of being born and the shock of leaving the comfort of the womb and being exposed to the cold realities of the outer world leaves the individual with a lasting unconscious desire to return to the womb. The cure consists of persuading patients to relive this harrowing experience with the help of the love and support of the therapist. They are encouraged to 'work through' their fear of asserting their own identity and separateness, a fear derived from the experience of birth. To achieve this the patients may walk beneath a row of other clients standing in line with their legs astride: their emergence at the far end symbolizes birth. The resolution of transference, that enables the patient to function without the therapist's help, is equivalent to the resolution of the birth-trauma.

Rank may have influenced the originators of one of the currently fashionable but least credible therapies, that based on the primal scream. Invented by a Californian psychologist, Arthur Janov, it has the attraction of extreme simplicity. He thought that in early infancy we all acquire a primal pool of pain, mainly from our parents' treatment of us. The only way to overcome the resulting tensions and anxieties is to summon up the pain and give vent to the primal scream. Primal therapists encourage their patients to stand around, sometimes in groups, screaming 'love me, love me' or shouting abuse at their absent parents.

Yet another analyst who parted company from Freud was Wilhelm Reich. He was subsequently expelled in successive years from the Communist Party and the International Psychoanalytical Association. After emigrating to

America in 1938, he became, by the lime of his death in 1957, a cult figure and folk hero. His ideas, especially in later life, were a curious combination of mysticism and pseudo-science. He believed that all neurosis arose from sexual repression—particularly from toilet-training, punishment for masturbation, and sanctions against sexual freedom in adolescence. He thought that from the age of 15 everyone should be encouraged to have sexual intercourse freely, and that marriage was an unnatural and undesirable institution. He claimed that sexual attraction could not last: he liked to be precise, and gave its natural term as four years. His desire for precision also led him to state that 'biologically speaking the healthy human organism calls for three to four thousand sexual acts in the course of a sexual life', a figure that in the present era of sexual licence will strike many as rather on the low side.

Reich earned the esteem of the feminists by being one of the first to stress the importance of orgasm for women. Although the young admired him for his promulgation of sexual freedom, he was himself in many ways curiously Victorian. He refused to accept homosexuals as patients, saying, 'I will have nothing to do with such swine.' According to his third wife he was happy to live up to his own standards of sexual freedom himself while forbidding her to emulate him. He never left to go on a trip without making her promise fidelity, and was savagely jealous.

He thought all life was sustained by a form of vital energy which he termed 'bio-energy'. He claimed that the presence of this energy could be detected under the microscope, with thermometers and with Geiger counters. The energy existed in packets called orgones, which were blue in colour, oscillated continuously and had size but no mass. In the healthy individual, the life force was discharged periodically through orgasm, which united the individual with the cosmos, but he thought that today most people were incapable of having proper orgasms: too often sex was an expression of anxiety rather than of desire.

Reich is perhaps best known, or most notorious, for his invention of the orgone box, a device intended to accumulate orgones from the atmosphere and concentrate them on anyone lucky enough to be sitting in it. He claimed not only that bio-energy helped to cure neuroses but that patients who sat in his orgone box could also be cured of cancer and psychosomatic illnesses. The United States Food and Drug Administration placed an injunction on the distribution of orgone accumulators on the grounds that Reich's claims for their efficacy were fraudulent. He refused to obey, and in 1955 was sentenced to two years' imprisonment for contempt of court. In prison he was diagnosed as suffering from paranoia and was transferred to a psychiatric penitentiary, where he was declared sane. He died shortly thereafter of a heart attack. In America, some states declared his books pornographic: they were seized and burnt. His supposed martyrdom at the hands of the US government only served to increase the appeal of his teachings.

In his pursuit of the orgasm Reich attempted to reduce muscle tension, an obstacle to it, both by direct manipulation of the patient's body and by forcing the patient to concentrate on his own facial expressions and to change them. By all accounts, he treated his patients harshly, and pointed out their neurotic defences and weaknesses in no uncertain terms: one of his own disciples referred to his 'cruel and penetrating technique' and thought that many of his patients were crushed by him. Reichian analysis is still practised both in Britain and in the United States; his followers subscribe to the importance of the orgasm, but each tends to use his own method of helping patients to reach it.

The flavour of dottiness that surrounds Reich can be brought out by a personal experience of my own. In 1954, out of idle curiosity, I visited a community of Reich's disciples. They lived in a commune some time before this style of life became fashionable with the young. The commune occupied several Nissen huts in a pine wood on the edge of a deserted airfield. Leaving my car outside a gate bearing the name 'Communitas', I walked through the trees towards the nearest hut. On the way, I stooped to pick up a pine-cone. A window shot up and a voice bellowed: Put that down—it's mine.' Evidently, their ideas about sharing property did not embrace myself. Nevertheless, I was received with kindness and given a cup of tea.

The commune had been founded by 11 adults—5 men and 6 women. They were vague about the number and the parentage of the children, but there appeared to be about thirty or forty running about naked and unkempt. Walking round the airfield, I was puzzled by the fact that one strip of runway had been carefully weeded and levelled—the other runways were long since disused, and were covered with weeds and cracks. The in-habitants, so they told me, had received a message from the master (Reich) that if they tended a strip of runway they might expect a visit from a flying saucer. When I asked whether they were looking forward to this visitation, they replied: 'Of course—the crew will be Martians dressed in green, and they will bring a free issue of orgones, enough to last us for years.'

They proudly showed me their orgone box, conveniently placed next to an excessively large double bed. The box was made of layers of plywood, zinc, steel wool and other substances thought by Reich to accumulate orgones from the atmosphere. It was about five feet high and big enough to accom-modate an adult sitting on a chair. I regretfully declined their invitation to spend half an hour in the box, largely because in order for the experience to be efficacious one had to sit in the nude, and the temperature was little above freezing. I explained that my middle-class morality would prevent me from taking advantage of the accumulation of orgones with any of the assembled women who offered themselves, and honour was satisfied on all sides.

The group with whom I was talking (four women and a man) had told me that they had an exceptionally good library of the works of Reich and his disciples, and I expressed an interest in seeing it. They explained, rather shamefacedly, that although they had originally intended to share every-thing, there had been a schism in the commune over a doctrinal point: the remaining four men and two women were in a separate building, so was the library, and the two groups were not on speaking terms. They pointed out the building, where I was again received with kindness and was given an opportunity to inspect the library. The second faction explained with sadness that they were excluded from the orgone box and described the suffering they were undergoing as a result. Since the first group had more academic inclinations than they had, it would have been a better arrange-ment if they had occupied the hut with the orgone box while the others had had access to the library. I was reminded of W. S. Gilbert's tale of the two castaways who divided a desert island between them to their mutual disadvantage:

> On Peter's portion oysters grew—a delicacy rare,
> But oysters were a delicacy Peter couldn't bear.
> On Somers' side was turtle, on the shingle lying thick,
> Which Somers couldn't eat, because it always made him sick.

Dotty though Reich undoubtedly was, some of his ideas were in advance of his time, particularly the stress he laid on the female orgasm and his insistence on the quality rather than the quantity of orgasms. Nevertheless his therapy has little to recommend it.

Bioenergetics, invented by a psychoanalyst called Alexander Lowen, carries some of Reich's ideas to their logical conclusion. In order to observe and correct muscular tension and bad posture, he sometimes treats patients in scanty dress. He believes that most patients both desire and fear bodily contact, and to remove this conflict the therapist touches, massages, and cuddles the patient. Bioenergetics, sometimes known as 'cheap thrills therapy', has given rise to more extreme forms of treatment by some of Lowen's followers: it is alleged that sessions may culminate in sexual exchanges between patient and therapist.

* * *

Yet another technique is known by the acronym 'ASCID'—Altered State of Consciousness Induction Device, which is supposedly copied from a swing used by medieval witches. The patient is strapped in and rocked around with the intention of producing 'deep trips' and visions. Perhaps, however, the prize for the most bizarre form of psychotherapy yet invented should go to Bindrim, the inventor of nude marathon groups, who has more recently devised 'crotch-eyeballing therapy'. He notes that the crotch is the central locus of three kinds of hang-up—difficulties in toilet training, guilt about masturbation, and adult problems. His method of over-coming these problems is to have two naked patients spread-eagle a third on the floor with his or her knees up and legs held wide open: the remainder of the group gather round and stare long and hard at the 'offending target organ'.

There are many other barmy forms of psychotherapy, most of which dignify themselves with scientific sounding names. For example, Neuro-Linguistic Programming attempts to teach people how to communicate, but the term 'neuro' is meaningless in this context since the therapy has nothing to do with either neurons or the brain. Its founder, Richard Bandler, was charged with the murder of a prostitute. Although he was acquitted, he admitted having threatened to kill her and having left her alone to die, afterward tempering his own distress with gin and cocaine. Not all therapists are caring people.

A further recent development is the use of astrology in psychotherapy: the therapist's advice to patients is based not merely on what they have revealed about themselves, but on the present position of the planets. The husband of a well known English novelist, Fay Weldon, left her on the advice of one such therapist. Here are quotations from two therapists: 'astrology is taking its place among the helping professions', 'Psychological astrology can . . . provide a surgical scalpel which cuts through to the underlying motives, complexes and family inheritance which lie behind the manifest problems and difficulties which the individual faces.' Other therapists base their advice on Tarot cards, while 'psychic therapy', in which the therapist relies on occult information, is on the increase. There are too many outre psychotherapies to list: all have impressive names that would do an advertising consultant credit, for example, transpersonal therapy, object relations, and psychosynthesis.

The gullibility of the clients of modern psychotherapy is almost unbelievable. If you are desperately mentally ill, it is common to clutch at straws—I myself became involved with psychoanalysts. But Freudian analysis is almost plausible when compared to the Primal Scream and the other therapies outlined in this chapter. The fact is that people are credulous: 80% of British adults believe in astrology, and many believe in alien space craft and UFOs. Our ancestors believed in the powers of witchcraft. All that has changed is fashion.

Although the encounter movement has attracted an undue proportion of quacks and charlatans, it should not be supposed that it has a monopoly of them. In 1972 the New York State Attorney brought a successful action against Albert and Maya Wood, the proprietors of the Long Island Institute for Emotional Disorders. The action was successful and the Institute was closed down. Its proprietor, Albert Wood, had sold books on psychology and psychiatry for a New York publisher. He was caught thieving and was sacked. He decided to become a psychotherapist, and accordingly listed himself in the telephone book as 'Albert D. Wood, Ph.D., Psychological Counselling'. Having no Ph.D., his only qualification was one introductory course on psychology. His wife joined the business, she too having awarded herself a non-existent doctorate.

By 1972 the Woods were earning $500,000 a year. They had branched out from individual therapy for adults, and now treated retarded children and ran group therapy sessions. In addition, they conducted a school for training in psychotherapy and offered unaccredited doctoral degrees costing $5,940 each. This also secured them the unpaid services of 13 trainee therapists who treated members of the public as a requirement for their sham Ph.D.s. When one of their patients committed suicide, his wife subsequently brought a legal action claiming that through fraud and misrepresentation they were responsible for her husband's death.

Enterprising amateurs are also found in Britain, though the existence of the National Health Service makes it harder for them to find patients. As a result of the newspaper articles I published on my own breakdown, I received several offers of help from such lay therapists. One was written by a woman claiming to be a "specialist in mind* aware*ness' (her asterisks). She wrote (her punctuation and spelling are preserved)

> My Accurate *analysis* does not rely on questions; but is based on The Fundamental Principals upon which we are all created.

> My assessment is correct and effective; Scientifically told reliable and lasting. and speedy two sessions.

I had other equally kind offers. A gentleman describing himself on impressively headed paper as 'Psycho-Therapist' wrote disarmingly: 'Although (and perhaps because) I am in the "unqualified" sector of psychologists, I continually see and help patients with exactly those symptoms which you mention.' He was kind enough to enclose his own diagnosis of my case:

> The basic cause of your breakdown is certainly repressed sexual guilt, probably arising from a masturbation contact with boys or a boy between the age of 11 and 14. Had I treated your case, I would have expected a recognisable though slight improvement in 3 weeks, marked improvement in 6 and boredom (you not me!) indicating recovery in 10 weeks.

From his description of his successes with other patients, I could have saved myself much misery had I only known of his existence, though at the expense of emerging from my treatment rather bored. On his headed paper, there appeared the impressive initials 'M.N.C.P.', standing for member-ship of an institution with the awe-inspiring title 'National Council of Psychotherapists'. On investigation, it turned out that this body is an association of lay therapists. Its rules state that the only qualification for membership is that two members of the Council 'shall vouch for the candidate's fitness for membership'.

It is true that lay therapists do just as well as professionals: indeed if the ability to exercise warmth, empathy and genuineness is all that matters, they are as likely to possess these qualities as anyone who has undergone a training analysis or taken a doctoral degree in clinical psychology. Nevertheless, you run less risk of being exploited if you seek treatment from a qualified psychiatrist or clinical psychologist than if you seek it from a layman, if only because members of genuine professional bodies, if detected in malpractice, risk losing their licence or certificate. The risk of misconduct may be minimized, it is not eliminated: a recent survey of American clinical psychologists showed that up to 25% of male therapists had slept with one or more of their patients as well as 10% of female therapists.

The litany of the bizarre or evil behaviour of therapists, as described in this and previous chapters, makes one wonder about their sanity, but I have only skimmed the surface: for example, Bettelheim, who ran a school for disturbed children, beat them without mercy, but was applauded for his compassion by the psychotherapeutic community.

It would appear that among psychotherapists the dottiness count is much higher than in the general public or in related professions such as psychiatry. It may be that psychotherapy attracts people who are themselves disturbed: to put it in their own terms, intervening in others' problems can be seen as a cunning defence mechanism for concealing one's own.

21

Behaviour therapy

In the late 1950s a new form of treatment came into being—'behaviour therapy'. This method was developed and is practised mainly by clinical psychologists. The treatment is paradoxical: it is the closest to common sense, while being based on the scientific findings of experimental psychology. Instead of viewing neurosis as the outcome of dynamic and unconscious processes, the behaviour therapist sees it as the result of having learned maladaptive habits. The method of treatment is simple and direct: the therapist attempts to teach the patient new and more suitable ways of responding, using our knowledge of the learning process derived from the work, mainly with animals, of experimental psychologists.

One of the first systematic attempts to employ behaviour therapy was made by Joseph Wolpe in South Africa in 1958: the therapy was promulgated by B. F. Skinner in America and by Hans Eysenck in England. In 1960 there were five papers published on the subject in learned journals: today there are many thousands a year. The ideas behind behaviour therapy have influenced therapists who would not themselves claim to make direct use of its methods. Behaviour therapy is not a cure-all, but works well for certain specific types of mental disorder, particularly phobias.

Phobias are hard to overcome because of the persistence of fear. In the case of the agoraphobic woman who was frightened by an indecent proposition made in public (described in Chapter 11), she became afraid of public places in general and because the more she withdrew from them the safer she felt, she withdrew more and more. Again one of Freud's cases was a small boy called Little Hans, who was terrified of horses. Freud, as usual, diagnosed an Oedipal complex: being jealous of his father's relationship with his mother, the boy feared his father (symbolized by the horse) would castrate him. Freud had no difficulty supporting his view by selecting evidence in favour of his case: the horse's muzzle symbolized his father's moustache and its blinkers his father's glasses. In fact it is small wonder that Little Hans feared horses, Oedipal complex or not, for he had seen a horse pulling a bus fall down and writhe on the ground: he had also seen one of his friends bitten by a horse.

Not all phobias have such clear-cut precipitating causes as the two described. Some are probably caused by a genetically determined tendency (shared by monkeys) to fear certain things, such as blood, worms, snakes, and heights.

Whatever the cause of a particular phobia, the treatment is basically the same. The oldest and best known treatment is 'systematic desensitization'. It is based on two principles discovered in the course of work on learning in animals. First, the startle response to an alarming stimulus can be greatly diminished if the stimulus is initially introduced at such a low intensity that no startle ensues, and if it is then gradually increased in strength. The animal is thus enabled to tolerate an intense stimulus that in the absence of training would have produced a massive fear response. Second, it has been found that animals may overcome their fear of an object if they are induced to approach gradually closer to it by rewarding them with food or some other pleasurable experience: this technique is known as 'counterconditioning' —the conditioning of a new response (eating) that is incompatible with an existing undesirable response (fear).

In preparation for treatment, the patient is first taught, as I was, progressive relaxation. Next, the therapist, in interviews with the patient, establishes a hierarchy of the situations that cause the phobic reaction, ranging from those of which the patient is only mildly afraid to ones that produce intense levels of anxiety. In the case of spider phobia, the hierarchy might range from seeing an old spider's web with no spider present, through a small spider at a distance, up to allowing fearsome-looking spiders to crawl over one's body, with many intermediate cases. After these preliminaries, the patient is instructed to relax and the therapist asks her (most phobics are women) to imagine the least frightening item in the hierarchy. The relaxation is antithetic to feeling fear (counterconditioning). This procedure is repeated until she can tolerate imagining that item without anxiety and while remaining completely relaxed. The therapist then proceeds progressively through the whole hierarchy, reverting to less fearful items whenever the patient experiences any discomfort on the presentation of a particular item. The treatment normally requires between 20 and 30 sessions, and once the patient can tolerate in imagination the most dreaded scenes in the hierarchy she is encouraged to approach them in real life.

A second method is known as 'flooding'. The patient is asked to imagine from the outset the scenes of which she is most terrified; for example, allowing large hairy spiders to crawl all over her naked body. This normally arouses extreme fear, but the patient is told to keep on imagining the terrifying scenes until the fear subsides. Put another way, the subject comes to realize that imagining the phobic object is not followed by harm and the fear subsides. The method has the danger that if the patient cannot bear to continue until she no longer feels fear, the reduction in fear when she stops imagining the terrifying scenes will actually reinforce avoidance of the object of the phobia and may make it worse rather than better. Where the patient is able to endure until the fear begins to subside, the method works at least as well as systematic desensitization. Nowadays, flooding is often carried out while the patient is calmed by tranquillizing drugs. This greatly reduces anxiety, and imposes less stress on the patient. Both systematic desensitization and flooding can be achieved by presenting the patient with the real object or situation she fears rather than having her merely imagine it.

'Modelling' is another method; it takes advantage of the fact that we all tend to model our behaviour on those we respect. The therapist first tries to persuade the patient that her fears are irrational by demonstrating that the phobic situation is in fact harmless. He then places himself in the situation to show that no harm comes to him and induces the patient to copy him. This sort of treatment is again usually accompanied by graduating the fear-provoking stimuli and in successive sessions persuading the patient to approach closer and closer to the situation that she originally found most terrifying. One of the women on my ward suffered from agoraphobia: she was particularly afraid of cemeteries and funerals and her life had been incapacitated for years, since she dared not board a bus or go into the streets for fear of catching sight of a cemetery or funeral. Several times a week she was led by a behaviour therapist to a nearby cemetery, which she was taught to approach closer and closer and finally to enter. She had been through a protracted and expensive analysis to no avail, but by the time I left hospital she was better able to cope with her problem. Modelling always contains an element of flooding. Behaviour therapy is, however, not the best treatment for agoraphobia: as described in the next chapter, it should be combined with cognitive therapy.

Nor can all other phobias be alleviated by behaviour therapy. In general, the stronger the phobia, the more difficult it is to treat, and if it is accompanied by other symptoms such as depression, withdrawal or generalized anxiety, it may be impossible to persuade the patient to cooperate with the therapist sufficiently to allow the treatment to work. The suffering of the girl with a phobia of spiders was not relieved during my stay on the ward: she spent nearly 24 hours prostrate on the floor in a corner of the day-room, and had to be removed to another ward.

Many people, particularly women and children, have phobias that are not completely disabling but that can be a nuisance: they may, for example, have unreasonable fears of examinations, thunderstorms, public speaking or, like Kingsley Amis, flying and travel by underground. Carefully controlled experiments have been performed on treating such minor disabilities, and it has been found that behavioural methods not only work but work better than any other method tested, such as counselling or analysis. In one of the most impressive of these experiments, 96 students who complained of fears of speaking in public were assigned at random to different treatment conditions, and to a no-treatment condition. All treatment was conducted by traditional psychotherapists who believed that the most effective technique was to give the patient 'insight' into his problem. These psychotherapists were trained to give behaviour therapy, and although they themselves did not believe in its efficacy, even as practised by them it turned out to be greatly superior to their own methods, whose results were no better than those produced by chatting with the clients and encouraging them.

The progressive development of behavioural methods for the treatment of phobias is impressive. Instead of the random and untested theories based on clinical hunches that characterize the history of psychoanalysis, hypotheses have been put forward about the causative factors responsible for producing improvement and have been carefully tested and refined by experiment. In 1966, a psychiatrist at the Maudsley Hospital using systematic desensitization brought about a mean reduction of 0.9 points on a rating scale for the strength of phobias. In 1974 the same psychiatrist working at the same hospital and with similar patients used a flooding technique conducted on groups of patients and produced a mean change of 2.8 points. Not only had the treatment greatly improved in its efficacy, but far less therapist time was spent on each patient (about 3 hours as against 60 in the earlier treatment). Systematic desensitization has been described as 'the first psychotherapeutic procedure in history to withstand rigorous evaluation', but it is now clear that flooding, when it can be used, is even more effective.

Behaviour therapists have also treated patients with obsessive-compulsive disorder, for example, compulsive washing for hour after hour. The theory behind the treatment is that the patient has developed an irrational fear of leaving a ritual undone: since he always goes through his compulsive acts, he can never find out that omitting them will not produce untoward effects. Because no harm occurs when he obeys his compulsions, he is reinforced in his belief that they are necessary to ward off evil. If he can be persuaded to omit his compulsive acts, he has a chance of learning that they are unnecessary. The therapy uses the techniques of progressive relaxation and modelling, and attempts to get the patient to expose himself in real life to the situations that bring on his compulsive rituals—wearing dirty clothes, touching sticky food, or looking at objects out of place on his desk—while allowing no opportunity to practise the rituals. Behaviour therapists have had some success with obsessions, though they are more resistant to therapy than are phobias: when an obsessive patient reduces his compulsions there is an all-round improvement in his condition, and no symptom substitution appears.

* * *

Behaviour therapy has been used in the treatment of many other forms of neurosis, but despite its promise its efficacy has not yet been properly validated for neurotic disorders other than phobias, panic attacks and obsessive compulsions. Although it has been used for depression, it has not been markedly successful. Psychologists try to induce depressive patients to undertake some task that will 'take them out of themselves', even if they can only concentrate on it for a few minutes at a time: it has been found that such treatment does produce a temporary elevation of mood, but the effects are usually short-lasting, and it is not known whether the treatment actually shortens the term of the illness.

Many behaviour therapists believe that neuroses can either be originated or perpetuated by other people rewarding or punishing the sufferer inappropriately. Freud himself postulated the concept of 'secondary gain', whereby a neurosis could be maintained because the symptoms served some function other than their original psychodynamic role. For example, someone who dislikes his job may, unintentionally, develop neurotic behaviour to avoid a return to work: it is well established that, in the USA, neurotics without disability insurance go back to work after a breakdown sooner than those who are so insured. The tearful or fractious child may be trying to gain attention, and the neurotic woman may use her neurosis to keep her husband out of bars and to extract sympathy. Florence Nightingale suffered from neurasthenia and spent much of her life in bed. It was probably the only place in a Victorian household where she could find peace from the daily round expected of middle-class women and could concentrate on her reading, writing, and devotion to administration.

For these reasons, behaviour therapists dealing with neurotic patients sometimes make a point of seeing the patient's family, friends and colleagues to persuade them to reward the patient for behaving well: a husband might be encouraged not to express too much solicitude when his wife complains of a headache, but to be particularly nice to her whenever she acts in a brighter way. Behaviour therapy is often combined with talking therapy, in which the patients are encouraged to express their current conflicts and an attempt is made to resolve them. Much treatment of this sort relies heavily on common sense, and is comparatively unsystematized, though the common sense is often supplemented with ideas introduced from developments in the theory of learning. For instance, a husband who is prone to sulking may be told to sulk only on a special stool placed in his garage, and to repair there every time he wishes to sulk in the hope that sulking may be brought under the control of this one situation, and hence be reduced in others.

* * *

Apart from its use in the classical neuroses, behaviour therapy has been applied to many other problems. As a further instance, we may consider the treatment of alcoholics on my ward. They were all voluntary patients and knew that if they drank they were likely to be summarily discharged: they would therefore have wasted the misery of withdrawal experienced during the first days after admission. This in itself was a strong incentive not to drink. Various methods were used to give them control over their urge to drink. For example, part of their treatment was to enter with another alcoholic a pub in the nearby village and to order and drink non-alcoholic beverages. Many patients failed this test—not by breaking down and drinking, but because having arrived at the pub they felt they dared not enter for fear they would be unable to resist temptation.

Moreover, the alcoholics gave one another considerable support through group therapy. Some became extremely cheerful after the first five or six days, and treated the hospital as a free holiday camp. About 75% stuck it out and left hospital free from their addiction—for the time being. Unfortunately, follow-up studies show that even patients who have gone through a full course of treatment tend sooner or later to resume drinking.

Some of the methods used in weight reduction based on experimental findings are of interest. Stanley Schachter has found that obese people tend to eat more food than normals when they are tempted by the sight of readily accessible food, but if they have to make an effort to obtain food they eat less. In addition, fat people suffer less discomfort than those of normal weight if they are not allowed to eat at regular mealtimes, particularly if nothing happens to remind them of food. Schachter suggested that eating behaviour in the obese is under the control of external stimuli such as the smell of food instead of being regulated by internal stimuli signalling hunger.

Prompted by these findings, behaviour therapists encourage obese patients to bring their eating behaviour under the control of a limited set of external cues to which they will not be too often exposed. In particular, they are recommended never to eat anywhere except sitting at table. They are also taught to chew each mouthful with great care, to savour the food as much as they can and to avoid all other activities such as reading or watching television while eating. They are instructed to finish each mouthful before commencing the next and to leave an interval between mouthfuls. During therapy, their weight is constantly monitored, and they are reinforced with praise for weight-loss. Although derived from experimental findings, these methods again have a ring of common sense, and if only partially successful they are likely to be more efficacious than the attempt to persuade patients that they overeat because their libido is fixated at an oral stage. In fact everyone has their own fixed physiological target for weight and it is very hard to maintain weight below that target.

Nor is behaviour therapy for giving up smoking particularly effective. Most people who want to give up can be persuaded to stop for a time—a day, a week, or a year—but all but about 5% return to it sooner or later. Nicotine replacement therapy (the nicotine gum, patch or spray) combined with supportive psychotherapy in a group has the highest success rate— about 30% still abstaining after a year. For several reasons, both the US and Britain have failed to support nicotine replacement sufficiently. The ostensible reason is the fear that people might become addicted to the nicotine supplied by these devices. In fact, they are already addicted through smoking; moreover, the main danger of smoking is the inhalation of carbon monoxide and tar, which is eliminated by nicotine replacement therapy. It may be that in Britain, the fear of the loss of the vast revenue from tobacco taxes (equivalent to a two pence addition to income tax) plays a part.

A further instance of the use of behaviour therapy on my ward was the treatment of a patient with anorexia nervosa. She was a rather handsome upper-middle-class woman in her mid-forties, with blue-grey hair; she was fastidious about her appearance but since she ate almost nothing she was in a skeletal-like state. She constantly begged food from other patients and then hoarded it: she would also carry tidbits of food away from the table to ward off night starvation, but they remained uneaten. At one point in her treatment, and of course with her own agreement, she was confined to her room and all privileges were withdrawn including contact with her family, access to television and the reception or sending of letters. She was weighed once a day, and whenever she gained weight some privileges were restored: when she lost weight, they were again removed. She discharged herself prematurely. This is a crude application of the effects of rewards and punishments on behaviour: it may work in a few cases, but anorexia nervosa is difficult to treat by any method.

* * *

Rewards and punishments have also been used for such problems as dystonic homosexuality, transvestism, exhibitionism and various forms of fetishism. The homosexual is shown pictures of nude men and women in suggestive poses: those of men are accompanied by shocks, those of women by some pleasant stimulus such as a favoured morsel of food. Patients are also encouraged to masturbate while fantasizing images of attractive women or while examining *Playboy's* girl of the month. The method is crude, and of doubtful effectiveness. Nevertheless, appropriate sets of slides together with the apparatus for delivering shocks are commercially available in the United States. At psychological conferences, the stands of firms exhibiting such slides are a favourite attraction both for heterosexual and gay psychologists: on such occasions no shocks are delivered.

Trying to rid someone of a habit they want to give up—such as homosexuality, fetishism, alcoholism or exhibitionism—by punishing them for indulging it is known as 'aversion conditioning'. Though widely practised at one time, it has now been almost completely abandoned: it simply does not work. Giving electric shocks or making the patient violently ill for drinking or looking at pictures in homosexual magazines does not carry over into everyday life: patients know they will not be punished for practising the habit there.

When my literary agent read an early draft of the above paragraphs, she was horrified that behaviour therapists should seek to impose their own view of what constitutes normal sex by attempting to change patients' sexual proclivities in this way. This is a common misconception. Even in these enlightened times, there are many homosexuals who at a conscious level would much prefer to be heterosexual. Some are tortured by moral scruples, others would like to have children and a normal family life. No behaviour therapist would attempt to change the sexual habits of a patient against his will. Apart from its being unethical, it is wholly impracticable, since the methods of behaviour therapy demand the whole-hearted co-operation of the patient. Only after a very full discussion, in which alternatives are explored, would a therapist agree to help patients to change their sexual orientation. The alternative is to help them reduce the anxiety they feel about their habits and to accept and fulfil their own nature as it is: many behaviour therapists to this end keep directories of gay clubs and act as marriage bureaux for homosexuals.

Most neurotics have difficulties in their personal relationships. Some behaviour therapists tackle this problem head-on by giving extensive coaching in social skills. Patients are rehearsed in the appropriate way in which to ask a woman to go out with them, or on how to approach their boss in order to request a rise in salary. One form of such therapy is 'assertiveness training', in which the patient is taught to act in a more assertive and aggressive fashion. It could be argued that many need not assertiveness training but de-assertiveness training, but maybe that is more difficult to instil.

* * *

All the applications of behaviour therapy so far discussed are made with the full consent of the patients. When they seek help voluntarily, it is important to obtain agreement between patient and therapist on the precise aims of therapy and on the methods to be used. Many behaviour therapists draw up a written contract between therapist and patient, which specifies the objectives and methods of treatment. In institutional settings, however, particularly with patients confined by law, it is possible to apply behavioural methods without the patient's consent.

The best-known example is 'token economy', which has been used, particularly in the USA, in the treatment of long-stay mental patients, usually psychotics. Such patients often suffer as much from being institutionalized as from their mental disorder. It becomes difficult to disentangle how far the maladaptive behaviour of patients who have spent years on a psychotic ward is due to their original illness, how far it is due to the apathy induced by institutionalization. The patients live in conditions of extreme monotony, and because they are freed from taking decisions and become accustomed to being cared for by others, they may lose all sense of responsibility. Long-stay patients may cease to care for their appearance, develop slovenly eating habits and become completely passive.

Token economy provides rewards for good behaviour: the patients can earn tokens by behaving in responsible ways, for example by washing themselves, cleaning their teeth, making their beds, helping other patients, or performing hospital chores like washing dishes, waiting at table, sorting laundry, or gardening. The tokens can be exchanged for goods or privileges, for sweets, cigarettes, access to television or a chance to talk with the hospital staff. There is evidence that some token economies have helped patients to become more responsible, but the method has dangers of its own. In order to set up a system of rewards, it is often necessary to deprive patients of other methods of gaining whatever is used as a reward. Hence, although staff may see patients as working for rewards, the patients themselves may feel that they are working to escape a punishment they have done nothing to deserve: in consequence, they may become alienated from the staff. Furthermore, the system can never be any better than those administering it, and the power to give rewards can always be misused to persuade patients to do things that are patently for the good of staff members but are not so obviously for the good of the patient. Although this may sometimes happen, it should be remembered that a mental patient who is unkempt and besmeared with faeces not only has little self-respect but makes it difficult for other people to be kind to him. Persuading him to adopt more sanitary habits is in his own interests, if only because it will predispose others to treat him better.

Perhaps a more important reason for not using coercive methods of behaviour therapy is that its benefits do not normally extend beyond the institutional situation. A patient who brushes his teeth or helps another patient because he wants to earn a token is unlikely to continue such activities once he is out of hospital and tokens are no longer forthcoming. Everything we know about learning suggests that as soon as the rewards are withdrawn, the behaviour will simply 'extinguish'; when patients are discharged from institutions run on token economy lines, this has often proved to be the case. The answer may lie in attempting to work out ways of providing patients with endogenous motives for continuing to behave in ways that will benefit them on discharge, for example, better relations with others.

In an experiment with surprisingly good results, long-term hospitalized schizophrenics (with an average stay of 17 years) who initially did little but either gibber or retreat into themselves were put on a token economy. They were rewarded for dressing properly, making their beds and so on, but also for socializing and participating in classes. They were systematically taught how to interact with others and joined in groups to solve problems. At the end of treatment all the untreated control groups were still taking pills for their disorder, against only 11% of the token economy group. Moreover, the effects of the treatment continued after discharge, since on average the token economy group remained out of hospital longer than the control group. This raises the question why their new habits did not extinguish. The experimenters believe that the role of the token rewards was to gain the patients' attention so that they could be taught. It is moreover known that praise has a longer-lasting effect on behaviour than does money or tokens.

Despite this remarkable success, token economies seem to be going out of fashion. One research worker found that if no tokens were given but the rest of the economy programme was carried out (for example, carefully observing what patients were doing and encouraging them to behave) the patients behaved just as well as when tokens were earned, so it may be not the tokens, but the attention and care of the staff that produces the benefits of a token economy.

* * *

One behavioural method of reducing stress is the use of a technique known as biofeedback. Part of the autonomic nervous system is excited under any strong emotion and the aim of biofeedback is to reduce this excitation when the patient is anxious or under stress. The patient sits before a screen that displays measures of his autonomic activity—heart rate, blood pressure and the electrical resistance of the skin, all of which alter during anxiety. The patient concentrates on attempting to change the indications on the screen in a way that corresponds to reducing the activity of the autonomic system, a change that would normally accompany the onset of a calmer mood. The rationale is that by seeing the physiological indications of their anxiety displayed, patients are given immediate feedback for reducing them.

Although a few normal people seem able to learn to lower their auto-nomic activity in this way, and may even learn to produce patterns of brain waves associated with tranquillity, the changes in the measures of anxiety and arousal brought about by biofeedback are almost certainly too small to be of significance. Moreover, they may well be due to a placebo effect—the patient's expectation that the elaborate display of his inner functions will help him. Indeed, one study reversed the display so that the clients thought their blood pressure was rising when in fact it was falling. Their blood pressure dropped just as much as in those seeing a correct display, though in both cases there was only a small effect. The best attested use of biofeed-back is for tension headaches caused by contracting the muscles of the head and neck. Electrical activity from these muscles is displayed on the screen and the patient's task is to learn how to reduce it. Even in this condition relaxation training is at least as helpful as biofeedback. Yet one more ingenious psychotherapeutic idea bites the dust. Nevertheless, it became a popular craze in America and the equipment needed is now marketed and sold to the general public.

* * *

There has been a considerable outcry about the dangers of using behavioural methods to shape people in ways that society deems desirable. Consider, for example, such works as *The Manchurian Candidate* or *A Clockwork Orange*. The alarm has been partly provoked by intemperate and downright silly statements made by proponents of behavioural methods. B. F. Skinner, an extreme behaviourist, vastly exaggerated their potential for dealing with the problems of society. In fact, psychologists are little better at designing methods of improving our educational system than are economists at devising means to ensure full employment without inflation. One advocate of behavioural methods, J. V. McConnell, wrote in an article entitled 'Criminals can be brainwashed now': 'We should reshape our society so that we would all be trained from birth to want to do what society wants us to do. We have the techniques now to do it.' Fortunately, we do not have the techniques. A great stir was made about the methods of brainwashing used by the Chinese against American prisoners captured in the Korean War. Despite the fact that the Chinese had complete control over every aspect of these men's lives, at the end of the war only 22 American prisoners out of a total of 4,450 elected to remain in China.

The use of punishment is counter-productive: it may stop you doing something you want to do, but it tends to make you want to do it all the more—if it weren't pleasurable, why would you need to be punished? In fact punishment, 'aversive conditioning' is nowadays used less and less by behaviour therapists. It can lead to rigid and inflexible behaviour and though it can be applied to suppress certain actions in the laboratory, it is impossible to apply it to those actions in real life, which is what matters.

People are not stimulus-response animals: they think. In consequence even reward has one unexpected result: it has been repeatedly shown that if people are given money or other rewards for performing a task they enjoy, it devalues the task and when the reward is withdrawn, people give the task up. They argue to themselves that if it was intrinsically interesting, there would be no need to reward them for performing it.

There are of course genuine ethical issues involved in the practice of behaviour therapy. Autistic children have been prevented from savagely mutilating their own bodies, but only by giving them strong electric shocks for any attempt at such behaviour. How dangerous to themselves do children have to be before we punish their behaviour in this way? Are we justified in asking homosexual patients to accept strong shocks even with their consent? One psychologist voluntarily exposed himself to the level of shock used: he was amazed by the degree of pain and observed 'How strongly motivated towards change a male homosexual would have to be to subject himself to a series of such shocks, visit after visit.'

In fact nowadays punishment is rarely used. It can suppress certain actions in the laboratory, but since it cannot be consistently applied in the real world it has no useful effects.

Dynamic therapists object to behaviour therapy on several grounds. They claim, rightly, that it does not give the patients insight into themselves; but there is no evidence that such insights are helpful. Some, in the Freudian tradition, believe that if one symptom is removed without delving into the patient's unconscious conflicts, another will be substituted; we have already seen that exactly the reverse is true. Removing one symptom ameliorates the others. Finally, behaviour therapy is sometimes thought to be a mechanical and dehumanizing process. In fact, in one study comparing the attitudes of dynamic and behaviour therapists, the behaviour therapists were rated (from tapes) as exhibiting more empathy and genuineness than the dynamic ones. All these objections are irrelevant: to the patient with a mental disorder, all that matters is recovery. It has been demonstrated that, particularly in combination with cognitive therapy, behaviour therapy is the most effective method for the treatment of phobias, and obsessive compulsion. This seems a small gain, but it has transformed the lives of many of the sufferers from these disorders.

Cognitive therapies

There is a second newly discovered type of therapy that is, like behaviour therapy, partly based on common sense, partly on fashions within experimental psychology. Until the early 1960s, most experimental psychologists, following the tradition of Pavlov, Thorndike, Watson and Skinner, saw their task as explaining behaviour by investigating the formation of links between stimuli and responses. But the possibility of simulating thought processes on computers opened up a whole new approach in which memory, language, reasoning and other cognitive activities were studied. As already described, Beck and Seligman proposed that the origins of depression were at least in part cognitive: it was caused by faulty thinking. If gloomy thoughts can lead to depression, then it might be possible to alleviate it by teaching more positive ways of thinking: that was how 'cognitive therapy', as originated by Aaron Beck, was born. The term is ambiguous, since it is sometimes used to refer only to Beck's approach and at other times to any therapy that concentrates mainly on patients' current problems and that attempts to change the way they think about them.

The disorder for which cognitive therapy has been most used is depression, a condition for which behaviour therapy appears to be only marginally useful. In essence, cognitive therapy attempts to cheer the patients up by making them take a more optimistic view of life. Cognitive therapists, particularly Aaron Beck, have evolved some specific techniques for preventing patients having gloomy thoughts about themselves and the world. For example, they may point out errors in the logic the patient uses to infer gloomy conclusions. Patients disliked by someone may falsely conclude they are disliked by everyone. The therapist argues with them trying to make them see that it is unreasonable to draw a general conclusion from one example and pointing out that they have many friends (if indeed they do).

Again, the patient may have failed at some task, such as taking an examination, and blame themselves for it, thinking they are no good at anything. The therapist will point out that they have done well at other courses or that the exam was in a subject that did not interest them. Or patients may blame themselves for some trivial misfortune, like causing a flood by failing to turn off the bathroom tap. The therapist will say that this is of little consequence—everyone (or almost everyone) at some time does the same thing. The patient will be told to watch out for negative (despondent) thoughts, particularly ones that recur and to try to stop thinking them: whenever they catch themselves at it, they should think of something pleasanter or divert themselves in other ways. In addition, the therapist looks for a task that patients may just be able to perform and encourages them to tackle it; for example, my clinical psychologist persuaded me to start making an index of a set of articles. If the patient succeeds at a worthwhile task, he or she will gain confidence. Great emphasis is placed on ways to increase patients' self-esteem and to persuade them that the future is not as bleak as it appears.

Largely in order to escape from the charge that cognitive therapy is just common sense, its practitioners, like behaviour therapists and psychoanalysts, have invented a large number of rebarbative and unnecessary terms. The 'cognitive triad', for example, is having negative thoughts about one's own capacities, about one's current experience and about one's future. 'Arbitrary inference' is inferring an unjustified gloomy conclusion from an event; 'selective abstraction' is latching on to an insignificant but depressing detail of a situation rather than looking at it as a whole and taking into account its more promising aspects; 'magnification' is exaggerating in one's mind the impact of a bad event while 'minimization' is playing down the significance of a good one; and so on and on.

It is clear that cognitive therapy depends upon the skill of the therapists: since they are trying to argue the patients out of their gloom, they must themselves be good at gentle persuasion and must have enough insight into their patients to present the arguments that will be most convincing to them. Again they must understand the patients' state of mind well enough to know what tasks they can tackle: if they are too difficult, the patient will fail and his poor self-image will be confirmed.

There is clearly considerable overlap between behaviour therapy and cognitive therapy: modelling (a behaviour therapy technique) involves persuasion and reassurance, while cognitive therapy uses reward in the form of praise when patients succeed in controlling their negative thoughts. Again, both therapies set tasks for the patients. The difference is merely one of emphasis—behaviour therapists believe that by changing behaviour they can change the patient's thoughts, whereas cognitive therapists believe that by changing thoughts they can change behaviour. They are both right and in practice the techniques of both kinds of therapy are usually practised together, hence giving rise to the expression 'cognitive-behaviour therapy', which adds yet another name to the awesome list of therapies. The two kinds of therapist also have in common that they ignore patients' childhood experiences, unless they are consciously troubled by them, and they concentrate on the patients' conscious motives and worries, not upon putative and speculative unconscious ones. Indeed both behaviour therapy and cognitive therapy are the sort of help your grandmother might have offered, provided of course she had not had her natural instincts overruled by reading Sigmund Freud.

As I have described it, cognitive therapy may sound a simple-minded and rather crude technique. It should be remembered however, that the errors in thinking just listed are only pointers for the therapist on what to look for in the patient's thought processes. The textbooks do not sufficiently stress that good cognitive therapists must acquire a good understanding of their patients, if they are to persuade them to see their problems in a different light. As a matter of fact, the so-called errors of thinking to which attention has been drawn may not be errors at all: it has been found that depressed patients are actually more accurate about their own capacities and their situation than are normal people, who consistently exaggerate their talents and prospects. Compare my own realistic worries about the trees pushing down my house. Maybe, *pace* Freud, nobody can face the truth about themselves or their situation—it leads to depression.

By now at least 20 studies of the outcome of cognitive therapy for unipolar depression have been undertaken. In all cases it has been shown to have a beneficial effect. When compared with other forms of psychotherapy, particularly dynamic therapy, it has always been shown to be superior. Although it takes longer than drugs to reduce depression (about eight weeks as opposed to about four), all studies comparing the two treatments have found that in the long run it is as effective as drugs or superior to them. For example, in one study on patients who had been depressed for at least a year 79% of those given cognitive therapy were much improved as against only 29% receiving drugs. Moreover, several studies suggest that, unlike drugs, it reduces the recurrence of depression, which is unfortunately extremely common. More surprisingly, some studies show that whereas giving both cognitive therapy and drugs is better than giving only drugs, it is no better than giving the therapy without drugs.

These studies have been undertaken with patients suffering moderate to severe forms of unipolar depression. It is doubtful whether psychotherapy can shorten the course of bipolar manic-depression or even very severe unipolar depression. Although at a conscious level, anyone depressed would give anything to overcome it, patients suffering from depression, myself included, often give the impression of being determined to cling to their sorry state. What are cognitive therapists to do with a patient who is cleverer than they are and insists on refuting all their well intentioned, but sometimes naive, arguments? This was to some extent the stance I took with my psychoanalysts. It would be interesting to discover whether less intelligent patients do better under cognitive therapy than cleverer ones, thus inverting Freud's belief that only intelligent people can benefit from psychoanalysis. The studies comparing the accuracy of normal and de- pressed people about their own abilities suggest that cognitive therapy teaches one to live by lying to oneself, whereas psychoanalysis purports to teach one to accept nasty truths—which is perhaps why it, as Freud admitted, is both unpleasant and ineffective for depressed patients.

* * *

Cognitive therapy has been successfully applied to several other disorders, for example to panic attacks, which are extremely common, affecting as they do about 2% of the population. Moreover, the comparative failure of behaviour therapy to ameliorate agoraphobia is almost certainly because it does not deal adequately with the panic attacks which so many agora- phobics experience and which are both a symptom and a cause of the disorder.

To understand the rationale for treating panic attacks it is necessary to describe the cause. Everyone when anxious is likely to have physical symptoms, such as palpitations, dizziness and breathlessness. Some people misinterpret these symptoms as signs of an impending heart attack or even death. Such a misinterpretation increases anxiety and hence exacerbates the symptoms, thus leading to a panic attack. In the case of agoraphobia, one reason that patients cannot go into public places is that they are afraid of having an attack and receiving no help or simply afraid of making a scene in public. Cognitive therapists systematically teach the patient that the physical symptoms of panic attacks are not life threatening. Over-breathing can produce panic attacks: hence patients may be asked to hyperventilate until they have an attack and then shown that it is simply the result of excessive breathing and is not dangerous. The therapist uses such means to break the vicious circle—symptoms of anxiety leading to terror which itself increases the symptoms: he convinces the patients that the critical symptoms are perfectly normal by demonstrating that they are not dangerous. If, for example, a patient's attacks start with dizziness, the therapist may revolve the patient in a chair to induce dizziness and then explain how it is that this can lead to a full blown panic attack. The patient is given practice in coping with the critical symptoms and understanding their origins in the safety of the therapist's office. Several different investigators have shown that this treatment can reduce or abolish panic attacks in all patients and is much more effective than taking drugs for the condition. As already explained, in the case of agoraphobia the treatment of panic attacks is combined with modelling and exposure: the therapist accompanies the patient to public places while reassuring her (most agoraphobics are women) by showing that there is no danger.

Cognitive therapy has been applied to many other disorders for which it appears to be reasonably successful, though strict scientific proof is sometimes lacking. I will illustrate this with the case of a woman who was raped and in consequence developed post-traumatic stress disorder, accompanied by appalling nightmares, obsessive brooding, extreme anxiety and inability to concentrate. The therapist would tell her to imagine the rape scene with the man approaching her. She is asked what she would have liked to have done to him and is encouraged to imagine doing it—to knife him, wounding him in the testicles, or whatever. She is asked to visualize such actions as vividly as she can. The therapist asks questions to make her imagery as detailed as possible: for example, when she imagines herself attacking the rapist the therapist might ask how he responded or whether he said anything. Eventually she sees herself overpowering her assailant and avoiding the rape. If the rape occurred in childhood, it is usually impossible for the adult coming under treatment to imagine herself as a child over-coming the rapist. She might therefore be asked to picture herself as an adult coming to the rescue of herself as a child. In both cases the patient will be instructed to use her mastery techniques and the imagery she has learned to produce, whenever she thinks of the rape. This technique sounds crude, but it is claimed that it works. Like the dynamic therapists, cognitive ones are never stuck for a catchy name—the method is called 'imagery re-structuring'.

The second example is anger management, which has been used on prisoners. They are taught that anger is normal but should be kept under control. People who do so are more likely to achieve their objectives (a belief that could surely be questioned). The prisoners are then asked to think carefully about what makes them angry (some might be tempted to respond 'anger management courses') and to recognize when they are in danger of becoming angry. They are trained to make calming statements to themselves in different anger provoking situations, such as 'If I keep calm, he might listen to my argument', 'I won't let them get me angry—that's what they want' or 'There's no need to take this personally'. They are encouraged to prepare themselves in advance if they are about to put themselves in a situation that is likely to make them angry. For example, before entering a shop to complain about an unsatisfactory purchase they are to say to themselves 'They'll take no notice of me if I shout my mouth off'—a belief that is unfortunately blatantly untrue. In addition to the attempt to change their attitudes by making self-statements, the prisoners receive training in progressive relaxation to be used to counter incipient anger. They also role play: for example, they are asked to behave as they would if someone called them a coward.

Some success is claimed for both imagery restructuring and anger man-agement, but neither has been adequately tested. The prisoners may have improved merely because of the attention they have received or because, as I showed earlier, they take pleasure in fooling their psychologists. As already emphasized, it is probably impossible to change the behaviour or cast of mind of anyone who does not want to change.

* * *

Cognitive therapy had a precursor—Rational Emotive Therapy (yet another splendid name), which was developed by Albert Ellis in the late 1950s. Like Beck, he believed that anxiety and depression were caused by irrational thoughts and like Beck he tried to reduce such thoughts in his patients. He thought people often expected too much of themselves and he would argue with them vociferously. If someone was worried about being a bad parent or a bad lover, he would argue that it did not matter—many people were like that. Whereas Beck would try to convince them that they were wrong about their faults, Ellis would insist that they should accept them and stop worrying about them. To the many people who believe that they have to be good at everything they do, Ellis would insist that this was nonsense. If someone felt anxious in a particular situation, he would try to convince them to see it differently—it was not the situation, say a cocktail party, that made them anxious, it was their attitude towards it. Clearly there is a great deal of overlap between Beck's Cognitive Therapy and Rational Emotive Therapy. The main difference is that Ellis harangued his patients, whereas Beck and his followers try by gentle persuasion to make them see the world and themselves in a more optimistic light. Rational Emotive Therapy has not been so thoroughly tested as cognitive therapy, but it appears to be of some benefit for anxiety neurosis and depression.

A third type of therapy, used mainly for depression, is closely allied to cognitive therapy: it is known as 'interpersonal therapy' and stems from the belief that depression is usually caused by unsatisfactory relationships. In consequence, it focuses on the most important current relationships in the patient's life. It emphasizes four failures: interpersonal role disputes, for example, a wife feeling that her husband does not attend sufficiently to her needs or dominates her; role transitions such as becoming divorced or being promoted but feeling unable to cope with the extra responsibility; interpersonal difficulties, meaning the inability to get on with others; and over-reaction to bereavement which goes beyond normal grief. Although the therapy concentrates on current relationships, a history of previous ones is taken to discover whether there is any pattern: it may turn out that the patient has never been able to make or maintain friendships and the reason for this failure will be sought and an attempt made to change the client's behaviour. Depending on the way in which social relationships have broken down, the therapist tries to help the patients clarify their feelings, by persuading them to communicate more openly with their spouse; to behave less angrily; to stand up for their rights; to be more or less assertive; if they lack friends not to be too abrasive; to make the right amount of eye contact; and even to bath regularly. Unlike cognitive therapy, interpersonal therapy deals with feelings of which the patient may be only half conscious. The bereaved often feel guilty or angry without recognizing it: the interpersonal therapist would try to make them abreact and recognize that their half-felt emotions are not abnormal and should be accepted, though not necessarily acted upon.

After preliminary discussion of the patient's problem, the nature of their disorder is explained to them together with the techniques of interpersonal therapy. As in behaviour therapy, it is usual to draw up a contract specifying the problems to be tackled and ways of solving them: both patient and therapist sign the contract, which usually states that the therapy will last for a specified number of sessions, normally about 16, and will then terminate. Such 'time-limited' therapy is used in other types of psychotherapy, including cognitive therapy. The idea behind it is that knowing how long the therapy will last may prevent the patient becoming too dependent on the therapist, a problem that besets Freudian analysis.

Despite its focus on the present, interpersonal therapy contains some elements of dynamic therapy, particularly abreaction and the attempt to get the patients to recognize unconscious motives. Although not as thoroughly tested as Beck's cognitive therapy, it has a good record, at least for depression. Indeed, in one exceptionally careful study, it did as well as Beck's cognitive therapy or drug treatment. In all three cases 50% of patients had recovered after 12 weeks of treatment, whereas there was only a 29% recovery rate in a control group who received a placebo pill and standard interviews with psychiatrists.

Both psychotherapies are superior to drug treatment in one respect: they have no unpleasant side-effects. They are probably better in two other ways. First, because of their side-effects, patients are more likely to drop out of treatment when on drugs than under cognitive therapy. Second, as we have seen, there is evidence that cognitive behaviour therapy prevents relapse more than does drug treatment and the same may apply to interpersonal therapy.

Like cognitive-behaviour therapy, interpersonal therapy depends heavily on the insight of individual therapists and their skill at addressing the patient's problems. Like both behaviour therapy and cognitive therapy, it has a manual which details the stages of therapy and instructs the therapist what to look for and how to respond. Unfortunately, no manual can contain all the problems from which the mentally disordered suffer and their possible environmental causes nor can it adequately teach how to interpret the patient's facial expression, gestures and tones of voice. In fact several studies have shown that therapists who have read manuals are less successful than those who have not.

A further form of cognitive therapy, developed about 20 years ago, is known as 'stress inoculation': patients are taught a completely general method for coping with anxiety. The theory behind it is that people can learn to control their reaction to stress. This is supported by several experiments. In one, subjects were given an inert drug; some were told incorrectly that it was a pain-killer, others were informed correctly that it was not. All of them were then exposed to electric shocks which were increased to the highest level they could tolerate. After an interval long enough for any supposed effects of the drug to have worn off, both sets of subjects were retested to discover the highest shock they could now take. The subjects who had been told that the drug was inert and who had therefore gained confidence in their own ability to withstand shock without the drug were able to tolerate more severe shocks at the final stage than were those who thought they had previously been helped by the drug. The pain (or stress) a person can tolerate depends on the level with which they believe they can cope.

In the therapy itself patients may learn how to withstand moderately strong electric shocks delivered at unpredictable intervals, and they are given practice in muscular relaxation and in slow breathing, both of which are antithetical to the arousal of anxiety. They are also taught to give instructions to themselves to help in coping with stressful situations. For example, they may be taught to say to themselves: 'Relax, I am in control of the situation, I can handle it; in the long run there is nothing to fear." These techniques are practised until they reach a point where they can endure the expectation of shock without anxiety. They then practise the same anxiety-reducing procedures in the real-life situations of which they have developed phobias, or whenever they feel anxiety. One study found that this procedure was more effective than the behaviour therapy technique of desensitization in helping patients to overcome phobias. More recently, it has been found that victims of rape suffering from stress are helped by a combination of stress inoculation and flooding (recalling while relaxed the events of the rape).

What is particularly interesting about stress inoculation is that people can employ it quite generally in any stressful situation in which they find themselves. We have in fact come full circle. In Victorian times neurotics were told to pull themselves together and exert some will-power. The techniques of stress inoculation were used in Ancient Greece in the upbringing of Spartan children. They were—at least until recently—also practised in many boarding schools in Britain, many of whose alumni say that they suffered so much at school that they could never be seriously worried by anything in later life.

It will be interesting to see whether the key to helping some of the mentally ill lies in an old-fashioned remedy, the strengthening of the will by practice and auto-suggestion. If this turns out to be the case, psychotherapy will have travelled a long and circuitous route only to find itself back where it started. At least the experience gained on the way should be of some help. We now realize the dangers of accepting methods of treatment that have not been objectively validated and the importance of testing the components of each method carefully and developing it step by step. We may be in danger of adopting our grandmothers' methods, but before doing so, they will be scientifically validated.

In summary, cognitive-behaviour therapists agree that it does not matter how their clients got to be the way they are, what is important is to change maladaptive thinking and behaviour and the best way to do this is by teaching them and encouraging them to think and behave in more adaptive ways. This rather obvious approach is the most successful of current therapies, but it should be remembered that it is little help to the psychotic and works well only for certain types of neurosis. It is, for example, doubtful how far it can ameliorate general anxiety disorder.

Moreover, as already noted, the theory behind cognitive therapy for depression is inadequate. It is not clear how faulty thinking can lead to sleeplessness, agitation, or the loss of appetite; these are known as the biological symptoms of depression. The answer surely lies in the two-way influence of mood and brain function. Depressive thoughts may alter the working of the parts of the brain underlying mood, making the depression worse, while as in bipolar manic-depression changes in brain function may induce low mood and the depressive thoughts that accompany it. The problem can be tackled from either end—cognitive therapy to change thinking or drugs to affect the brain directly.

23

Psychotherapy assessed

It has been said of psychotherapy that '[It is] an undefined technique applied to unspecified problems with unpredictable outcomes. For this technique a rigorous training is required. Everyone needs it.' The evaluation of the efficacy of psychotherapy (called 'outcome research') is beset with difficulties.

First, patients are likely to enter therapy when they are at their worst. Most patients recover, at least to some extent, of their own accord. In consequence, the fact that a patient feels better after therapy than when they entered it does not mean that the therapy was responsible for the improvement.

Second, as we shall see, regardless of the techniques they use, therapists vary in their ability to help patients. If it is found that one type of therapy does better than another, this could simply be due to it being practised by more empathic, more directive, or more caring therapists than those administering the other type of therapy.

Third, in many of the studies conducted the results have been evaluated by the therapists themselves. Clearly they are likely to be biased towards seeing improvement even where none exists.

Fourth, different therapies may be appropriate for different forms of mental disorder.

Fifth, a surprisingly large number of clients drop out of therapy: one study showed 45% terminated therapy after two sessions, another found 70% had dropped out by the tenth session. There is no means of knowing whether clients abandon therapy because they feel better or because they think the therapy is making them worse.

Sixth, the editors and readers of learned journals are not interested in negative results—research workers who find a particular therapy has no effect are often unable to get their findings into print. This biases the results of published papers towards showing that therapy works.

Seventh, by seeking out therapy the patients are taking a step towards recovery: hence, they are likely to be the ones who will recover of their own accord.

Eighth, it is not easy to determine the outcome of therapy. In some cases, such as anxiety disorders or phobias, physiological measures can be used, for example, to find how far the bodily symptoms of anxiety have been reduced. The opinion of the patient may be sought, possibly by giving a questionnaire. As already noted, the patient is likely to say that therapy has helped, whether or not it has: people who spend time or money on any activity cannot admit even to themselves that it has been wasted. Or, the patient may be rated through an interview given by someone who does not know what treatment he or she has had: even then the patient may reveal the treatment in the course of the interview. Again, a technique rarely used, the opinion of the patient's family or friends may be taken.

Finally, for unknown reasons different measures often do not agree. Recovery from a phobia may be measured by how near to the phobic object the patients can approach, by their own report of anxiety or by physiological measures such as heart rate. For unknown reasons there is little or no agreement between these three measures.

The best but still not entirely satisfactory way round these problems is as follows. Take a large group of patients diagnosed as suffering from the same disorder. Divide them into three (or if more than one therapy is under test, more) groups, taking care that the average severity of the disorder is the same in each group. The three groups are: those who have the therapy; those who have no therapy—a 'waiting list control' who for ethical reasons are promised therapy after the trial is over; and a placebo group who are given sham therapy. The third group should see a sham therapist as often as the first group sees a genuine one: the sham therapist encourages them to talk and may make supportive noises, but does not apply the techniques of the therapy under test. In practice these conditions have seldom been fulfilled in the thousands of reported tests of different therapies. Moreover, the studies yield almost every possible result from little or no improvement to massive improvement due to therapy. In every single relevant study the placebo group, which receives sham therapy, shows more improvement than the group given neither therapy nor placebo treatment.

Using a cunning technique, psychologists have attempted to put together the results of many different studies. The problem is how to compare them, as each will use different measures of efficacy. How does one compare patients who have moved up five points on a scale of self-esteem with ones whose ability to interact socially is thought to have risen from 'poor' to 'good'?

This paragraph gives a simplified account of how it works. It is not easy to follow and may be omitted by the faint-hearted. There is an ingenious statistical method for combining the results of studies using different criteria. The question is how much better (or worse) are patients at the end of treatment than those who have had no treatment. The trick, known as 'meta-analysis', is to convert the measurements of all the different studies to the same type of score (technically a score that has the same mean and the same standard deviation for all the studies). Using this score it is possible to make meaningful comparisons between the average success of studies that have examined different kinds of therapy compared with their control groups, which have received no therapy. Essentially, the technique measures the percentage of the treated group who, after therapy, are better on the relevant measures than is the untreated (control) group (this is slightly over-simplified). Thus if 70% of the treated group are better than their control group average, the therapy has been moderately efficacious and will be said to have moved patients to the 70% point. If it had not worked at all the figure would be 50% with half the patients faring worse than the control group and half better, since the control group were selected to have the same severity of disorder as the treated group. Remember, however, that we are comparing the treatment group with a group of disturbed people (the control group): even if all the treatment group were better after therapy than any of the control group, they might not have made a full recovery, since all the control group have psychological problems.

The important point is that the technique of meta-analysis allows meaningful comparison between studies that use different measures of the efficacy of therapy and whose subjects differ in the severity of their disorder. It was expected that the use of this technique would settle once and for all the vexatious question of whether psychotherapy works: instead, it has led to violent controversy, but then almost everything in the field of psycho-therapy ends in violent controversy. Dynamic therapists have hailed the findings of meta-analysis as proving that all therapy works: behaviour and cognitive therapists strongly disagree. Whenever the results of meta-analysis have been broken down by type of treatment, cognitive-behaviour therapy and its allied therapies have proved superior when used to treat the disorders at which they are specifically aimed. When the efficacy of dynamic therapy is estimated, it is in fact little different from a placebo control group and sometimes actually worse. Moreover, a shift in the scores of the treatment group to the point where 70% he above the average of the measures for the control group (a result often found for dynamic therapy) sounds greater than it really is. Because the scores of most patients in the untreated group will cluster close to the average, it will only require a small improvement in the treated group to bring them to the 70% level (that is, less disturbed than 70% of the control group). Compare the way height is distributed in members of the same sex: since most are only an inch or so away from the average height, someone of average height would only have to gain about an inch to be taller than 70% of the population of the same sex.

There are further difficulties. The use of meta-analysis does not overcome the problem that negative results are rarely published so we cannot be aware of them. The fact that in meta-analysis psychodynamic therapy is rarely better than the placebo group is particularly sinister. The placebo group rarely receives as many sessions as the treatment group and the sham therapist tends to intervene less than genuine therapists: if all that mattered were the attention given to the patient, not the form of therapy, one might expect the placebo group to be marginally worse. As Hans Eysenck has pointed out, many of the studies fed into meta-analysis were poorly con-trolled and suffered from some or all of the defects mentioned at the beginning of the chapter. As computer experts say, 'Garbage in, garbage out'. Again, with the exception of behaviour and cognitive therapy, all other therapies do about as well (or badly) as one another. But each is based on a different theory of the causes of mental illness and each uses different techniques of treatment. If any of these theories or techniques were valid, one would expect that some therapies would be more efficacious than others; they are so different that they cannot all be right, but they could of course all be wrong. Despite all this, it has to be granted that dynamic therapies have a marginally beneficial effect, an effect that is equal to that of having no therapy at all but merely the chance to talk to someone who is mildly supportive (the placebo treatment).

In meta-analyses, both behaviour therapy and cognitive therapy have shown upward shifts to between 84% and 99%. Although none of these figures imply that all patients made a complete recovery, the latter figure shows that after cognitive therapy patients were functioning at the same level as the least disturbed control patients. In studies breaking down the results for different disorders, cognitive-behaviour therapy produces good results for depression, panic disorders and agoraphobia, while behaviour therapy did well with phobias and obsessive-compulsive disorders.

Curiously, it has been alleged by psychotherapists on the basis of these analyses not only that all psychotherapies are effective, but more surprisingly that all are equally effective. One writer even applied to the psychotherapies the remark of the Dodo bird in *Alice in Wonderland:* 'Everyone has won and all must have prizes.' This remarkable conclusion, which flies in the face of the evidence, is achieved by lumping together the results of many different therapies, including with those of doubtful value the ones that are now known to work. Moreover, the analyses have produced three further damning findings on which everyone is agreed.

Amazingly, when comparisons have been made, professional psycho-therapists have actually done worse overall than untrained or minimally trained ones, surely a terrible blow to the profession but one which it continues to ignore. In one of several studies patients who were anxious, depressed or obsessional were randomly allocated for treatment either to licensed psychologists or to professors in other subjects who had no training in psychology whatsoever. At the end of the therapy, there was no difference between the two groups of patients. The reason for the possible superiority of untrained or minimally trained therapists is not far to seek. They are not blinded by narrow and often implausible theories so that they can use common sense in interpreting their clients' behaviour rather than ignoring everything that does not fit with a rigid theory.

Second, it is well established that the length of time for which a therapist has been practising does not affect the extent to which she (three-quarters of psychotherapists are women) helps her patients. Beginners do just as well as those who have been treating patients for 30 years.

Third, the length of therapy is unrelated to its success. Patients tend to improve slightly over the first 25 sessions or so but show little or no further improvement (a conclusion based on over 2,000 different studies). So much for the lengthy treatments favoured by orthodox psychoanalysts.

One may ask why so many therapists choose to practice therapies which are known to provide little benefit. So! Garfield, who is both a therapist himself and a trainer of psychotherapists, reports that, 'Students choose one type of therapy . . . because it is more interesting and exciting than another . . . They do not make any reference to the effectiveness of the respective therapies, but rather to the personal satisfaction secured by one approach over another." This hardly needs comment; do such therapists continue to put their own good before that of the patient when they start practising?

* * *

Since the previous section was written, *American Consumer Reports* have published the results of a survey suggesting that psychotherapy has some beneficial effects. A questionnaire was sent to all 180,000 members of the organization asking them to return it if they had experienced 'stress or any other emotional problems' over the last three years. It turned out that 2,738 of those replying had consulted a mental health professional. Of those who were originally feeling 'very poor', 87% claimed to be considerably improved as a result of therapy, while of those who were feeling 'fairly poor' at the outset, 97% claimed to have improved. Those who went to psychiatrists, psychologists or social workers all improved equally; those who had therapy from marriage counsellors or ordinary doctors showed less improvement. The fact that social workers did as well as psychiatrists and psychologists confirms the finding that training is largely irrelevant, since social workers usually have less training than the other two professions. Doctors may have had less time to devote to their patients. Those who attended Alcoholics Anonymous—a non-professional body—claimed to have benefited most. The most surprising finding, however, is that the longer the treatment, the larger was its effect, in direct contradiction to previous studies. It is possible that those who stayed longest did so because they thought the therapy was helpful. In other words, the fact that they were feeling a lot better made them stay in therapy longer, not the other way round. This would not apply to the experimental studies discussed earlier, since in them it was decided before therapy started how many sessions there would be.

This report is suggestive but no more. It does not overcome the problem that anyone who has expended considerable time and exertion (and in many cases money) on treatment is likely to justify their effort by thinking it must have done them good. Again, most people recover from mental disorder of their own accord and if those who responded began treatment when they were at their worst, they are likely to have improved with or without treatment. Moreover, only 4% of the sample replied. We have no means of knowing what has happened to those who had had a mental disorder, but did not reply. Were they too fed up with therapy, or even too unwell to be bothered to reply?

The fact that there was no untreated group makes the result hard to interpret. We simply cannot know whether a group without therapy would have recovered as much. Moreover, the therapy is not broken down into type so we cannot compare dynamic with cognitive-behaviour therapy nor can we know how much each of the different therapies contributed to the overall improvement. For all these reasons, the results cannot be said to support dynamic therapy: it is safer to rely on properly controlled experimental studies.

* * *

If all dynamic therapies work equally well, if amateurs are better than professionals, if length of training makes no difference, and if psychotherapy is only marginally if at all better than sham therapy, then all these therapies and also placebo treatments must surely have an ingredient in common that gives them a slight beneficial effect. It could be something as simple as Rogers suggests—the chance to talk about one's problem to a sympathetic and supportive listener.

On the other hand, the techniques of cognitive-behaviour therapy appear to work comparatively well, albeit for a limited range of disorders. But there is no reason why this method should be administered mainly by highly trained clinical psychologists. Surely a doctoral degree is no help in mastering the simple—one is tempted to say 'simple-minded'—techniques of these forms of treatment. Nurses and social workers could be trained within a month or so and could practise them just as well and at far less cost: indeed some already are so trained.

If in addition to the special techniques of cognitive-behaviour therapy, sympathy and support are helpful, the personality of the therapist and the relation between him or her and the patient will be important. Perhaps the most dramatic demonstration to date that the value of psychotherapy depends upon the characteristics of the individual therapist was a study carried out by a New York psychiatrist, David Ricks. He investigated the effects of treatment by two different therapists on twenty-eight 13- or

14-year-old boys attending a child guidance clinic. Fifteen were treated by a therapist whom the boys themselves had a very high regard for: they had in fact given him the name 'Supershrink'. The remainder were treated by a therapist whom Ricks refers to as therapist B.

Of those treated by Supershrink, only four were found to be suffering from schizophrenia in adulthood, whereas 11 of those treated by the other therapist received this diagnosis as adults. Ricks examined the protocols made by the therapists at the time of treatment, and concluded that although they were both psychoanalytically orientated, they differed in the following ways. Supershrink made fewer psychoanalytic interpretations of behaviour and concentrated more on giving the boys support: he encouraged them to be autonomous and to take responsibility for their actions more than did therapist B. He also met the boys' parents more often and gave them more direct guidance. Therapist B allowed himself to be caught up more readily in his patients' depressions, and seems to some extent to have fostered depression by telling the boys how miserable they sounded. Supershrink also gave more practical advice on attending camps, obtaining jobs and so on than did therapist B. It would of course be unwise to place too much reliance on an isolated study of 28 children, but the differences in therapeutic style and outcome are suggestive. Recent studies indicate that the characteristics of the therapist may be more important than the type of therapy practised. One found that the best therapists were successful in almost all their cases, while the worst helped less than 50% of their clients.

Unfortunately, we still do not know for certain what aspects of the therapist's character are important for success. Several thousand studies have obtained widely different results: it is likely that an optimal degree of warmth and genuineness on the part of the therapist plays a part, but, as we have seen, even this is unproven.

We do not know whether psychotherapy works—if it does—by supporting patients, by providing a confidant, by offering sensible advice, by relieving their guilt, by making them feel less lonely, by making them confront their problems or by suggesting they ignore them. As already remarked, the apparent success of some therapy may even be due to patients being unwilling to admit to themselves that they have spent time, effort and money in vain. A recent study of 225 depressed out-patients found that the success of therapy depended on 'the therapeutic bond', that is how much the patients liked their therapists and how far they confided in them. Only one thing is certain: the relation between patient and therapist is important—patients who like their therapists do better than those who do not.

Clinical psychologists" claims to be 'experts' in assessing human behaviour are as fraudulent as their claim to be expert at helping people in distress. One therapist even claimed to be able to detect whether a woman had been raped 'within ten minutes' of meeting her. There is no evidence that they are any better than laymen at making such judgements. In one study it was suspected that a child, Melissa, had been sexually abused by her father. A clinician interviewed Melissa alone, Melissa with her mother, and Melissa with her father. When other psychologists were shown videotapes of the interviews, their independent opinions of the probability of her having been raped varied from 5 to 75%. There is no reason to suppose that other judgements made by psychologists are more reliable. Scandalously, many continue to rely on 'projection tests' such as the Rorschach; the use of such arcane and completely discredited tests cannot aid judgement, but they can fool the patients into believing psychologists have an expertise they do not possess. Psychologists love designing tests: there is one—often a dozen—for almost all human activities, including the probability that a married couple will be divorced. Most are meaningless, but businessmen, perhaps the only professional people that are more naïve than psychologists, waste millions of pounds for the right to use them.

* * *

If the success of psychotherapy depends more on the character of the therapist than on the type of therapy practised and if untrained therapists are as good as trained ones, why is it that clinical psychologists have multiplied so much over the last forty years, and why both in America and Britain do they need a higher degree (a Masters or even a Doctorate) in order to be licensed? Part of the answer is that the *American Psychological Society* and *The British Psychological Society* act as trade unions: by persuading their governments (or states) to license clinical psychologists, they lay claim to a non-existent expertise and ensure that in the face of a gullible public they can charge higher fees than psychotherapists who are not licensed. In addition the considerable fees charged for registering clinical psychologists help to support the vast bureaucracies that these two self-important bodies have created. Having recently succeeded in making registration a condition for calling oneself a 'clinical psychologist', the British Society is now lobbying parliament to prevent anyone claiming to be a 'psychologist' of any type who is not registered with it.

Since the Second World War there has been a vast growth in the so-called 'helping professions'. In the US the number of clinical and counselling psychologists rose from a mere 2,500 in 1959 to about 90,000 today: the number is at present doubling every ten years. Psychiatry, which is more prestigious, and requires a longer and more rigorous training, has approximately doubled its practitioners over the last 30 years. These figures do not include psychiatric social workers (who only became licensed in most American states about 1980), nor nurses practising therapy, nor the army of lay therapists, who outnumber professionals many times over. Britain lags behind in the growth of clinical psychology, but according to *The Times* newspaper the welfare of its citizens is now secured by a staggering two million counsellors (including social workers) and a mere 250,000 members of the armed forces.

Part of the growth has occurred because of changes in society, part through the sheer pushiness of psychologists. The decay of the church is a further factor: in 1949, 49% of Americans who were mentally disturbed went first to their local priest, now largely replaced by the local psychologist. In addition, the break-up of the nuclear family, the replacement of small shops by supermarkets, increased geographical mobility and tower blocks may all have produced a dearth of close friends or relatives. It will be remembered that one secure finding is that having someone to confide in is some protection against depression. But perhaps above all is the naive belief, originating mainly in America, that there is a remedy for all ills and the self-interested propagation of this belief by psychologists and drug companies, which have made psychiatric services available to far more people than in the past.

Psychiatrists have played their part in extending the need for their services by inventing new categories of mental disorder, such as multiple personality, hyperactive attention-deficit disorder, and dysthymic personality disorder (meaning sadness and lack of liveliness). And psychologists have made specious promises, most of which they cannot fulfil: the shy can become confident; the sad cheerful; the morose lively; the lonely the belles of the ball; the gauche prepossessing; and the insecure brim full of self-esteem, the current catchword of clinical psychology. Here is a typical quotation from a humanistic psychotherapist on that subject: 'I cannot think of a single psychological problem—from anxiety and depression, to fear of intimacy or of success, to spouse battery or child molestation—that is not traceable to the problem of poor self-esteem." As so often in clinical psychology, there is no evidence to support this claim. A task force on self-esteem established by the California State Assembly reports that: 'One of the disappointing aspects of *every* chapter [in its report] (at least to those of us who adhere to the *intuitively correct* models sketched above) is how low the association between self-esteem and its consequences are in the research to date,' Note the refusal to accept the very evidence gathered—if the report does not show that self-esteem is important, you continue to believe 'intuitively' that it is. Low self-esteem has in fact been shown not to be a factor in child abuse, drug use, alcoholism or crime. It is of course pleasant to esteem oneself highly, but lack of self-esteem does not seem to lead to bad behaviour.

Psychologists and psychiatrists are taking over more and more of people's lives. If your marriage is in difficulties you run to RELATE; if your children play up, take them to a psychiatrist—in America there are now car pools for this purpose to ease the strain on the mothers (psychiatric buses may soon replace school buses); if your spouse dies, you may take an antidepressant; and if you don't know how to occupy your spare time, you consult a "leisure counsellor'. If you are involved in a trauma, you may not only have trauma counselling, you may sue for being subjected to post-traumatic stress disorder. Psychologists propagate the belief that everybody has a right to happiness and everything is always someone else's fault. If your father kissed you on your tenth birthday, you have been sexually abused and cannot help becoming a criminal. Whether it is beneficial to be absolved from accepting responsibility for one's actions and to seek psychiatric or psychological help for the misfortunes to which all of us are prone is open to doubt: if having control over one's own destiny staves off depression, it can only do harm.

* * *

Scientific psychologists are aware of the dangers of using data gathered in clinical sessions. It is only too easy for the clinical psychologist to select those of the patient's responses that suit his own biases and even easier to interpret them in any way he likes. The follies of some clinical psychologists are now so extreme that they are being battered from within their own profession. One President (R. E. Fox) of that august body, the American Psychology Association (APA), in his presidential address quoted from some of the attacks made by other psychologists on clinical psychologists.

> So-called clinicians have taken control of APA for no better purpose than to use it to push questionable treatments and to convince the public that they are a real profession with legitimate services to offer.
> Most clinicians should be confined to a preserve at least until such time as they could reliably tell the difference between real data and the hearsay they obtain from patients. In fact, psychology, APA and society would be a lot better off if they stayed in the preserve, treating and diagnosing each other rather than innocent members of society.

He also attacked some of the outrageously false claims made by clinical psychologists, for example 'On [a TV] program, a psychologist described the House-Tree-Person test as a "personality X-ray" capable of accurately predicting such things as future violent behaviour and marital compatibility.' The test is of course worthless. Scientific psychologists can also make errors, but their sophistication about control groups, statistics and observer bias makes them less likely to do so than clinical psychologists, for whom Freud set the pattern by relying entirely on clinical data.

Dynamic psychologists will undoubtedly criticize me for my assaults on their beliefs and practices. They will allege that my views are merely a defence mechanism to enable me to ignore the contents of my own unconscious of which I am scared. From Freud onwards they have used unhelpful, indeed despicable, *ad hominem* arguments of this sort. What matters is not my motives, but whether my views are correct and to decide that one has to turn to evidence. On that evidence, there is no question that psychotherapists (with the exception of cognitive-behaviour therapists) do little or no better than a placebo and they do not improve with experience, while professionals do rather worse than amateurs.

Manipulating the brain

An alternative to psychotherapy is the use of physical methods of treatment, based on direct manipulation of the brain itself. Psychoanalytically oriented psychiatrists often abhor physical methods, since they believe that patients are more receptive to psychoanalysis if the edge of their worries is not blunted by drugs: the scorn of my own analysts for drug treatment is a typical reaction.

Perhaps the most dramatic physical method of treating mental disorders is electroconvulsive therapy (ECT). It is dramatic both because it is a drastic procedure that is much feared and because it sometimes produces an instantaneous improvement in the patient's condition. On my ward several patients were in fact transformed by ECT while I was there. Half-way through my stay someone was brought in with severe paranoid delusions. He believed that money was the root of all evil and refused to use it; in addition he thought that there was a vast conspiracy against him. One night, when I was telephoning, he hung round interrupting my every word. He heard me saying: 'I'll see you tomorrow', and was convinced I was in a plot against him. 'I know you're in it with all the others. You're going to attack me tomorrow—don't deny it, you're plotting on the telephone. I heard you plainly. Who's that you're phoning?' Three weeks later, after six electroconvulsive treatments, he was outwardly composed and cheerful and could talk interestingly and rationally. Four weeks after admission, he became an out-patient spending most of the day at the hospital but returning home each evening; within three months he was back at work.

ECT is an effective treatment for severe depression. A large but carefully controlled electric current is passed through the head by means of electrodes applied to the scalp. The procedure is much less drastic than it used to be: when first introduced, it was given without an anaesthetic but nowadays the patient is always anaesthetized. Formerly, ECT produced gross convulsions, but nowadays a muscle relaxant is usually used to reduce their amplitude. They are so mild that they can only just been seen by an onlooker, but it is thought that ECT is ineffective if no seizure occurs. Any severe trauma to the brain produces a loss of memory for immediately preceding events: hence we can never know whether its administration to unanaesthetized patients was accompanied by pain, since they had no memory for it. For whatever reason, ECT was widely dreaded, and there are many reports from patients likening the atmosphere in hospital on days when ECT was to be administered to that of a prison on the day of an execution. In some hospitals the apparatus was wheeled along the centre of the ward and patients had to watch others having convulsions before their turn came.

Although the administration of ECT is now painless, it is still feared, perhaps in part because the tradition of how unpleasant it used to be has been handed down from one generation of patients to another. On my ward, there was usually an unnatural silence when preparations were being made for it, and although one rarely knew beforehand who was to be the recipient, he or she could always be identified afterwards by the small strip of sticking plaster covering the vein on the back of the hand where the anaesthetic had been inserted. Patients wearing such sticking plaster were treated with great solicitude by the others.

The method of giving ECT is in fact now so refined that it is administered in some hospitals to out-patients. They attend once or twice a week for about two hours, most of which time is spent recovering from the confusional state temporarily induced. When they come round from the anaesthetic, they may not realize where they are or what has happened, but this condition usually passes off within an hour or two, leaving a slight headache, and sometimes nausea or dizziness. A course of treatment normally consists of about half a dozen applications, given over a three-week period. Careful research suggests that ECT does not cause any permanent impairment of memory, except for the brief periods before and after each application. As a precaution it is nowadays sometimes administered to one-half of the brain only. In most people, language is largely controlled by one hemisphere, called the dominant hemisphere, which is usually located on the left side of the brain: trauma to the other hemisphere may have less severe effects on mental function. Hence, giving ECT only to the non-dominant hemisphere should minimize any adverse side-effects. The balance of evidence suggests, however, that ECT to one side of the brain is not as effective as when given to both.

ECT is used in the treatment of severe depression, usually only after other forms of treatment have failed, or if the patient is suicidal. A trial sponsored by the British Medical Research Council showed that it is a rapid and effective treatment, with a higher success rate than antidepressant drugs. Although I would have been reluctant to have ECT at the time of my first and most severe depression, knowing what I know now I would certainly consider it, if I had a really prolonged and severe depression. Unfortunately, it does not prevent relapses. Despite its drastic nature and our ignorance of its mode of operation, its dangers and its side-effects are probably no worse than those of antidepressant drugs. The death rate under ECT is about 4 per 100,000 applications, about the same as for any procedure in which a general anaesthetic is used: deaths are produced by the anaesthetic rather than the shock, particularly in patients with cardiovascular disease.

Several psychiatric treatments have proved to be both dangerous and useless, but it is worth emphasizing that such treatments abound in other forms of medicine. Tonsillectomy is a case in point. It is a more dangerous procedure than ECT both in terms of mortality rate and in its long-term effects. Removing the tonsils quadruples the risk of catching bulbar polio and triples the risk of Hodgkin's disease, a form of cancer that is usually fatal. Out of every thousand children who have their tonsils removed one used to be killed by the operation and sixteen were made seriously ill.

Moreover, there is much better agreement on the indications for administering ECT than for removing the tonsils. The American Child Health Association carried out an interesting study on the criteria used by doctors in recommending tonsillectomy. Of 1000 eleven-year-old children surveyed in New York schools, 61% had already had their tonsils removed. When the remaining 39% were referred to physicians, it was recommended that 45% of them should have their tonsils out. The 55% who had been passed as not requiring tonsillectomy by the first set of doctors were sent to other doctors who duly recommended that 46% should have their tonsils removed. This study suggests that many tonsils are removed more or less at random. It is of course true that one cannot justify the use of drastic procedures in psychiatry by comparing them with mistakes made in other branches of medicine, but in the case of ECT there is compelling evidence that it works.

The use of ECT has an interesting history. It was held in the eighteenth century that traumatic events, like ducking in icy water or exposure to snakes, could alleviate or cure mental illness, and in the nineteenth century some physicians attempted to cure the mentally sick by deliberately infecting them with malaria, smallpox and typhoid, and by giving seizures induced by camphor. In the 1930s, insulin injections were used to produce coma and convulsions in the insane. Insulin-induced coma is accompanied by writhing and moaning, and until recently it was quite common to bring on such comas in schizophrenics every day for periods of up to eight weeks. It was not until the mid-fifties that a careful appraisal of the effects of insulin on schizophrenics was made: it was discovered that it had no beneficial effects whatever. This appalling episode indicates that all that can be learned from clinical observations is that nothing can be learned from them. Systematically controlled trials are as essential in medicine as in psychotherapy. Although very occasionally still used, this treatment will not be discussed further.

Partly as a result of the belief that convulsions helped schizophrenics, investigations were undertaken to discover what proportion of schizophrenics had epilepsy: it was found to be much less common in them than in the general population, and this encouraged the belief that giving convulsions to schizophrenics might help them. At about the time that insulin treatment was introduced, a psychiatrist in Budapest began to induce convulsions in schizophrenics using injections of camphor, a drug used in the treatment of the insane in the late eighteenth century. He subsequently found that another drug, metrazol, caused convulsions more reliably, and switched to that. His work in turn prompted an Italian psychiatrist to experiment with convulsions induced by electro-shock, and this method completely supplanted the use of metrazol. Although the treatment has proved to be beneficial, it was discovered as a result of a series of false assumptions. It turned out to be of little use for schizophrenia but proved helpful in the treatment of depression; more recently it was discovered that it works just as well when given under an anaesthetic.

* * *

A second drastic physical treatment was also introduced in the late 1930s. It is called prefrontal leucotomy in England and prefrontal lobotomy in America. The procedure involves severing many of the fibres connecting the front part of the cerebral cortex to the remainder of the brain. It is now usually thought that the harmful effects of this operation outweigh any benefits. One of the saddest cases on my ward was a gently-spoken, slightly portly, middle-aged man who had been an accountant in a good post. He had had a breakdown in his twenties and had submitted to a prefrontal leucotomy (in a different hospital). He bitterly regretted having had the operation: he had been in and out of mental hospitals ever since, and was unable to hold down any job. He suffered from obsessive thoughts and complained that the leucotomy had made it impossible to follow any coherent train of thought: the only mode of thinking it had not destroyed were the agonizing obsessions for which the operation was performed in the first place.

Prefrontal leucotomy was introduced by a Portuguese psychiatrist named Moniz. He attended a talk given by two neurophysiologists, who reported the results of extirpating the prefrontal lobes of two chimpanzees: one animal that had previously been rather fractious was rendered tame and friendly. When Moniz told John Fulton, one of the neurophysiologists, that he was thinking of using the procedure on psychotics, Fulton was horrified. Although many now execrate the name of Moniz, he received a Nobel prize for introducing this operation. He considered himself the best judge of whether it helped his patients, and reported that of the first 20 operated upon, seven were completely recovered, seven much improved, and the rest unchanged. In investigating the effects of any method of treatment, perhaps the most basic principle is that the evaluation must be carried out by independent investigators using systematic methods of assessment, not by the doctor who gives the treatment. Unconscious bias may lead him to see improvement where none exists. Moniz's career was terminated in 1944 when a leucotomized patient shot him in the spine, rendering him hemiplegic.

The history of leucotomy does little credit to the medical profession. It was introduced in the USA in 1936. In 1946 a new procedure was devised by Walter Freeman. He thrust an ice pick through the orbit of each eye and behind the eyeball into the frontal lobes. Initially, he carried out the operation in his office because the hospital would not give permission to have it performed on its premises. It is estimated that some 40,000 operations were carried out in the US in the next twenty-five years. British neurosurgeons were just as avid to use this new and unproven method of treatment and severed the frontal lobes of some 10,000 patients. Few adequate studies of the effects of the operation were carried out: it should be remembered that many mental patients improve spontaneously, and the fact that some people recover after leucotomy is meaningless unless it can be shown that a significantly higher percentage recover than after no treatment or after less drastic forms of treatment. The two most carefully conducted studies involving large numbers of operated patients and unoperated control patients matched for severity of illness showed no benefit from leucotomy.

It was known that removal of the frontal lobes in monkeys led to marked deficits in some tasks requiring intelligence, but no loss could be detected in leucotomized patients on standard intelligence tests; the operation may have rendered patients more tractable, and hence they may have cooperated on the tests more readily than preoperatively. There were many indications that the operation leads to more subtle deficits: in particular, most leucotomized patients are incapable of forming and executing long-term plans, they are easily distractible, and if they are interrupted in the performance of a task they do not resume it. Their emotions are often shallow and short-lived, with a tendency to euphoria, tactlessness and sudden changes of mood. Although a few patients appear to be improved by the operation, it is unclear how far the semblance of improvement is produced merely because they become easier for others to manage, how far they are genuinely more at ease with themselves. It has been said that the operation turns people into cabbages, and although this may not be completely true in all cases it is the general impression gained by many of the close relatives and friends of leucotomized patients.

It should not be assumed that the surgeons who undertook this sensational operation did so merely to further their own careers or out of indifference to their patients' welfare: they were often presented with cases of people in dire misery, and at the time the operation was most popular, other methods of treatment, such as psychotropic drugs, were not available. The real criticism that can be made of many of the doctors who performed the operation is that they did so without adequately exploring alternative methods of treatment and that they failed to undertake careful follow-up studies to determine its precise effects, a failure probably due less to arrogance than to ignorance of how to conduct the necessary research. Moreover, the operation came to be performed not just on desperate cases but on less severe cases. Leucotomy was also used for the relief of chronic pain: after the operation, patients would say their pain felt the same as ever, but it was more bearable because they did not pay so much attention to it. The wife of a patient who received a leucotomy for the relief of chronic back-ache told an investigating psychologist:

> That operation was performed on my husband in September 1949 and it has also been a very sad affair, and if the doctor had of spoke of it as you do we would never of had it done, but he said it would slow him up but he would be able to do the things he always did and even be able to get at his place of business, but he cannot do anything and do it right, he can't even take care of himself in the bathroom, and does not take any interest in anything. When he went into it mentally he was fine, kept in contact with his business, even done some of the book work, but he had suffered pain for years from back trouble I some days think I will lose my mind going through this with him.

The growing evidence that leucotomy led to intellectual deterioration coincided with the discovery of a series of drugs that could be used in the alleviation of mental disorder. Full-scale leucotomy was largely abandoned in the early 1960s. One would have supposed that the tragic history of its use would have made neurosurgeons more cautious about introducing irreversible damage to the brain without careful study of the consequences. Unfortunately, as far as I know, no such study has been conducted, but the American National Institute of Mental Health withdrew all supporting funds for the investigation of psychosurgery. Moreover, in 1996 Norway and some American states gave ex-gratia payments in compensation to those who had had the operation and were still alive.

Nevertheless, the number of brain operations for mental disorder is still running at several hundred a year in the US and about 25 a year in England, many of which are performed at the Maudsley Hospital. In Scotland a working party has proposed that the operation could be given to mental patients who are too ill to give consent. With advances in the techniques of neurosurgery, it is now possible to destroy selectively and accurately small areas of brain tissue so that the lesions made by modern psychosurgery are more restricted than those damaged by the large and poorly located cuts made in full leucotomy. The areas destroyed, however, are still of crucial importance to normal brain functioning, and are invariably parts of the brain thought to be implicated in emotion and in the deepest aspects of personality.

It is important to distinguish between psychosurgery and neurosurgery. In the operations so far discussed, the tissue removed is not, as far as we know, diseased or damaged. Where there is damaged tissue in the brain, as with a cerebral tumour or an epileptic focus, it is often essential to remove it. Both tumours and epileptic foci may produce psychiatric symptoms, but their removal can undoubtedly benefit the patient.

In the absence of clear-cut signs of brain pathology, brain surgery for the mentally ill is today normally given only to patients with a long history of severe anxiety or depression, or of serious and uncontrollable violence, and then only after all other forms of treatment have been tried and found wanting. Unfortunately, these conditions are not always met. Some years ago I came across a case of a 21-year-old girl who received psychosurgery for a severe phobia. She had been seen by a clinical psychologist who was of the opinion that she could be helped by behaviour therapy, but his judgement was overruled by the psychiatrist in charge of the case and she was referred for leucotomy. In America some brain operations for violence have been performed on children and prisoners: it is hard to see how they can give 'informed consent'.

One case aroused considerable controversy. In 1967, Mark and Ervin of the Massachusetts General Hospital in Boston operated on 'Thomas R.', a 34-year-old engineer who, according to them, was highly successful in his work but was given to outbursts of uncontrollable rage and violence, and who suffered from paranoia and occasional epileptic seizures. They destroyed the amygdala, a region of the brain known to be implicated in the emotions including anger. Before the operation they had implanted electrodes in the patient's brain and had repeatedly stimulated parts of it with electric current. Their own description of how they obtained his consent to the operation is as follows:

> We suggested to him that we make a destructive lesion ... He agreed to this suggestion while he was relaxed from lateral stimulation of the amygdala. However, twelve hours later, when this effect had worn off, Thomas turned wild and unmanageable ... it took many weeks of patient explanation before he accepted the idea of bilateral lesions being made in his medial amygdala.

In reporting the outcome, they state: 'Four years have passed since the operation, during which time Thomas has not had a single episode of rage. He continues, however, to have an occasional epileptic seizure with periods of confusion and disordered thinking.'

An independent psychiatrist reported that before the operation the patient 'had never been in any trouble at work or otherwise for aggressive behaviour'. Moreover, the hospital records prior to the operation revealed that he had no psychotic symptoms, no hallucinations, delusions, or paranoid ideas, and no signs of difficulty in thinking. His wife was having an affair with another man whom she subsequently married: it was this man about whom Mark and Ervin had alleged the patient was paranoid. An investigating psychiatrist discovered that after the operation the patient had become socially confused and was unable to cope with normal life. He moved to the West Coast, where he was admitted to hospital and sedated. His new doctors thought his reports of what Mark and Ervin had done to him so incredible that they decided he suffered delusions. The patient was unable to care for himself and had to be hospitalized periodically for violent and psychotic behaviour. Eight years after the operation, a neurologist stated that 'the patient would never be able to function in society'.

I once travelled to a conference with a young neurosurgeon who has since become well known. He explained to me that he hoped to win a Nobel prize by opening up the skulls of patients with terminal cancers and observing the results of electrical stimulation of different parts of the brain. The excuse for using patients as guinea-pigs in this way was that he might find an area of the brain which on stimulation would reduce pain and cause pleasurable sensations—such areas are known to exist. However, much of the work he described involved stimulating parts of the brain, such as the visual centres, that have nothing to do with pleasure and pain. These operations were subsequently performed under a local anaesthetic on fully conscious patients, as indeed is most brain surgery, since it is necessary to obtain patients' subjective reports on the effects of stimulation of various parts of the brain in order to discover whereabouts one is operating. The neurosurgeon in question, unlike Moniz, has not so far been awarded a Nobel prize, but he has achieved a certain degree of notoriety. Such cases of brain surgery are extreme, though there are similar ones on record. Moreover, the way in which cases of psychosurgery are followed up and reported by psychiatrists and neurosurgeons usually continues to fall short of acceptable standards of scientific objectivity.

Through the study of people who have suffered accidental damage to their prefrontal lobes, we now know much more about their function. They are closely connected to the amygdala (the structure on which Mark and Ervin operated). Damage to certain parts of the prefrontal lobes can lead to emotional flatness, indecisiveness and an inability to plan ahead. One of the foremost investigators in this field, Antonio Damasio, a Portuguese immigrant to the US, has argued that many decisions can only be taken if planning them is followed by emotional arousal. All this fits well with what we know of the effects of leucotomy on psychiatric patients. Recently, there have been some even more surprising findings: there is some evidence that the left prefrontal lobe can suppress strong emotions arising from the right one and that it gives rise to cheerfulness whereas the right side produces strong and unpleasant emotions such as fear or anger. The circuitry of the brain is, however, so complex that we are far from understanding it, let alone using our knowledge to alleviate depression through surgical intervention, but that may become possible at some unspecified time in the future. It is perhaps more likely that we shall be able to implant electrodes to deliver tiny shocks to selected areas of the brain, thus allowing people to become cheerful at the press of a button. Such techniques would have their disadvantages, for fear, anger and dismay are warnings that something is wrong and some action should be taken. Moreover, such interventions might well be unsuccessful or counterproductive in the long run because when interfered with the brain has an uncanny knack of restoring its pre-existing state, an ability that will be discussed in the context of drugs.

As a coda it is worth mentioning a much less severe biological manipulation of the brain that has been advocated recently for depression. Some psychiatrists believe that sleep deprivation—either eliminating a night's sleep completely or drastically decreasing its length—can greatly reduce depression. This suggestion has not as yet been properly tested. It is, however, of interest that James Boswell, who suffered severe depressions (or 'hypochondria', as he called them), repeatedly notes in his journals that if he slept little, he felt more cheerful the following day.

works well only for certain types of neurosis. It is, for example, doubtful how far it can ameliorate general anxiety disorder.

Moreover, as already noted, the theory behind cognitive therapy for depression is inadequate. It is not clear how faulty thinking can lead to sleeplessness, agitation, or the loss of appetite; these are known as the biological symptoms of depression. The answer surely lies in the two-way influence of mood and brain function. Depressive thoughts may alter the working of the parts of the brain underlying mood, making the depression worse, while as in bipolar manic-depression changes in brain function may induce low mood and the depressive thoughts that accompany it. The problem can be tackled from either end—cognitive therapy to change thinking or drugs to affect the brain directly.

The use of drugs

There is a more subtle way of influencing mental states than hacking out parts of the brain or giving electroconvulsive shocks: 'psychotropic drugs' are those that through their influence on the brain affect states of mind. Apart from medical drugs used to help mental disorders—or at least intended to help them—they include alcohol and nicotine, and many illegal drugs such as cannabis or cocaine.

Chloral and paraldehyde were employed in Victorian times to sedate patients, but the first modern group of tranquillizing drugs to come into general use were the barbiturates. They are effective, at least at first, in reducing anxiety and as sedatives, but if they are taken regularly the brain becomes less sensitive to them, a phenomenon known as 'tolerance'. In consequence, larger and larger doses are needed to produce the same effect. Like many other psychotropic drugs, they are highly addictive. Prolonged use leads to chronic intoxication accompanied by total deterioration of the personality: addicts cannot function in society and cannot hold down their job or keep friends. They become maudlin, moody and childish. In addition, whether by accident or design, people have often taken overdoses that have led to their death. In 1960, 350 patients suffering from barbiturate poisoning were admitted to one hospital alone in Scotland. In the US 10,000 people a year were at one time killed by barbiturates. They were the favoured method of committing suicide among film stars and the jet-set; moreover, many died by taking additional doses having forgotten in a drowsy state what they had already taken. Withdrawal produces delirium tremens, insomnia and anxiety. Dr William Sargant has called attention to a more curious but equally real danger. He reported cases of patients with chronic anxiety states who were given prefrontal leucotomies: only after the operation was it discovered that the anxiety was caused by barbiturate poisoning.

In 1967 there were an estimated 100,000 people in the United Kingdom with chronic dependence on barbiturates, as compared with about 70,000 chronic alcoholics. Although, when administered under strict medical supervision, these drugs helped in the control of anxiety, their dangers were not appreciated early enough.

The barbiturates have been largely superseded by a new range of tranquillizers thought to be less addictive. The first of the new tranquillizers, meprobamate, was put on the market in 1955. The British National Formulary for 1971, a Government publication, stated: 'Clinical trials have shown that meprobamate, once widely used as a tranquillizer, has no more effect than a placebo.' The 1993 edition of the same publication recommends 'short-term use of the drug in anxiety'—the effectiveness of drugs is clearly hard to determine. It is now known that meprobomate is almost as addictive and as fatal in overdoses as the barbiturates, but it is still sometimes prescribed.

It has largely been replaced by a new family of drugs known as the benzodiazepines, of which Valium, Mogadon and Dalmane are examples. These drugs have few side-effects and a vast number would have to be taken before any serious damage was done. Like most psychotropic drugs, they were discovered by accident not design. In their case, the accident was a particularly curious one. A Czech pharmacologist was synthesizing other chemical substances from dyes, in the hope that he would find one that had pharmacological effects on the body. In fear of the Nazis, he moved his laboratory to America. Some years later, the laboratory was cleared by a technician, who noticed that, of all the hundreds of compounds synthesized, one had not been tested. When it was given to animals, it sedated them. As with all new drugs the pharmaceutical companies began ringing the changes on the original benzodiazepine molecule, partly in the hope of finding a related compound that would be more effective, but also in order to circumvent their rival's patent on the original drug. There are now 14 different benzodiazepines on the market, each of which has slightly different effects.

When they were introduced in the early 1960s, they were hailed as being completely non-addictive, but in 1964, a leading textbook of psychopharmacology stated that the benzodiazepines, if taken over a prolonged period of time, could be addictive and could lead to 'hallucinations, restlessness and hostile-aggressive tendencies'. As in the case of the barbiturates, the addiction occurs because the brain becomes tolerant to benzodiazepines: if they are withdrawn, sleep is severely disrupted and unpleasant feelings of unreality and inability to concentrate occur in the daytime. Tolerance, that is, reduced sensitivity to a drug, produces another unfortunate effect. With continued use the original dose becomes less and less effective so that if a sleeping tablet is used, sleep will become as difficult as it was before starting the drug. Increasing the dose will increase the addiction. It took the medical profession 20 years after the first warning to recognize the dangers of the benzodiazepines: in the meantime they were doled out in massive quantities—100 million prescriptions a year in the US alone. There are no good estimates for the number of people currently dependent on the benzodiazepines, which can be obtained by prescription (or by raiding chemists' shops), but there are thought to be many more than are addicted to illicit drugs. Over 100,000 use heroin and increasing numbers use such drugs as amphetamines, cocaine, and ecstasy. All carry the risk of convulsions, psychotic symptoms, depression, and—through an overdose or shared needles—death.

All benzodiazepines tend to make one drowsy, but some more than others: these, such as Mogadon, are used as sleeping pills. Mogadon stays in the bloodstream for a long time: half of a given dose remains 24 hours later. Although it certainly helps sleep, it therefore tends to induce drowsiness in the daytime. Short-acting benzodiazepines have now become available: they help people who cannot get to sleep, but not those who wake too early.

Unfortunately, the finding that benzodiazepines are addictive has had one curious and unfortunate effect. Some general practitioners have sought to avoid their addictive effect by prescribing old fashioned drugs like chloral and the barbiturates. These drugs are far more addictive than the benzodiazepines which are relatively harmless. It's no good trying to be a clever doctor if you're not a knowledgeable one.

* * *

In the early 1950s more potent tranquillizing drugs, known as the major tranquillizers or neuroleptics, were discovered. The parent drug from which they were developed was originally an insecticide. They were widely used to calm patients who were intolerably agitated. They are powerful and bring about a pronounced reduction in levels of anxiety, excitement and aggression. I have already described their rapid mode of action on myself. In mental hospitals they reduced the incidence of broken windows, the extent to which patients had to be restrained and the number of assaults on staff.

Although they were called major tranquillizers, they are less used for this purpose nowadays since the benzodiazepines are usually as effective and have fewer side-effects. They are, however, still prescribed for agitated or anxious patients who have become tolerant to other drugs and for others whose aggression is exacerbated by benzodiazepines.

Their main use is for schizophrenia and to a lesser degree psychotic mania. Although they undoubtedly reduce many schizophrenic symptoms, to prevent relapse patients have to take them over many years. Unfortunately, the original neuroleptics had uncommonly serious side-effects, such as dryness of the mouth, impotence, lack of motor co-ordination and constipation. Moreover, they often produce much more severe side-effects, including restlessness, involuntary grimaces and protrusions of the tongue. They can also give rise to the symptoms of Parkinson's disease—an expressionless face, rigidity of the muscles, and severe tremor. Some of these side-effects can be partially controlled by administering other drugs, and they usually cease when the neuroleptic is stopped.

Unfortunately, there is a further side-effect, tardive dyskinesia, that occurs in about 30% of patients. It can develop after the neuroleptic treatment has stopped (and sometimes while the patient is still on it). The main symptoms are constant chewing and sucking movements, and grimacing. Patients usually recover from the other side-effects, but the tardive dyskinesia often remains. Because of these unpleasant effects, many schizophrenics stop taking neuroleptics. When they are prone to aggression, this can lead to assaults or murders by patients living in the community.

Chronic schizophrenics are frequently maintained on one or other of the neuroleptics, and their introduction was followed by a sharp fall in the number of hospital beds they occupied both in Britain and in North America. Despite their appalling side-effects, they have enabled many schizophrenics to function well enough to hold down jobs and to lead a semblance of normal life outside hospital. It has recently been discovered that the original neuroleptics are very much more effective for patients suffering the positive symptoms of schizophrenia—delusions, hallucinations, and severe disorders of thinking—than for those with negative symptoms such as withdrawal, lack of emotion and loss of interest in the world. It seems possible that different malfunctioning of the brain underlies these two types of schizophrenia.

Over the last few years several new drugs for schizophrenia have been introduced: one of the latest and most promising is Risperidone. Unlike earlier drugs it is effective for patients with negative symptoms such as withdrawal and flattened emotions. Moreover, it does not have severe side-effects such as tardive dyskinesia: in consequence patients continue to take it. Those on this drug have cut their visits to general practitioners by 30% and their visits to hospital by 60%. It is true that the new drugs are expensive, but they are much cheaper than keeping patients in hospital or under close care. Unfortunately, because doctors tend to be too conservative, new drugs of this type have not been widely used and most schizophrenics are still taking the neuroleptics available 25 years ago and suffering their unpleasant side-effects.

* * *

Tranquillizers calm patients, but do not elevate a depressed mood: various drugs are available for this purpose. The first were the amphetamines, discovered in the mid-1930s and widely used in the 1950s and early 1960s. They are highly addictive and did more harm than good, since withdrawal is accompanied by a rebound effect leading to even worse depression. In 1966, 200 million amphetamine tablets were prescribed by general practitioners working within the National Health Service in Britain. When first taken, they reduce appetite, and they were widely prescribed for people wanting to slim. Despite the claims of the drug companies, they are useless for this purpose: if taken for any period of time, their effect on appetite wanes, and it returns to its previous level as soon as the would-be slimmer abandons the drug.

When given intravenously, amphetamine and its derivatives lead to pleasurable 'highs', and following their introduction into medicine they began to be taken for this purpose: there are now a large number of 'speed' addicts. Amphetamines are as dangerous as heroin: chronic use can produce the same symptoms as schizophrenia and may cause permanent brain damage. In 1954 there were about half a million amphetamine addicts in Japan: in the same year, the then chief medical officer of the British Ministry of Health wrote complacently: '[Amphetamines] have the advantage of being relatively non-toxic, addiction to them is rare and there are no serious ill effects.' He was repeating a mistake made by Freud, who advocated the use of cocaine (which in many ways resembles amphetamine) as a cure for all ills.

The prescription of amphetamine compounds and barbiturates continued long after their dangers were known. Many of the alcoholics on my ward were dependent not merely on alcohol but on a variety of sedatives, sleeping tablets, and stimulants with exotic-sounding names like Mandrax, Moggies, Purple Hearts and Black Bombs, nowadays largely succeeded by a new crop of names, such as Ecstasy, Speed and Crack. They were often taken off all drugs on admission and experienced withdrawal symptoms including sleeplessness, terrifying and persistent nightmares and extreme levels of tension and anxiety. Many complained, rightly or wrongly, that they suffered more from having such drugs withdrawn than from alcohol withdrawal.

A new use has been discovered for the amphetamines: particularly in the USA, they are frequently employed in the control of badly behaved children diagnosed as having attention-deficit hyperactivity disorder. Large doses of amphetamines and related compounds (the most common of which has the trade name 'Ritalin') have a paradoxical effect on some agitated children: instead of exciting them, it frequently quietens them down and makes them more tractable both at home and at school. Although the child may appear to concentrate better, it has been shown that Ritalin does nothing to improve their poor scholastic performance. Moreover, we know that the long-term use of amphetamine may produce intellectual deterioration and permanent psychotic states. Nevertheless, an American psychiatrist, Wender, advocated that more naughty children should have the benefit of such treatment: 'Minimal brain dysfunction [the original name for attention-deficit hyperactivity disorder] is probably the single most common disorder seen by child psychiatrists. Despite this fact, its existence is often un-recognized and its prevalence is almost always underrated.' The disorder is diagnosed ten times as often in America as in Britain: it is likely that this is caused more by differences between the two countries' psychiatrists than by differences in their children.

One of the reasons why amphetamine is no longer used for depression is that a new group of drugs known as 'antidepressants' was discovered in the late 1950s. The first, the MAOIs (the monoamine-oxidase inhibitors), were originally employed in the treatment of tuberculosis, and an observant doctor noticed that some of the patients taking them became very cheerful. At about the same time a second class of antidepressants, known as the tricyclics, was discovered—again by chance. They were being used to treat schizophrenia when it was noticed that they seemed to cheer patients up, without removing their fundamental symptoms. The drug firms got busy producing variants, of which there are now 16 in Britain each with slightly different properties. The generic names of the two that have been most widely used are amitriptyline, which I was given, and imipramine. It is virtually certain that they are not addictive, possibly because they take so long (three or four weeks) to have any therapeutic effect. The elevation of mood they produce is not followed by deep depression as a rebound effect when they are withdrawn. It was not long before the tricyclics almost completely succeeded the MAOIs, which destroy a substance in the stomach and liver needed to break down a biochemical present in certain foods. While taking MAOIs, the patient therefore has to avoid cheese, yeast, red wines and beans. The tricyclics do not have this disadvantage.

As I have described in my own case, the side-effects of tricyclics can be very unpleasant: they include extreme dryness of the mouth, constipation (or sometimes diarrhoea), disorders of vision, impotence in men and loss of sexual drive in women, disorders in the functioning of the heart and vascular system, muscular weakness and tremor, and difficulty in urinating. With so many undesirable side-effects it is perhaps not surprising that no cases of addiction have been reported. Recently a new class of antidepressants, the SSRIs (the selective serotonin re-uptake inhibitors), has been developed: Prozac is one example. The side-effects are much less severe than those of the tricyclics, but it is usually thought that the new drugs are not as effective for severe depression. The means by which they were discovered—again more by luck than judgement—will be described in the next chapter.

Until recently it was customary to take patients off antidepressants soon after their depression had ceased, but nowadays it is common to prescribe maintenance doses for a further six months or year. This helps to prevent relapse during that time, but the likelihood of recurrence once off the drug is not decreased. Clinical trials have shown unequivocally that the tricyclics work in about 70% of cases, though this figure makes no allowance for the 30% of patients who would have recovered of their own accord nor for those who give up treatment.

* * *

Over the last 40 years or so, yet another substance—lithium—has leapt into the top ten of drugs in psychiatric use. It was originally employed in the treatment of mania, but well-controlled studies have shown that when manic-depressive patients are permanently maintained on lithium it reduces the severity and incidence of both mania and depression. The use of lithium has an interesting history. It was, yet again, discovered by a circuitous route. It occurs naturally in many mineral springs, and the drinking of such waters was advocated by a perspicacious Ancient Greek physician for the reduction of manic excitement. In 1949, its beneficial effects on mania were rediscovered by an Australian medical research worker, Cade: the discovery was made by chance on the basis of an incorrect hypothesis. Cade found that injecting the urine of manic-depressives into guinea-pigs often proved fatal to the animals, and he thought that this was caused by the presence of uric acid. To test this suggestion, he injected with the urine a salt of uric acid based on lithium, expecting to increase the toxicity, but found to his surprise that the mixture was less toxic than plain urea. Moreover, guinea-pigs given the lithium salt lost much of their natural timidity and became more tranquil. When he administered a lithium salt to manic patients, the mania was much reduced.

Many years passed before lithium became widely used in the treatment of manic-depressive disorder. Its toxic effects may have been partly responsible for this delay, but an article in the *American Journal of Psychiatry* suggested that the delay may have been caused by the fact that salts of lithium are very cheap to produce; moreover, because it is a naturally occurring substance, it cannot be patented. Hence the drug companies saw little profit in marketing and promoting it. It did not become commercially available until 1970.

Once introduced, it became the new wonder drug: it has been administered to control aggression, particularly in fractious children and adolescents, and has also been used in the treatment of schizophrenics, psychopaths, mental defectives, alcoholics and women with pre-menstrual tension. There is little or no evidence that it helps any of these conditions, but it does greatly reduce mania. Its main value is that it is extremely effective as a prophylactic for preventing both mania and depression in people with bipolar affective disorder. There is currently a debate about whether it is useful for unipolar disorder: it may potentiate the effects of antidepressants.

I have already described my own experience of the side-effects of lithium —extreme thirst accompanied by the need for frequent urination and a tremor that, in my case, was fairly slight. It can also cause damage to the thyroid and the kidneys, but such damage is usually reversible if the drug is stopped. If the dose is too high much more extreme side-effects occur, including severe vomiting and diarrhoea.

Properly administered, the risks of lithium therapy are no greater than those of any other psychotropic drug. There is, however, a rather small margin between the dosage needed to produce therapeutic effects and a highly toxic or even lethal dose. For this reason, the level of lithium in the blood needs to be monitored, and the dosage is adjusted accordingly. When patients are first placed on lithium, blood samples are taken every few days, but once the right dosage for the individual has been established, it is only necessary to monitor its level once every few months. When lithium was first introduced the recommended level in the blood was three times as high as that now thought to be optimal.

Manic-depressives given lithium on a long-term basis often become outwardly more normal, but some complain that their lives are flat and less colourful: some businessmen argue that a degree of manic energy is necessary for their work, while artists assert that lithium reduces their creative power. Many who at first make such complaints find to their surprise that once they become used to living without manic episodes and are adjusted to a more stable pattern of life, their productivity and creativity become as good or better than before.

* * *

Evaluation of the effectiveness of drugs is fraught with difficulty. For a variety of reasons, the opinions of clinicians who have prescribed the drug are useless. First, doctors who have faith in a given drug will prescribe it to all patients who have the condition for which they believe it is helpful, but many patients recover of their own accord and the doctor cannot know how many of his patients would have recovered without the drug.

Second, it is known that everybody pays more attention to positive results than to negative ones: doctors will therefore be impressed by the patients that recover and tend to forget those that do not.

Third, if the doctor has faith in the drug, he will convey this to the patients and such faith aids recovery, particularly in psychiatric cases.

Fourth, doctors are bombarded by advertising from drug companies (not to mention free meals and bottles of champagne). The aim of pharmaceutical companies is to make profits and they may make exaggerated claims for their products, or suggest by implication that powerful psychotropic drugs should be prescribed for comparatively trivial complaints. For example, in 1974 one new tranquillizer was advertised with four pictures of endearing children suffering from such 'complaints' as being picky eaters or troublemakers. Another was recommended as suitable for the anxious housewife with the caption: 'She welcomed marriage, children, domesticity. But sometimes the change seems too much, too sudden. She is frustrated and lonely. To lighten her load of worries comes . . . a new tranquillizer.'

These advertisements were withdrawn several years ago and there has been a tendency for the advertising of psychotropic drugs to be toned down, but it has not changed that much. The reader who wishes to find out how drug companies rate the intelligence of doctors has only to pick up a copy of any magazine aimed at them. Taking an issue of *World Medicine* at random, I discovered an advertisement for a tranquillizer showing an attractive young mother who is able to combine playing hockey with looking after two young children, presumably thanks to the action of the drug which is advertised as 'the tranquillizer for active patients', a fine oxymoron. The same issue carried an advertisement for an antidepressant: a picture of a happy if somewhat chaotic child's birthday party is accompanied by the slogan 'for the treatment of depression in general practice'. Each family doctor in Britain receives free between 25 and 40 different journals or newsletters published by the drug companies to promote their wares. Until recently, many of them were accompanied by female nudes, and they still appeal more to the doctor's emotions than to his reason. As a senior advertising copy writer put it: 'Razzle-dazzle promotion has come to play a more decisive role than scientific evaluation of drugs in determining the career of a pharmaceutical product.'

Fifth, the general public have too much faith in medicine and are prone to accept claims for new drugs, a tendency to which the media pander and which by so doing they increase. Once the word gets around, patients put pressure on their doctors to prescribe the drug. When, as in America, the doctor depends on his patients' fees. it must be hard for him to resist such demands. The 'hype' surrounding Prozac, known as 'the happy drug' for its effects on the moods of people who were not depressed, made it one of E. W. Lilly's best-selling drugs. The idea that Prozac was a cosmetic drug (i.e. one that would help anyone) was abetted in a book by Peter Kramer, which was a paean of praise to it. One *New Yorker* cartoon showed it being fed to a cheerful looking cat. In 1993 Lilly tried to reduce its use for normal people (and cats) presumably fearing that it would trivialize both depression and Prozac; they declared that it should only be taken 'if a clear medical need existed'.

The randomized control trial is the only way round the difficulty of evaluation: it was introduced in agriculture and psychology at the beginning of the century, but shockingly was not used in medicine until 1952. Medical control trials follow the same procedures as those used in research on psychotherapy substituting a drug for therapy. A large number of patients are selected all with the same illness; they are divided into two groups matched for the severity of the disorder; one group is given the drug to be tested, the other a pill that is inert—a placebo that has no physiological effects on the body. To prevent the person administering the drug from accidentally showing more faith when the drug is genuine than when it is not, the drugs are (or should be) administered by a doctor who does not know which is which, while at the end of the trial the patients are assessed by someone unaware of who has received the genuine drug. During the trial careful checks are made to discover whether there are any undesirable side-effects. Before such trials are undertaken the drug is tested on animals to discover whether it has any beneficial effects and whether it is safe. It is then tested for safety in young, healthy volunteers and only then is it administered to a small number of patients, at first in very low doses to see whether it helps them and to examine side-effects. If the drug appears both safe and useful, full randomized control trials begin.

The reason why the medical profession was slow to adopt the randomized control trial (one of the first was that of the Salk polio vaccine in 1954), was that like most so-called experts, doctors believed their own intuitions about diagnosis and treatment were more accurate than trial results could ever be: slavishly following the findings of scientific control trials would belittle their power of judgement and derogate from their responsibility. Unwarranted conceit is a mark of almost all experts. There were two other reasons why control trials in medicine were slow to come about. First, they are expensive and time consuming. Second, it was thought unethical to withhold from the control group a treatment that might prove effective. The second objection is easily met. The control group often turns out to do better than the group given the treatment. Against considerable medical opposition, the first test of coronary care units was conducted in 1971. All patients had had heart attacks: the control group was treated at home, the rest in coronary care units. Those treated at home did considerably better. Again, calomel, one of whose ingredients, mercury, was a deadly poison, was used in many teething powders until 1948, when it was noticed that it caused 'pink disease' from which many babies suffered. Had a clinical trial been undertaken, much misery would have been averted.

The situation today is better, largely because of the setting up of the Food and Drugs Administration (FDA) in the US and in 1968 very belatedly the Committee of Safety in Medicine (CSM) in Britain; the latter body came into existence largely as a result of the thalidomide disaster. These bodies require proof of both the efficacy and safety of a drug before it becomes available through licence to the general public. In the absence of a complete control trial the USA refused to license thalidomide. It was introduced as a sedative in Britain in 1960 although a closely related drug was known to cause deformities in infant rats. A letter of warning had appeared in the *British Medical Journal* in December 1960 and by May 1961, when it was banned, over 1,300 cases of inflammation of the nerves caused by the drug had been reported. As late as November 1960, an advertisement had stated that the drug 'can be given with complete safety to pregnant women—without adverse effects on mother or child'. The drug caused deformities in over 10,000 babies.

Even randomized clinical trials have many difficulties. Usually several different hospitals are involved and their treatment of patients may differ; patients have to volunteer for a trial and particularly for psychiatric disorders those who do so may differ in ways that are relevant for their prognosis from those who do not; we have already seen that psychiatric diagnosis is hazardous and if diagnostic procedures are not standardized, different disorders may be under test without the experimenter's knowledge;

it is essential to ensure that all patients take the drug or placebo prescribed, a difficult task when drugs have unpleasant side-effects; trials are confounded by patients who drop out. Finally, adverse long-term effects of a drug may not be picked up, for example, tolerance for and addiction to the benzodiazepines.

Despite these difficulties, clinical trials are the only method of discovering whether a drug is safe and efficacious. It is to be hoped that they will spare us in future from the kind of damage produced by amphetamines and barbiturates, which though less sensational may have been even greater than that caused by thalidomide. Since drug companies have to perform clinical trials before a drug is licensed almost all the drugs mentioned here are effective (at least in the short-term) and reasonably safe. It is, however, not unknown for drug companies illegally to suppress unfavourable results and it might be more sensible to have all tests performed by a body controlled by the state, with the drug companies paying the full costs of the tests.

How drugs work

This chapter is the most difficult in the book and may be skipped by anyone with no interest in how drugs affect the brain. The going becomes easy in the following chapter.

The processes at work in a nerve cell are of unbelievable complexity. Quite apart from performing its function, which as far as we are concerned is to carry messages from sense organs, to muscles, or between other nerve cells, it has to take in nutrients (the biochemicals it needs) from its environment and to excrete its own waste products. Even more complex are the processes that occur at the junction between cells and the changes within a cell that mediate learning. In addition, cells regulate themselves in such a way that over the long term their activity tends to remain constant with changes in the amount of stimulation they receive from other cells.

To understand how drugs act on the brain and hence on the mind, it is necessary to give a brief (and grossly oversimplified) account of how nerve cells (shortened to 'cells') work. They transmit electrical impulses, which can indirectly cause the cells to which they are connected to fire or in other cases to reduce their tendency to fire. The junctions between nerve cells are known as synapses. To give an idea of the complexity of the system there are over a 10,000 billion nerve cells in the brain and each has of the order of about a thousand synapses (contacts with other cells), making an unimaginable number.

A nerve cell is said to 'fire' when an electrical impulse is created at one end, which travels down the cell to arrive at other nerve cells. All behaviour is (almost certainly) determined by which brain cells are firing and their firing underlies conscious experience. Two qualifications should be made.

First, there are other cells in the brain that might possibly influence the firing of nerve cells: we do not know whether or not they do. Second, the nature of consciousness and its relation to the brain is a mystery and always will be.

In order to understand how drugs affect the brain, it is necessary to describe what happens at a synapse. Although when they 'fire' nerve cells transmit electrical impulses, most do not affect other cells electrically. Instead, they communicate by discharging a biochemical substance, which because it transmits a signal from one cell to another is known as a 'neurotransmitter' For simplicity, I shall call the cell that influences another the 'first cell' (technically known as the 'presynaptic cell') and the cell influenced by it the 'second cell' (technically the 'postsynaptic cell'). Although we know that neurotransmitters excite or inhibit the second cell (that is raise or lower the probability of it firing), we do not fully understand the details of the biochemical mechanism by which they do so.

When an electrical impulse arrives at the end of the first cell, it causes some of that cell's neurotransmitter to be released into the tiny gap between it and the second cell (the 'synaptic cleft'). Molecules of the transmitter attach to special sites, known as receptors, on that cell. When they are received by this cell's receptors they may make it fire (or prevent it firing) provided enough molecules are received more or less simultaneously. Any transmitter remaining in the cleft between the two cells is taken back by the first cell ('re-uptake') where it may be destroyed by a special substance (an enzyme) present in the first cell.

As already noted, the effect on the second cell depends on how many molecules of neurotransmitter attach to its receptors. If over a period of time there is an unusually large (or small) amount of excitatory neurotransmitter released, the number of receptors on the second cell decreases (or increases): this device ensures that the tendency of the first cell to fire the second will be roughly constant. We have no idea how these increases and decreases are brought about, but they are clearly designed to stabilize the effects of the first cell on the second and may play a part in tolerance to drugs, since if there is an unusually large amount of a given transmitter present in the cleft the second cell will become less receptive to it. The whole process is ill-understood and is almost inconceivably complex -much more complex than my description.

It is known that there are at least 40 different neurotransmitters: some local areas of the brain contain mainly one kind, others another. Nobody knows why so many are needed, particularly as the same neurotransmitter is often present in parts of the brain with very different functions. We do know, however, that increasing or decreasing the activity of certain neurotransmitters can affect mental states and it is thought that psychotropic drugs operate by causing such changes in the activity of one or more of the forty or so neurotransmitters. They can increase activity in the following ways.

1. They may contain a substance (a 'precursor') needed by the first cell to manufacture the transmitter, thus increasing the amount at the synapse. It may be wondered why the drugs used do not simply contain the transmitter itself rather than a precursor. The reason is that most transmitters cannot enter the brain because there is a barrier that only allows certain molecules to pass from blood to brain.

2. The drug may contain a chemical substance that prevents the neurotransmitter being broken up by the enzyme when it is returned to the first cell, thus increasing the amount of the transmitter present in the synaptic cleft.

3. The drug may contain a substance that prevents re-uptake of the transmitter from the synaptic cleft by the first cell, again increasing the activity of the transmitter.

4. The number of receptors on the second cell may be increased, thus making it more sensitive to the transmitter released by the first cell.

5. The drug (or one of its derivative substances) may increase the tendency for the transmitters of the first cell to bind to those of the second cell, thus increasing their activity; it may even bind to them itself.

If any of these operations are reversed, the activity of the transmitter at the synapse will be decreased. This occurs when the amount of precursor is reduced; when the amount of the transmitter destroyed after re-uptake is increased; when the re-uptake by the first cell is increased causing more of the transmitter to be broken down; when the number of receptors on the second cell is reduced: or when a molecule similar to the transmitter attaches to the receptors of the second cell without directly influencing them, thus blocking the receptor, and preventing the normal transmitter attaching to it.

* * *

Benzodiazepines increase the activity of a neurotransmitter called GABA, probably by increasing the tendency for it to bind to the receptors of the second cell. GABA itself reduces the firing of the cells on which it is discharged. Hence, if the activity of GABA is increased, there will be a decrease in the tiring of cells secreting other neurotransmitters, including those discharging the transmitter noradrenaline. Noradrenaline increases arousal both in anxiety and in pleasurable excitement. If its activity is reduced by increased firing of cells secreting GABA, the organism will become calmer. The benzodiazepines are therefore used as tranquillizers (for example, Valium) and as sleeping tablets (for example, Mogadon).

* * *

It is highly probable that schizophrenia (in which there is a large hereditary influence) is caused by over-activity in another transmitter—dopamine. One might therefore expect that drugs to combat schizophrenia would reduce the activity of dopamine. The evidence for this is considerable. First, the most widely used drugs (neuroleptics) that ameliorate schizophrenia produce the symptoms of Parkinson's disease, which is itself thought to be caused by too *little* activity of dopamine, and which is ameliorated by a drug (L-dopa) that is a precursor of dopamine. Decreasing dopamine activity in the part of th brain involved in schizophrenia would be expected to reduce it in other parts thus giving rise to the symptoms of Parkinsonism, which occur when neuroleptics are administered for some time. Second, prolonged use of amphetamine produces the symptoms of schizophrenia and it is known to increase the release of dopamine from the first cell. Third, post-mortem examinations of the brains of schizophrenics have shown that in certain regions of a part of the brain called the limbic system there has been abnormally high dopamine activity. Finally, it has been shown directly that neuroleptics do reduce dopamine activity by attaching to receptor sites on the second cell and hence blocking the amount of dopamine that can adhere to this cell's receptors.

* * *

The mode of action of antidepressant drugs is less well established. It was found through work with animals that the first two classes of antidepressants to be used—the MAOIs (now rarely prescribed) and the tricyclics—increased the activity of a class of transmitters called amines: noradrenaline, serotonin and dopamine. Although it is probable that too little amine activity is associated with or even causes depression, this has not been firmly established. Dopamine is found in the 'pleasure centres' of the brain: animals will learn to press a lever and continue to press it furiously if each press is followed by a tiny electric shock to certain cells in these centres. It is plausible to assume that if there is not enough activity in the neurotransmitters found there, the organism will lose the capacity to feel pleasure—it will become depressed. Furthermore, although the MAOIs and tricyclic antidepressants increase the activity of all the amines, each does so by a different means. MAOIs destroy the enzyme responsible for breaking up the amine neurotransmitters in the first cell, while the tricyclics decrease the re-uptake of amines by that cell, thus in both cases increasing the transmitters' activity. The fact that these two types of antidepressant produce the same effect in a different way suggests that it is this effect that is crucial.

Unfortunately, the story does not end there. The level of antidepressant peaks in the bloodstream a few days after the patient starts taking it, but the effect on depression does not become apparent for a further three or four weeks. This remains one of the many outstanding puzzles of psychopharmacology. One possibility is that when the amount of neurotransmitter in the synaptic cleft is increased, the second cell compensates by reducing the number of its receptors and that this decrease overshoots, thus actually reducing the effects of the neurotransmitter in the cleft. We cannot therefore at present be certain whether depression is caused by too much or too little activity in the amines, serotonin, noradrenaline and dopamine.

The fact that these three transmitters are affected by antidepressant drugs strongly suggests that one or more are involved in depression, but there is no agreement about which are responsible. The part of the brain that mediates emotion contains all three and changing the activity of any one would change the firing of cells discharging on the other two.

There is now a third type of antidepressant in common use. As usual, it was discovered partly by chance. All the other antidepressants affect many other neurotransmitters apart from the three mentioned so far. In particular they suppress the activity of a transmitter called acetylcholine and it is this suppression that leads to many of their unpleasant side-effects including a dry mouth and difficulty in urinating. An American research worker, therefore, set out to find a drug that would not affect acetylcholine but that would enhance noradrenaline activity, since at that time noradrenaline deficiency was believed to be the main cause of depression. By accident he synthesized a drug that had little effect on noradrenaline, but boosted the activity of serotonin. It did so by preventing serotonin re-uptake by the first cell. Hence this class of drug came to be known as 'selective serotonin re-uptake inhibitors' or SSRIs. Since SSRIs have less effect on the acetylcholine system than previous antidepressants, their side-effects are less severe.

The trade name of the first SSRI to be synthesized is Prozac, at the moment both the most famous—or according to some the most infamous —of all psychotropic drugs. In America it received enormous hype both from the manufacturer (Lilly) and from the media. Soon many completely normal people were besieging their doctors for a supply of this wonder drug. It was claimed that it made everyone (or almost everyone) confident and happy and came to be known as 'The happy drug'.

These claims received some support from work with monkeys. In a group of male monkeys there is always one who dominates the others (he is head of the 'pecking order'). It was found that the dominant monkey had on average 50% more serotonin in his bloodstream than the others. Even more strikingly, if the dominant monkey was removed from the group and another was given Prozac, it was always that monkey that became dominant over the rest of the group. The degree of dominance in monkeys may be regarded as an analogue of self-confidence in people. There are two problems in interpreting this experiment. First, in his absence from the group the dominant monkey's serotonin dropped to normal levels, but when he was replaced he again became the dominant one. Second, only 2% of the total serotonin in the body is actually in the brain. It is found in much larger quantities in the stomach and elsewhere. How then can a 50% rise in the blood be attributed to its presence in the brain?

Some people believe Prozac increases not only self-confidence, but also aggression, a belief that recently led to a sensational trial in Louisville, where a man who was taking Prozac shot 12 people dead and injured 8 others. The relatives and survivors sued E. W. Lilly, the manufacturer of Prozac for not having a warning on the label that the drug could cause aggression, particularly in people who had previously shown aggressive tendencies. The trial was settled out of court when Lilly agreed to pay an unknown sum to the plaintiffs. The American media have often presented Prozac as a drug that could render patients homicidal or suicidal. According to John Cornwell, who wrote a fascinating book on the Louisville trial, by 1990 Lilly had been cited in 54 civil and criminal cases for the manufacture and sale of Prozac.

Although in the USA Prozac is the most sought after antidepressant, there are now at least three other SSRIs manufactured by rival drug companies. As far as we know, they are just as efficacious in alleviating depression as Prozac. One nice piece of irony is that Prozac was intended to be a 'designer drug', that is one deliberately constructed to target a specific neurotransmitter, while having minimal effects on others. In fact, as we have seen, it targeted a different neurotransmitter (serotonin) from that intended (noradrenaline), but on top of that it turned out to be the *least* selective drug of any of the SSRIs, as it has a considerable effect on many different transmitters. Although all SSRIs, including Prozac, have fewer side-effects than the tricyclics, they are not free from them: among the effects of Prozac listed in the British National Formulary are 'rash, nausea, vomiting, diarrhoea, headache, insomnia, anxiety, tremor, dry mouth, dizziness and difficulty in reaching orgasm'. Not everyone suffers these effects, indeed some are quite rare, but it is clear that there is no such thing as a free lunch when taking psychotropic drugs.

The SSRIs appear to work as well as the tricyclics for most depressions, though many psychiatrists believe they are less effective for severe depression. Since the newer SSRIs affect mainly serotonin, this would appear to point a finger at that transmitter as being the one mainly implicated in depression, but because of the complexity of the system and the interconnection of neurons with different neurotransmitters even this conclusion is premature.

There is a very recent and very exciting finding that appears to implicate too little activity in one or more of these neurotransmitters as the cause of depression and too much as producing mania. One experiment measured the activity of nerve cells in a region of the prefrontal lobes which is rich in all three transmitters. Activity was significantly lower than normal both in unipolar and bipolar patients when depressed, and higher in bouts of mania (all patients had a family history of depression). It was already known that damage to this area (by, for example, a stroke or a tumour) tends to produce flattened emotions particularly in interactions with other people.

Oddly, little or nothing is known of the way in which lithium ameliorates manic-depression. It is given as a salt (lithium chloride) and replaces some of the sodium chloride (table salt) that is found in all cells.

* * *

Over a period of time many drugs lead to tolerance, that is it requires a larger dose to produce the same effect that the drug originally had. Tolerance is brought about by the subtle regulatory mechanisms that tend to keep the activity of each neurotransmitter constant. One mechanism already described is that if the drug increases the activity of a neuro-transmitter at the synapse, the number of receptors on the second cell is decreased. A smaller proportion discharged by the first cell will therefore adhere to the second and to obtain the original effect more of the drug will be needed. Moreover, once such tolerance has developed, the person may find it hard to give the drug up: if they do, because of the reduced number of receptors, the neurotransmitters affected will be even less active than before the drug was first taken. Of the pharmaceutical drugs mentioned here only the benzodiazepines produce marked tolerance.

The meaning of 'addiction' is disputed and the term 'dependence' is often used in its place. This appears to be a distinction without a difference. In the case of drugs, both words surely mean 'A state of mind marked by compulsive use of a drug that gives pleasure (even when its effects are deleterious) and by a craving for the drug if its use is stopped." There is usually an element of compulsion in taking the drug. The reasons why it is difficult to stop the drug may be the immediate pleasure derived from it or inability to tolerate the withdrawal effects. The term can be extended to cover other activities such as gambling or overeating. Physiological withdrawal effects, caused by tolerance, may be weak or absent, even when dependence (or addiction) exists; they are, for example, comparatively mild in the case of nicotine. Addiction seems to occur only when there is a fairly short time interval between taking the drug and its pleasurable effects.

Illegal drugs work in similar ways to pharmaceutical ones. For example, cocaine increases the activity of the amine systems, by preventing re-uptake; amphetamines do the same thing but also block the degradation of amines by the enzyme responsible. Opiates, such as morphine or heroin have a chemical structure so similar to that of some neurotransmitters occurring naturally in the brain that they stimulate the same receptors (the opiate receptors). Indirectly they increase the activity of the amine systems, particularly that of dopamine. All three classes of drug can produce intense pleasure—even in rats, who will work hard at pressing a bar to receive injections of them. The reason why they are so addictive, unlike most pharmaceutical drugs, is probably that their effects are immediate whereas most drugs for mental illness (except sedatives) take weeks to work and even then do not normally produce the extreme highs of drugs of abuse.

* * *

It should be emphasized that there is a great deal we do not know about the mode of action of the drugs that are used for mental disorders. They all affect many different neurotransmitters and we are not aware of all or possibly even of most of their effects on the brain. Each neurotransmitter appears in several of the brain's different systems and it is not easy to discover which system is crucial for a given form of mental illness. Again, it may not be the absolute level of activity of a given neurotransmitter that matters but the amount of activity relative to that of other transmitters.

Moreover, even if, for example, it were firmly established that anti-depressants work by raising serotonin activity, there would still be a huge gap in our knowledge. How is it that raised serotonin activity leads to a more cheerful frame of mind and to the behaviour that accompanies it? This must be mediated by neural pathways of which we have no knowledge. It has been suggested that Prozac has raised the possibility of designing people's personalities through drugs—making the meek self-assured, the glum cheerful, the conceited modest and the antisocial better behaved. Such a brave new world is not impossible, but given the paucity of our current knowledge of the brain, it is a long way off. Despite repeated stories in the press, there is no drug that is known to improve intelligence or the ability to concentrate without in the long-run having seriously deleterious effects. The human brain has developed and improved through many millennia of evolution: it may not be perfect, but we alter it at our peril.

What goes wrong

This chapter examines some of the mistakes made by psychiatrists and psychotherapists in treating the mentally ill: the errors for the most part have the same adverse effects on the patients, whether they are undergoing psychotherapy or physical methods of treatment. The description of un-intentional mistakes is partly based on my own experiences, partly on the reports of others—mainly pseudo-patients—who have investigated psychi-atric hospitals by admitting themselves when perfectly sane; so common has this practice become that the pseudo-patient is now the main occupational hazard of psychiatrists. Although none of the other studies make all the points made here (which I have described in more detail elsewhere), their agreement with my own experiences is striking. The most interesting and detailed of the other accounts is by D. K. Reynolds who having obtained false papers showing he had been in the American Army, slashed his wrists and had himself admitted to a prestigious Veterans Hospital as a potential suicide. Although sane when admitted, he claims the treatment drove him mad: he found a rope in the hospital grounds and picked it up to hang himself, abandoning the idea just in time.

Intemperate attacks on psychiatry are common and though they some-times contain elements of truth, they are often wildly exaggerated. They were particularly popular in the 1960s when books and films appeared with bizarre titles, like 'One Flew Over the Rose Garden' and 'I Never Promised You a Cuckoo's Nest'. My own account differs from these in three ways. It is not exaggerated; it is mainly about the best psychiatric care available in Britain, not about grossly underfunded state hospitals in Alabama; and it acknowledges the dilemmas and difficulties that psychiatrists experience: as we shall see, they too have their problems.

Most mentally disordered people (with the exception of those with mania) are unduly sensitive: although psychotherapists and psychiatrists are aware of this, they do not always sufficiently bear it in mind. Indeed some, for example, my second analyst, seem to set out to hurt their patients. It was not helpful to be told that I 'had missed out on all the best things in life', that I 'had to get worse before getting better', or that I was a latent homosexual, particularly as I was in a state of total panic at the time. Even the innocuous remark of the black nurse 'You're always blaming your troubles on something else' upset me considerably. From the psychiatrist's side of the fence, Aaron Beck, the inventor of cognitive therapy, writes 'The depressed patient is prone to read insults, ridicule or disparagement into whatever other people say to him.'

There are good reasons why psychotherapists should avoid hurting their patients. First, it is cruel. Second, if there is anything in cognitive psychology, in the case of depression it can only make patients despise themselves even more and hence make them worse. Third, with severely depressed patients, there is always a risk of suicide and there is a danger of driving the patient over the brink.

There is a dilemma for the therapist. In order to recover, the patient has to change. But if too much change is demanded, the patient cannot meet the request and will feel even more of a failure, as I did when my first analyst told me that I must become more sensitive to my feelings, something that I regarded as completely beyond me. A good therapist will try to discover a task that the patient can perform in his current condition and this is precisely what my clinical psychologist did when he persuaded me to prepare an inventory of learned papers. Finding goals of the right level of difficulty is not easy.

A second problem that is often ignored is that patients become very dependent on those treating them, as Freud himself realized. In hospital my fellow patients would often approach a doctor on his way through the ward asking 'When can I see you?' The doctor would answer carelessly, This afternoon' and usually make no attempt to keep the appointment. Reynolds also notes this habit and although he was supposedly sane was very upset by it. I was dismayed by two other broken promises—the first analyst's failure to tackle the cause of my lack of crying and of more importance, my clinical psychologist's failure to attempt to rid me of my agonizing thoughts. Once again there is a dilemma for doctors and therapists. They are too busy to stop to speak to everyone on the ward and cannot possibly devote as much time to their patients as the patients would like. This, however, is no excuse for broken promises, which not only upset the patient but destroy the relationship of trust that is important for recovery. Psychiatrists should remember that even though they may not be serious when they say they will see a patient 'this afternoon', the despairing patient is likely to consider it a firm promise.

Both I and Reynolds felt that much of the therapy we received was artificial and had nothing to do with our problems. The first analyst's remark about 'a woman who had seen a flower for what it is for the first time and burst into tears' had no relevance for me. Nor did the marital therapist's claim that my wife's grandfather was 'a faceless penis'. The false emotions that the woman registrar tried to whip up in group therapy seemed equally pointless. Reynolds attended a form of group therapy, psycho-drama, in which a patient was asked to re-enact a telephone conversation with his wife, who had asked for money to buy more furniture for the living room. In the discussion a young black patient asked whether the therapist could afford it, a sensible enough question one might think. But the psychiatrist crushed him by responding That raises a "reality problem". We aren't concerned with that here but with emotional problems that usually have their roots in early childhood . . . blah, blah, blah.'

Avoiding artificial forms of therapy creates no dilemma for its practitioners. Why then do they employ them? The answer lies in their dogmatic adherence to their own often absurd beliefs ranging from my first analyst's faith in the effectiveness of crying over flowers to Janov's conviction that repeating the primal scream will work wonders.

One of the most damaging aspects of treatment is the failure to take the patient seriously. Freud was of course the first and perhaps worst offender—nothing the patient said or did was to be taken at face value: it was put down to unconscious conflicts usually about parents. It will be remembered that the amiable con-man on my ward said he would rather spend two years in prison than two weeks in a mental hospital, because his warders took him seriously whereas his doctors and nurses did not. The nurses simply smiled at me when I told them I was being given the wrong tablets. Rosenhan in his pseudo-patient study also comments on the failure to take patients seriously. He found that psychiatrists meeting a patient on the ward casually would make eye contact on only 29% of occasions. By comparison strangers, when asked the way, made eye contact 100% of the time. Janet Gotkin, who wrote a moving book about her experience as a schizophrenic in American hospitals, argues that psychiatric jargon is dehumanizing: 'Wanting to know your diagnosis is "morbid curiosity". Sad? No. You're depressed. Angry at your shrink? Resisting therapy. Like your doctor? Positive transference. Make a joke your doctor can't understand? Thought processes disturbed.'

Except for psychotics, most patients are reasonably sensible most of the time: failure to take them seriously is demeaning and is likely to exacerbate their problems. I have mentioned the boost I received, when the otherwise contrived woman registrar stopped her car to talk to me as a person not a patient. Perhaps the real reason for this failure to take patients seriously is that psychotherapists do not want to involve themselves too closely with people undergoing the agony of mental illness.

A further problem is boredom. Once again, this was one of Reynolds greatest worries as well as my own. The occupational therapists were excellent at distracting me, but they only worked from ten o'clock until four in the afternoon. Moreover, the nurses did their best to occupy patients in the evening by engaging them in Scrabble or ping-pong, but despite their efforts there were too few nurses to make much impact. This problem is no fault of the psychiatrists—it would require a great deal of money to have occupational therapists on the go all day long. There is a temptation for psychotherapists to try to turn patients into someone like themselves or someone they approve of as an ideal (usually one and the same thing). For example, Gestalt therapy is extremely anti-intellectual. It also encourages selfishness in patients, with such mottoes as 'Do your own thing' and 'Live in the here and now'. All dynamic therapy urges patients, as I was urged, to get in touch with their feelings—fine for the introvert, but not so good for the extravert, like myself, who is more interested in the outside world than himself. Clearly Maslow's therapy, with its impossibly high goals, is strictly for the elite—perhaps he never encountered the man-in-the-street, let alone the man in the bar. There are many ways to live and—provided you do not hurt others—every single one of them is right. You may be a good family man or you may be a brilliant physicist living in a fantasy world of quarks and neutrons: you are unlikely to be both.

Psychiatrists often preach to other doctors that they should give the patient full information. Numerous studies show the benefits of this. For example, some patients about to undergo abdominal surgery were told in advance how long the operation would last, the circumstances under which they would regain consciousness, the nature of the pain they were likely to feel and so on: other patients went through the standard hospital procedures. The group given the additional information needed fewer sedatives and pain-killers, and were discharged from hospital three days earlier than the other patients. Unfortunately, psychiatrists often do not follow their own advice. I was met with evasive answers when I asked whether they could prevent my wife visiting me. Reynolds complains bitterly about the same type of problem: he could not discover what his rights were. His hospital was like Dante's *Inferno*—because he had pretended to be suicidal he started on a locked ward. He could not discover what he had to do to be allowed onto the next rung, nor once there how to recover other privileges such as walking round the grounds or going out in the street. It took him nine days to find how to get clean sheets. He was lucky —it took me three weeks. I suffered agonies because of the constipation induced by the drugs I was taking. When I complained to a doctor he expressed surprise that the nurses had not told me I could have laxatives on demand. A more serious case is that of the patient who was taken to another hospital to have his electroencephalogram recorded. He thought he was having ECT (electroconvulsive therapy) and experienced searing pains: nobody had thought to tell him that the procedure was completely painless. There is no dilemma here: psychiatrists could easily provide more information to patients and their families than they do.

Lack of information contributes to the final problem, namely, power-lessness, which is acknowledged in all of the many accounts by pseudo-patients: it is humiliating not to be allowed to make one's own decisions. One pseudo-patient writes 'I found the loss of control over my own life to be the greatest threat . . . Suddenly tremendous feelings of anger overwhelmed me as I sensed a loss of personal control ... I was jealous of those staff people who could come and go.' Of course, as in any institution patients have to follow a regime, but the reasons for the regime should be explained to them. A group of nurses who were pseudo-patients, were told on admission to strip off their clothes without being given any reason: it turned out it was to have a shower. A student of mine had an episode of schizophrenia and admitted himself to hospital voluntarily. When I visited him, I found his clothes had been removed. Unless he walked abroad naked (which would of course confirm the diagnosis of schizophrenia), he could not leave the ward, let alone the hospital. I questioned several nurses and a junior psychiatrist about his rights but only received evasive answers. A journalist who entered hospital sane, once more as a pseudo-patient, could not discover her rights: she was accused by the staff of being paranoid. She writes 'Because I was acting out paranoia, I began to feel somewhat paranoid.' I cannot see that there is any dilemma here. Patients should not be kept in hospital by tricks like removing their clothes or evasiveness about discharge: if they present a danger to themselves or others, they can be sectioned. They should be told both how the hospital is run and what are their rights.

It is of course true that there is no such thing as a perfect institution any more than there exists a perfect human being. Psychiatrists and psychologists are as prone to lack of tact and failure to understand the needs of others (including their patients) as are the rest of us. Moreover, coping with the extreme sensitivity of patients requires a great deal of empathy. Psychiatrists are usually short of time, though a little reflection would reveal to them the importance of information and the need to alleviate the patients' feelings of powerlessness as much as they can. I have in fact given colloquia on this theme many times to psychiatrists and invariably one or two of them has approached me afterwards to confess that they had recently been guilty through thoughtlessness of one of the faults to which I had drawn attention. Most of the problems listed affect almost all institutions, such as schools, churches, sports clubs and firms, but their effects are magnified in mental hospitals because of the sensitivity and genuine powerlessness of the patients.

Therapeutic folly

So far I have dealt with mistakes made in hospitals, but there is no reason to suppose that therapists treating patients out of hospital are more sensitive to their needs. It will be sufficient to deal with two topics in which singular arrogance and stupidity has been exhibited, both in Britain and the US.

In 1986 a man living in the Orkneys was jailed for physically harming his children. Later one child told the mother that she had been sexually abused by her father. The mother told the police and her husband was sentenced to a further term in jail. Two of her children subsequently refused to go to school because their classmates taunted them about their father's practices. The local social workers then intervened: at first the mother trusted them, believing, 'They were genuinely trying to help me . . . for they were elegant girls in designer clothes who talked sweetly.' The mother agreed to one daughter going away for three weeks' 'assessment'. In fact she was held for six months, most of the time in isolation. The child was told she would only be allowed to eat or to sleep when she revealed details of continuing sexual abuse in the family. When she grew up she claimed she, 'Had been turned into a zombie. Every word the social workers claimed I said was untrue.' Many of the interviews were not recorded (or the recordings were destroyed). In one that has survived—an interview with another daughter only four years of age—the social worker suggests ten times that someone had inserted his 'dickie' into her 'fanny', an allegation that she consistently denied.

On the unsubstantiated allegations of continuing sexual abuse made by the social workers, eight of the children were taken into care. They were eventually released on the direction of a legal officer responsible for child care, who had been horrified by the social workers' bullying interviews with the children, as revealed in the surviving tapes. Eighteen months later, all the children were again taken into care and remained there: the mother was refused all contact with them. Two of the older ones subsequently brought law suits for their release and returned home. The youngest was three years old and was not sent home for several years.

Not content with the damage they had already done, the social workers, in collaboration with the police, made a further raid at dawn and removed another nine children belonging to four separate families, whom they accused (along with the local minister of religion) of taking part in satanic abuse involving sexual acts with children. These families had in fact merely supported the distraught mother and her children; in the eyes of the social workers they were guilty by association. For five weeks the nine children were separated from their parents and from one another. The parents were not allowed to communicate with them even by letter. Eventually, a sheriff examined the evidence and was outraged by the tapes of the interviews. He ruled the proceedings incompetent and the children were released. Later the parents sued the local council for damages, which were duly awarded both to them and to their children. Not a single prosecution was brought against any member of the four families suspected of child abuse.

As a result of this and similar cases, two commissions were set up in the UK (one by the Department of Health and one by the police) to examine the issue of satanic rituals. They both reached the same conclusion, as did a similar commission in the US: there was no evidence for satanic rituals having occurred anywhere in Britain or America. When people claiming to be eye witnesses were examined, it was found that their statements were completely inconsistent. It was also concluded that, if sufficiently brain-washed, children could be forced to say anything the interrogator wanted. As for the two main social workers involved, they resigned their posts and set up as freelance consultants on child abuse, for which their experiences must have made them well qualified. The latest development is that a 17-year-old boy is trying to clear his parents of the allegation of sexual abuse. He was carried off by the social workers who offered him (spuriously) a ride in a helicopter if he would describe the (non-existent) abuse. He claims to have been traumatized by his six-week enforced absence from his parents. The events in the Orkneys were repeated on a grander scale in Cleveland, England where 200 children were taken away from their homes in dawn raids. There was no substance to the allegations and they were later released.

The craze to hunt down sexual abusers began in the US, where there have been hundreds of cases in which people subsequently found to be innocent have been persecuted and imprisoned. One of the first was a hysterical attack on care-givers at the McMartin Preschool in California. It was started by a social worker but continued by the children's parents, who claimed not merely that their children had been sodomized but had had their eyes jabbed with scissors: one baby was said to have been killed in order that his blood could be drunk. Several of the school's care-givers were prosecuted and spent years in prison in the course of the longest trial ever held in California. All were found innocent. As in England, an American commission set up to investigate satanic rituals, found no evidence of their existence.

From the 1960s onwards, more and more members of the psychiatric professions came to believe that child abuse was widespread and that it was the main cause of aberrant behaviour ranging from schizophrenia, through depression to playing truant and dressing sloppily. They reasoned as follows. All mental illness is caused by child abuse. Therefore anyone mentally ill has been abused. Because the mental illness can only be cured if the person abreacts by reliving with the appropriate emotions the events of the abuse, the only way to help the mentally ill is to make them uncover memories of their abuse: that is the therapists' duty. The mental health professions, aided by the media, persuaded the lay public that child abuse was rife. This belief was formed and propagated for three reasons. First, many if not most people take a morbid delight in a witch-hunt—it is always good to be able to blame one's troubles on someone else: Nazi Germany singled out the Jews, eighteenth-century Britain the Catholics. Second, most people are titillated by sex in any form. Third, as I have already pointed out, 'experts' must lay claim to knowledge, however false, that the general public does not possess. Therapists claim to be 'expert' at detecting abused people, both children and adults, a claim for which they have produced no evidence whatever.

Many people who have alleged that they were abused as children have subsequently retracted. From their accounts it is clear that their therapists had prompted them to confabulate memories of child abuse. I have already mentioned patients' desire to please their therapists, a powerful motive for recalling something that never happened. But the therapist can bring even stronger pressure to bear by telling the patients that they cannot recover from the psychiatric problem which brought them into therapy until they manage to recall an incident of sexual abuse. The therapist may also make suggestions about the nature of the abuse and lead patients gradually from one 'memory' to another until they become convinced that they are recalling something that actually happened. This does not mean that the therapists are acting dishonestly. They may simply be naive. They may genuinely believe that abuse has occurred and that recovery depends on the patient recalling it. Even if their behaviour is honestly intended to help the patient, it is inexcusable. Stupidity combined with dogmatism can be as harmful as malice.

It is known that even memories only a few minutes old can be distorted by the way a question is framed. In one experiment people who had watched a video of a car crash imagined they had seen a non-existent barn after being asked 'Did the car pass the barn before it crashed?' How much more susceptible to suggestion are children's memories or those of adults for events that occurred many years ago, particularly when they are in therapy and are looking for any crutch to ease their agony.

Psychotherapists find what they seek. For example, in *The Primal Scream,* written in 1970, Arthur Janov only mentions one patient—a schizophrenic with delusions—who claimed to have been sexually abused as a child. Twenty years later, in *The New Primal Scream,* he wrote 'I have treated a great number of incest patients.' Psychiatrists find, and patients claim, the fashionable causes for distress. In 1960, patients complained of lack of parental love, in 1990 of sexual abuse. It seems unlikely that parents have changed their habits so drastically.

Apart from using persistent suggestion and persuasion, psychotherapists have invented a number of other methods that enable them to claim, often if not usually falsely, that their patients have been abused. To back up their judgement, psychologists have invented, as is their wont, 'tests' for whether someone has been sexually abused. They present adolescent or adult patients with lists of symptoms that they believe are typical of child abuse, which include 'poor self-esteem', 'excessive daydreaming', 'feelings of guilt', 'fatigue', 'fear of being left alone', 'loss of appetite', and so on. The list is remarkably similar to those of the 'symptoms' of masturbation put forward at the end of the last century. A high score on such a check-list is said to be associated with sexual abuse as a child. It would be remarkable if anyone could give honest answers to such questions without being diagnosed as having suffered child abuse. Moreover, it should be remembered that the people with whom the therapist is dealing are almost all mentally disturbed—that is the reason they contacted a therapist in the first place. They are therefore likely to have most of the symptoms listed regardless of whether they have been abused. Few if any will escape the net spread by the questionnaire.

Another method of determining abuse is to ask the child to play with dolls: the observer often biased, notes any aspect of the play that might have to do with sex or might reveal a precocious knowledge of sex. Despite the fact that the test has never been validated and is almost certainly useless, 92% of child protective services in North Carolina employed it in 1987. The construction of such tests by psychologists using pure guess work and with no attempt to validate them, is a disgrace, but then there are many other tests, such as the Rorschach, which though repeatedly shown to be useless, are still employed. It cannot be too much emphasized that, until the score on a test has been shown to be related to the presence or absence of a certain characteristic or illness, the test should not be used.

If therapists have to hammer at their patients for session after session in order to persuade them to 'remember' an episode of sexual abuse, it is necessary to explain why they did not remember it sooner. Therapists have invented a neat but false explanation. Anyone suspected of sexual abuse, either as the result of bogus tests or because they present some of the lengthy list of 'symptoms', is deemed to be 'in denial' until they eventually 'remember'—a process called 'recovered memory'. Borrowing from Freud, therapists allege that the memory has been repressed, and their job is to help the patient recover it through suggestion and persuasion. There is no evidence to support the concept of repression. Indeed very disturbing events are usually particularly well remembered and in post-traumatic shock disorder they tend to prey upon the patient's mind. Loss of memory can, of course, follow a blow to the head. It can also occur occasionally after a psychological trauma, but a whole section of the person's life is blotted out not merely the traumatic event and memory usually returns after a brief period measured in days not years. Furthermore, it is surely more than a coincidence that the spate of claims for recovered memory began only after the publication of a self-help book, *The Courage to Heal,* in which the possibility was first drawn to the public's attention.

Even more scandalously, some therapists have used hypnosis to extract memories of child abuse. Hypnosis does not help to recover true memories of any description, but because it renders people highly suggestible, it can certainly implant false memories. Such is the American judiciary's naive trust in the efficacy of psychological techniques that memories 'recovered' under hypnosis are admitted as evidence in some American states. Perhaps the most damning indictment of the concept of repressed memory was presented by two American psychiatrists. They examined studies of over 500 patients who claimed to have been abused and found not a single case in which it could be confirmed that the patient had both suffered abuse and had lost, and then recovered, the memory of it.

Taking repressed memories at face value can be very harmful. In America, George Franklin was jailed for life after his daughter under therapy recovered a repressed memory of his killing a friend of hers 20 years earlier. A psychiatrist had sworn in court to the accuracy of the daughter's testimony: how could he possibly know and how could the judge and jury know he knew? Five years later Franklin was released on the order of a federal judge. In Britain, a father was sentenced to eight years in prison for sexually assaulting his daughter on the sole basis of her uncorroborated testimony, extracted from her while under psychiatric care. Apart from such cases and those in which children have been forcibly removed from their parents on false allegations of child abuse, there are many more in which the families have been wrecked without the allegations being made public. A daughter convinced by a therapist that she has been abused by her father, is likely to flee her family. Moreover, intervention by the authorities, usually in the shape of social workers, can be extremely damaging to the very people it is designed to protect—the children who are alleged to have been abused. This is abundantly clear in the Orkneys case, but just as much damage can be done when abuse has actually occurred. In a case known to me, the father had mildly molested his seven-year-old daughter. Unfortunately, a neighbour got to hear about it and informed the social services. Up to this point the daughter had regarded the whole event as fairly trivial and had not been at all disturbed by it, but she was now taken aside by a social worker and repeatedly grilled for hours. Not unnaturally she came to believe that something terrible had happened to her. She became thoroughly confused by some of the questions, for example, those trying to make her agree that full intercourse had occurred. Given the circumstances, the only sensible thing to do was to hush the whole thing up. Above all, the child should have been left alone—she did not need help until the social workers intervened.

Child abuse undoubtedly exists: indeed in Britain alone the Home Office recently reported that there are at present 100,100 people who have at least one conviction for paedophilia, most of whom are not related to their victims. This figure excludes exhibitionists. Sexual abuse occurs on a wider scale than would have been thought possible 50 years ago, but it is not necessarily between parent and child; it is particularly common in step-families. It seems unlikely that Woody Allen would have fallen in love with his natural daughter. In the US estimates vary from 0.5% of the population having been abused up to 90%. There is no good evidence for either figure. It does of course depend on what counts as abuse: is a kiss on the cheek or a hug to be included? In some parts of America it is dangerous to be seen kissing your child in public. One authority believes that having a child sleep in the same room as the parents is abuse, although young children often sleep in the same bed, let alone the same room, and in many societies there is no alternative. In 1990 a US presidential panel made the hysterical declaration that child abuse was a 'national emergency'. It is rarely noticed that in some societies, such as the Trobriand Islanders, child sexual abuse is not merely tolerated but is a conventional practice. That does not excuse it, for in other societies the cruel practice of clitorectomy is the norm.

As we have seen childhood trauma appears to do little permanent harm. This is also true of sexual abuse, though some of the results are hard to interpret since the abuse often only comes to light because the person has psychiatric symptoms, which may have nothing to do with having been abused. Despite this biasing factor which will lend to exaggerate the symptoms of the abused, it is apparent that sexual abuse does little or no permanent damage, provided it does not involve physical cruelty or penetration (itself painful for the young). If abused children are compared with non-abused, where both have psychiatric symptoms, their condition is better, not worse. Many studies have now found little or no effect of child abuse on adult personality, including one by the Howard Reform League. One of the most recent reviews of the subject concludes that provided there is no brutality 'early sexual experiences . . . have little or no influence on later development'; and another that 'Permanent harm [from non-penetrative sexual molestation] is rare and the effects are small on the average.' Even Finkelhor (and his associates), who has devoted most of his career to child abuse, finds that two-thirds of sexually abused children have completely recovered within 18 months of the incident. Again, he writes 'The role of disturbance to self-esteem [caused by sexual abuse] and of a child's . . . vulnerabilities has not been well substantiated.'

It is commonly believed that those who have suffered sexual abuse as children become sexual abusers as adults, but this is a myth. As one author remarks, 'There are few in the scientific community who would embrace such [a view].' There is a slightly increased tendency to delinquency after any form of abuse, but the sexually abused are no more likely to become sexual abusers than others. Moreover, the increase in delinquency may be genetically caused: nobody has succeeded in sorting out genetic from environmental influences in this connection.

There are two facts on which all investigators are agreed. First, sexually abused children exhibit a precocious interest in sex: whether this is a good or bad outcome is open to question—in many previous ages young children were exposed to sex much more openly than at present. It is possible that such exposure would reduce some of the guilt and furtiveness associated with sex in the Western world. Second, poverty is very much more closely associated with mental illness than is child abuse, though how far this is caused by genetic factors and how far by environment is again not known. As has frequently been noted, nations shy away from the cost of alleviating poverty and concentrate on less important but more circumscribed problems like sexual abuse.

In view of the recent evidence it is unclear where to draw a line between the harmless physical display of affection and potentially damaging sexual behaviour towards children. Although the long-term effects of sexual abuse may not be severe, some children become disturbed in the short-term, but it is unclear whether this is caused by the abuse per se, or by the salacious cross-examination that tends to follow it. We know too little about these immediate effects, which are rarely studied because it is difficult to locate the children. Hugging and kissing are surely harmless, penetration is not. One absolute rule should be never to do anything to a child that it does not welcome and never to cause physical pain (except possibly as a punishment). Most people are probably revolted at the thought of sexual contact with a child, particularly at the thought of someone else making such contact with their own child. Maybe this is a healthy instinct and should be followed. On the other hand the thought of homosexual behaviour revolts most heterosexuals—and vice versa—and this is a poor argument against homosexuality. There is, however, a difference: the child has not enough knowledge to consent. It is safest to avoid paedophilia in any form, but that does not mean we should show no compassion for non-violent paedophiles, and we should certainly not exaggerate the damage they do.

To return to the hunt for sexual abusers, many psychotherapists believe that anyone who claims to have been sexually abused must have been sexually abused (though they do not accept that anyone who claims not to have been abused is equally correct). But memory does not work like that. Elizabeth Loftus and others have repeatedly shown that we do not preserve an exact image of our experiences: we try to reconstruct them and we make grievous errors, mixing fantasies with reality, distorting what happened to make it support our other beliefs and fit in with our current mood, and confusing with the experience we are trying to recall earlier or later events. Moreover, we are often deceived by our memories. One psychologist was convinced he heard an announcement of the attack on Pearl Harbor while watching a baseball match on television. He subsequently realized that this was impossible since the baseball season ends in October, while the attack occurred in December. Although he now knows he is mistaken, he continues falsely to recall the incident. There are many studies showing that people are over-confident about their memory. They may think they are always correct when they are in fact scarcely performing above chance.

In these circumstances nobody should be convicted of sexual abuse on the unsupported evidence of a report whether by a child or adult. The evidence of a psychiatrist or psychotherapist is worthless—they cannot know, any more than you, the reader, whether the child's memory is accurate.

There are signs that the American courts are becoming more cautious about repressed memory. In two cases they have rejected testimony from a plaintiff claiming repressed memory for sexual abuse. In one the court concluded: 'We are deeply sceptical of . . . the clinician's ability to weed out the most patently groundless claims', adding that the allegations were 'fanciful, far-fetched and uncorroborated'. It is, however, still easy to find psychologists who will swear to the truth of recovered memories. British courts have also become more cautious about claims to have been abused, unless they are supported by other evidence.

If some social workers are too keen on looking for signs of sexual abuse, others have failed to take action where there is clear evidence of children being physically abused. Recently in England, a boy called Rikki, aged six, was repeatedly beaten up by his mother to the point where he could not go to school because of bruises on his head. Neighbours reported the case to the social services alleging that Rikki had been repeatedly shaken and kicked like a football and had washing-up liquid poured down his throat among other tortures. Social workers were called in, but did nothing despite the neighbours' reports. Eventually Rikki was murdered. His mother was charged with his killing but acquitted. She was, however, convicted of cruelty. This is but one case out of dozens over the last few years, in which social workers have been outrageously reluctant to separate children from evil parents—except on the grounds of sexual abuse.

* * *

A second area in which psychotherapists have often behaved in too dogmatic and arrogant a fashion is sex therapy. This topic would be light relief were it not for the harm some therapists have inflicted on their patients. Most therapists are united in their insistence that every-one should have a rip-roaring sex life. It is of course true that many forms of mental illness, particularly those involving extreme depression or anxiety, are accompanied by a lack of sexual drive. As we have seen, even for normal people their sexual desires and practices are one of their major worries.

Many patients and many normal people are surprisingly ignorant of sexual techniques and do not know how to give either themselves or their partners the maximum sexual pleasure. The psychotherapeutic profession can clearly play a useful role in providing such knowledge, provided it does so with tact. If and only if the client wants to know, it can only do good to teach him where the clitoris is located and that most women benefit from clitoral stimulation. The problem is that not everyone does want to know, and that it is often difficult for the therapist to refrain from imposing his own views on what is normal or desirable. For example, Masters and Johnson, on the basis of physiological measurements, have concluded that the vaginal orgasm is a myth, and partly thanks to them, many therapists teach that there is no benefit to be derived from simultaneous orgasm based on penetration. In the opinion of the Family Planning Association 'Foreplay . . . can be as enjoyable as intercourse', while the Terrence Higgins Trust maintains that neither penetration nor coming is 'essential'. One wonders whether these officious bodies realize that the biological purpose of sex is to produce babies and that to maintain the drive the maximum pleasure occurs at the end of the sex act not the beginning. Moreover, their views ignore the psychological implications of simultaneous orgasms: some patients (known to me) have become very upset because they cannot enjoy mutual masturbation as advocated by many therapists. As some wag commented, 'After all, sexual intercourse is no substitute for masturbation.'

Again, the vibrator may be a useful device for some women, but if others find it distasteful, preaching its benefits is likely to make them more rather than less worried. I know one woman who attended a clinic for marital therapy. She had a normal sex life but was undergoing a stormy emotional passage with her husband. She revealed in an aside that she never masturbated. The therapist seized on this remark and advised her to buy a vibrator and practise. She duly did so, and proved to her satisfaction that using this device she was sufficiently normal to obtain several successive orgasms: she then proceeded to throw the vibrator away, having decided that she preferred sexual intercourse.

Some of the official pronouncements of the bodies which concern themselves with sexual relationships are risible. RELATE—an army of do-gooders who enhance their self-esteem by misguiding others—is one of the worst offenders. Its *Guide to Sex in Loving Relationships* 'shows you . . . how to draw up a better sex plan'. It argues that 'Sex in a loving relationship is better than sex without love', a sentiment with which the considerable number of Conservative MPs caught in *flagrante delicto* would surely disagree, Both RELATE and The Terrence Higgins Trust advocate more open communication. As Aric Sigman comments, 'Tell me what you want me to do next' sounds rather like 'Can I take your order?' RELATE's dislike of spontaneity is further evinced in the advice it gives to couples who have 'a discrepancy in libido', because one wants more sex than the other. 'One of the best ways . . . is to agree when you will make love—say, once a week . . . The one with the lower sex drive has to participate fully and willingly on the agreed date'—an extraordinary plea for sex by numbers. It is not merely about sex that men should 'open up' according to RELATE: they should reveal their vulnerability, their insecurities and their need for support. Elsewhere RELATE counsels that some women did not welcome the increased communication when 'the feelings [were] negative, or when the men exposed fears and insecurities and appeared weak and in need of support". Pity the poor man who is urged to expose his weaknesses at the cost of being disliked by his partner.

Sexual activity varies greatly from person to person, but the myth that it is necessary for well-being is now widely spread in the Western world, partly as a result of the activities of sex therapists; there is as little evidence for this belief as for the Victorian idea that women should not seek sexual pleasure or that masturbation leads to insanity. It is of course hard to say how far therapists fall in with the myths of their day and how far they create them, but we have moved from a situation in which people felt ashamed of liking sex too much to one where people are made to be ashamed if their sexual performance does not match that of the sexual athletes who report their real or imaginary sexual triumphs in *Forum*—a magazine to which almost all psychotherapists subscribe.

I recall one patient in the hospital who was in a truly sorry state. He was about 45 and shy but friendly. He was upset by the efforts of therapists to persuade him to masturbate: he lived alone and was desperately shy of women. Although he was provided with a liberal supply of pornographic pictures, his puritanical conscience was revolted, and so far from turning him on, they gave him an even deeper aversion to sexual activities.

The great variation in sexual tastes presents obvious difficulties to the sexual therapist who has the delicate task of providing information without imposing his or her predilections on patients who may be quite otherwise inclined. In *The Joy of Sex,* Alex Comfort puts the Good Sex Guide's seal of approval on bondage but not on flagellation, which surely provides more insight into his own tastes than guidance for the general public.

* * *

It is clear that there are fashions in therapy: apart from the two topics reviewed in this chapter—the hunt for child abusers and the promulgation of non-penetrative sex. I have sketched earlier in the book the diagnosis of multiple personality. Part of the problem is that psychotherapists want to be experts—to have knowledge and techniques not shared by the general public. In addition there is their tendency to be dogmatic. Their arrogance is of course fed by their clients, who tend to cling to them admiringly out of dependence. It would help if they could be brought to realize that not all their clients are the same and that they have different needs. But above all else, they should develop humility and ask themselves repeatedly whether what they are doing is beneficial—or harmful.

Ethics

In the 1960s and 1970s Thomas Szasz and others attacked psychiatrists for classifying people as mentally ill. They argued that where there was no physical pathology, people should not be treated by doctors and that labelling them as mentally ill was simply society's way of controlling their deviant behaviour. They also pointed to the discrepancies in diagnosis and alleged that there was a continuum of feelings and behaviour between normal people and those classified as mentally ill. Szasz believed that psychiatric treatment merely disguises the fact that the unjust organization of society is responsible for all psychiatric problems. In support of this belief he noted that symptoms differed markedly from one country to another. These points will be dealt with in approximately reverse order.

1. Does society cause mental illness? Symptoms for some disorders vary from country to country. *Koro,* the fear that one's penis is retracting inside one's body, is not found in the West. It is, however, a form of phobic or anxiety disorder: as already pointed out, the way in which such disorders manifest themselves depends on the beliefs of the society. We have seen that even in the West, there are copycat disorders such as multiple personality. The fact that symptoms vary with culture does not mean that the underlying disorder differs. There is just as much schizophrenia in underdeveloped countries as in the West, though the content of the hallucinatory voices differs from one culture to another.

The evidence on whether society causes mental illness is hard to evaluate. In the West the poor have more illness than the better-off, but this is at least partially explained by those who are ill drifting downwards in class. Taking this into account, the effect cannot be a large one. Severe mental illness is certainly not caused by living in towns, as in America the rural community has more psychoses than the urban one. In a study of Israeli immigrants it was found that the upper social classes actually had a higher incidence of schizophrenia than the lower ones. Moreover, *pace* Szasz, it would be callous to withhold treatment from those who need it in order to draw attention to the hypothesis that poverty creates mental illness.

2. Is mental illness on a continuum with normal behaviour? It is of course true that neurotic symptoms are on a continuum with normal behaviour. Szasz argues that this makes it impossible to distinguish between different types of neuroticism and to decide how severe a neurosis must be before it is labelled as a mental disorder. Most people have some curious but harmless obsession, like not stepping on the cracks of the pavement or not flying on the 13th of the month. Only when obsessions become severely maladaptive are they counted as neurotic, but there is no clear dividing line between neurotics and normals. However, physical illnesses also lie on a continuum. Neither for respiratory function nor blood pressure, is there a cut-off point at which we can say everyone on one side is healthy and everyone on the other side is ill. Nor can we lay down that everyone having fewer than a specified number of hairs is bald, and everyone with more is not. There are, none the less, clear-cut cases of baldness and of clinically high blood pressure, and there are also clear-cut cases of people who are mentally ill and of people who are not. As we have seen, diagnosis of mental illness is far from perfect, but that applies, perhaps to a lesser extent, to physical illness and is not a reason for failing to make diagnoses; without them, it would be impossible to provide the best method of treatment.

3. Should mental illness be treated by doctors? It is now known that psychoses are caused by organic malfunctioning of the brain and they can be alleviated by drugs. This disposes of Szasz's claim that psychosis is not a medical condition. In a previous edition of this book, I suggested that psychosis is caused by a major defect in the brain comparable with a failure of part of a computer's hardware, whereas neurosis is due to faulty organization of nerve cells in the brain, comparable with a mistake in a computer program. The analogy no longer holds. Obsessive-compulsive disorder, for long thought to be a good example of a neurosis, is associated with a gross defect in the brain: it can be inherited, and can be treated by drugs that increase serotonin activity. Attention-deficit hyperactivity disorder is thought by some to be due to poisoning by lead or mercury. There is a considerable genetic influence on anxiety disorders, which suggests they are not merely due to faulty learning (programming) but at least in part to an inherited defect in the brain. Indeed, recent research shows that inheritance is much more important in determining personality than was once thought: studies of adopted children show that criminals tend to have biological fathers who are criminals, while their adoptive fathers who bring

them up are no more prone to crime than anyone else. Research suggests, then, that deficits in brain function underlie some if not all neurotic behaviour, a belief to which Freud himself subscribed.

Doctors have made great progress in the treatment of the mentally ill. In 1700 lunacy was ascribed to witchcraft, demons or the misalignment of one's astrological signs. Lunatics were far worse off then than now, being manacled in chains, and subjected to whippings, cold douches and purges. Despite Szasz, the realization that their condition is a medical one has improved their lot. Once it was fashionable to go to Bedlam (now the Royal Bethlem) on a Sunday afternoon to watch the lunatics like creatures in a zoo. It was not until the nineteenth century that doctors began to take over the care of the insane, admittedly from the discreditable motive that they could earn more money by so doing. Far from degrading them, the medical approach has improved their lot, though the increasingly humanitarian views that have developed over the last century have also played their part.

4. Is the term 'mental illness' demeaning? The expression 'mental illness' is becoming more and more appropriate, as an increasing number of disorders have been shown to be caused by malfunctioning of the brain. Ironically, particularly in America, the politically correct (PC) expression 'mental disorder' has largely been substituted and most British psychiatrists nowadays would only use the term 'illness' of psychotics, but then in the language of PC, prostitutes are now known as 'commercial sex workers', putting them almost on a par with social workers. It is certainly true that there is a stigma attached to mental illness, but doubtless as 'mental disorder' takes over, that expression will acquire the same connotation. Far from increasing the stigma, the knowledge that much mental illness, if not all, comes from brain dysfunction should surely reduce it. Although there is no good evidence, I believe that it is a relief to be told that one's abnormal thoughts and behaviour are caused by an illness—an organic malfunctioning of the brain: it partially absolves one from the guilt of not being able to control oneself. Moreover, all known languages have a word for 'madness' and it is hard to see how one could do without some descriptive term for this condition.

There is, however, an appalling lack of understanding about mental illness among the general public. A television presenter in Britain, who had a child suffering from mylencephalic encephalitis (ME), recently became very irate because a doctor she was interviewing denied that ME was a physical illness. She seemed to think that if it was a mental illness it was the child's own fault. This misguided view is widespread, for it is likely that television presenters are no more ignorant than the public at large.

Although there is considerable stigma attached to the mentally ill, much of it is caused by their own behaviour. They are difficult to handle—they may talk and act inappropriately and they fail to listen to reason. Dealing with them is frustrating, while their strangeness induces fear. Since in many ways they are normal, others may suspect that their abnormalities are of their own making. Even psychiatrists find it hard to make eye contact with them—in some ways they may seem not wholly human. People always have a tendency to disparage others who are different: only if other groups are worse than your own can you claim any prestige for your in-group. And myths have grown up about the mentally ill. For example, they are thought to be more violent than others, whereas in reality they are less. Because of his oddity, a newspaper article about a murder by a schizophrenic is more likely to be remembered than one committed by a carpenter.

Apart from suffering from such prejudices, people who have been mentally ill may find it difficult to obtain employment. This is not as unreasonable as it sounds, for anyone who has been mentally ill is at greater risk of a further episode than someone who has never been ill. Not so long ago, the American Embassy used to ask applicants for a visa to state whether they had ever been mentally ill. With the increasing emphasis on the rights of the underprivileged, attitudes are changing. The US Equal Employment Opportunities Commission has just (1997) issued new guidelines about the employment of the mentally ill, making it illegal not to make special provisions for them, for example by providing sound-proof rooms for schizophrenics so that they are not disturbed by others' conversation. Employers are also told to make allowances for employees being late or aggressive if they are mentally ill. Applicants for employment cannot be rejected on the grounds of mental illness—it has to be shown that they are incapable of doing the job. There are other groups, including the blind and deaf, that through no fault of their own find it hard to get employment. All that is possible is to make a careful assessment of each person to decide whether they can do the job and the probable likelihood and consequences of another episode of illness.

5. Is psychiatry just a means of protecting society from deviants'? It has certainly sometimes been so used. Russian psychiatrists declared hundreds of thousands of dissidents insane, committed them to hospital and administered electroconvulsive therapy (ECT) and major tranquillizers. It is less well known that many German psychiatrists in the 1930s did exactly the same to Jews. More recently, in Paris psychoanalysts attempted to discredit the rebellious actions of university students by labelling them as suffering from an 'omnipotent infantile fixation'. As recently as 1851 psychiatry was used in the American South to keep slaves in order. A Dr Samuel E. Cartwright wrote an article in a learned journal naming two diseases peculiar to Negroes—drapetomania and dysthesia aethiopsis. The symptoms of the first were running away from plantations and of the second 'a tendency to do much mischief, to slight the work and to generally raise disturbance'. He claimed the 'diseases' had a medical cause, poor respiration, but they were 'easily curable . . . by anointing the slave with oil and slapping the oil in well with a broad leather strap.' These examples

show how easy it is to misuse psychiatry. One wonders whether hyperactive attention-deficit is a modern example.

Nevertheless, there is a clear distinction between deviants who dislike the way in which society is organized and who seek to change it in well thought out ways such as forming political parties, writing pamphlets or planting bombs, and the inconsequential behaviour of a psychotic, which serves no realistic goals.

Although even today some psychiatrists may abuse their powers, few cases have come to light in Britain, where the vast majority of patients seek help voluntarily. Some of the state mental hospitals in the US are an exception: until recently half of all admissions there were under compulsion and one suspects that some commitments were made to keep tramps and down-and-outs off the streets. Nevertheless, it is unarguable that many (though not all) forms of mental disorder can be helped by modern drugs and by cognitive-behaviour therapy. Despite their afflictions, the mentally ill are better off than they have ever been.

6. Should patients be involuntarily committed? Szasz argued that commitment was a form of slavery, but since slaves are forced either to work or to provide sex, the comparison is silly. In fact, both in Britain and America people can only be committed if they are a danger to themselves or to others. The British Mental Health Act of 1983 distinguishes between compulsory admission for 'assessment' and for 'treatment'. Admission for assessment is the more common. Two criteria must be satisfied. First, the patient must have a mental disorder that 'warrants' their stay in hospital for assessment or assessment followed by treatment. Second, admission must be necessary for the patient's own health or for the protection of others. Admission requires an application from the patient's nearest relative or a social worker approved for this purpose together with recommendations from two doctors, one of whom is normally a psychiatrist. The act has various other sections governing emergency admissions, the commitment of voluntary patients who want to discharge themselves and orders to receive treatment. Moreover, in 1983 a Commission was set up (as I advocated in the first edition of this book) to safeguard the interests of sectioned patients. Its members can visit them in hospital to ensure they are being properly treated and can obtain their release where it is justified. As already noted, there is little fear that psychiatrists and social workers will commit patients unreasonably, at least in Britain, for they have no incentive to do so. Under the National Health Service there is a shortage of beds and an extra patient is more work. As a psychiatric textbook notes, 'An experienced psychiatrist can often avoid the use of compulsory admission by patiently and tactfully persuading the patient to accept care voluntarily', thus gaining the patient's cooperation.

In the US the laws governing commitment vary from one state to another; the emphasis is again on being a danger to oneself or others or being incapable of surviving on one's own. In most states, the case has to go before a law court if committal is to last more than 48 hours. Although American laws appear more liberal, at least in the past there have been more committals per head of population there than in Britain.

It is, however, impossible even in principle to decide who, if not detained, will injure either themselves or someone else: they do not wear badges proclaiming 'I am a potential murderer' or 'suicide'. The behaviour even of normal people is unpredictable and subject to chance events that cannot be foreseen; the behaviour of the mentally ill is even more erratic. It does not matter how 'expert' a psychiatrist or social worker is, they will often be wrong. In Britain, over the last two decades 39 schizophrenics released from hospital have perpetrated murder, but the only way to stop this happening would be to commit every paranoid schizophrenic in the country. The difficulty of taking a decision is insufficient reason to shirk it. As a matter of fact, the best way to predict future violence is to base the judgement on whether the person has been violent in the past: this applies as much to sane criminals as to psychotics. It is, however, far from accurate.

To my mind, no case can be made against involuntary commitment. Freedom is not the only goal of society: aircraft have to meet safety standards at vast expense to their passengers and planning laws restrict the house one can build. We are regulated at every turn. If it is sensible to protect the sane from dangerous drugs or gas leaks, how much more reasonable is it to prevent the deranged from killing themselves or someone else.

7. Should compulsory treatment be given? Both in Britain and America this is possible, but only in an emergency, for example, where without the treatment the patient would seriously deteriorate or injure himself or others. In America and England (but not Scotland) giving psychosurgery without consent is banned, and special procedures are used for ECT.

Most people would agree that at least in emergencies compulsory treatment should be given to those committed, but only if it is known to be helpful. Until recently there were no treatments that helped psychotics. Some of the useless and damaging treatments to which the mentally ill were subjected over the last hundred years include cold douches, removal of the ovaries or thyroid, castration, hysterectomy, cooling almost to the point of death (and at least once beyond it), extracting the teeth and tonsils, enucleating the cervix, drilling holes in the skull, inducing coma through insulin, using metrazol to cause convulsions and slashing through a large chunk of the frontal lobe. Only treatments that have been validated by scientific trials should be given compulsorily.

Some American states offer persistent sex-offenders parole on condition that they allow themselves to be castrated or to take drugs that reduce the sex drive. Although this practice may horrify liberals, provided the prisoner has a free choice and the consequences are carefully explained a reasonable case can be made for the practice, particularly as many such offenders probably act under a compulsion and have no choice but to reoffend. American courts have also given parole to criminals in return for undertaking behaviour therapy. This may be innocuous, but in most cases it is merely silly. Nobody changes unless they want to change and most people do not change even if they want to. One criminal committed to an institution remarked, 'Look, man, most of us are good at shamming . . . You spill your guts out in a nice kind of way and act as if you're gaining all these insights . . . Hell, everything I've told them is a lie.' The institution in question was Patuxent in Maryland where much of the therapy depended on administering electric shocks as a punishment. In 1971, the US Supreme Court ordered the release of a criminal who had been there six years instead of the eighteen months he would have spent in prison. In the same year a court ruled that some of the punishments meted out at Patuxent were 'contrary to the rehabilitation of the inmates and serve no purpose of any kind'. Patuxent has been closed, and punishment 'negative reinforcement' is today rarely used by behaviour therapists. None the less, this example suggests that where prisoners either voluntarily or by compulsion receive therapeutic treatment instead of gaol, their treatment should be overseen by an independent body.

In recent years behaviour therapy to redeem criminals has been re- placed by another fad which is likely to be just as unsuccessful. An attempt is made to train prisoners to respect others, to control responses governed by anger, and to learn 'moral reasoning'. Alcatraz, now closed, might have become a latter-day Lyceum. Consider the following quotation 'Violent youths who received ART [Aggression Replacement Therapy], compared with those who did not, showed significant increases in constructive personal behaviours . . . within the institutional setting. They also advanced significantly in moral reasoning. However, the ART youths did not differ from controls in either the number or intensity of acting out behaviors.' 'Acting out' is psychotherapese for 'violence'. The authors are naïvely idealistic. Unlike the prisoners at Patuxent they cannot see that it means nothing for the youths to behave themselves within the institution: it may give them a kick to fool their mentors. But as far as reducing loss of control and violence, the programme was worthless.

In a new development, California has passed a law under which paedo- philes with more than one conviction will under compulsion either be castrated or receive weekly injections of a drug that reduces the sex drive; they may choose between the two treatments. The drug is known to have dangerous side-effects including damage to the heart and vascular system. In the interests of protecting society their option about receiving treatment has been removed. It is an unresolved ethical question whether the benefits to society are sufficient to justify such draconian measures, particularly as neither castration nor the drug can be relied upon to remove the sex drive. Such compulsory treatment of sex offenders has been legal for some time in

Germany and Denmark. As in so many moral dilemmas, there can be no rational resolution to the problem of whether it is desirable to castrate or otherwise reduce the sex drive of persistent sex offenders. How is one to balance the liberty of the individual against the common good?

As a matter of fact, the line between compulsory treatment and treatment with informed consent is a thin one. Few patients have the knowledge to give really informed consent. To decide whether to take a particular drug, they might have to read and evaluate several hundred articles, many of which would present results that disagreed with one another and all of which would be unintelligible. Psychiatrists do not have the time to explain in detail the pros and cons of a given treatment and they often rely on their own fallible clinical experience, with which the patient can hardly argue. Most psychiatrists do not like their 'expertise' to be challenged and it has to be a brave patient who does so.

It is difficult merely by persuasion to make patients take their drugs when out of hospital, particularly those for schizophrenia (the neuroleptics), which have unpleasant side-effects (though as already noted, some recently developed neuroleptics have far less unpleasant effects). Lithium can elim-inate enjoyable spells of hypomania while many people feel they are not themselves if their moods are being controlled by drugs. Even Kay Jamison, herself a clinical psychologist, who should have known better, repeatedly stopped taking her lithium thus producing attacks of mania.

It is paradoxical that the nanny state does not force treatment on those who are seriously ill, whether mentally or physically. After all we ban addictive drugs and at least in America, make it as difficult to smoke as possible. It is a fallacy, common to all branches of medicine, that one should prevent people actively harming themselves but leave it to them to take steps that will benefit them.

A related issue, which has been fought in some American state courts, is whether committed patients have a *right* to treatment. Under the NHS this is taken for granted. The state courts have always affirmed this right but there is no federal ruling on it.

8. Do mental hospitals infringe patients civil rights? Abuses exist in almost all institutions: mental hospitals, particularly some state hospitals in America, are no exception. Even voluntary patients may have their civil rights infringed. In the US, on admission, patients may be asked to sign an agreement that they will remain in hospital for a minimum specified time. Such agreements are not legally binding, but many patients presumably do not appreciate this. They may be restricted to closed wards, or allowed access to the hospital grounds but not allowed outside the institution—grounds parole (compare Reynolds's experiences, Chapter 27). Some hospitals censor patients' mail, a practice of doubtful legality. It is of course necessary to have some discipline in any institution and patients' freedom (to have visitors, get out of bed and so on) is limited even in

ordinary hospitals. Nevertheless it is questionable whether the restrictions imposed on voluntary patients by many psychiatric hospitals, particularly in America, are justifiable.

A number of cases have come to light where patients have been abused or robbed by their nurses and children have been tied to their beds, but such behaviour is uncommon and it is impossible to keep evil-doers out of any institution whether it be the army, the American Congress, the British Parliament, or mental hospitals.

The American courts have recently been increasingly concerned with the rights of mental patients. In one of the most important cases (Wyatt v. Stickney. 1971), an action was brought against the state of Alabama for depriving a patient of his legal rights. The court found against the state, deciding that psychiatric patients have a constitutional right to a comfortable bed with screens or curtains to ensure privacy, a locker for personal belongings, nutritionally adequate meals, visitors, regular physical exercise and access to the outdoors, interaction with the opposite sex, and (a nice touch) a television set in the day room.

The Alabama court also decided that there should be a minimum of two psychiatrists and four other doctors in addition to four clinical psychologists to every 250 patients. By English standards, this is far too few, but at the time of the ruling two Alabama hospitals had one doctor with some psychiatric training and three psychologists per 5,000 patients. In another case, the Supreme Court affirmed that non-dangerous patients could not be held in confinement if they were able to live safely outside an institution.

The expense of implementing legislation of the type described and of providing treatment has reduced the number of patients in state hospitals in the US declined drastically—from 559,000 in 1955 to 110,000 in 1985. The fact that such a large decline was possible and that in 1955 committed patients were often not treated suggests that at least some patients were detained not for their own good but to keep them off the street. A second reason for the decline was the recognition that long stays in mental hospitals could cause 'institutionalization'—a state of apathy induced by the monotony of hospital life, by inability to take one's own decisions and by having to do very little to look after oneself. Finally, the development of drugs for psychosis and depression enabled many patients who would formerly have had to be admitted to live out of hospital. For the same reasons, a similar decline in the number of psychiatric beds took place in Britain.

* * *

In this section, I tackle the minor ethical issues which have been the subject of hue and cry particularly in the US. The first is the problem of therapists having sex with their patients: estimates in America and Australia suggest that about 25% of male therapists do so as against about 5% of female therapists. In England only about 4% of male clinical psychologists admit to making love to their patients, but some of the reasons given for not indulging, such as 'lack of opportunity', are not entirely creditable. Both in Britain and America clinical psychologists (and of course medical doctors but curiously not nurses) can lose their licence for this offence and rightly so, for the patient who is mentally disturbed is in a particularly vulnerable position: she is likely to become heavily dependent on her therapist and the relationship is the most intimate of any between professionals and their clients. Apart from the fact that the therapist is taking advantage of his role, sex between therapist and patient is likely to increase the patient's dependence, which is hardly conducive to recovery and termination of therapy. In an article with the portentous title 'Harmful relationship effects of postterminal sexual and romantic relationships between therapists and their former clients', Laura Brown describes five such damaging relation-ships, all of which were between lesbian therapists and clients. She claims, startlingly, that 'Many lesbians are in therapy, and going into therapy is seen as a positive, almost civic minded action.' Although, then, you run the risk of being seduced, entering therapy is all for the greater glory of your town. Just how long an interval should elapse between the end of therapy and the beginning of an affair is much debated. Brown thinks for ever, but others recommend two years by which time one would think all passion would be spent. So seriously is the topic taken in America, that workshops on 'How to avoid sleeping with your patients' have been set up as part of trainee psychologists' courses. Psychotherapists have remarkable faith in their own techniques.

A new and important issue will arise in the future when more of the genes responsible for mental illness have been discovered. One ethical problem is whether prospective mothers should be encouraged or even allowed to have their foetus's genes examined and to abort if the genes carry a strong predisposition to severe mental illness. There are four arguments against permitting this. First, it is dangerous to eliminate a particular gene or even to reduce its frequency in the population at large. Genes that can produce defects often carry advantages as well as disadvantages. One well known example is the gene that when present on both matched chromosomes causes sickle cell anaemia, but when present on only one, protects against malaria. Although we may know enough to discover that a particular gene predisposes to mental illness, it is likely to be a long time before we are able to assess all its other effects.

A second argument is that it is already known that bipolar manic-depression (and possibly other forms of depression) is more common in people who are highly creative in the arts than in the general public. In *Touched With Fire* Kay Jamison provides a long list of famous poets, painters and musicians who have suffered depression, including Byron, Handel and van Gogh, while Arnold Ludwig, in a careful analysis of biographies of great figures in the present century, came to the same conclusion but extended Jamison's findings to include schizophrenia. Interestingly, there is no excess mental illness in scientists. Whatever the genes are that produce creativity, they may do so even in people who do not become mentally ill.

Third, there is the questionable issue of whether one is justified in taking the life of a foetus, on which there are conflicting opinions that can never be resolved. These arguments have to be offset against the appalling misery that severe mental illness causes.

Fourth, genetics cannot predict the development of mental illness with any certainty. Furthermore, new and better methods of treatment are constantly being devised, so there is always some hope even for the severely mentally ill. These two considerations mean that any attempt to use genetic techniques to abort foetuses that have a predisposition to mental illness would also destroy many who might have grown up perfectly healthy.

A second dilemma raised by genetics is whether to screen the foetus for genes that would render it a danger to others. The fragile-X chromosome has a genetic defect that leads to mental retardation and—it is thought—criminal tendencies. The question has been raised whether foetuses with the fragile-X should be aborted. It cannot be resolved. Unlike Down's syndrome children, those with the fragile-X syndrome are not happy. Rationally one might choose to abort: as there are far too many people in the world, why preserve one who is likely to be miserable and bring misery to others? But this is no reply to anyone who believes in the sanctity of life starting with the foetus.

There are at this moment a large number of commissions throughout the world considering ethical questions arising from advances in our knowledge of genetics. In some cases, scientific knowledge is relevant, for example, on whether one should eat genetically modified plants. But few people realize that it is pointless to argue about such matters as abortion. Only in the rare (or non-existent case) in which one can agree a common hierarchy of ends can there be any rational discussion. Otherwise the level of argument is reduced to 'I believe this', 'No, I believe that'—or 'Ya' 'Boo'. There is no belief so irrational as the creed that there is a solution to all problems.

There is a sense in which all behaviour and all feelings are the products of our nervous system. One extreme case is that there are patients with epilepsy caused by spreading excitation in the cells of a small region of the temporal lobe. These patients become saint-like: they relinquish all forms of addictive drugs including alcohol, adopt religious attitudes and give up sex. When the epileptic focus is removed, their interest in sex revives, their religious beliefs are abandoned, and they return to whatever addictive drugs they took before the epilepsy developed. All the existing evidence suggests that there is a complete parallel between brain activity on the one hand and behaviour and feelings on the other. This raises the question of when one should blame or punish people. If one believes that there is a cause for a certain action whether it be inheritance, schizophrenia, or sexual abuse in childhood, there is a tendency not to hold the person responsible: this raises the vexed and unsolved problem of the freedom of the will. The tendency to absolve people of responsibility for their actions if a cause for their behaviour can be found is surely a mistake. If all behaviour is caused by the activity of our brains, why should we distinguish between activities whose cause is known and those for which it has yet to be discovered? Moreover, praise and blame, and punishment and reward are needed to sustain society.

We do, however, feel reluctant to punish people for an action that they perform not voluntarily, but from a compulsion. This again raises the problem of how to recognize a compulsion. In practice, some psychiatrists regard someone as acting from a compulsion if they have constantly fantasized about the compulsive act, largely to the exclusion of other thoughts, particularly if they cannot control their fantasies.

A novel way of cutting through these problems is to define a voluntary act as one that could be influenced by praise or blame or the expectation thereof or by the expected consequences of the action, and an involuntary act as one that could not be so influenced. Thinking in such terms is more specific than resorting to the concepts of free will and compulsion, although it does not guarantee that we can always know in which category a given action falls. Interestingly, psychopaths are not influenced by praise or blame. Moreover, from a pragmatic point of view it is clearly sensible to punish only those who will be affected by the punishment or the threat of punishment. Punishing people who act from a compulsion will not deter them, but punishing bad behaviour performed voluntarily is likely to do so. As a rider, it should be noted that some 'punishments', such as locking up violent criminals are intended not as a deterrent but to protect society. If this is the reason for a custodial sentence, it is appropriate regardless of whether the violent act was voluntary or committed under a compulsion.

The belief that people are not responsible for acts that have a cause whether it is an indulgent upbringing or a bad cold is producing a society in which nobody takes responsibility for their actions or state of mind. There are rights but no duties. Nothing is your fault, it is always somebody else''s. As Stephen Sondheim wrote: 'I'm depraved 'cos I'm deprived.' Blame your parents, blame your wife, blame the police or blame the government. There is no longer any such thing as bad luck. As already mentioned, the policemen who took care of the dead after the stadium collapse at Hillsborough claimed to have developed post-traumatic stress disorder (PTSD). They successfully sued their own police force and were awarded damages. One thing is certain—if people can obtain damages for PTSD, its course will be prolonged, though it is likely to show marked improvement after the damages are awarded. It is even possible to sue for feeling sexual jealousy. After a gynaecological operation that went wrong, a woman sued the surgeon on the grounds that since she no longer felt like sex, her husband was consorting with other women, making her feel jealous. The successful search for causes in psychiatry and genetics and the rash pronouncements of psychologists (and some psychiatrists) mainly on parents being the cause of disorders or deviance in their children have helped to create the current failure to accept responsibility, and to promulgate criminal or antisocial behaviour.

The question of how much and what kind of care society provides for the mentally disordered remains an important issue. Both in Britain and North America the use of psychiatric and counselling services has enormously increased over the last 50 years. The number of attendances at out-patient departments of psychiatric hospitals in Britain increased threefold between 1964 and 1970. Such increases do not necessarily reflect a change in the prevalence of mental illness or neurotic disorder. Neurotic unhappiness is a permanent part of the human condition. The increase in the extent to which society cares for the mentally disordered is part of a general tendency for the state to assume responsibility for its weaker or more unfortunate members, whether they be the unemployed, the old, children in need of education, the physically ill or the mentally disabled. As already pointed out, despite the good intentions, such care may be counter-productive. People may lose charge of their own destiny, if when in emotional trouble, they seek help from outsiders, thus inducing learned helplessness and depression.

It may be that many of those currently attending psychiatric clinics would be better cared for within a family, but in the Western world the closely knit family is becoming increasingly rare. We cannot, however, legislate to recreate it, and in its absence some of the roles it formerly performed must be taken over by paid professionals.

It is possible that modern society presents its members with more psychological problems than any previous civilization, if only because of the accelerated rate of change. Within the span of a lifetime, we have had to accustom ourselves to radically new ways of living. Much of this is due to technological innovations—this is the age of the motor car, the aeroplane, television, the birth-control pill, the computer and Prozac. Perhaps as important as any of these, it is the age of psychotherapy. Sudden and radical changes in our artefacts have been accompanied by and have in part produced equally drastic changes in mores and attitudes. Whether or not they are realized, the expectations of women, the poor, and the under-privileged are today completely different from fifty years ago. Few people are content, as during most of history, merely to accept their lot in life.

The rate of change in our artefacts means that the slow process of trial and error, by which in the past houses, spoons, or chairs evolved, no longer occurs; millions of copies of a new product may be made before its use has stood the test of time. It was many years after high-rise flats began to be built before research revealed the psychological problems they created. We have therefore had to substitute self-conscious design criteria based on psychological research for the gradual evolution of new artefacts, though we clearly have a long way to go in this respect. For the first time in history we have the technology to control fire, flood, pestilence and starvation.

We have yet to learn how to control ourselves, and until we do so we are likely to put our technological knowledge to bad use. If we are to improve our lot—and perhaps if we are to survive as a species—we need a greater understanding of humankind, and it is hard to see where this is to come from except from the systematic investigation of men and women. One might hope that psychologists would contribute to this endeavour and also to the design of our new toys and our adaptation to them, but some of their asinine pronouncements in the media make one feel the hope is unlikely to be realized.

Choice of treatment

My views on what you should do if confronted by a breakdown either in yourself or in someone close to you have been made obvious throughout the book. At the risk of repetition, I will summarize some of the lessons I learned as a result of my own experiences and of the reading I undertook in preparing this book, by providing some advice about what treatment to choose if you or someone close to you becomes disordered. The views are my own and many may disagree with them.

1. Only enter Freudian analysis if you are well balanced, reasonably wealthy, and enjoy fairy stories. If you are at all mentally disturbed, stay away from analysis.

2. If you are depressed or have a phobia, panic attacks or obsessive-compulsive disorder, try to find a cognitive-behaviour therapist. In Britain the waiting-list on the National Health Service is so large that you may have to pay to go privately.

3. I personally would also seek a cognitive therapist for other neurotic conditions, but the advantage over psychodynamic therapy is not so well proven.

4. If you really believe that poking around in your childhood will help, then see a psychodynamic therapist or better an eclectic one. Avoid ones with dogmatic and far fetched theories such as Gestalt psychologists or those who believe in the primal scream.

5. Try to pick a therapist whose ideas and views on life are similar to your own. If you are a feminist, this will not be difficult, but if you are anti-feminist you may have a long search.

6. If you don't trust or don't like your therapist, leave them at once. Faith in your therapist is perhaps the single most important indicator of the likely success of therapy.

7. Before commencing any psychotherapy in earnest you should agree with the therapist on its aims and methods, preferably through a written contract. If you cannot agree, seek another therapist.

8. Mistrust any therapist who tells you must get worse in order to get better.

9. If you are depressed to the extent that your functioning is seriously impaired, antidepressants are an alternative to cognitive therapy. The new ones, SSRIs, are as effective for mild depression as the tricyclics, which are probably more effective for severe depression but have worse side-effects.

10. Take any drug prescribed for the period laid down by the doctor. Even if you feel better after a few weeks you may relapse.

11. An exception is if prescribed a sleeping tablet or sedative, try to give it up as soon as you can. Most benzodiazepines are highly addictive and it is likely that newer drugs of this sort will also turn out to be addictive.

12. Most mental hospitals have an emergency department. If a relative or friend appears psychotic (out of touch with reality), try to persuade them to go to one.

13. If a psychiatrist suggests you enter hospital, do so. He does not want unnecessary admissions, though the only reasons for entering a hospital are if you are a danger to yourself or others, if you cannot maintain yourself, if you need a respite from your home background, or if the treatment you require can only be given in hospital.

14. If you need voluntary hospitalization, try to find out what conditions are like in different hospitals in your area. In general, teaching hospitals are likely to have better facilities and to have more and better staff than non-teaching hospitals.

15. If you are sleepless, anxious, given to bouts of anger, very depressed without external cause or suffering severe headaches, insist on a physical examination before starting therapy. Even if you have none of these conditions, it is wise to have a physical examination.

16. If you are British and using the National Health Service, remember that you are entitled to the opinion of a second consultant, if you are dissatisfied with the first one you see. If you think you need psychiatric help and your doctor refuses to refer you, there are many hospital psychiatric departments that will see patients without a referral.

17. If you live in Britain and run into difficulties over psychiatric treatment either for yourself or for a friend or relative, try contacting MIND

(formerly, the National Association for Mental Health—addresses in several telephone directories including London).

18. Unless you are reasonably robust psychologically, avoid 'personal growth' groups, particularly ones run by an aggressive therapist.

19. In dealing with friends or relatives undergoing a breakdown, take what they say seriously. Unless they are psychotic, most of their remarks will be based on reality and should not be treated merely as a symptom of an illness. Be sympathetic without being sentimental and try to restore their faith in themselves. Anything good you can point to in their past or present behaviour is likely to be helpful. Avoid recrimination or passing moral judgements. Try to give them hope for the future: the restoration of hope is often the most significant step towards ultimate recovery. Never make remarks like, 'God, you do seem awful today'; if possible, tell them they seem a bit better. Finally, try to distract them by getting them interested in something outside themselves.

20. Remember that although most depressives feel they will never recover, that is a symptom of the illness. In Britain, the great majority of psychiatric patients admitted to hospital are discharged within a month. Moreover, the rate of production of new drugs and advances in psychological methods of treatment provide some hope even for the chronically ill.

21. Finally, remember that it is no disgrace to be mentally ill. Indeed, mental illness is particularly common in artists, musicians, poets and other writers.

* * *

I am conscious that by emphasizing the shortcomings of those caring for the mentally disordered, I may have said too little about the difficulties they face and the devotion that many of them display in their attempts to help. Many of their difficulties stem from our ignorance of the subject and from insufficient resources: neither problem is easily overcome. Psychiatry is still a much maligned profession. In another context, I wrote:

> The psychiatrist is in danger of becoming a greater scapegoat than his patients. Pilloried by the press and on the screen and stage, he finds himself continually impaled on the horns of multiple dilemmas. If he commits a dangerous or suicidal patient, he is accused of being a jailer; if he discharges one, he is thought to be incompetent. The public besiege him for drugs and then accuse him of treating them as machines. If he gives psychotherapy, he can be simultaneously charged with using techniques of doubtful therapeutic value and with imposing on the patient his own view of how to live. If he preserves an eclectic approach to treatment, he is indecisive or wishy-washy: if he opts firmly for one or other of the

dozens of fashionable varieties of psychotherapy or physical treatment, he is a bigot. His patients often start by ascribing to him the wisdom of a God, and end by hating him for his failure to produce a magical solution to their problems. If he conducts careful trials of a new therapeutic method using a no-treatment control group, his colleagues write letters to *The Times* accusing him of unethically withholding a treatment intuitively known to be valuable; if he fails to conduct controlled trials, the remainder of his colleagues write to *The Times* pointing out that he is an unscientific quack.

The psychiatrist, then, is caught in a series of double-binds that make the nuclear family seem a refuge of sweetness and reason. Nevertheless, sympathy for his plight should not blind us to the need to improve the treatment and care of the mentally ill and with this need in mind, I may have perhaps concentrated too much on the failings of contemporary psychiatry and too little on its virtues and achievements.

In conclusion, I hope that I have provided enough information to enable those confronted with the problem of mental illness to avoid making some of the mistakes I made by being talked into unsuitable forms of treatment. Many, if not most or indeed all, of the arguments I have rehearsed will be familiar to members of the mental health professions: they are, however, often ignored by those ensnared by the dogma of a particular method of treatment, and are not sufficiently pondered by those embarking on a career in mental health. There is no one method that is suitable for all patients, just as there is no one end that all men should pursue. Indeed whatever we choose to do precludes us from doing something else: we develop our emotional sensitivities only at the expense of using time and energy that someone else might devote to artistic, academic or business pursuits. Nor do J believe in the concept of the well-rounded man who cultivates in equal parts his body, his feelings and his intellect. Great achievements in literature, art, science, medicine, politics or business are often attained by individuals who are driven by a single purpose to the detriment of other sides of their lives: without such people the world would be a poorer place. We should never presume to dictate ends: the most we are entitled to do is to ask that people should not pursue their own goals at the expense of others. As my old aunt used to say, 'It takes all types to make a world'.

Further reading

Reading on specialized topics is provided at the beginning of the notes to most chapters.

Bergin, A. E. and Garfield, S. L. (ed.) (1994). *Handbook of psychotherapy and behavior change.* (4th edn). Wiley, New York. A massive compendium on psychotherapy, but quite strongly biased towards dynamic therapy.

Davison, G. C. and Neale, J. M. (ed.) (1994). *Abnormal psychology.* (6th edn). Wiley, New York. A comprehensive textbook on mental illness, most of which will be intelligible to laymen. Rather bland.

Dawes, R. M. (1994). *House of cards, psychology and psychotherapy built on myth.* The Free Press, New York. An extremely well argued and well documented attack on all aspects of dynamic therapy.

Dryden, W. and Feltham, C. (ed.) (1992). *Psychotherapy and its discontents.* Open University Press, Buckingham. A critical review of psychotherapy, allowing some of its practitioners a hearing.

Garfield, S. L. (1955). *Psychotherapy, an eclectic-integrative approach.* (2nd edn). Wiley, New York. An interesting appraisal of psychotherapy. Although written by a leading therapist, it contains criticisms and doubts about its value.

Gelder, M. , Gath, D. and Mayou, R. (ed.). (1989). *Oxford textbook of psychiatry.* (2nd edn). Oxford University Press. An excellent and comprehensive textbook on psychiatry. Well organised and well written, though it falls over backwards to be fair to all schools of thought.

Jamison, K. R. (1995). *An unquiet mind, a memoir of moods and madness.* Knopf, New York. An account of her own manic-depressive illness written by a clinical psychologist; very frank about herself, less so about her therapists but a fascinating read.

Herman, E. (1995). *The romance of American psychology, political culture in the age of experts.* University of California Press, Berkeley. A devastating history of the failure of psychology to justify its increasing use over the first seventy years of this century.

Pendergrast, M. (1996). *Victims of memory, incest accusations and shattered lives.* HarperCollins, London. A good account of the recovered memory syndrome and other aspects of sexual abuse.

Rosenhan, D. L. and Seligman, M. E. P. (1995). *Abnormal psychology.* (3rd edn.). Norton, New York. Norton's answer to Wiley's Davison and Neale. The two books are not dissimilar and both are excellent.

Sutherland, N. S. (1992). *Irrationality, the enemy within.* Penguin, London. An account of the systematic mistakes in reasoning made by most people, including, of particular relevance here, psychotherapists.

Notes

No reference is normally given for two kinds of item in the text: (1) Facts that are well known and non-controversial; (2) Information taken from newspapers. Where possible, I have referred not to learned articles but to books, which are more accessible to the general reader. References listed in the bibliography and ones listed in the general section of each chapter are referred to by authors' names and date only. If any references are missing, it is due to carelessness on my part.

Of the two numbers to the left of each entry, the first indicates the page number, and the second the paragraph on that page.

Chapter 10   Who's Who

91, 4   For number of visits to GPs, see Kerwick, S. W. and Jones, R. H. (1996). *Primary Care Psychiatry,* **2**, 107-17.

92, 2   For training of psychiatrists, see Brook, P. (1973). *British Journal of Psychiatry, Special Publication,* No. 7.

92, 2   On psychotherapy by trained and untrained therapists, see Dawes, R. M. (1994), pp. 55-6.

92, 3   Brewer, C. and Lait, J. (1980). *Can social work survive?* Temple Smith, London.

94, 4   Study on truants is described in Brown I. *et al.* (1990). *Educational Review,* **42**, 231-45.

94, 6   Quotation from *American Psychological Association Monitor* (1975). **6**, No. 7, 4 from an address given by J. Spiegel.

94, 7   On growth of clinical psychology, see Dawes, R. M. (1994), and Humphries, K. (1996). *American Psychologist,* **51**, 190-7.

97, 5   Weiss, J. R. *et al.* (1995). *Journal of Consulting and Clinical Psychology,* **63**, 688-701.

98, 3   Quotation from Bellak, L. (ed.) (1974). *A concise handbook of community psychiatry and community mental health,* p. 9. Grune & Stratton, New York.

Chapter 11   The nature of mental illness

General   In this and the two following chapters more information can be obtained from any good textbook of psychiatry or abnormal psychology, for example, Gelder, M. *et al.* (1989), Rosenhan, D. L. and Seligman, M. E. P. (1995), or Davison, G. C. and Neale, J. M. (1994).

99, 2   Quotation from *A glossary of mental disorders* (1968). HMSO, London.

100, 3   On witches and drugs, see Rothman, T. (1972). *Bulletin for the History of Medicine,* **46**, 562-7.

101, 4   Jamison, K. (1995), pp. 79-83.

102, 3   On genetics of affective disorder, see Goodwin, F. K. and Jamison, R. (1990). *Manic-depressive illness,* pp. 373-401.

103, 1   Bonanno, G. (in press) *Journal of Personality and Social Psychology.*

103, 3   For anxiety disorders, see Rosenhan, D. L. and Seligman, M. E. P. (1995), pp. 209-309.

105, 3   On prevalence of hysteria, see Gelder, M. *et al.* (1989), p. 210.

105, 3   On confusing neurological symptoms with hysteria, see Davison, G. C. and Neale, J. M. (1994), pp. 168-9.

106, 1   On ME, see Report of Royal Colleges of Physicians, Psychiatrists and General Practitioners (1996). *Chronic fatigue syndrome. Royal College of Psychiatrists,* London.

107, 3   The figures on the frequency of mental illness are based on four studies. For a review of the two earlier ones, see Agras, W. S. *et al.*(1969). *Comprehensive Psychiatry,* **10**, 151-6, and for the later two undertaken in 1984 and 1994, see Rosenhan, D. L. and Seligman, M. E. P. (1995), pp. 163-5.

Chapter 12   Diagnosis

110, 3   Cooper, J. E. *et al.* (1972). *Psychiatric diagnosis in New York and London.* Maudsley Monograph No. 20, Oxford University Press, London describes the study on schizophrenia.

111, 2   For two types of schizophrenia, see Gelder, M. *et al.* (1989), pp. 290-1.

111, 3   On the Rorschach test, see Dawes, R. M. (1994), pp. 14654.

112, 3   On diagnostic reliability, see Rosenhan, D. L. and Seligman, M. E. P. (1995), pp. 193-200.

112, 3   Or pseudo-patients, see Rosenhan, D. L. (1973). *Science,* **179**, 250-8.

113, 3   Goldberg, L. R. (1968). *American Psychologist,* **23**, 483-96.

114, 1   For a thorough but rather convoluted history of multiple personality, see Hacking, I. (1995). *Rewriting the soul, multiple personality and the science of memory.* Princeton University Press. The next two pages are mainly drawn from this book.

114, 2   Thigpen, C. H. (1957). *The three faces of Eve.* McGraw-Hill, New York.

114, 2   Schreiber, F. R. (1973). *Sybil.* Warner, Chicago.

114, 3   Bass, E. and Davis, L. (1988). *The courage to heal: a guide for women survivors of child abuse.* Harper Perennial, New York.

114, 3   Rettersol, N. (1993). *Suicide, a European perspective.* Cambridge University Press.

115, 3   Belsky, J. (1993). *Psychological Bulletin,* **114,** 413-34.

115, 5   Merskey, H. (1992). *British Journal of Psychiatry,* **160,** 327-40.

116, 2   On Ritalin, see Gelder, M. *et al.* (1989), pp. 195-7, and Editorial (1996). *British Medical Journal,* **313,** 77-9.

Chapter 13   Origins of mental illness

General   See any recent textbook on psychiatry or clinical psychology for an account of the genetics of mental illness. For more detail, see Hull, L. L. (ed.) (1996). *Genetics and mental illness: everyday ideas for our society.* Plenum, London.

118, 3   On prefrontal lobe activity and depression, see Drevets, W. C. *et al.* (1997). *Nature,* **386,** 824-7, and Damasio, A. R. (1997). *Nature,* **386,** 769-70.

118, 4   On OCD, see Rapoport, J. L. (1990). *Neuropsychopharmacology,* **5,** 1-10.

118, 4   On genetics of OCD, see McGuffin, P. *et al.* (1994). *Seminars in psychiatric genetics.* Gaskell, London.

119, 5   On genetics of schizophrenia, see Gelder, M. *et al.* (1989), pp. 292-6.

119, 3   Quotation from Heston, L. L. and Denney, D. (1968). In *The transmission of schizophrenia,* (ed. D. Rosenthal and S. S. Kety), p. 371. Pergamon, New York.

121, 1   On DNA and schizophrenia, see Gelder, M. *et al.* (1989), pp. 298-300.

121, 2   On mental illness and genius, see Jamison, K. R. (1993). *Touched with fire.* The Free Press, New York and Ludwig, A. M. (1993). *The price of greatness: resolving the creativity and madness controversy.* Guilford, Brighton.

121, 4   On genetics of neuroses, see Gelder, M. *et al.* (1989). pp. 165, 180-1, and Stone, O. C. *et al.* (1995). *American Journal of Human Genetics,* **57,** 1384-94.

121, 5   Bock, G. R. and Goode, S. A. (ed.) (1996). *Genetics of criminal and anti-social behaviour.* (CIBA Foundation, Vol. 194). Wiley, Chichester.

121, 5   For genetic influences on delinquency, see Plornin, R. *et al.* (1997). *Behavioural genetics.* Freeman, New York, and Rowe, P. C. (1994), *The limits of family influences.* Guildford, Brighton.

121, 5   On viruses and schizophrenia, see Gelder, M. *et al.,* (1989), p. 300.

121, 3   For Rutter's previous beliefs, see, for example, Rutter, M. and Madge, N. (1976). *Cycles of disadvantage.* Heinneman, London.

122, 3   Quotation is from Rutter, M. L. (1997). *American Psychologist,* **52,** 390-8.

123, 1   On Head Start, see Atkinson, R. L. *et al.* (1996). *Introduction to Psychology.* 10th edn. Harcourt, Brace, Johanovich, San Diego, pp. 267- 9.

123, 3   On comparison of mental illness between countries, see Dohrenwend, B. P. and Dohrenwend, B. S. (1974). *Annual Review of Psychology,* **25,** 417-52.

123, 4   On suicide both here and later in the chapter, see Rettersol, N. (1993). *Suicide: a European perspective.* Cambridge University Press.

124, 2   On Hutterites, see Eaton, J. W. and Weil, R. (1955). *Culture and mental disorder.* The Free Press, New York.

124, 3   On mental illness in Massachusetts, see Goldhamer, H. and Marshall, A. W. (1949). *Psychosis and civilization*. The Free Press of Glencoe, New York.

124, 3   On depression in the young, see Lewinson, P. M. *et al.* (1993). *Journal of Abnormal Psychology*, **102**, 110-20.

124, 5   On suicide, see Rettersol (1993). *Suicide a European perspective*. Cambridge University Press.

125, 3   On poverty and mental illness, see Dohrenwend, B. P. *et al.* (1992). *Science*, **255**, 946-52.

125, 4   Malinowski-Rummell, R. and Hansen, D. J. (1993). *Psychological Bulletin*, **114**, 68-79.

125, 5   Laing, R. D. and Esterson, A. (1964). *Sanity, madness and the family*. Tavistock, London.

125, 5   Bateson, G. *et al.* (1956). *Behavioral Science*, **1**, 251-64.

125, 5   On schizophrenia and the family, see Gelder, M. *et al.* (1989), pp. 302-3.

125, 5   Clay, J. (1996). *R. D. Laing, a divided self* Hodder and Stoughton, London.

126, 2   Vaillant, G. E. (1977). *Adaptation to life*. Little Brown, Boston.

127, 1   On kibbutzim and Guatemalan children, see Rowe, A. C. (1994), *The limits of family influence*, p. 10. Guildford, New York.

127, 2   On Brown's studies, see Gelder, M. *et al.* (1989), pp. 240-3.

127, 3   For children's ability to recover from severe deprivation, see Kagan, J. (1996). *American Psychologist*, **51**, 901-8.

127, 3   Clarke, A. M. and Clarke, A. D. B. (1976). *Early experience: myth and evidence*. Open Books, Shepton Mallet.

127, 3   On deprived monkeys, see Harlow, H. F. (1964). In *Unfinished tasks in the behavioral sciences* (ed. A. Abrams *et al.*), pp. 154-73. Williams and Wilkins, Baltimore.

127, 4   For orphans brought up in a concentration camp, see Moskovitz, S. (1983). *Love despite hate*. Schocken, New York and for children homeless through war, see Winnick, M. (1975). *Science*, **190**, 173-5.

127, 4   Seligman, M. E. P. (1994). *What you can change and what you can't: the complete guide to successful self-improvement*. Knopf, New York.

128, 1   Mansfield, M. G. and Widom, C. S. (1996). *Archives of Pediatrics and Adolescent Medicine*, **150**, 390-5.

128, 2   Belsky, J. (1993). *Psychological Bulletin*, **114**, 413-34.

128, 3   On failure of punishment, see Sutherland, S. (1992), pp. 113-14.

128, 4   For a list of life events, see Davison, G. C. and Neale, J. M. (1994), pp. 192-3.

128, 3   For experiment on dogs, see Seligman, M. E. P. and Maier, S. F. (1967). *Journal of Comparative and Physiological Psychology*, **74**, 19.

128, 4   For effects of self-blame, see Sweeney, P. O. *et al.* (1986). *Journal of Personality and Social Psychology*, **50**, 974-91.

Chapter 14   Freudian theory and practice

General   Freud is much the best expositor of his own ideas. His *Introductory lectures on psychoanalysis* (delivered between 1915 and 1917) is an excellent starting point. *The interpretation of dreams* and *The psychopathology of everyday life* are also highly readable. Recently, a great many books have been written attacking Freud; far fewer have been written in his defence. The clearest onslaught is Eysenck, H. J. (1985). *Decline and fall of the Freudian empire,* Viking, Harmondsworth; the most vicious is Masson, J. (1985), *The assault on truth,* Penguin, Harmondsworth; and the most ponderous (in both senses) but also the most scholarly is Webster, P. (1995) *Why Freud was wrong,* Harper Collins, London. All references to Freud given below are from the Standard Edition of the Complete Psychological Works of Sigmund Freud (1953-64) (ed. J. Strachey). Hogarth Press, London.

133, 1   On seeing others as similar to oneself, see Sutherland, S. (1992), pp. 195-6.

134, 4   On over-valuation, see Sutherland (1992), pp. 115-17.

134, 4   Valentine, C. W. (1939). *The psychology of early childhood,* Methuen, London.

135, 2   On waiting room, see Freud, XVI, p. 248.

136, 1   On the history of child rearing, see Aries, P. (1974). *Centuries of childhood: a social history of family life.* Vintage Books, New York.

137, 5   On Freud's view of the couch, see Roazen, P. (1976). *Freud and his followers,* pp. 138-9. Allen Lane, London.

Chapter 15   Evaluation of Freud

140, 2   Quotation from Freud XV, p. 179.

140, 2   Quotation from Freud XVIII, p. 50.

140, 4   On tests of Freudian theory, see e.g., Eysenck, H. J. and Wilson, G. D. (1973). *The experimental study of Freudian theories.* Methuen, London, and Rachman, S. J. and Wilson, G. D. (1980). *The effects of psychological therapy* (2nd edn). Pergamon, New York.

141, 3   On repression, see Schacter, D. (1996). *Searching for memory,* pp. 232-62. Basic Books, New York.

141, 3   Quotation from Holmes, D. S. (1974). *Psychological Bulletin,* **81,** 632-53.

141, 4   On sexual fantasy, see Leitenberg, H. and Henning, K. (1995). *Psychological Bulletin,* **117,** 469-86.

142, 1   On American Psychoanalytic Association's survey, see, Eysenck, H. J. (1992). In Dryden, W. and Feltham, C. (1992), pp. 100-24.

142, 1   On symptom substitution, see Rosenhan, D. L. and Seligman, M. E. P. (1995), p. 230.

142, 1   On analysts' confessions of failure, see Hamburg, D. A. *et al.* (1967). *Journal of the American Psychoanalytic Association,* **15,** 841-62.

142, 2   Malan, D. H. (1973). *Archives of General Psychiatry,* **29,** 719-29.

142, 3   Kernberg, O. F. *et al.* (1972). Psychotherapy and psychoanalysis: final report of the Menninger Foundation's Psychotherapy Research Project. Menninger Foundation, Topeka, Kansas. For a critical review, see Rachman, S. (1973). *Bulletin of the British Psychological Society,* **26,** 343-6.

Chapter 16   The Freudian cult

143, 2   Quotation from Freud, *XII,* p. 115.

143, 3   Malan, D. H. (1973). *Archives of General Psychiatry,* **29,** 719-29.

143, 3 Medical Director's pronouncement is quoted in Dewald, P. C. (1975). *Contemporary Psychology,* **20**, 492.

143, 4 Quotation from Landis, C. (1940). *Journal of Abnormal and Clinical Psychology,* **35**, 17-28.

144, 5 On over-valuation, see, Sutherland, S. (1992), pp. 102 4.

145, 2 Quotation from Freud, *XI.* p. 142.

145, 2 Quotation from Freud, *X,* p. 104.

146, 4 On need for achievement, see McClelland, D. C. (1961). *The achieving society.* Van Nostrand, Princeton, NJ.

147, 3 Eysenck, H. J. (1971). *Penthouse,* **6**, No. 9.

148. 2 Quotation from Freud, *XVI,* p. 452.

148, 2 Quotation from Freud, *XV,* p. 50.

148, 2 On masturbation, see Greenbank, R. K. (1961). *Pennsylvania Medical Journal,* **64**, 989.

149, 6 See Sutherland, S. (1994), p. 167.

150, 4 Quoted from Stein, M. K. by Lussier, A. (1972). *International Journal of Psychoanalysis,* **53**, 13-9.

150, 4 Cooper, I. S. (1974). *The victim is always the same.* Harper & Row, New York.

Chapter 17 The wars between the analysts

General None of Freud's successors wrote with his clarity and élan, but Adler, A. (1929). *Problems of neurosis.* Harper and Row, New York, and Horney, K. (1939). *New ways in psychoanalysis.* International Universities Press, New York are reasonably intelligible. Storr, A. (1973). *Jung.* Collier, London, makes sense of that scoundrel's ideas, no mean feat. A recent biography, McLynn, F. (1996), *Cart Gustav Jung,* Bantam Press, London, reveals his extreme selfishness, but the book is heavy-going. Kiernan, T. (1974). *Shrinks, etc.: a consumer's guide to psychotherapy,* The Dial Press, New York, is a breezy introduction for the general reader and clearer than any more recent books I know of.

152, 2 Quotation on Jung's value as a Gentile is from Abraham, H. C. and Freud, E. L. (eds.) (1965). *A psychoanalytic dialogue: the letters of Sigmund Freud and Karl Abraham. 1907-1926,* p. 34. Basic Books, New York.

152, 2 Freud on sexual theory as dogma is quoted in Jung, C. G. (1965). *Memories, dreams and reflections* (ed. A. Jaffe), pp. 146-69. Vintage Books, New York.

153, 3 Quotations on extroversion-introversion are from Jung, C. G. (1959). *Collected works.* Vol. VII, p. 64, Routledge & Kegan Paul, London.

154, 2 The famous episode of the penis appears in Cohen, E. D. (1975). *C. G. Jung and the scientific attitude.* Philosophical Library, New York and is taken from Jung's works.

154, 5 Quotation is given in Storr, A. (1973), p. 88.

155, 5 For Adler and common sense, see Mosak, H. H. and Dreikurs, R. (1973). In *Current psychotherapies* (ed. R. Corsini), pp. 35-84. Peacock, Itasca, IL.

Chapter 18   Psychotherapeutic sects

General Reading the works of Rogers and Perls requires little or no previous knowledge, but makes considerable demands on one's patience. Rogers, C. (1954). *Client-centred therapy*. Houghton Mifflin, Boston is as good an introduction to his ideas as any. For an account of Gestalt therapy with do-it-yourself exercises, try Perls, F. S. *et at.* (1951). *Gestalt therapy: excitement and growth in the human personality*. Julian Press, New York, or Fagan, J., and Shepherd, I. L. (ed.) (1970). *Gestalt therapy now*. Science and Behavior Books, New York. For briefer accounts, see Corsini, R. (1973). *Current psychotherapies*. Peacock, Itasca, IL or Davison, G. C. and Neale, J. M. (1994). *Abnormal psychology*. (6th edn), Wiley, New York. The writings of the existential therapists are impenetrable. Unless you have time on your hands, use secondary sources. Sigman, A. (1995). *New improved? Exposing the misuse of popular psychology*. Simon and Schuster, London is a witty but devastatingly accurate debunking of modern psychotherapy.

159, 2 Number of therapies—Garfield, S. L. (1995), p. 1.

160, 5 For the ineffectiveness of therapy for therapists, see Garfield, S. L. (1995), pp. 68-70.

160, 5 On the therapist's choice of what therapy to use, see Garfield, S. L. (1995), pp. 301.

161, 3 For tests of CARE, see Garfield, S. L. (1995), pp. 74-6.

162, 3 For computer program, see Weizenbaum, J. (1976). *Computer power and human reason: from judgment to calculation,* pp. 3-10. Freeman, San Francisco.

164, 2 The quotation is from Perls, F. S. (1970). In *Gestalt therapy now.* (ed. J. Fagan and I. L. Shepherd), p. 19. Science and Behavior Books, New York.

165, 5 Binswanger, L. (1975). *Being in the world*, p. 291. Souvenir Press, London.

166, 4 Quoted from Maslow in Hernan, E. (1995). *The romance of American psychology,* p. 273. University of California Press.

167, 1 Quotation is from Maslow, A. H. (1967). *Journal of Humanistic Psychology,* 7, 93-127.

167, 2 Braginsky, B. M. and Braginsky, D. D. (1974). *Mainstream psychology: a critique,* pp. 79-80. Holt, Rinehart & Winston, New York.

167, 3 Quotations are from Sigman, A. (1995). *New improved: exposing the misuse of popular psychology,* p. 23. Simon and Schuster, London.

168, 2 On task force, see Dawes, R. M. (1994), pp. 236-43.

168, 4 On teachers' so-called 'moral reasoning', see Goleman, D. (1995). Emotional intelligence: why it can matter more than IQ. Bantam, New York.

169, 1 On psychotherapists' lack of expertise, see Dawes, R. M. (1994). and Herman, E. (1995). *The romance of American psychology*. University of California Press, Berkeley.

Chapter 19   Group therapy

General Yalom, I. D. (1995). *The theory and practice of group psychotherapy* (4th edn). Basic Books, New York, is a sensible account of group therapy; it is clearly written and can be read by the general reader. There are many popular books on encounter groups. Maliver, B. (1973). *The encounter game*, Stein & Day, New York, gives their history in the USA and was written primarily for the general reader. Lieberman, M. A. *et al.* (1973). *Encounter groups: first facts.* Basic Books, New York reports the most systematic investigation yet conducted on the effects of encounter groups. Bednar, R. L. and Kaul, T. (1994). In Bergin, A. E. and Garfield, S. L. (1994), pp. 631-88 give an up-to-date but slightly tendentious account. I have drawn on all three sources.

170, 2   Moreno laid down his creed in three volumes published over 23 years—Moreno, J. L. (1946, 1959 and 1969). *Psychodrama.* Beacon Press, Boston.

170, 3   Berne is his own best expositor, for example Berne, E. E. (1966). *Games people play: the psychology of human relationships.* Grove Press, New York.

171, 2   Yalom, I. D. (1995).

173, 3   For research on group therapy, including casualty rates, see Bednar, R. L. and Kaul, T. J. (1994). In Bergin, A. E. and Garfield, S. L. (1994).

173, 4   Information on T-groups is from Maliver, B. (1973), pp. 179-99.

174, 3   The quotation from Perls is given in Maliver, B. (1973).

175, 3   On Task Force, see American Psychiatric Association, Task Force Report. (1970). *Encounter groups and psychiatry,* American Psychiatric Association. Washington, DC.

176, 2   Quotation from Maliver, B. (1973).

176, 3   The Stanford study is reported in Leiberman, M. A. *et al.* (1973).

177, 1   Braginsky, B. M. and Braginsky, D. D. (1974). *Mainstream Psychology: a critique,* p. 85. Holt, Rinehart & Winston, New York.

Chapter 20   The wilder shores of therapy

General   Sigman, A. (1995). *New improved? exposing the misuse of popular psychology,* Simon and Schuster, London, is a hilarious onslaught on current practices. Braginsky, B. M. and Braginsky, D. D. (1974). *Mainstream psychology: a critique,* Holt, Rinehart & Winston, New York covers the past with the same élan. Kiernan, T. (1974), *Shrinks etc.: a consumer's guide to psychotherapy,* Dial Press, New York, provides a critical but accurate account of most of the therapies described in this chapter.

179, 1   On Rank, see Kiernan, T. (1974), pp. 136-40.

179, 2   On Janov, see Kiernan, T. (1974), pp. 225-7.

179, 3   Reich himself is unreadable, but Rycroft, C. (1973). *Reich.* Collier, London is an excellent account.

182, 4   On Bioenergetics, see Lowen, A. (1971). *The language of the body.* Collier, New York.

182, 5   For ASCID, see Braginsky and Braginsky (1974), pp. 79-80.

183, 2   For misconduct by Bandler and other therapists, see Masson, J. (1988). *Emotional tyranny and the myth of psychological healing.* Atheneum, New York.

183, 3   On how to apply astrology to mental illness, see Greene, L. and Sasportas, H. (1987), *The development of the personality: Seminars in psychological astrology.* Routledge and Kegan Paul, London.

183, 5   The Woods case is described in Kiernan, T. (1974), pp. 1-5.
185, 1   For therapists having sex with patients, see e.g. Garrett, J. (1993). *The Psychologist,* **8**, 303.

Chapter 21   Behaviour therapy

General   Rosenhan, D. L. and Seligman, M. E. P. (1995) contains a good account of behaviour therapy.
186, 3   On Little Hans, see Wolpe, J. and Rachman, S. (1960). *Journal of Nervous and Mental Disease,* **130,** 135-48.
188, 1   For flooding under tranquillisers, see Marks, I. M. *et al.* (1972). *British Journal of Psychiatry,* **121,** 493-505.
189, 2   Study on speech phobia—Paul, G. L. (1966). Insight vs desensitization in psychotherapy: an experiment in anxiety reduction. Stanford University Press.
191, 2   The psychiatrist was Isaac Marks and his findings are reported in Hand, I. *et al.* (1974). *British Journal of Psychiatry,* **124,** 588-602.
191, 3   For high rates of recidivism after treatment for alcoholism, see Bergin, A. E. and Garfield, S. L. (1994), p. 402.
191, 3   Schachter, S. (1971). *Emotion, obesity and crime.* Academic Press, New York.
191, 5   On quitting smoking, see, for example, Stapleton, J. A. *et al.* (1995). *Addiction,* **90,** 31-42.
193, 4   On token economies, see Davison, G. C. and Neale, J. M. (1994), pp. 558-61.
194, 3   For attempts to provide motives for good behaviour, see Paul, G. L. and Lentz, R. J. (1977). *Psychosocial treatment of chronic mental patients: milieu versus social learning programs.* Harvard University Press, Cambridge, MA.
194, 4   On token economies for schizophrenia, see Baker, R. *et al.* (1974). *Journal of the Royal College of General Practitioners,* **28,** 621-6.
195, 1   On praise, see Sutherland, S. (1992), p. 108.
195, 2   On biofeedback, see Davison, G. C. and Neale, J. M. (1994), pp. 215-17 and 577-8.
196, 1   McConnell, J. V. (1970). *Psychology Today,* April, p. 14.
196, 1   On brainwashing, see Sutherland, S. (1979). In Duncan, R. and Weston-Smith, M. *Lying truths: A critical study of current beliefs and conventions,* pp. 107-20. Pergamon, Oxford.
196, 2   n increased liking for any activity that is punished, see Sutherland, S. (1992), pp. 113-14.
196, 3   On adverse effects of reward, see Sutherland, S. (1992), pp. 113-14.
196, 4   Strength of shocks—see Russell, A. W. (1974). Journal of Chemical Psychology, **30**, *Special Monograph Supplement,* 111-36.
197, 1   On dynamic therapists being less empathic than behaviour therapists, see Sloan, R. B. *et al.* (1975). *Psychoanalysis versus behavior therapy.* Harvard University Press, Cambridge, MA.

Chapter 22   Cognitive therapy

General Good accounts of cognitive therapy are to be found both in Rosenhan, D. L. and Seligman, M. E. P. (1995). and Davison, G. C. and Neale, J. M. (1994).

198, 1 Beck, A. T. (1967). *Depression: clinical, experimental, and theoretical aspects.* Hoeber, New York, and Beck, A. T. (1976). *Cognitive therapy and the emotional disorders.* International Universities Press, New York, are easy to read and reasonably definitive.

200, 2 On accuracy of depressives' judgements, see Lewinsohn, P. M. *et al.* (1980). *Journal of Abnormal Psychology,* 89, 203-12, and Taylor, S. E. (1989). *Positive illusions; creative self-deception and the healthy mind.* Basic Books, New York.

200, 3 For efficacy of cognitive therapy, see Rosenhan, D. L. and Seligman, M. E. P. (1995). pp. 748 9, and Blackburn, I. M. (1995). In Aveline, M. and Shapiro, D. A. *Research foundations for psychotherapy practice,* pp. 232-45. Wiley, Chichester.

201, 2 For panic attacks, see Salkovskis, P. M. (1995). In (ed. Aveline, M. and Shapiro, D. A.) *Research foundations for psychotherapy practice,* pp. 231—46. Wiley, Chichester.

202, 1 Accounts of treatment for rape victims and of anger management are based respectively on Smocker, M. R. *et al.* (1996). *Image rescripting, a treatment manual for survivors of childhood sexual abuse expressing PTSD,* and McDougall, C. (1990). *How to run an anger management course.* Both unpublished.

203, 2 On rational emotive therapy, see Davison, G. C. and Neale, J. M. (1994), pp. 563-5.

203, 3 On interpersonal therapy, see Klerman, G. L. *el al.* (1984). *Interpersonal psychotherapy of depression.* Basic Books, New York.

204, 3 For a description of this study, see Rosenhan, D. L. and Seligman, M. E. P. (1995), pp. 395-7.

204, 5 On deleterious effects of manuals, see Lambert, M. J., Bergin, A. E. and Garfield, S. L. (1994), pp. 143-89.

204, 6 On stress inoculation, see Meichenbaum, D. (1995). *Stress inoculation training.* Pergamon, New York.

205, 1 For experiment on pain, see Davison, G. C. and Vallins, S. (1969). *Journal of Personality and Social Psychology,* 11, 25-33.

205, 2 For study on victims of rape, see Foa, E. *et al.* (1991). *Journal of Consulting and Clinical Psychology,* 59, 715-23.

Chapter 23   Psychotherapy assessed

General Judgements of the value of psychotherapy tend to be polarised, with those in favour relying largely on their own intuition and sceptics relying on research results. For a moderate defence, see Bergin, A. E. and Garfield, S. L. (1994); for a reasoned onslaught, see Dawes, R. M. (1994).

207, 6 On drop-outs, see Garfield, S. L. (1995), p. 45.

208, 4   On measures of phobia, see Alloy, L. B. and Abramson, L. Y. (1988). In *Cognitive processes in depression* (ed. L. B. Alloy), pp. 223-65. Guilford, New York

209, 1   On meta-analysis, see Smith, M. L. *et al.* (1980). *The benefits of psychotherapy.* Johns Hopkins University Press, Baltimore, and Bergin, A. E. and Garfield, S. L. (1994).

209, 2   For failure of psychodynamic therapy, see Shapiro, P. and Shapiro D. (1982), *Psychological Bulletin,* **92,** 581-604

210, 1   Eysenck, H. J. (1992). *British Medical Journal* **309,** 789-92.

210, 3   For the three damning results, see Dawes, R. M. (1994), pp. 54-63.

211, 4   Quotation from Garfield, S. L. (1995). *Psychotherapy: an eclectic-integrative approach* (2nd edn), p. 31. Wiley, New York.

211, 5   The Consumer Report is summarized in Seligman, M. E. P. (1995). *American Psychologist, 50,* 965-74; see also further comments by several authors in *American Psychologist,* **51,** 1072-88.

212, 6   Supershrink, see Ricks, D. R. *et al.* (1974). *Life history research in psychopathology,* Vol. 3, pp. 275-97. University of Minnesota Press, Minneapolis.

213, 2   On importance of therapists' characteristics, see Garfield, S. L. (1995), p. 238.

213, 4   On bond with therapist, see Orlinsky, D. E. *et al.* (1994). In. Bergin, A. E. and Garfield, S. L. (1994), pp. 270-376.

213, 5   On therapists' judgements, see Dawes, R. M. (1994), p. 181.

214, 1   For Melissa study, see Dawes, R. M. (1994), pp. 163-4.

214, 1   On projective tests, see Dawes, R. M. (1994), pp. 150-4.

214, 3   For number of clinical psychologists in USA, see Dawes, R. M. (1994), p. 12.

214, 3   Figures come from *The Times* newspaper. The two million must include everyone with even the slightest pretension to being a counsellor.

215, 3   The quotation is reported in Dawes, R. M. (1994), p. 234.

215, 3   On the California Task Force, see Dawes, R. M. (1994), pp. 236-46.

216, 2   The quotations in the presidential address are reported in Fox, R. E. (1995). *American Psychologist,* **51,** 779.

Chapter 24   Manipulating the brain

General   For the horrific treatments given to mental patients in the past in attempts to alter their brains, see Valenstein, E. S. (1973). *Brain control.* Wiley, New York—a terrifying but salutary book.

217, 1   On ECT, see Clare, A. (1980). *Psychiatry in dissent* (2nd edn). Tavistock, London and Gelder, M. *et al.* (1989), pp. 679-89.

218, 4   On the large-scale study of ECT, see Clinical Psychiatry Committee (1965). *British Medical Journal,* **282,** 881-6.

219, 1   For mortality in tonsillectomy, see Ministry of Health Report on in-patient enquiry for the year 1961, (1962). HMSO, London, and Wolman, I. J. (1956). *Quarterly Review of Paediatrics,* **2,** 109. Fewer tonsillectomies are undertaken now, but referrals for surgery are likely to be almost as random.

219, 3   On random choice of children for tonsillectomy, see Bakwin, H. (1955). *New England Journal of Medicine,* **232,** 691.

220, 1   For the development of ECT, see Valenstein (1973). pp. 1-197, and Gelder, M. *et al.* (1989), pp. 679-89.

220, 2   On prefrontal lobotomies, see Valenstein (1973). pp. 53-5 and 279-93, and Gelder, M. *et al.* (1989), pp. 689-90.

222, 4   Number of psychosurgical operations is reported in *British Medical Journal,* September 1996, **313,** p. 813.

223, 3   On the treatment of this patient, see, Mark, V. and Ervin, F. (1970). *Violence and the brain.* Harper & Row, New York, and also Chorover, S. (1974). *Psychosurgery: A multidisciplinary symposium,* pp. 15-32, Lexington Books, Lexington.

224, 3   Damasio, A. R. (1994). *Descartes' error: Emotion, reason and the human brain.* Putnam, New York.

Chapter 25   The use of drugs

226, 2   On admission for barbiturate poisoning, see Malleson, A. (1973), *Need your doctor be so careless.* Allen & Unwin, London.

226, 2   Sargant, W. (1958). *Proceedings of the Royal Society of Medicine,* **51,** 353.

227, 1   On the number of people dependent on barbiturates, see Bewley, T. (1967). *Bulletin of Narcotics,* **13,** 20-7.

227, 4   The textbook was Valzelli, L. (1973). *Psychopharmacology: an introduction to experimental and clinical principles,* p 173. Spectrum, New York.

229, 4   On Resperidone, see e.g. Edwards, J. G. (1994). *British Medical Journal,* **308,** 1311-22.

229, 5   Amphetamine prescriptions and doctors' complacency, Malleson, A. (1973). *Need your doctor be so useless!* pp. 63-4. Allen & Unwin, London.

230, 2   Quotation given in Malleson, A. (1973), pp. 63—4.

230, 4   On Ritalin, see Mayor(?), S. (1996). *British Medical Journal,* **313,** 770.

230, 4   Quotation from Wender, P. (1971). *Minimal brain dysfunction in children,* p. 12. Wiley, New York.

232, 1   On lithium, see Gelder, M. *et al.* (1989), pp. 666-73, and Goodwin, F. K. and Jamison, K. R. (1990). *Manic-depressive illness,* pp. 603729. Oxford University Press.

232, 2   On drug firms and lithium, see Cole, J. O. (1968). *American Journal of Psychiatry,* **125,** 556-7.

233, 2   On creativity under lithium, see Goodwin, F. K. and Jamison, K. R. (1990). *Manic-depressive illness,* pp. 365-6.

233, 3   On being too impressed by positive results, see Sutherland, S. (1992), pp. 133-43, 159-61.

234, 2   Kramer, P. (1993). *Listening to Prozac.* Fourth Estate, New York.

235, 2   For a history of early random control trials in medicine, see Cochrane, A. L. (1972). *Effectiveness and efficiency, random reflections on the Health Service.* The Nuffield Provincial Hospitals Trust, London.

235, 2   On calomel, see Malleson, A. (1973), p. 25. Allen & Unwin, London.

Chapter 26   How drugs work

General   As far as I know there are no good popular accounts of how psychotropic drugs affect the brain. Much theorizing in this area is very speculative, and opinions change with great rapidity.

239, 8   On dopamine and schizophrenia, see Gelder, M. *et al.* (1989), pp. 307-8.

241, 3   For development of SSRIs, see Kramer, P. (1993). *Listening to Prozac,* pp. 60-4. Fourth Estate, New York.

241, 5   On Prozac and confidence, see Kramer, P. (1993), pp. 198-222.

242, 2   For a riveting account of the Prozac trial, see Cornwell, J. (1996). *The power to harm.* Penguin, London.

242, 2   Selectivity of SSRIs—see Stanford, S. C. (1996). *Trends in Pharmaceutical Science,* **1**, 150-4.

Chapter 27   What goes wrong?

General   Most of this chapter is a shortened version of Sutherland, S. In Dryden, W. and Feltham, C. (1992). pp. 169-86. Open University Press, Buckingham where further references may be found.

245, 1   Reynolds, A. K. and Fairberow, N. L. (1976). *Suicide, inside and out.* University of California Press, Berkeley, CA.

247, 3   Rosenhan, D. L. (1973). *Science,* **179**, 250—8.

247, 3   Quotations are from Gotkin, J. and Gotkin, P. (1977). *Too much anger, too many tears.* Jonathan Cape, London.

Chapter 28   Psychotherapeutic folly

General   On the search for child abusers, both Nathan, D. and Snedeker, M. (1995). *Satan's silence, ritual abuse and the making of a modern American witch-hunt.* Basic Books, New York, and Pendergrast, M. (1995). *Victims of memory.* Upper Access Books, New York, are thorough and readable. Much of the information in this chapter is taken from them.

250, 2   My account of the Orkneys case is taken from newspapers.

251, 4   On McMartin PreSchool, see Pendergrast, M. (1995), pp. 399-402.

252, 4   For the imaginary barn and numerous similar errors, see Loftus, E. F. (1979). *Eyewitness testimony.* Harvard University Press, Cambridge, Mass.

253, 1   Janov, A. (1970). *The primal scream: primal therapy, the cure for neurosis.* Dell, New York and Janov, A. (1990). *The new primal scream.* Dell, New York.

253, 2   On questionnaire, see Dawes, R. M. (1994), pp. 157-9.

253, 3   On doll play, see Dawes, R. M. (1994), pp. 159-63.

254, 1   Bass, E. and Davis, L. (1988). *The courage to heal, a guide for women survivors of child sexual abuse.* HarperPerennial, New York.

254, 1   The failure to find any case of recovered memory is reported in Pope, H. G. and Hudson, J. I. (1995). *Psychological Medicine,* **25**, 121-6, 297-304.

254, 3   On people falsely accused of child abuse, see Pendergrast, M. (1995), pp. 78-80.

255, 2   On step-families, see references in Belsky, J. (1993). *Psychological Bulletin,* **114**, 425.

255, 2   On what counts as sexual abuse, see Pendergrast, M. (1995), pp. 30-1, 297-304.

255, 3   For lack of symptoms in adults after child sex abuse, see Hacking, I. (1995), pp. 63-6, Pendergrast, M. (1995), pp. 618-20 and Rind, B and Harrington, E. (in press). In *False memory syndrome, therapy and forensic perspectives* (ed. D. A. Halpern). American Psychiatric Press, Washington, DC.

255, 3   On non-abused psychiatric patients having more severe symptoms than abused, see Kendall-Tackett, K. A. *et al.* (1993). *Psychological Bulletin,* **113**, 164-80.

255, 3   First quotation is from Kendall-Tackett, K. A. *et al.* (1993).

255, 3   Second quotation is from Rind, B and Harrington, E. In *False memory syndrome.*

255, 3   Finkelhor's views are given in Kendall-Tackett, K. A. *et al.* (1993).

256, 1   Belsky, J. (1993). *Psychological Bulletin,* **114**, 413-34.

256, 2   On sexually abused becoming sexually precocious, see Kendall-Tackett, K. A. *et al.* (1993).

256, 2   On damaging effects of poverty, see Belsky, J. (1993). Psychological Bulletin, **114**, 425.

256, 4   Loftus, E. F. (1979). *Eyewitness testimony.* Harvard University Press, Cambridge, MA.

257, 1   The psychologist keen on watching baseball was Neisser, U. (1982). In *Memory observed, remembering in natural settings* (ed. U. Neisser), pp. 43-8. Freeman, San Francisco.

257, 1   Sutherland, S. (1992). pp. 236-45.

257, 3   Ewen, C. P. (1996). *Monitor of American Psychological Association,* **July,**14.

258, 2   For absence of female orgasm, see Masters, W. H. and Johnson, V. (1970). *Human sexual inadequacy.* Little Brown, Boston.

258, 2   I have filched the following quotations from Sigman, A. (1995). *New improved? Exposing the misuse of popular psychology.* Simon & Schuster. London.

259, 4   Comfort, A. (1972). *The joy of sex.* Modsets Securities, London.

Chapter 29   Ethics

General   Thomas Szasz's books are repetitive. The views mentioned here are to be found in Szasz, T. S. (1961). *The myth of mental illness,* Dell, New York; and Szasz, T. S. (1963), *The manufacture of madness,* Dell, New York.

261, 2   For why rates of mental illness differ with socio-economic class, see Dohrenwend, B. P. *et al.* (1992). *Science,* **255**, 946-52.

262, 3   On abnormalities of the brain and obsessivecompulsive disorder, see Rosenhan, D. L. and Seligman, M. E. P. (1995), pp. 275-7.

262, 3   A fuller discussion of the genetics(?) of criminal behaviour is given in Chapter 13.

263, 2   For a readable history of the treatment of madness in Britain, see Scull, A. (1993). *The most solitary of afflictions, madness and society in Britain 1700-1900.* Yale University Press,

264, 1   On violence, see Dawes, R. M. (1994), pp. 205-6.

264, 3   On Cartwright, see Chorover, S. (1973). *Psychology Today,* **October,** 43.

265, 4   On 1983 Mental Health Act, see Gelder, M. *et al.* (1989), pp. 897-909.

265, 4   Quotation from Gelder, M. *et al.* (1989), pp. 860-1.

266, 5   On history of savage treatments for the mentally ill, see Valenstein, E. S. (1973). *Brain control.* Wiley, New York.

267, 1   On Patuxent, see *American Psychological Association Monitor,* 1974 and 1975, almost all issues.

267, 2   Quotation on 'acting out' from Tate, D. C. *et al.* (1995). *American Psychologist,* **50,** 777-88.

268, 6   On restrictions on patients' liberty, see Reynolds, A. K. and Farberrow, N. L. (1976). pp. 13-163.

269, 3   On the Wyatt case, see *American Psychological Association Monitor* for 1974 and 1975, most issues.

269, 5   For occupancy of beds for mentally ill, see Herman, E. (1995), p. 243.

269, 6   For figures on therapists having sex with their patients, see *American Psychological Association Monitor,* 1996, **August,** 8, and Garrett, T. (1995). *The Psychologist,* **8,** 303.

270, 1   Brown, L. S. (1988). *Psychotherapy,* 25, 249-85.

271, 5   On curious effects sometimes accompanying epilepsy, see Davidson, J. M. and Davidson, R. I. (1980). *The psychology of consciousness.* Plenum, London.

273, 4   On high-rise flats, see Fanning, P. (1967). *British Medical Journal,* **1,** 382-6.

Glossary

The meaning of all technical terms used is explained as they are introduced in the text. Only those terms that recur in different parts of the book are defined in the glossary. (I am grateful to The Macmillan Press Ltd for permission to use some of the definitions provided in my own *Macmillan Dictionary of Psychology.*)

actualization The full development and use of all one's talents and potentialities; in practice, only potentialities for good are included and a highly successful bank-robber would not be considered to be actualized.

affective disorders Disorders of mood, *see* manic depression.

agoraphobia A morbid and irrational fear of public spaces.

antisocial personality disorder Extremely antisocial behaviour beginning before the age of 15 with a disregard of sanctions or punishment.

bipolar manic-depression *see manic-depression.*

CARE An acronym standing for the three qualities thought to be required in a client-centred therapist, namely, Communicated Authenticity, Regard, Empathy (or genuineness, warmth, and understanding).

cognitive behaviour therapy The use in combination of the techniques of cognitive therapy and behaviour therapy.

cognitive therapy The systematic attempt to persuade someone suffering from a mental disorder to see the world and himself in a more sensible and adaptive way, based on the belief that maladaptive emotions are caused by maladaptive thought processes. In practice, it is often unclear how the approach of the cognitive therapist differs from that of most laymen confronted with mental disorder in others.

defence mechanism In psychoanalysis, any process by which the ego protects itself from recognizing the demands of the **id,** e.g. projection, **repression** and sublimation.

desensitization In psychotherapy, reducing the power of thoughts, events or situations to disturb the patient, by exposing him to them.

ego   In psychoanalysis, the part of the mind that is in touch with reality and that mediates between the libidinous urges of the **id** and the puritanical disapproval of the **superego.**

ego strength   **In** psychoanalysis, the extent to which the **ego** can handle without disruption the demands of the **id** and **superego** and can reconcile them with the environment. An individual with a strong ego is strong-willed, and can withstand frustration. According to many psychoanalysts he is also the most suitable case for treatment: he may not need it, but at least it won't upset him.

flooding   **A behaviour therapy** technique for extinguishing anxiety, in which the patient is exposed to the situation (or to the thought of it) of which he is most anxious and is kept in it until the anxiety reduces. It is used to alleviate **phobias.**

free   association   A technique, used in psychoanalysis, to overcome **defence mechanisms,** in which the patient gives vent to his thoughts without any attempt to suppress them or make them logical; patients or experimental subjects may also be presented with words and asked to respond as fast as they can with the first word they think of.

id   The unconscious part of the mind from which, according to Freud, drives (particularly the libido) emanate, and which contains forbidden wishes and associated thoughts that have been repressed.

individualization   *A synonym for* **actualization.**

manic-depression   A severe affective disorder in which the patient has episodes of depression or mania (or hypomania). It is called **unipolar manic-depression** if it is marked by episodes of either depression or mania but not both, and **bipolar manic-depression** if the patient oscillates between these two extremes of mood.

neuroleptic   Any drug that has a therapeutic effect on schizophrenia in particular, and more generally, on any overactivity or agitation that is a symptom of a psychotic illness (e.g. mania). These drugs are also known as major tranquillizers since they have a large calming effect.

neurosis   A mental disorder in which the patient does not lose contact with reality. It is usually accompanied by anxiety.

neurotransmitter   A chemical substance secreted at a neuron's terminal, which attaches to the receptor of a second neuron, and has an excitatory or inhibitory effect upon it.

phobia   A morbid, irrational and often incapacitating dread of something, which the sufferer usually realizes is unrealistic, although it remains uncontrollable.

projective test   Any personality test in which the subject is required to respond freely to material that can be interpreted in different ways. The assumption is that his responses will reveal needs, wishes, or ways of seeing the world that he will not explicitly disclose because of repression, shame or shyness.

psychopathy   A synonym for antisocial personality disorder.

psychosis   A severe mental disorder, marked by lack of contact with some aspects of reality, e.g. by delusions, hallucinations, or incoherent thought processes.

receptor   A molecular configuration on the surface of a nerve cell to which neurotransmitters (and some other substances including certain hormones and drugs) can attach, thereby increasing or decreasing the tendency of the cell to fire.

repression   In psychoanalysis, the process of removing from consciousness, or preventing the emergence into consciousness, of material or wishes which would produce anxiety or guilt; it is the most important single **defence mechanism.**

serotonin   A neurotransmitter thought to be implicated in depression.

superego In psychoanalysis, the part of the mind into which the attitudes of the parents and possibly other important figures have been introjected, and which constitutes a person's conscience by barring the **id** from gratifying itself in unacceptable ways.

synapse The point at which one nerve cell influences the firing of another.

unipolar manic-depression *See* **manic-depression.**

Name index to Part II

Subject index to Part II

biofeedback 195
birth trauma 179
boredom 248
British Psychological Association 90,
    214
bulimia 116

Californian Task Force to Promote Self-
    Esteem and Personal Growth 215
calomel 235
CARE (Communicated Authenticity,
    Regard and Empathy, otherwise
    known as sincerity, warmth and
    empathy) 143, 161-2, 184, 197,
    212
castration complex 134
child abuse 114, 125, 127-8, 141; *see
    also* child sexual abuse and
    nurture
child neglect, *see* child abuse
child sexual abuse 115-16, 214, 250-7
chloral 226
chronic fatigue syndrome 116, 125, 263
civil rights, mental hospitals and 268-9
clinical psychologists 90-1,94—5,
    214-16
cocaine 228, 230, 243
cognitive behaviour therapy 198-206,
    209-10, 212
cognitive triad 199
commitment, compulsory 96, 265-6,
communicated authenticity, *see* CARE
Community Mental Health Centres
    97-8
complexes 153
compulsions 110, 243, 272
contract, *see* therapeutic contract
conversion hysteria 105
convulsions 220
coronary care unit 235
counsellors 92
counterconditioning 187
criminality 122-3, 127, 271
crotch eyeballing therapy 182

defence mechanisms 132-3
delusions 100, 226

denial 133, 253
dependence on drugs, *see* addiction
dependence on therapists 246
depression 101, 107, 108, 124-5, 203,
        210, 209-22, 234, 242; *see also*
        manic-depression
    antidepressants and 200, 240-3
    behaviour therapy and 190
    cognitive therapy and 130, 198-203,
        204
    endogenous vs reactive 102
    learned helplessness as cause of 120
    leucotomy and 220-5
    secondary vs primary 102
deprived children, *see* child abuse
desensitization 186-8, 205
diagnosis 109-16
Diagnostic and Statistical Manual of
        Mental Disorders (DSM) 109,
        111, 112, 113
diagnostic manuals 112; *see also*
        Diagnostic and Statistical Manual
        and International Classification of
        Diseases
displacement 123
Dissociative Experience Scale 115
dissociative hysteria 105
DNA 121
dominance hierarchy 241
dopamine 239-40, 243
Down's syndrome 271
dreams 135, 140, 141, 149, 154-5
drop-outs 173, 204, 207
drugs, illicit 243 -4
drugs, pharmaceutical 204, 226-36
DSM, *see* diagnostic and statistical
        manuals
dynamic therapy 160, 197, 200, 204,
        209-10, 211-13; *see also* under
        individual dynamic therapies, e.g.
        Gestalt therapy

Ecstasy 230
ECT. *see* electroconvulsive therapy
ego 132, 157
ego strength 137, 142, 146
electroconvulsive therapy (ECT) 217-19
emotional intelligence 168